MASTERPIECES OF CHIKAMATSU

I0646896

MASTERPIECES OF CHIKAMATSU

The Japanese Shakespeare

Translated by
ASATARO MIYAMORI

Revised by
ROBERT NICHOLS

Volume 58

Routledge
Taylor & Francis Group

LONDON AND NEW YORK

First published in 1926

This edition first published in 2011
by Routledge
2 Park Square, Milton Park, Abingdon, Oxon, OX14 4RN

Simultaneously published in the USA and Canada
by Routledge
711 Third Avenue, New York, NY 10017

Routledge is an imprint of the Taylor & Francis Group, an informa business

© 1926 Kegan Paul, Trench, Trübner & Co., Ltd.

British Library Cataloguing in Publication Data
A catalogue record for this book is available from the British Library

First issued in paperback 2013

ISBN 13: 978-0-415-84945-6 (pbk)
ISBN 13: 978-0-415-59122-5 (Volume 58)
eISBN 13: 978-0-203-84352-9 (Volume 58)

Publisher's Note
The publisher has gone to great lengths to ensure the quality of this reprint but
points out that some imperfections in the original copies may be apparent.

Disclaimer
The publisher has made every effort to trace copyright holders and would
welcome correspondence from those they have been unable to trace.

MASTERPIECES OF CHIKAMATSU

THE JAPANESE SHAKESPEARE

TRANSLATED BY

ASATARO MIYAMORI

*Professor of English Literature in
The Oriental University, Tokyo*

REVISED BY

ROBERT NICHOLS

*Formerly Professor of English Literature in
The Imperial University, Tokyo*

With 74 Illustrations

THE YAMATO SOCIETY
TOKYO

LONDON
KEGAN PAUL, TRENCH, TRUBNER & CO., LTD.
NEW YORK: E. P. DUTTON & CO.
1926

PRINTED IN GREAT BRITAIN BY
THE EDINBURGH PRESS, 9 AND 11 YOUNG STREET, EDINBURGH

PREFACE

WITH the exception of *The Tethered Steed*, the following are unabridged translations of the best *jōruri* (puppet plays) of Chikamatsu Monzaémon, known as "The Japanese Shakespeare". All episodical details are omitted from *The Tethered Steed*, and passages consisting of "words, words, words," have been very much condensed, so that the play as it is now offered to the reader is less than half the length of the original. With regard to the other plays, the translation has been invariably made with such conscientious fidelity as is consistent with clarity. It must be borne in mind, however, that certain narrative elements and, in particular, the *michiyuki* or "songs of travel", which abound in classical quotations, similes, metaphors and above all in the most exquisite word-play, offer almost insuperable obstacles even to the hand of a master-translator. Where such difficulties are encountered any attempt at literal translation is of necessity abandoned and I have endeavoured to convey the general sense in my own phraseology. This unavoidable paraphrasing is the more unfortunate in that half the special significance and grace of Chikamatsu is to be found in these very passages, written in excellent verse and displaying to the fullest advantage the beauty and music of the Japanese tongue.

Sometimes for the sake of euphony the poet sacrifices sense to sound and is content to remain inconsistent, a tendency which it is not hypercritical to regret. An illustration of the weakness is to be found in *The Love Suicide at Amijima*, where in the first act the hero is spoken of as being in narrow circumstances, while at the beginning of the second act, the audience is given to understand that the hero's business is in a thriving condition.   I have given myself a free hand in rendering such contradictory information and avoiding such discrepancies.

The reader would do well, moreover, to remember that these selections are puppet plays intended to be chanted by professional reciters to the music of the samisen, the finest of all Japanese instruments, and to be performed by beautiful marionettes, skilfully manipulated; let him reflect that puppetry is a synthetic art in which dialogue, poetry, music, song and the motion of marionettes all combine.   True and perfect appreciation of Chikamatsu, therefore, is not to be gained by a mere reading of the texts; even less is it reached by a reading of any translation of them.   It may assist the reader's imagination to notice that to impart life and animation to the puppets demands a certain exaggeration in the action, a leaven of bombast in the language throughout the piece.

Throughout this volume, in the case of personal names of Old Japan the surname precedes the given name (equivalent to " Christian name "), while with present-day names the position is reversed.   The reason for such an arrangement is that in olden times given

names were the more important; to-day, as happens
with European names, the surname is of the greater
importance.   Again, many names used in olden times
occur to one's mind, of which it is absolutely impossible
to write the given name first.   Let me instance the
name Taira-no-Shigémori, which cannot be written
Shigémori Taira, since the surname Taira is always
followed by the postposition *nŏ*.   I enlarge on this
somewhat trifling matter because a reviewer in an
American magazine, in the course of his notice of my
" Tales from Old Japanese Dramas", laid upon me
the reproach of an apparent inconsistency.   The titles
of many Japanese classic dramas are, for a reason into
which it would be inconvenient to enquire here, both
long and quaint, and consequently are among the
troubles of the translator.   I have thought it helpful
to translate some of these old superscriptions very
literally in the course of my introduction, that the reader
may more easily identify the plays by means of the
original titles, clumsy though the titles may sound.

My hearty thanks arc duc to Mr. Kidō Okamoto,
Mr. Yonétarō Matsuyama, Mr. Seitarō Atsumi, Dr.
Tsukuru Fujimura, Dr. Mankichi Wada, Mr. Saburō
Sakamoto and Mr. Kaisō Nonomura, all of whom gave
me valuable suggestions.   I am also under obligation
to Mr. Hōgin Kidani, who kindly supplied me with
a few photographs and further granted me ready
permission to avail myself freely of his " Comments
on Chikamatsu's Complete Works".

ASATARO MIYAMORI.

Tokyo.

A LETTER FROM DOCTOR SHŌYŌ TSUBO-UCHI, THE BEST
AUTHORITY ON JAPANESE DRAMA.

(Translated from the Japanese.)

ATAMI,
May 20, 1924.

DEAR MR MIYAMORI,

I have read with a great deal of interest a manuscript copy of your recent work, *Masterpieces of Chikamatsu, the Japanese Shakespeare,* which was kindly sent to me by the Yamato Society. I am impressed with the learned Introduction as well as the excellent translations from the *Japanese Shakespeare.* In the event of your book being brought out and widely read by the English-speaking communities, it cannot be long before the unique stage art of Japan is introduced abroad in its true light.

Our marionette and *Kabuki* (popular) dramas have no parallel, for the remarkable complexity of their form and technique, in the world's dramatic history, extending over twenty-five centuries ; and, to my regret, so far no book in any European language has appeared, fully qualified to make foreigners realize their peculiar development and the true significance of their form and contents. Now the present Introduction, which is concise, yet comprehensive and to the point, will exactly serve this purpose ; and I do not hesitate to say that it will prove a most trustworthy guide, setting Europeans free from the glaring errors concerning our dramatic literature which have been caused by over-hasty observations of foreign visitors to this country.

The *nō* plays, which are comparatively simple though they form one branch of our stage art, are understood by foreigners to some extent ; but, nevertheless, some resemblance in form which they bear to the old Chinese dramas has regrettably led astray even some of our scholars who have ventured the idle conjecture that the *nō* plays are an imitation of the Chinese dramas. The case being so, it is nothing to wonder at that foreigners have failed to grasp the essential meanings of our puppet and popular dramas. But when your book sees the light, I am sure Western readers, who have been hitherto in the dark about our histrionic art, will be encouraged to undertake voyages of discovery to the *terra incognita* of puppet and *Kabuki* plays.

Japanese classics, which are written in a language entirely different in construction and idiom from the European languages, are extremely difficult to translate into these tongues ; above all, Chikamatsu's puppet plays, which are in characteristic verse and abound in the most ingenious word-play, are perhaps almost impossible to render word for word into even present-day colloquial Japanese. I can well imagine, therefore, what a painstaking task you must have carried out, in order to execute such a faithful, and at the same time, such a clear translation, which often endeavours to reproduce these plays upon words.

If the day comes when our drama, which is peculiar, yet possesses unique merits and characteristics, is widely recognized, appreciated and digested by Western literary circles as our pictures of the *Ukiyo-é* school are studied and appreciated by them, it may be that the Western drama, influenced by ours, will make a new departure in form and technique. Supposing that such a metamorphosis happens, the credit of giving the inducement towards the movement will be accorded chiefly to your valuable work. In prospect of such a development, I look forward to the publication of your volume with great interest and pleasure.

Thanking you for the privilege of reading your manuscript.

I am yours most cordially,

SHŌYŌ TSUBO-UCHI.

CONTENTS

LIST OF ILLUSTRATIONS

xi

INTRODUCTION

INTRODUCTION

I

LITERATURE AND THE POPULACE IN OLD JAPAN

DURING the middle and latter part of the archaic period of Japanese history (660 B.C.–A.D. 700) the entire people, high and low, were in the habit of composing poems of various types under the impulse of momentary emotions. Emperors and noblemen, peasants and fishermen, were alike poets, in the widest interpretation of the term. Love was the theme of most of the poems and next in importance to love came war and wine. These poems were transmitted orally, since the Japanese possessed no characters by which to commit their language to paper. Somewhere about the fourth century A.D., Chinese characters, having been introduced as a partly phonetic and partly literal transcription of speech,[1] the whole forming an extremely complicated process, the educated classes began to write their poems, inaugurating thus a great advance in Japanese culture. To acquire the mastery of thousands of the cumbrous ideographs now introduced, however, demanded hard study, and the recording of poems was consequently beyond the capacity of the populace, who lacked a school education.[2] As a result, while verse-making

---

[1] Chinese characters thus employed are called *Mannyō Gana* or *Mannyō* Letters, because they were used mainly in recording the famous anthology *Mannyō-Shū* or "The Collection of A Myriad Leaves".

[2] All the schools of this period were exclusively for the education of the sons of noblemen and of officials of high rank.

3

was less practised by the populace, it became more and more an aristocratic accomplishment.

During the Nara Period (709–784), when the Emperors ruled at Nara, the study of Chinese literature and the writing of Chinese became very much the vogue among the leisured classes. This circumstance raised the literary standard far higher than before, and consequently there grew up a literary circle composed of court nobles and ladies and other persons of rank. Other classes of the population, on the contrary, almost entirely abandoned the production of literary compositions. The writing of poems, particularly odes of thirty-one syllables, was the most important literary accomplishment of this period; and it was then that the famous anthology *Mannyō Shū* or " The Collection of A Myriad Leaves " was compiled. The actual number of poems assembled in this work is four thousand, four hundred and ninety-six, of which four thousand, one hundred and seventy-three consist of odes of thirty-one syllables. Among the six hundred and thirty-one writers of the selections there are seventy poetesses and a certain number of persons of humble station. At the beginning of the Heian Period (794–1186), so called because the Emperors resided at Heian, the present Kyoto, two systems of syllabary, the ninety-five characters of which are much simplified forms of complicated Chinese ideographs, came into use. Their introduction enormously facilitated writing, and gave a great impetus to literary activity, although pedantic persons continued to record their poems in Chinese characters according to the complicated process above mentioned even to as late a date as the end of the Yedo Period (1603–1868).[1] The practice of writing stories,

---

[1] Nowadays *Mannyō* Letters supplemented by the above-mentioned two systems of syllabary are used not only in recording poems, but also extensively in everyday writing; and almost all personal and geographical names are written in *Mannyō* Letters. To give an instance interesting to the English-speaking

diaries, accounts of travel and miscellanies was added to the art of versification. The most eminent masterpieces of this period are *The Story of Genji*, a novel; *The Pillow Sketches*, a miscellany; *The Collection of Odes Ancient and Modern* and *An Anthology for All Ages*. Nevertheless, authorship still remained the province of a small group of persons of rank, which now included Buddhist priests. It is worthy of note that in the above two periods, and particularly during the Heian, woman's social standing was high, and the sexes mixed freely in social intercourse. Women figured prominently in literature and a number of brilliant authoresses appeared, among whom the most celebrated were Murasaki Shikibu and Sei Shōnagon (the respective writers of *The Story of Genji* and *The Pillow Sketches,* above mentioned) and Akazomé Emon and Izumi Shikibu, all court ladies.

The next period worthy of mention is the Muromachi Period (1338–1565) during which the Ashikaga Shoguns, the *de facto* rulers, had their seat at Muromachi, Kyoto, while the powerless Emperors dwelt in gilded captivity. The representative masterpieces of this period are the *nō* plays (lyric dramas) and *kyōgen* (comic interludes), both of which were monopolized by the Shoguns and the samurai, to the exclusion of the populace.

This state of affairs underwent a considerable modification during the Yedo Period (1603–1868), when the Tokugawa Shoguns ruled at Yedo, the present Tokyo. After a long period of anarchy, the nation enjoyed under this régime a profound peace, and the government encouraged the study and printing of Chinese classics and the propagation of Confucianism. One result of these new conditions was a general extension of education, based upon the Confucian

public, the names Oxford and Cambridge are often represented by Chinese characters signifying respectively " Cattle Ford " and " Sword Bridge ", the character for " Sword " being pronounced somewhat like " Can ".

doctrines. Higher education, it is true, was confined to the samurai, priests and physicians, and the education imparted at the *terakoya* (common schools) was far from satisfactory ; but there is reason to believe that many scholars of Chinese and Japanese classics kept private schools in Kyoto, Osaka and Yedo, amongst the pupils of which were to be found the sons of merchants and sometimes of peasants. Thus a portion of the populace was enabled to gain access to that treasury of knowledge from which they had been excluded for more than ten centuries. Yet another important consequence of the peaceful Shogunate régime was the steady growth of national wealth and prosperity. Cities and towns throughout the land grew opulent and a rich merchant class came into existence. In Osaka, the greatest centre of commerce, there were numerous millionaires, to whom samurai and daimio turned for financial assistance, insomuch that Gamō Kumpei, a celebrated scholar and patriot, is said to have exclaimed, " When the rich Osaka merchants become angry the daimio of all Japan tremble ".

There was, however, another side to the Shogunate's administration—its extreme despotism. The people at large experienced the tyranny which a saying, almost proverbial in the days of the Shogunate, ironically denotes : " Let the people obey absolutely ; let them never know anything of politics." For the people there was no freedom of speech and conscience ; nay, even the security of life and property was lacking to them. They had no shadow of popular rights ; the strictest class distinctions were in force and the people were divided into peasantry, artisans and merchants, the samurai or warrior gentry forming the ruling hierarchy. Of the three lower classes, the merchants were held in the greatest contempt,[1] in accordance with the theory of the

---

[1] It was not uncommon to find at the entrance of a well-regulated village a notice-board reading " Merchants not admitted ".

Chinese metaphysicians of the Chu-Hi school,[1] which despises riches and frowns upon material wants. Bushido, the canon of moral principles of Japanese knighthood, also despised commerce as being conducive to effeminacy and the decline of the martial spirit. To make matters worse, the government imposed severe restrictions and prohibitions on the merchants' mode of life and these restrictions and prohibitions extended to the minutest detail.[2] The merchants were not only subjected to the maximum of scorn and oppression, but were also debarred from engaging in any enterprise of foreign trade by the policy of exclusion followed by the government, a policy which forbade any subject to cross the seas under penalty of death. It was the same regrettable policy which isolated Japan for nearly two centuries from international currents of thought and culture.

Thus it was but natural that the populace, and in particular the rich shopkeepers and merchants, should seek eagerly for some outlet for their pent-up energy and discontent. Some turned to arts and literature; others to sensual pleasures. It was to such sources as those just touched upon that we may trace the rise of popular literature, such as *haiku* (seventeen syllable odes), *senryū* (a variety of *haiku*), comic odes of thirty-one syllables, humorous essays, novels and regular and puppet plays. The nation at large,

[1] Chu-Hi, one of the most famous of Chinese commentators on the Confucian doctrines, says: " Riches, like oil, defile men. Where there is any government there is sure to be revenue." This saying is justly considered to be a misinterpretation of Confucius' saying in *The Great Learning*: " Virtue is the primary consideration; riches are the secondary consideration." The Chu-Hi theory of Confucianism was adopted and established by the Tokugawa Government. Dissenters were punished as heretics. Yamaga Sokō, a famous Confucianist and tactician, was punished for a criticism of the established doctrine; and Kamei Nammei, another distinguished Confucianist, was driven out of his mind by the controversy and finally died of it.

[2] Among prohibitions issued in 1652 may be found: " Tradespeople and servants must not wear silk "; " Tradespeople must not give splendid dinners "; " Tradespeople must not have lacquered utensils "; " Tradespeople must not have three-storied houses built."

high and low alike, took with enthusiasm to the composing of the above-mentioned odes and regular odes of thirty-one syllables. Indeed the Japanese of this period might well have been called a nation of poets and poetesses. Such was the popularity of verse-making that the better educated peasants and merchants were in the habit of holding frequent poetical competitions, the best of the resulting extempore poems being copied out in a fair hand and hung when framed in the temple of the tutelary deity as votive offerings. " Poetry in Japan is universal as the air. It is felt by everybody. It is read by everybody. It is composed by almost everybody — irrespective of class and condition." These remarks of Lafcadio Hearn on modern Japan might well be applied to Old Japan, and with greater truth. The people were also diligent in learning the tea-ceremonies and flower-arrangement, accomplishments previously limited to the privileged classes ; amateur painting ; music of several kinds ; and calligraphy, which in Japan is an art in itself. The publication of novels and essays attracted excellent lists of subscribers ; above all, the Osaka shopkeepers and mer-chants patronized with extreme liberality the theatre, and particularly the puppet theatre, with the consequence that the puppet play achieved a remarkable development in their city.

The seat of learning and literature during the first half of the Yedo Period was at Kyoto, and later at Osaka, although Yedo was the political centre and the capital of the Shogun ; and it is worth while to examine for a moment the reasons for this peculiar phenomenon. The military classes dominant in Yedo still retained a warlike spirit and cared little for refinement, so that the metropolis remained as yet a soil un-favourable to arts and literature. Kyoto, on the other hand, a city which had been the capital of the Emperors and of the Ashikaga Shoguns for centuries, inherited refinement and a taste for the elegant arts. Osaka, so far as the rise of popular arts and literature was concerned, fared better still, because there the merchants were the masters, the military class having comparatively little influence.

In this city then it was, that two of the three outstanding literary figures of the period, the novelist Saikaku and the dramatist Chikamatsu (the third figure being the *haiku* writer Bashō) came to reveal their genius.

There is, however, a reverse to the shield. While some of the merchant class, as has been observed, sought refuge in the arts and literature, others became devotees of sensual pleasures. Courtesans were much patronized ; merchants frequented the gay quarters where every visitor, were he shopkeeper or samurai, was treated on a footing of equality, the courtesans being no respecters of persons. The demi-monde quarters were the only places in the entire Empire where the merchants started level with the samurai and even with the daimio. Here alone could they display their real power. That this was not a trifle we see by the fact that among these frail ladies were many accomplished girls who, unlike the courtesans of to-day, were versed in etiquette, the tea-ceremony, flower-arrangement, *koto*-playing [1] and also in the composition of poems. They occupied a rather higher social position than the modern geisha, in this somewhat resembling the Greek hetairai ; and samurai and even daimio did not disdain to patronize them. Courtesans of the best class were not without dignity and pride, and would never yield to the desire of patrons for whom they had no esteem.

This is the reason why the courtesan figures so prominently in novels and dramas of the period, and why the scenes in both are so often laid in the pleasure-quarters. On the other hand, girls and women of good family appear but rarely as heroines in the literature of those days. The Chinese custom that women should be kept as far as possible in a

---

[1] A sort of zither.

state of absolute subjection and seclusion was so universally prevalent that the wives and daughters of samurai and merchants were but rarely seen or heard of in public life. Buddhism, which holds women to be sinful souls, and Confucianism, which declares " women and mean men are alike hard to manage ", delighted in lowering women's status and ultimately turned them into spiritless dolls. So dull and helpless were they that they dared not give expression to their feelings. For this reason, then, if for no other, they were unfitted to be the heroines of novels and dramas.

II

THE ORIGIN OF THE JAPANESE DRAMA AND ITS VARIETIES

In Japan, no less than in Greece and many other European countries, religion is the mother of the drama. There can be no doubt that the *kagura* or sacred dance, still performed during festivals in Shinto temples, is the progenitor of all forms of Japanese drama.

Mythology has it that the Sun Goddess, disgusted at the conduct of her brother, the God Susano-ono-mikoto, hid herself in a cave. There followed darkness throughout the universe—to the great perplexity of the myriad gods, who were at a loss to know what to do. At this critical and gloomy moment, the witty and jovial Goddess Uzumé performed a comic dance at the mouth of the cave and succeeded in enticing the Sun Goddess from her hiding-place. Thus, to the immense joy of the myriad gods, light was restored to the universe. Such is the traditional origin of the sacred dance. Whatever the significance of the legend may be, certain it is that the sacred dance has existed from time immemorial. The sacred dance is a pantomime in which the actors imitate the deeds of the different deities whom they impersonate. They wear grotesque masks and dance to the accompaniment of singing and of flutes and drums. So simple and so primitive in plot is the sacred dance that it possesses no literary value, but it is interesting none the less as being the parent of all forms of Japanese literary drama.

The literary dramas of Old Japan are divisible into four classes : the *yōkyoku* or *nō* play, the *kyōgen* or comic interlude, the *kabuki* play or drama for the regular theatre, and the *jōruri* or puppet play.

III

THE *YŌKYOKU* OR *NŌ* PLAYS

The *yōkyoku*, or texts of musical dramas known as *nō*, are short, serious plays, generally in two scenes. Their plots are chiefly derived from Japanese history, myth and folklore, and from certain Japanese stories such as *The Story of Genji*, and *The Story of the Taira Family*. They contain, in addition to dialogue and monologue, descriptive passages. The loveliest inspirations in the whole piece are often found in the monologue of the protagonist and in the so-called *michiyuki* or " songs of travel ", which indeed form the most important part of the descriptive passages and narrate in a few exquisite lines the journey, sometimes covering hundreds of miles, made by some person in the drama. The greater part of this type of drama is written in the colloquial language of the Kamakura Period (1186–1332), which just preceded the authors' birth, and the greater portion of the descriptions and occasionally some of the dialogue and monologue is of a piece with the lyric and epic poetry of the latter half of the Heian Period (794–1186), with the lyric element predominating. The verse is largely composed of a succession of seven and five syllable lines, the standard metre of Japanese poetry. Profusely adorned with classical Japanese and Chinese poems, this order of drama also abounds in historical references and in quotations from Buddhist scriptures. For this reason the *nō* plays prove too difficult for ordinary comprehension without special study. These dramas disclose another pronounced characteristic in the frequent use of ingenious plays upon words, a device which is a distinguishing feature of Japanese classics and one which adds considerably to the beauty and melody of such compositions. It detracts from the originality, but not from the merit, of the *nō* plays, that the most beautiful passages in them are upon examination only too often found to be undigested borrowings from *The Story of Genji*, *The Story of the Taira Family*, *The Rise and Fall of the Minamoto and Taira Families*, *The Record of Great Peace*, *The Collection of Odes Ancient and Modern*, etc., so that the *nō* plays are often with justice likened to a patchwork of brocade.

The plan of these plays is generally the same, simple framework—being often but a narration of the ups and downs of fortune of some historical or fictitious character and a sermon on the uncertainty of human life. First, for instance, appears a Buddhist priest making a pilgrimage through several provinces; next appears a ghost in human shape, who relates to the priest his experiences and adventures as a mortal and confesses that he is a ghost; finally the priest prays for the peace of the departed and upon this the ghost vanishes. Such is the most typical plan. Buddhist doctrines, in particular the doctrine of Karma, pervade these plays; and in some of them, called " god-

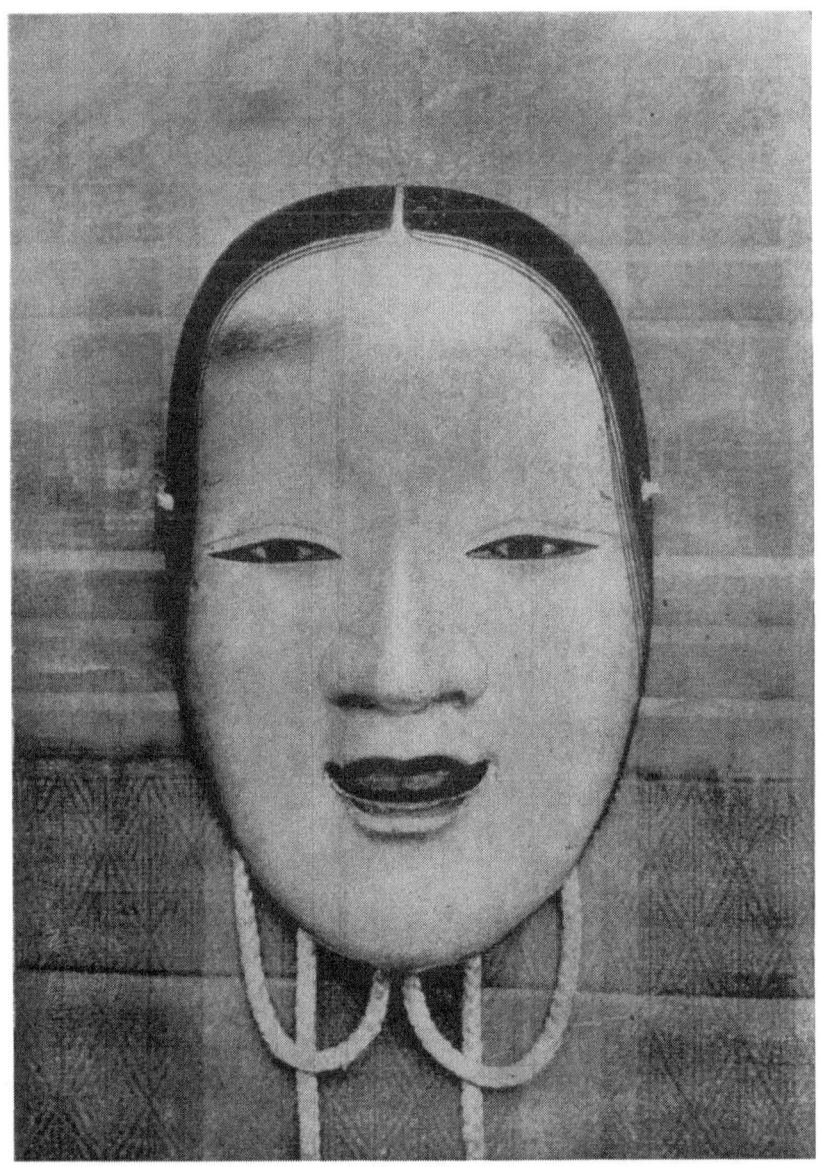

A YOUNG WOMAN'S MASK MADE BY KONGŌ MAGOJIRŌ, WHO
LIVED IN THE SIXTEENTH CENTURY

THE DEMONESS, THE PROTAGONIST OF *THE BLACK MOUND*,
A *NŌ* PLAY, ACTED BY MR. KINNOSUKÉ KONGŌ

plays ", the history of certain Shinto shrines is related, or the spirits of Shinto deities appear and perform miracles.

The actors impersonating the principal rôles wear masks of wood and dance to the accompaniment of a flute, two hand-drums and, in some cases, of a drum beaten with a stick. The manner of the dancing is usually extremely slow, full of dignity, solemn. The play, from start to finish, is chanted, somewhat like an oratorio; and the chanting of the protagonist's part while he dances falls almost entirely to the chorus. This chorus consists of ten or twelve men, seated motionless at the side of the stage. These also sing the narrative portions. The technical principles governing the nō plays are symbolism, conventionalism, mysticism and unrealism, if I may be permitted to use such a term, for these plays seem to aim at carrying the imagination of the audience away from real life. Let me cite one or two instances of this pure convention. Upon the nō stage a palace, a house, a cottage, a hovel, are all alike represented by four posts covered with a roof; the fan which the actor usually carries does duty often enough as a lute, a shield, a wine-holder, a wine-cup or some such object; the walking of a few steps on the stage often signifies the travelling by the character of hundreds of miles and the attainment of a far-off destination. The nō plays are somewhat deficient in lucidity and coherence but exceedingly beautiful both in style and content, so that only to read them tends to elevate one's feelings and thoughts. Brevity and quietness characterize these dramas and their performance: their plots and sentences are simple but charged with significance; chanting is done in "cloudy" and subdued voices, and the difference between the voices of male and female characters is hardly noticeable save to a specialist; the music is calm and grave; mystic, lustreless masks are used; acting and dancing are slow, dignified and to the casual eye extremely simple.

These essential peculiarities were due, in a great measure, to the influence of the Zen sect of Buddhism, generally adhered to by the military classes during the Muromachi Period, whose teachings inculcate silence, quietude and the simple life for spiritual training. A similar influence came from the tea-ceremonies much in vogue among the military classes of those days, which none the less primarily aim at tranquillity of the mind.

The word *nō* signifies "performance" or "accomplishment". Etymologically the word is an abbreviation of *sarugaku-nŏ-nō*, *sarugaku* being a corruption of *sangaku* or "scattered music", that is "popular music". Tatéki Ōwada asserts as a fact beyond all possible doubt that *sangaku*, which flourished in the fourteenth century, was a development from a somewhat comic song-dance performed in Shinto shrines. Perhaps it is well here to mention that in the Muromachi Period the religion of the nation at large was a mixed system of Buddhism and Shintoism and that the service in most of the Shinto temples was performed by Buddhist priests.

The majority of the *nō* plays were written in the Muromachi Period (1338–1565), the Dark Age of Japan. Their performance was favoured and encouraged by the Shogun, at that time the actual ruler of the Empire, and other noblemen. From the Muromachi Period down to the fall of the Tokugawa Shogunate (1868) the *nō* was a ceremonial function of the military classes. In the early days of the *nō* dance when the *nō* was still called *sarugaku-nŏ-nō* its performers were known as *sarugaku-nŏ-hōshi* or "priests of *sarugaku*" and ranked lowest in the priesthood ; but later their status gradually rose till, during the Yedo Period (1603–1868), they came to be regarded with high respect and ranked socially on a level with the samurai. Furthermore, the art of performing the *nō* was eventually classed as a knightly accomplishment. There is in existence an authentic document which states that on a certain occasion the leading parts in a *nō* play were acted by Hidéyoshi and Ieyasu, the two greatest warriors and statesmen Japan has ever possessed.

About one thousand *nō* plays are said to have been composed, of which some eight hundred survive, and of these two hundred and forty-two are now actually performed. It would appear that, in the lifetime of the authors, *nō* plays were sometimes performed in public, but since then they have never or very seldom been performed in public, and at present the mere singing of them at home, without action, is much in fashion among the upper and middle classes throughout Japan.

Of the four types of Japanese drama the *nō* plays were the first to attract foreign notice and to-day they are highly appreciated by cultured Europeans, presumably because they appeal to a taste which recognizes in them certain curious resemblances to Greek tragedy. These resemblances, as may be readily inferred from the above account, consist in the fact that the plays are entirely chanted, that they are pervaded by religious ideas, that the principal characters wear masks, that the chorus sings certain metrical portions and that the manner of the acting is dignified and reserved. None the less it is the truth, and it cannot be disregarded, that the puppet plays and the dramas of the regular stage, both of which reflect in a decidedly greater degree actual Japanese character, beliefs and moral ideas, are considerably more enjoyed by our countrymen at large and that from a literary point of view the puppet plays are more highly esteemed by Japanese scholars than the *nō* plays.

Apart from the question of public enjoyment and critical preference, the *nō* plays are the prototype of puppet plays and of plays for the regular theatre, to which attention will be given a little later in the present sketch.

A large number of the *nō* plays were written by the famous *nō* actors Kwan-ami (1333-1384) and his son Sé-ami (1363–1444), both favourites of the Shogun Yoshimitsu, an admirer and patron of the arts. Of two hundred and forty-two pieces now in actual performance, more than one hundred, including *The Robe of Feathers, Matsukazé, The Miidera Temple, Kagékiyo, The Sumida River* and several others of the best, are by Sé-ami. Sé-ami also wrote music for his own plays and for most of the other pieces, and, in addition, it was by him that the technique of the *nō* play and its dance was brought to such perfection that subsequent actors and writers were unable to contribute anything further to it. It was indeed Sé-ami and Sé-ami alone who combined and unified the merits of several styles of *sarugaku* and of several styles of dancing and who, almost single-handed, created the *nō* dance as we see and hear it to-day. He was, moreover, an able literary critic—the only man of letters in Old Japan who created a philosophy of art which he could justly call his own. His essays known as *Sé-ami's Sixteen Treatises* are excellent lectures on the æsthetics of drama and worthy of any authority on the drama of to-day. His philosophy of art may be condensed into two words, " mimicry " and *yūgen* [1] or " graceful ". Art consists, according to him, in the harmonization of the imitation of nature with graceful taste, or, in other words, in a harmonious combination of realism and idealism. " It is essentially," Sé-ami avers, " the aim of the *nō* performance to beguile all people, high and low." From this it would appear that he intended his art to be enjoyed by all classes,

[1] *Yūgen* nowadays signifies " abstruseness " or " mystic " ; but from his use of the word in his treatises it is evident that Sé-ami intends by it " graceful " or " beautiful ".—From *A New History of Japanese Literature*, by Professor Tsutomu Igarashi.

OLD MEN'S MASKS MADE BY BUNZŌ, WHO LIVED IN THE
FOURTEENTH CENTURY

THE PROTAGONIST OF *THE ROBE OF FEATHERS*, PLAYED
BY MR. KINNOSUKÉ KONGŌ

and it is, therefore, contrary to his purpose that the *nō* play should have been so long monopolized by the upper classes.

IV

THE *KYŌGEN*, OR COMIC INTERLUDES

The *kyōgen* are one-act comic interludes of slight construction, generally performed on the same stage as the *nō* plays and in the intervals between the more serious pieces. Their purpose is to relax that strain on the nerves of the audience which is produced by the lyric dramas. The *kyōgen* are the only plays of Old Japan which have no musical accompaniment, and they exactly resemble European dramas in form. Not a few of these comic interludes are witty satires on human failings and social evils, but the majority are such primitive and naïve farces as tickle the fancy of the audience with amusing portrayals of innocent follies. As for the material which goes to make up the *kyōgen*, no contemporary events concerning any class of society were neglected which could entertain the sense of humour. Their authors also make use of not a few fairy-tales concerning deities, the King of Hell, and the *tengu*, or long-nosed goblins.

It is a singular fact that among the *kyōgen*, these sister plays of the *nō* dramas which flourished under the patronage of the Shogun and daimio, there are some pieces which dare to hint at the ignorance, stupidity and cowardice of daimio, such as *Hagi Daimio*, *The Inky Woman* and *The Nightingale*. It is also noteworthy that in the Muromachi Period, when Buddhist priests had great influence and *nō* actors were chosen exclusively from that class, some comic interludes were written and played which treat of dishonourable priests

B

who neglect their preaching and are only anxious for the offertory, such as *Fish Preaching, Hanaori* and *Daihannya*. The plots of two or three naïve and simple *kyōgen* may be here related. There is, for instance, the absurd story of the Shogun Yoritomo's favourite steed, Ikézuki, who, having fallen into a fit of violent frenzy, is brought under control by the application of a sort of ointment. In *The God of Thunder*, the horrific deity, missing his footing, falls headlong into a corn-field, is petrified with terror, and a peasant who certainly appears anything but heroic makes fun of him. In *Aunty's Wine* the young nephew of a miserly old woman, a wine-seller, disguises himself as a demon, scares the old lady and proceeds to drink like a lord, but, growing top-heavy, presently forgets himself and endeavours to compose himself for slumber with his head on her lap. This leads to the discovery of the fraud and the interlude closes with the rogue being compelled to take to his heels. In *The Inky Woman* we see a cunning creature who feigns tears to deceive a daimio into sympathy for her and who for this purpose sprinkles her cheeks with the contents of a water-bottle. The nobleman's servant secretly substitutes black ink for the water. The unsuspecting woman smears her face pitch-black and thus loses the game. In contrast to the *nō* plays, composed of a patchwork of classic quotations and of dialogue in the colloquial language of the Kamakura Period, the *kyōgen* consist entirely of dialogue and monologue in the colloquial of the Muromachi Period, and are devoid of narrative elements, and lyric and epic poetry. Although the language used is the colloquial of that far-off era, these farces are quite intelligible even to uneducated people of the present day. Far less incisive than modern satires, their naïvety and absurdity prove all the more amusing to the modern Japanese. They are assuredly excellent dramas, suitable for all classes, and yet they are generally performed in connection with the *nō* plays. It is a matter for regret that they have been used as "side-dishes" to these plays and that opportunities to see and hear them have been limited in this way to the upper classes.

The *sarugaku*, the progenitor of the *nō*, as is clearly stated in *The Record of New Sarugaku*, originally consisted of comic performances, but during the Kamakura (1186–1332) and Muromachi Periods (1338–1565) a gradual transformation came over them, until they lost their original characteristic and became serious performances. From that original vein of comedy, however, descended incomplete farces, which were introduced into the serious dramas as episodical scenes, not to become until later distinct pieces complete in themselves. Such is the origin of the *kyōgen* as they are known to-day.

The surviving comic interludes number nearly two hundred and eighty. The probability is that they were composed during the same period as the *nō* plays, but the names of their authors remain uncertain.

V

THE *KABUKI* PLAYS, OR PLAYS OF THE POPULAR THEATRE

Kabuki plays, that is, plays of the popular theatre, are in form distinctly similar to European drama. In them the dialogue and monologue are sometimes in part metrical. Such portions are spoken to the accompaniment of the samisen, a three-stringed guitar, the finest of all Japanese instruments.

Kabuki plays are divisible into three varieties : in *sewa-mono*, that is, domestic plays, human nature is the central theme, and the playwright selects for his materials " some natural sorrow, loss, or pain " of the people around him. In *jidai-mono*, that is, historical plays, although the heroes and heroines are drawn from the pages of history, the plots are nevertheless far removed from the actual events of history and the realities of life. Even more distant from life is a special variety of historical play, *aragoto*, that is, drama of robust acting, which treats of Herculean warriors, terrible deities or weird spectres. In these pieces fantastic action, heightened dialogue and grotesque painting of the face provide highly legendary scenes appealing strongly to the imagination.

Shosagoto, known also as *furigoto*, posture-dramas with music, are the most characteristic form of *kabuki* plays. Largely influenced by *nō* plays and to a considerable degree by the airy dances of the marionettes, *shosagoto* possess but a slight plot, simple dialogue, descriptive dances and symbolic movement, the whole welded together by the rhythms of drum, flute, samisen and the voices of the chorus of Nagauta, Tokiwazu and Kiyomoto, the three styles of stage music. The best *shosagoto* are adaptations of *nō* plays and of these *The Kanjinchō* or " The Subscription Book " is without doubt the most perfect. Many adaptations of the comic interludes referred to above are to be found among *shosagoto*.

All varieties of these performances are to a lesser or greater degree accompanied by song and music. The same even applies to domestic plays, the most realistic pieces of all, for songs in low voices and to the accompaniment of the samisen, off-stage, are heard throughout half the performance. In all these different performances dialogue is spoken, or rather chanted, in highly artificial voices; the miming is much exaggerated, often approaching dancing, and the make-up is strongly accentuated. These productions are

THE SOGAS' NIGHT ASSAULT AT THE DAWN OF A HUNTING-FIELD, A KABUKI PLAY BY
MOKU-AMI, PERFORMED BY FAMOUS ACTORS OF OLDEN DAYS

From a colour print by Kunichika

[face p. 20

A SCENE FROM *KAMPEI AND O-KARU*, A *KABUKI* PLAY
MR. SHŌCHŌ AS *O-KARU* (left)
MR. SUMIZŌ AS *KAMPEI* (right)

therefore generally known as *kabuki-shibai* or "song-dance theatricals". According to Mr. Toshirō Ihara, *kabuki* was originally a slang expression signifying "humorous" or "amorous", but Chinese scholars later came to represent the word by three Chinese characters signifying "song-dance performance". Be that as it may, the fact remains that this appellation exactly characterizes what is typical of this form of drama.

Just as brevity and quietness are the characteristics of the *nō* production, so exaggeration and expressiveness are the distinguishing features of the *kabuki*, as exemplified in the painting of the actor's face, and in the costumes, scenery, dancing, acting, and rhetoric.

Tradition asserts that a priestess named O-Kuni of the great Shinto temple of Izumo invented the *kabuki-shibai*. At some period of the Keichō era (1596–1615) she proceeded to Kyoto and there, clad in a clerical robe, tinkling a tiny bell and singing simple religious lyrics, she performed a sacred dance for public benefit. She soon found an able assistant in her handsome lover Nagoya Sanzaburō, a Don Juan, who supplied her with simple farces adapted from comic interludes. The couple erected a rough stage in the dry bed of the Kamo River, which runs through the capital, and there the ex-priestess and a few other girls performed, to the accompaniment of the music of flutes and drums. The citizens received them enthusiastically, and their reputation rapidly spread far and wide, so that many girls joined the profession. In 1607 O-Kuni went to Yedo where her performances were also much admired, and, after that, actresses multiplied in Yedo, Osaka and Kyoto, some of them developing great brilliance. Theatre-going became fashionable among townsfolk, but, as the theatre of actresses developed, it exercised an evil influence on public morals. In 1629 the appearance of actresses on the stage was therefore forbidden by the authorities. The rise of the actors' theatre, which had but recently been established, followed, and some of these actors were obliged to play women's rôles. This unnatural art of *onnagata*, or actors playing feminine parts, gradually developed and we hear at different periods of great *onnagata*. Certain of the famous ones were at great pains, even in their daily lives, to train themselves for the feminine rôle, going so far as habitually to wear women's garments and to use women's toilet accessories and articles. A thin, high, falsetto voice, cultivated for the theatre, was used in ordinary conversation. When accomplished *onnagata* perform on the stage it is impossible to realize that they are men, so supreme is their art. The law prohibiting actresses continued in force throughout the greater part of Japan until the middle of the nineteenth century; and for this reason there have been but few actresses until quite recent years.

In 1633 stage music was greatly improved by the addition of the samisen. Later were written many serious dramas adapted from *no* plays or founded on history and stories, for the express purpose of *kabuki* representation, and much improvement was achieved in stage settings and properties, and more particularly in acting. Great actors arose. Among these three paramount figures may be cited : Sakata Tōjūrō (1645–1704), the founder of the realist school; Segawa Kikunojō (1691–1749), an *onnagata*; and Ichikawa Danjūrō the First (1704–1760), the originator of the *aragoto*.

The pieces first produced in the popular theatres were the compositions of ignorant actors, but toward the close of the seventeenth century the writing of plays became a special profession. Noteworthy among *kabuki* playwrights are Chikamatsu Monzaémon (1652–1724), whose work in this sphere, however, has fallen into comparative obscurity owing to the universal acclamation of his puppet drama;

MR. FUKUSKÉ (TOKYO) AS *HANAKO* IN *THE MAIDEN AT THE DŌJŌJI TEMPLE*

MR. KŌSHIRŌ AS THE HERO OF *THE SHIBARAKU*, A DRAMA OF ROBUST ACTING

Sakurada Jisuké (1734–1806), the author of *Your Favourite Kanjinchō* and *Hirugakojima;* Segawa Jokō (1738–1794), the author of *Yosaburō and O-Tomi;* Namiki Gohei [1] (1745–1808), the author of *The Temple-Gate and the Paulownia Flowers* and *Godairiki;* Kawataké Shinshichi (1746–1795), the author of *The Kanjinchō* and *Hōkaibō;* Tsuruya Namboku (1755–1829), the author of *The Love News of Hisamatsu and O-Somé, Suzugamori Forest* and *The Ghost Story of Yotsuya;* and Kawataké Mokuami (1815–1893), the author of *Murai Chōan, Benten Kozō, Seishin and Izayoi, Kōchiyama,* and *The Three Kichisas.* With the exception of these writers, most of the *kabuki* playwrights were of second or third-rate ability. For this reason the popular theatres which flourished in the Genroku era (1688–1704) could not compete with the marionette theatres for which Chikamatsu Monzaémon and many other able writers wrote with genuine gusto. Why, one may ask, did not the regular drama attain perfection during the Yedo Period ? The answer is that the actors reigned supreme in the popular theatre, and the playwrights, being in some sort their slaves, were compelled to adapt their scripts to the demands of the actors. Moreover, the nobility despised the regular theatre ; knights were forbidden to visit it and the actors were looked down upon as " vagabonds ". Under such conditions able writers of an independent spirit would not write for them. But in the latter half of the eighteenth century and in the beginning of the nineteenth, the above-mentioned great *kabuki* writers appeared ; and by the middle of the eighteenth century the regular theatre had effected remarkable improvements by, among other things, borrowing liberally from the doll theatre, not only appropriating its plays, its stage settings and costumes, but even going so far as to adopt the movements

[1] Gohei, an Osaka man, removed to Yedo during the era of Meiwa (1764–1772) and devised the revolving stage there.

of the marionettes. Slowly the regular theatres became more popular than the marionette theatres, until at last they were able to drive them almost out of existence.

VI

THE *JŌRURI* OR PUPPET PLAY

The *jōruri*, or puppet play, differs in form from European drama in that it contains poetic portions, largely written in a series of seven and five syllable lines, which describe the scenery, the expressions, action and moods of the characters, and also voice the author's judgment upon their deeds. The beautiful epic and lyric verse is written in such simple, easy, and often colloquial language that it is quite intelligible even to the uneducated. The *jōruri* is emphatically a literature for all classes.

The poetic narrative passages and often portions of the dialogue are sung or chanted to the agreeable music of the samisen by a chorus seated on a platform on the spectator's right and overlooking the stage. The chorus also declaims the speeches of the puppets. In the regular theatre, where puppet plays are often acted, the actors sustain the greater part of the dialogue and act and dance to the choric recitation of the poetic parts in a manner similar to that employed in the puppet theatre.

Exaggeration and expressiveness are the spirit of the *kabuki* productions; exaggeration and expressiveness are also the distinctive characteristics of the puppet plays and to an even greater degree, since to give life and animation to the puppets, demands extravagance in action and bombast in language. The fact is that the exaggeration of

TADANOBU IN *THE ONE THOUSAND CHERRY-TREES*

JŌRURI CHANTERS AND SAMISEN PLAYERS OF THE BUNRAKU-ZA, READY TO PERFORM

the *kabuki* plays was adopted largely from the puppet performance.

Puppet plays comprise two classes, historical and domestic, called *sewa-mono*. The former generally run to five long acts, while the latter are usually completed in three. Most of the historical plays afford excellent illustrations of patriotism, loyalty, justice, benevolence, honour, self-control and the other virtues of Bushido, the moral code of Japanese knighthood. The plots, like those of the *kabuki* histories, are far removed from the true course of historical events and from the actualities of life. The domestic plays, on the other hand, are studies of real life and are distinguished by their direct portrayal of human nature.

It is significant of popular approval that the puppet play enjoys an extensive popularity when merely chanted or sung. In *yosé* or variety-halls, of which Tokyo boasts at least a hundred and fifty, among the nightly performers one or two *jōruri* singers are always a feature, and there are in addition about ten halls where girl singers perform. A *jōruri* singer combines the functions of an opera singer and an elocutionist, so that it may with justice be claimed that two centuries ago a unique form of elocution was originated in Japan. Beside these professional singers of drama, successful amateur singers abound throughout the Empire, for the singing of puppet plays is traditionally popular among all classes, nor would it be a serious exaggeration to maintain that certain passages of the more famous puppet dramas are as familiar to our countrymen as the national anthem.

Puppet plays which are established as the representative literary masterpieces of the Yedo Period are of such distinguished style and content that modern scholars are agreed in considering them not only the best of all the various types of dramas, but the supreme achievements of Japanese literature.

During the Muromachi Period (1338–1565) the profession of chanting or reciting stories, popular histories and more particularly Buddhist legends came into existence. The style of recitation was modified from the chanting of the *nō* plays and the usages of other styles, the recitations being accompanied by fan taps for the marking of time or the lending of emphasis. Toward the close of the sixteenth century was added the music of the samisen, introduced shortly before, by way of Loochoo, from China. The effect of this improvement was to give a stimulus to the profession of chanting and it became more and more popular. It was about this time that there appeared a story in twelve short parts, entitled *The Story of Lady Jōruri*, which was a great favourite among the story reciters. Tradition avers that its author was Ono-no-Otsū, maid of honour to the famous General Nobunaga, although authority for this belief is lacking. The story treats of the love of the famous warrior Yoshitsuné and a fictitious heroine of supreme beauty named Jōruri, supposed to have been born in fulfilment of her father's earnest prayers to a Buddhist deity. Simple in plot, it nevertheless contains the rudiments of a drama. Henceforward this style of recitation came to be known as *jōruri*, while compositions used by the professional reciters were called *jōruri-bon*, and the reciters themselves *jōruri-katari*, that is *jōruri* chanters. Such is the origin of the term *jōruri* [1] now applied to the puppet play.

During the Keichō era (1596–1615), a noted samisen player of Kyoto, Menukiya Chōzaburō, working with a certain Hikita, a puppet showman of Nishinomiya in Settsu Prov-

---

[1] More exactly *jōruri* is also a generic term for several kinds of chanting to the accompaniment of samisen music, such styles for instance as Tokiwazu, Kiyomoto, Shinnai, Itchū, Tomimoto, Katō, Ōzatsuma and Sonohachi. Nevertheless the term is most frequently used to signify "puppet-play".

ince, invented the art of manipulating puppets [1] to the accompaniment of *jōruri* recitation and samisen music. This marionette show grew rapidly in general favour; so much so that the Emperor Go-Yōzei was pleased to summon the troupe to his palace that their performances might be seen there. Ere long marionette performances were taking place in several quarters of the Imperial capital, attracting large audiences, amongst whom were to be *incognito* found not a few of the warrior class.

Toward the middle of the seventeenth century there came into prominence in Yedo a great *jōruri* chanter, by name Satsuma Jōun, a native of Kyoto. This man's bold and energetic manner of recitation admirably matched the martial spirit then prevalent in the Shogun's capital. Not only did his theatre command large audiences, but daimios and other noblemen extended their patronage to him. After his death, many of his pupils continued for several years to enjoy great popularity, and an author named Oka Seibei is said to have written for them a number of stories, some of which, known as Kimpira-Bon, are still in existence. Their subject is the adventures of Kimpira, a legendary hero of Herculean strength and gigantic stature who achieves warlike feats, destroys demons and slaughters savage beasts. The general public was all ears for these stories and in particular the ignorant samurai of those days could never have enough of them.

The Shogun Ietsuna thrice summoned the *jōruri* players to his palace that he might witness their performances, once in 1678 and twice in 1680.

---

[1] These puppets were in all probability more than two feet high. They were supported by the operator, who was in full view of the spectator. They were not worked with strings from above. Gradually the puppets increased in stature. To-day they are at least two-thirds life size. Further details of the puppets will be found in the chapter entitled "Present Condition of Puppetry—Two Types of Puppets".

Toraya Gentayū, one of Jōun's pupils, moved to Kyoto, where his art was greatly admired, and his school produced a number of famous chanters, each of whom originated a particular style. Of these Inoué Harima and Uji Kaga are the best known. None of them, however, was of such pre-eminent ability as to overshadow the others and the composers of *jōruri* were as yet minor authors whose pieces hardly deserve the name of drama.

Toward the close of the seventeenth century a great *jōruri* chanter, Takémoto Gidayū (1650–1714), made his name in Osaka. He had taken lessons from a pupil of Inoué Harima and later from Uji Kaga, whose stage assistant he had been for some years. He had a powerful voice of excellent musical tone, and from the uncommon qualities of his masters' styles he blended a style of his own. The year 1685 saw the establishment by him of a marionette theatre named the Takémoto-za at Dōtombori, the most bustling quarter of Osaka. The following year he began to chant pieces which had been written at his request by Chikamatsu Monzaémon, destined to become the Shakespeare of Japan. His other partners were an able samisen player, Takézawa Gonnemon, and two extraordinarily dexterous puppeteers, Tatsumatsu Hachirobei and Yoshida Saburobei. An era of peace and refinement had now, under the Tokugawa régime, endured for many years ; and the Osaka citizens had grown tired of the unsophisticated pieces written by minor authors and chanted after a simple and monotonous manner. They hungered for novelty and exhilaration, and the Takémoto-za supplied exactly what they wanted. Gidayū's fame spread throughout Japan and his style surpassed that of any other artist of his day. As time passed his school gained so many disciples that at last almost all *jōruri* reciters adopted his style and the *jōruri* itself began to be known in popular parlance as *gidayū*, and the reciters as *gidayū-katari*. To-

[face p. 28

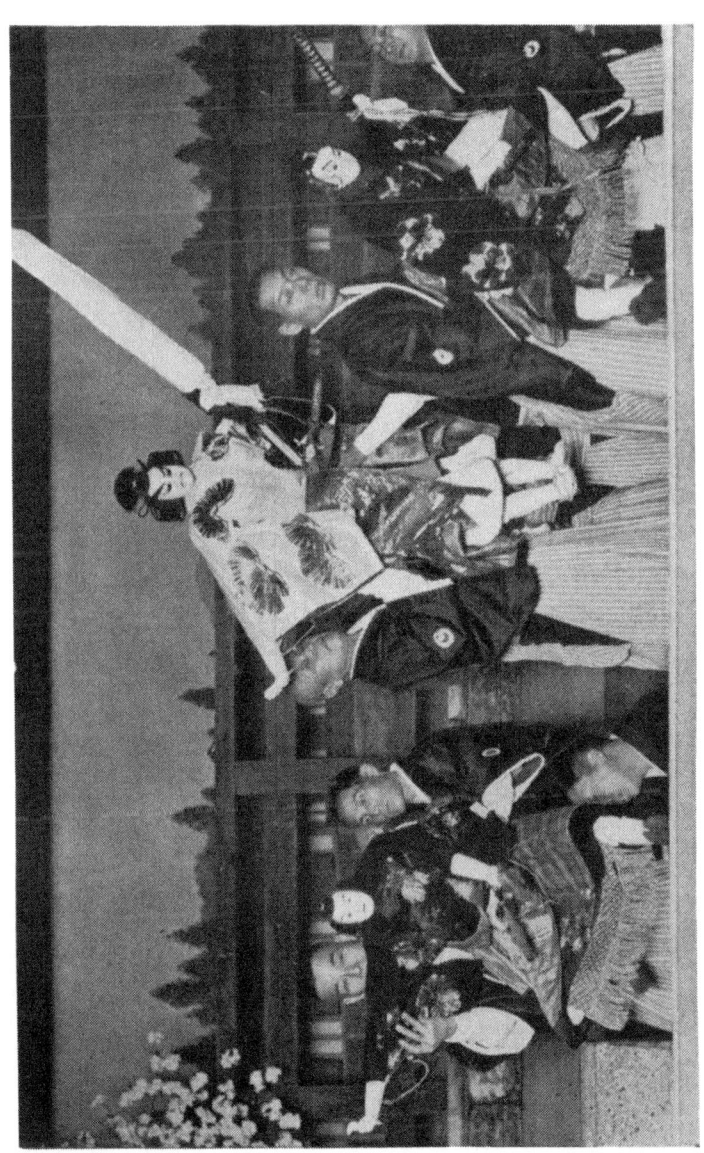

A SCENE FROM *SUGAWARA'S SECRETS OF CALLIGRAPHY*

No. 2

A SCENE FROM THE *EMPEROR YŌMEI*, PERFORMED BY THE BIG THREE OF THE TAKEMOTO-ZA

From an illustration in *The Annals of Puppet Performances*

TATSUMATSU HACHIROBEI (left).   TAKÉMOTO GIDAYŪ (middle).   TAKÉZAWA GONNÉMON (right)

day *jōruri* and *gidayū* are interchangeable terms for the puppet play. The popularity of the Takémoto-za was challenged by a powerful rival and the competition between the two had much to do with the improvement of the marionettes and stage settings, as well as the development of the dramas. This rival was Toyotaké Wakatayū (1680–1764), an ambitious man and an excellent pupil of Gidayū. During 1702 he established an independent marionette theatre, the Toyotaké-za, in the same quarter as the other theatre, having Ki-no-Kaion, an able author, as its playwright. On Gidayū's retirement from management, which ill-health occasioned three years later, the new theatre prospered nearly as much as the old, but we will now leave the subsequent development of these puppet theatres and proceed to the life and works of Chikamatsu.

VII

LIFE AND WORKS OF CHIKAMATSU; *SHINJŪ MONO* OR PLAYS
    TREATING OF LOVE SUICIDE AND THE CAUSES OF LOVE
    SUICIDE

Much of the life of Chikamatsu Monzaémon remains to this day shrouded in mystery. No certainty exists as to where he was born and where his bones lie buried ; nor is anything known of his parents, wife and children. This is, after all, but natural, as Japanese historians have interested themselves almost exclusively in the lives of people of the upper class. The memoirs of a man engaged in literary work for the masses, particularly one of the so-called " theatre people ", who were generally looked down upon in olden times, no more attracted the pens of these biographers than the life of a cat or dog. Among the facts which have definite authority, one is that Chikamatsu died in 1724 aged seventy-two, from which we infer that he was born in 1652.

As various towns disputed the glory of having produced Homer, so there are contestants for the birthplace of Chikamatsu. No less than nine places have claimed the honour, and among these either Kyoto or Hagi, in the province of Nagato, is generally considered to have the best title to the distinction, most scholars favouring Kyoto. For myself I may say, basing my belief on the fact that our dramatist, even in poetic narratives, often makes use of the dialect spoken in Nagato, Suwō and Aki, from the last of which I come, that Hagi is the likelier. Brief examples of the language clue must suffice,—the expression *taguru*, " coughing ", is to be found in the third act of *The Love Suicide at Amijima ;* and again the expression *nobutoi*, " bold ", is used in a descriptive section of the second act of *The Adventures of the Hakata Damsel.*

Tradition asserts that in his youth Chikamatsu was a Buddhist acolyte, the supposition being that he studied in the Kinshōji Temple at Karatsu in Hizen Province, or at the Gonshōji Temple attached to the famous Miidera Monastery in Ōmi Province, and that he called himself Chikamatsu after one of these temples, because the titles of these temples form the name in Chinese ideographs. The poet's true name is Suginomori Nobumori, a name, however, familiar to none but specialists, Chikamatsu Monzaémon being his *nom de plume.* The priests in those days were the most learned class, and if the tradition is to be trusted, we may assume that Chikamatsu's great erudition, and in particular his peculiar knowledge of Buddhist scriptures, a knowledge which blossomed so richly in his immortal masterpieces, was for the most part acquired during his sacerdotal period.

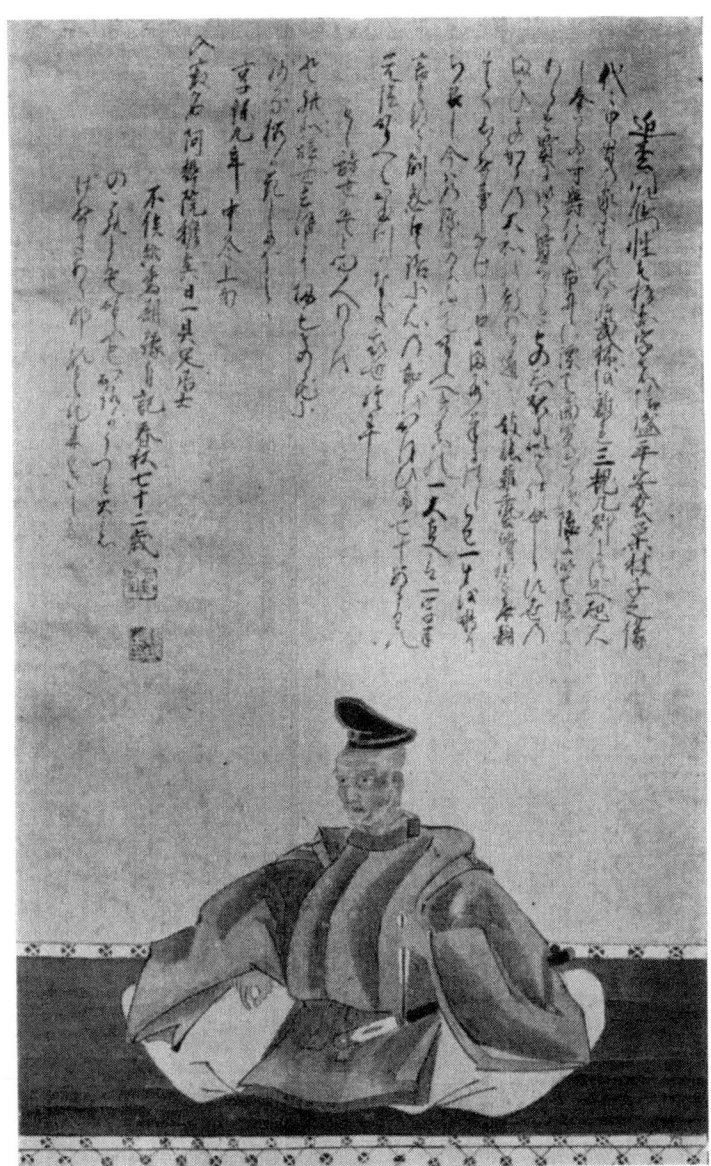

A PORTRAIT OF CHIKAMATSU

From a coloured picture by an unknown artist. The writing
above the portrait is the poet's famous *jisei* or death-bed message,
and is in the master's handwriting. This valuable picture is
in the possession of Mr. Yonétarō Matsuyama, the translator's
close friend.

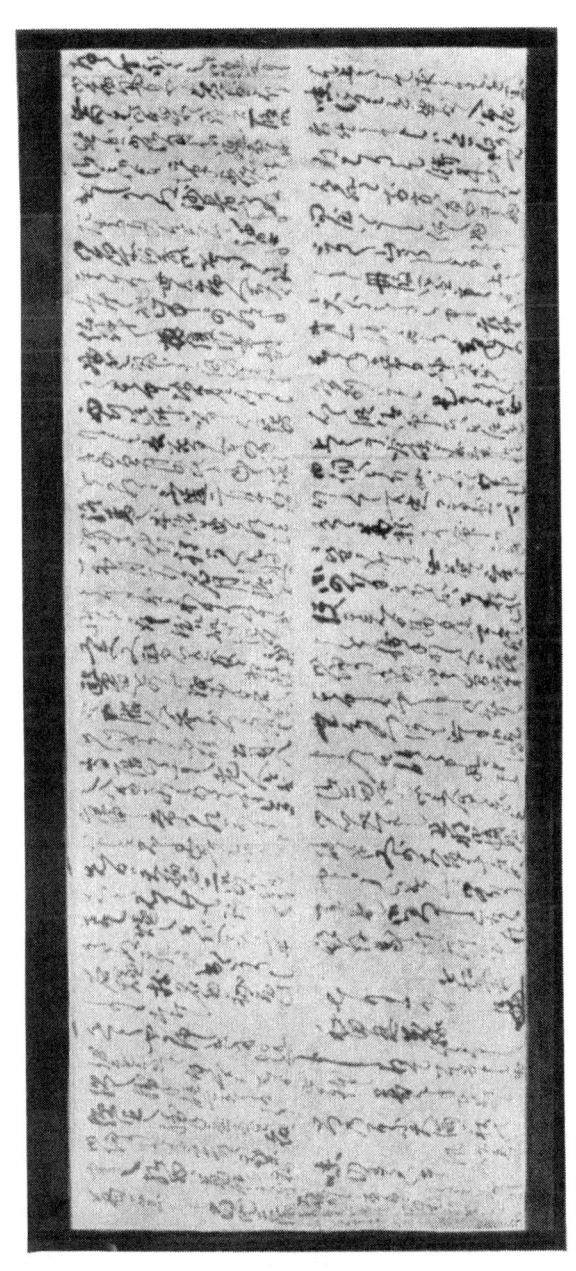

FAC-SIMILE OF A LETTER WRITTEN BY CHIKAMATSU MONZAÉMON

Although both birthplace and boyhood remain obscure, yet a volume named *Takaragura*, that is " The Treasury ", containing one of his *haiku* odes, proves that at the age of nineteen he was a resident in Kyoto ; because the volume is a collection of poems by writers residing in the Imperial capital. The ode in question is as follows :—

> *Shirakumo ya*
> *Hana naki yama no*
> *Haji kakushi.*

> " White clouds—they hide the dishonour
> Of a mountain which hath no flower."

From another document entitled *Okinagusa*, that is " An Old Man's Memorandum ", we glean : " Chikamatsu, in his younger days, served Lord Ōgimachi, a nobleman of the Kyoto court. This personage, a celebrated comic poet, wrote plays for the *jōruri* chanter Uji Kaga. So it came to pass that Chikamatsu was often dispatched on errands to this chanter. Literary talent was his and so he did sometimes assist his master in dramatic composition. In later days it was he who enticed Kaga's oldest pupil, Gidayū, to originate a new style of recitation, which was named Gidayū style, and he himself became Gidayū's playwright."

The statement that Chikamatsu served a court noble is corroborated by a passage of his famous *jisei* [1] or " death-bed message " : " I was born of a warrior's family, but severing my connection with the soldier class, I served more than one noble house."

In 1677, at the age of five-and-twenty, he wrote a *kabuki* play entitled *The Evil Spirit of Lady Wisteria* for the company of the great realistic actor, Sakata Tōjūrō, who performed at Kyoto. With this drama he emerged into sudden fame as a dramatist. We may suppose that it was

---

[1] The *jisei* was an ode or brief composition written on the death-bed by persons of literary taste : a custom of Old Japan.

not his maiden effort, and that prior to this he had turned playwright. From 1677 to 1704 he wrote *kabuki* plays for Tōjūrō's company and certain others, applying his skill now and again to puppet plays for the famous *jōruri* chanters, Inoué Harima, Uji Kaga and in particular Takémoto Gidayū. How many regular plays he wrote during these twenty-seven years has not been positively determined, but twenty-six historical and domestic plays have been attributed to him. The majority of these domestic plays were composed for Tōjūrō's company and it would appear that he wrote them in such a manner as to suit the characteristics of two or three chief actors of the company. In this he was only conforming to the custom of all other *kabuki* playwrights, who, as I have pointed out above, were little better than the creatures of the actors. None of these plays is comparable to the masterpieces he wrote later for the puppet theatre, but it is nevertheless worth chronicling that he took the lead in writing domestic plays which deal with shopkeepers, merchants, peasants and courtesans in place of the customary heroes and noblemen. Furthermore, these plays served as the pioneers to the excellent domestic plays, composed many years later for the puppet theatre, such as *The Love Suicide at Amijima* and *The Courier for Hades*. In 1678 he wrote the first and best of his domestic plays for the regular theatre, *The Last New Year for Yūgiri*, which depicts the life of a courtesan. It is not without interest to recall that George Lillo's domestic tragedy, *The London Merchant*, which also treats of the same subject, was performed in 1731, and that both in plot and in the choice of characters Lillo's play bears a remarkable resemblance to our dramatist's famous puppet-play *A Hell of Oil*, first produced in 1721.

Chikamatsu continued his activities as a *kabuki* dramatist, in addition to his work as a puppet dramatist, until his fifty-first year. By this time Tōjūrō, who had a high opinion of

Chikamatsu's ability as well as a great respect for his writings, was already an aged man about whom clung the mere shadow of former greatness, while the other actors, ignorant and supercilious, were unable to appreciate our author's merits. Then the dramatist, in a mood of discontent, resolved upon a great step. Without regrets he cast aside his pen as a *kabuki* writer and, leaving the Imperial capital, where he had resided since youth, he installed himself at Osaka, there to devote himself to writing puppet plays for his friend, Takémoto Gidayū. He thus entered upon a new life of great usefulness, congenial both to his genius as a writer and to his character as a man. Had he remained a slave to the actors, oblivion might have blotted out his name. This change was the crisis in his life; it likewise marks a great turning-point in the history of the Japanese drama. It is to be observed that, upon Chikamatsu's retirement, the regular theatres of Kyoto and Osaka gradually lost their prestige and were overshadowed by the theatres of Yedo, while the *jōruri*, which had welcomed him, advanced with a new vigour and entered upon the brightest period of its history.

Chikamatsu's career as a *jōruri* writer lasted for over forty-five years, that is from 1680, when he was twenty-eight, to 1724, the year of his death. The pieces written during these years number eighty historical and twenty-four domestic plays, one hundred and four works in all. Which was actually his first composition in this series cannot be definitely established, but the earliest pieces, so far as scholars can decide, are *The Story of Akazomé Emon's Prosperity, Lord Higashi-yama's Diversion on the Day of the Rat* and *Gleanings from My Leisure Hours*, the first written in his twenty-eighth year, the second two in his twenty-ninth. These pieces and certain others belonging to his apprenticeship period are either clumsy adaptations of *nō* plays, both as to plot and technique, or imitations of the old *jōruri*. Tales strung out with hardly any dramatic construction, they set time and space at naught. In style also they are but little superior to their prototypes. Many of his later masterpieces also bear traces of the *nō* play. In all probability Chikamatsu made the acquaintance of Gidayū when the great chanter-to-be was studying under the instruction of Uji Kaga at Kyoto. Gidayū, from the circumstance that he had been a pupil of Shimizu Rihei, who was in turn the greatest pupil of Inoué Harima, was at that time using the name of Shimizu Ridayū. He had but recently left his native city Osaka for Kyoto and was working as pupil-assistant to Uji Kaga. It was not long before his strong voice, excellent musical sense, and engaging manner of recitation, brought him fame. The probability is that it was during these days that he chanced upon Chikamatsu, and the two artists agreed to collaborate in future. Soon afterwards Ridayū deserted Uji Kaga's company and, entering into a triple alliance with a certain Takéya, a financier, and Takézawa Gonnemon, a great samisen player, started a puppet theatre in the Western Theatre at Dōtombori, Osaka, placing over the door a pretentious sign-board which read " The New School of *Jōruri* ". Having established this theatre, he proceeded to adopt the name of Takémoto Gidayū, to chant in a style of his own, and to avail himself to the utmost of original plays possessing literary merit. At his first performance in the new theatre, Gidayū recited Chikamatsu's piece *The Round Fan of Soga* (later renamed *One Hundred Days' Soga*), previously recited with great success by Uji Kaga. This he followed up by the same author's *Story of the Japanese Syllabary* and *The Wise Woman's Practice of Penmanship and the New Almanac*.

And then an interesting event in Japanese dramatic history occurred, an event which resulted in a literary contest between Chikamatsu and Ibara Saikaku, the novelist. Uji Kaga, learning that his erstwhile pupil and assistant Gidayū had established a theatre at Dōtombori, determined to put a spoke in the interloper's wheel. He therefore proceeded with his troupe to Osaka, and at the Eastern Theatre of Dōtombori entered into direct competition with his rival. His challenge took the form of a performance of *The Almanac* by Ibara Saikaku. The younger player replied with *The Wise Woman's Practice of Penmanship and the New Almanac*. Victory remaining with Gidayū, Kaga reorganized his forces and recited another piece by Saikaku; but luck was against him; a fire unfortunately broke out in his theatre, and reduced it to ashes; so that the crestfallen old chanter was reluctantly compelled to beat a retreat to Kyoto. This combat greatly contributed to the reputation both of Gidayū and Chikamatsu.

The year 1686 is a memorable one in the literary annals of the Yedo Period, for during this year three great men of letters embarked upon voyages of discovery. In this year the *haiku* writer, Bashō, dissatisfied with the old schools of Teimon and Danrin, made public a new style of his own as exemplified in his famous ode :—

> *Natsu-gusa ya*
> *Tsuwa-mono-domo no*
> *Yumé no ato.*
> "Haply the summer grasses are
> A relic of the warriors'[1] dream."

In this year the novelist Saikaku published his master-pieces *The Five Amorous Women* and *The Life of an Amorous Woman*. As for our dramatist, it was in February of the same year that his historical drama *The Successful Kagékiyo*, was first performed by Gidayū. The epithet " successful " preceding the name of the warrior was a sign that the author

---

[1] Of the warriors' dream of power and glory nothing remains but the high grasses waving upon the moor that is their tomb.

wished a successful future to the young artist in his new style of recitation. This play marks a departure from the old-fashioned *jōruri* in plot, characterization, scenes, dialogue, etc. ; the musical elements have diminished and the dialogue has proportionately increased. By this one play the dramatist revolutionized the nature of *jōruri*, for he brought home to an audience, accustomed to consider the musical and lyrical elements the chief essentials of *jōruri*, his new conception of the dialogue and action of the characters and the development of the plot as of an equal importance. *The Successful Kagékiyo* was pre-eminently suited to Gidayū's style of recitation, and by this performance a sudden access of fame rewarded both author and chanter. A new epoch in the literary and the chanters' world had commenced. As year followed year, *The Successful Kagékiyo* was succeeded by new dramas, including *Matsukazé and Murasamé, Shaka-muni's Nativity, The Annals of Urashima, Semimaru* and *The Five Soga Brothers.*

Another new stage of development was signalized in 1700 by the appearance of *The Woman's Harakiri at Long Street.* This realistic drama, the first of Chikamatsu's domestic plays for the puppet theatre, received a warm welcome from the public. The Osaka citizens naturally enough discovered much to interest them in a work representing the joys and sorrows of persons of their own class. The year 1703 saw the performance of *The Love Suicide at Sonézaki*, a play which deals with a *shinjū* or double-suicide of young lovers and is the first of the so-called *shinjū-mono* or plays of love suicide, a variety of *sewa-mono*. The originality of the theme, Gidayū's excellent production and the perfected talent of the puppeteer Tatsumatsu Hachirobei, combined to assure it a brilliant success. So enthusiastic was the reception accorded this play by the public that love suicide became a favourite theme for the contemporary dramatists of puppet and regular theatres. Indeed the story goes that *The Love Suicide at Sonézaki*, *The Love Suicide at Amijima* and other *shinjū-mono* by Chikamatsu, describing this tragic mode of death in language of amazing beauty, so fascinated the audience that on their appearance the number of cases of suicide among lovers showed an alarming increase, although it is impossible to ascertain what amount of truth there is in this tradition. The historian has no data on which to base an opinion, but the very existence of the tradition testifies to the great influence, both for good and evil, exerted by the plays of Chikamatsu.

Japan has the unenviable reputation of being the only country in the world where double suicide for love almost amounts to an institution. Only recently the public was greatly shocked by the love suicide of one of our greatest men of letters. When a pair of passionate young lovers despair of obtaining their parents' permission to marry, or when any other obstacle to their hopes arises, they elect often enough, instead of eloping, to die together, aspiring thus to become united in the next world. So frequent is this form of suicide that there exists for it the word *shinjū*, although it is uncertain at what period this special word was coined. It would appear likely that love suicide was unknown during the Nara and Heian Periods when, as may be inferred from the contents of *The Story of Genji*, love and marriage were comparatively unrestricted. The word *shinjū*, in any case, is not to be found in any document of the time. Later, during the Kamakura and Muromachi Periods, the military spirit so coloured the mentality of all classes that indulgence in love was considered shameful. A warrior counted it the supreme reward of his life to die fighting for his liege lord, even though this involved the sacrifice of the love of wife and family. Suicide for love can hardly have occurred under such conditions. The supposition is—

and nothing contradicts it—that this tragic form of death, and the word *shinjū*, originated during the Yedo Period when complete feudalism reigned, a feudalism characterized by class distinctions, the family system and by Bushido, or the moral principles of knighthood. It is obvious that class distinctions interfered with marriage between persons of different classes, and the family system, which is still in force, often compels a man to divorce a wife he loves dearly on account of discord with her parents-in-law. A result of the family system was the institution of compulsory marriage. Furthermore, the universal prevalence of Confucianism, which teaches that boys and girls of the age of seven and upwards should not sit together, prevented social intercourse between the sexes and the free choice of a life-companion. Again, the spread of the Jōdo and Shin sects of Buddhism, sects which emphasize the perfect bliss of a future existence called Jōdo or " Pure Land ", gave rise to an emotional way of counting as naught this earthly existence. Bushido, in turn, fostered the spiritual habit of making light of life and death, and taught that suicide was the best way of atoning for one's errors. Such were the factors that brought about the double suicide of thwarted lovers. To these must be added the *shinjū* literature of Chikamatsu and other writers and the influence of the pleasure quarters where, as we have emphasized above, all visitors, whether of the samurai or of the merchant class, so much despised in the outer world, found themselves on the same footing. To such persons the gay quarters were lands of liberty and a paradise on earth, and consequently their visits to the courtesans were frequent, and often enough resulted in financial ruin. In such situations the *shinjū* of sympathetic lovers, despite the saying that " there is no faith-keeping courtesan ", was common. Most of these influences, though moderated to a certain extent, continue in existence to-day :

hence the occasional occurrence of double suicide.[1] So much by way of explanation of *shinjū*.

From 1705, when he removed to Osaka, until the death of Gidayū in 1724, Chikamatsu continued to write a succession of excellent historical and domestic plays, amongst the more noteworthy of which are *The Snow-Woman and Five Battledores*, *The Courtesan's Frankincense*, *The Fair Ladies at a Game of Poem-Cards*, *The Almanac of Love*, *Tamba Yosaku*, and *The Courier for Hades*.

Gidayū's death in 1724 was a great blow to the Takémoto-za. Apart from the sorrow caused by the passing of the master-mind of the theatre and founder of the Gidayū style, great trouble arose over the question of succession to the chief recitership. In accordance with Gidayū's dying wish, it had been decided that Masatayū, one of the great chanter's younger pupils, should succeed to this post of honour; but the elder pupils, in indignation, seceded from the company and the public turned an eye of contempt upon Masatayū. Sudden unpopularity descended on the theatre, manifested in the steady falling-off in the size of its audiences. Something had to be done, and that quickly, to keep it " a going concern ". Chikamatsu, fully appreciative of Masatayū's uncommon degree of talent, threw himself unsparingly into action and produced the historical play entitled *The Battles of Kokusenya*. So enthusiastic was the reception accorded it on its appearance in November 1715, that it enjoyed a run of seventeen months. The theatre was saved. Chikamatsu's fame reached its zenith and Masatayū's name was made. The young chanter's position was thenceforth secure and the popularity of the Takémoto-za exceeded even that which it had known in the days of his predecessor. Such was the

---

[1] These remarks point to the evil influences of Confucianism, Buddhism and Bushido; but I am far from denying that the civilization of Old Japan owes to them almost all its essential elements.

success of *The Battles of Kokusenya* that not only was it revived at the Takémoto-za twice or thrice during the years that followed, but it was performed at several regular theatres in Kyoto, Osaka and Yedo, Danjūrō the Second playing the title rôle in the last-named city.

The Battles of Kokusenya is a drama founded on the career of Tei Seikō, the son by a Japanese wife of Tei Shiryō, a Chinese subject of the Ming dynasty. Shiryō came over to Japan in the way of business and lived for some years at Hirado, in Kyūshū, where by trading with Dutchmen coming to Japan, he managed to make a large fortune; and, presumably inspired by military ambition, he strenuously studied gunnery. Later, this adventurer crossed over to Formosa, where he soon became a pirate chief, built a strong fortress, and obtained such influence all over the island that the Ming Court found it expedient to appoint him Governor-General not only of the island itself but also of a large district in South China. In subsequent years, when the Chinese capital and Nanking were captured by the Tartar invaders, and the Emperor had sought refuge in his castle of South China, Shiryō fought bravely for his sovereign's cause. But after the assassination of the Emperor, he found it impossible to hold his own against the troops of the new dynasty and surrendered to them, in spite of strong dissuasion on the part of his relatives and followers. The army of his son Seikō, however, offered such stubborn resistance to the Tartars that the latter, hot for revenge, murdered Shiryō. This influenced Seikō to renewed resistance against the hostile troops. He occupied many towns and cities of South China for several years; but his army being greatly reduced in numbers, he was at last obliged to evacuate these places and cross over to Formosa, where he did his utmost for the restoration of the Ming dynasty. But, unfortunately, before his efforts bore fruit, a sudden illness carried him off at a comparatively early age. In the drama, Kokusenya—the fictitious name of Tei Seikō—crosses to China with his parents. There, aided by his sister-in-law's husband, General Kanki, after several battles he succeeds in conquering the usurpers and restoring the Ming dynasty.

The deftness of its stage technique, its grand scenes and gorgeous costumes, the great beauty of its style and above all its patriotic sentiments—the hero, half Japanese, half Chinese, is treated almost as if he were a Japanese patriot—conspired to make *The Battles of Kokusenya* an enthralling thing to the Osaka audiences. Viewed by modern standards the play cannot be called a great masterpiece and indeed it is inferior to other historical plays of the same author, such as *The Tethered Steed, The Courtesan's Frankincense* and *The Fair Ladies at a Game of Poem-Cards.*

We should be surprised if Masatayū, in view of what had occurred, had not felt a grateful affection to Chikamatsu, who in his turn returned the affection, and, as a fellow-artist, paid him the tribute of encouragement. To make up for the deficiences of his voice, which was of poor tone and small volume, Masatayū was at pains to bring out the strength of dialogue and to accentuate passages of human characterization rather than the purely narrative sections of the performance. Realizing the ability displayed by the reciter in conveying clearly the dramatic elements of his productions, Chikamatsu proceeded to write for him many excellent domestic plays, distinguished by acute human portraiture, with the aim of displaying the young chanter's talent to the best advantage. The increasing mastery of his craft which he displayed as years went on is in no small degree due to the perfect harmony which existed between the artistic conceptions of the chanter and the playwright. Noteworthy among the plays written for Masatayū are *Gonza and O-Sai, The Revenge of the Soga Brothers, The*

Adventures of the Hakata Damsel, The Taira Family and Nyōgo Island, The Love Suicide at Amijima, The Battle of Frogs, The Battles of Kokusenya, The Love Suicide on Kōshin Eve, and *The Tethered Steed.*

The Tethered Steed which was produced in January, 1724, proved to be his swan song, for the great dramatist breathed his last on November 22nd of the same year, having attained the advanced age of seventy-two. What complaint it was that occasioned his death is unknown; we may infer that, whatever that cause may have been, sheer old age was accessory to it. A conflagration which broke out in Osaka in March, 1724, may, it is conjectured, have been a shock to the aged dramatist, already declining. *The Tethered Steed,* which found the audience as friendly as ever, contains a scene descriptive of a bonfire built in imitation of one held every 16th of July on Mount Higashiyama near Kyoto. This bonfire is shaped like the Chinese character for " Great ", and has for its object the leading of souls astray in Hades back to the paths of righteousness. During the performance of the play an ominous rumour spread throughout Osaka to the effect that the character " Great " referred to Osaka, " O " signifying " Great " and " saka " " slope ", and therefore the city would be burnt. Strangely enough in March the greater part of the city was, in fact, destroyed by fire. The superstitious rumour having coincided so unfortunately with the event, the popularity of *The Tethered Steed* underwent such an eclipse that not only was the performance of it immediately stopped, but it was banished for ever from the repertory of both the puppet and the regular theatres. It is not, then, mere fantasy to think that this catastrophe so affected the invalid that his condition took a turn for the worse.

MISS TŌCHŌ, A TOKYO JŌRURI CHANTRESS, READY
TO SING

BEHIND THE PUPPET STAGE OF THE BUNRAKU-ZA.   MR. TAMAZŌ
YOSHIDA, A PUPPET-MASTER

VIII

CHARACTERISTICS OF CHIKAMATSU

Of Chikamatsu's one hundred and four puppet plays *The Battles of Kokusenya, The Revenge of the Soga Brothers,* and *The Snow-Woman and Five Battledores* used in days of old to be considered his masterpieces. This estimate has in recent years been modified and nowadays the palm is bestowed upon *The Love Suicide at Amijima, The Courier for Hades, The Almanac of Love,* and one or two other domestic plays. My own opinion, which chances to be endorsed by Dr. Oto-o Fujii, Mr. Hōgin Kidani and certain other authorities, inclines to awarding the first place among Chikamatsu's historical plays to *The Courtesan's Frankincense, The Tethered Steed* and *Fair Ladies at a Game of Poem-Cards.*

The modern reader of Chikamatsu finds something lacking in the historical plays, but holds the domestic plays in high esteem. When the playwright was alive, however, the histories enjoyed supremacy and the domestic plays were known as *ha-jōruri,* that is secondary plays, and were performed as after-pieces, although these, and in particular those dealing with love suicide, created at their first appearance sensation enough. The author, too, was of the opinion that his real power displayed itself better in the histories, and accordingly took great pains in the writing of them, especially as they afforded him ample opportunity for embodying his excellent knowledge of Shintoism, Buddhism, and Confucianism and of Chinese and Japanese classics, opportunity of which the dramatist availed himself to the full. The historical themes of which he has treated embrace a wide variety of subjects dealing, as they do, with Japanese myths, the more important events and personages of Japanese history, the life and teachings of Shaka Muni, certain incidents of early Christian missions in Japan, a number of Chinese historical personages, ghost stories, and still other motives. Our author's fertile imagination, his extensive learning, his magical colour, the fluency of his language, all these conspire to make these histories a matter for wonder.

Chikamatsu's histories were vastly effective in inspiring merchants and peasants with the spirit of the samurai. Be the period depicted the Age of Imperial Ascendancy or the Age of the Warriors' Ascendancy, be the scene at home or abroad, the basic spirit of the story is always Bushido or the precepts of knighthood. On this account, therefore, it is not amiss to style these plays " popular text-books of Bushido ".

In the histories the stress is laid on the unexpected development of events and the activity of the persons engaged. Consequently they show a tendency toward subordinating character to plot. And this leads to the inevitable query as to whether life-blood runs in the veins of the characters or not. Not only is distinct individuality often absent, but upon occasion not even the ordinary qualities of humanity are recognizable. The heroes of Chikamatsu are as brave as Hercules ; the wise as all-powerful as Gods. Anything the protagonist desires he can achieve. As a writer of histories Chikamatsu is a romanticist, an idealist and a mystic. The audience of his day was enraptured by miraculous incidents and fabulous characters. The public taste was low. And just as young people prefer flowery romances to the sobriety proper to the novel, so the audience preferred wild and exciting plots to the deliberate delineation of human nature.

The domestic plays are, generally speaking, based on actual occurrences of our author's era : dramatizations of

what might well be called the *chronique scandaleuse* of
the time. The events are ordinary and the characters such
as cross our path every day. Chikamatsu was such a rapid
writer of plays of this kind that *The Love Suicide at
Sonézaki*, referred to above, made its first appearance a fortnight after the suicide itself. These domestic plays are in
general characterized by unity of action and often even
by unity of time and place, and above all by just delineation
of fundamental human traits. The characters are for the
most part instinct with life, yet even among these the sharpness of individual personality is often lacking. Most of
them belong to a group of types; and Dr. Tsubo-uchi's
observation, " Chikamatsu was at pains to portray human
nature, not individual character", is applicable not only to
the histories, but in measure also to the domestic plays. In
these plays our author is a naturalist and a realist, and
contrives, strange to say, to be also an idealist, for ugly
events are beautified and contemptible characters idealized.
This is peculiarly the case with those dramas treating of
love suicide. " Chikamatsu saves the heroes and heroines
of his tragedies," says Dr. Tsukuru Fujimura, " by the
hope of a rebirth in the Pure Land or in the Lotus-Flower.
Such as commit suicide or are executed never fail to express
hopes of a rebirth in the Lotus-Flower.[1] In that respect the
hue of his tragedies differs from that of stock tragedies and
the darkness of the shadow of death is brightened with a
tiny flame. The painful sensations of the reader or spectator
of those days were relieved by the consciousness that the
souls of the dying lovers had found salvation and it would
appear that such consolation powerfully influenced the young
lovers of the dramatist's era who gave themselves to death.
The heroes and heroines of these plays indulged the following
reflections, ' Thwarted by social conventions and bound by

---

[1] A rebirth in the Lotus-Flower signifies a rebirth in the next world.

material ties, our lives, our mutual love have not been happy.
Since being crossed and thwarted as we are is contingent
upon the fact of our physical being, let us now destroy this
existence, cast off our bondage and, so doing, enter into the
spiritual existence of the future world, therein to enjoy to
the full a life of love that knows no barrier nor impediment.'
I do not believe that opinions like these generally obtained
in the society of that epoch. Indeed, I rather incline toward the supposition that the merchants and peasants were
more materialistic and more instinctive, and my notion is
supported by the work of the novelist Saikaku. This reading of the psychology of love suicide is in most cases a
creation of the poet, who displays a profound sympathy for
those unhappy lovers . . . Chikamatsu is called an artist
of love, and this appellation finds its appropriateness chiefly
in the sense that his plays are ardent with the warmth of a
great loving-kindness. He extends his sympathy and love
to men and women who, as the result of follies or of ' riotous
guilty courses ', take refuge in suicide. Nor does he hesitate
to show his benevolence also to unchaste wives, presenting the
matter in such a way that these unfortunates seem more
worthy of pity than of hate. It is hardly necessary to point
out that the girl characters Koharu, Umégawa and O-Hatsu
are of this type ; even the young profligates Jihei, Chūbei
and Tokubei are too luckless and too lovable to become the
object of detestation. Nay, one can hardly bring oneself to
be indignant even at Yohei, disobedient as he is to his
foster-father and his own mother and outrageously as he
behaves to both of them. The poet's strong and all-embracing
compassion wraps them round : he is their protector against
cold-hearted common-sense criticism and the conventional
moral censure of those days. Claims like these entitle
Chikamatsu to be called an artist of love."

Chikamatsu always paid due regard to the peculiarities

of the art of the samisen player, of the *jōruri* chanter and of the puppeteer, and the impression which his work produces is that he is a great poet combining in himself something of the musician, the elocutionist and the puppeteer. Thus his plays are primarily intended for spectacular and auditory effects; and it follows that, adequately to appreciate Chikamatsu, one should see his plays performed with marionettes to the accompaniment of the samisen and melodious chanting. I may be pardoned for again urging the axiom that exaggeration of acting and bombast of language are indispensable to effect in the puppet theatre. To this the poet himself bears witness: "The primary object of a *jōruri* consists in giving life and animation to marionettes. Words must, so to speak, become living things. Forasmuch as the object is to impart the semblance of a variety of passions and emotions to inanimate dolls, and this in competition with living actors, the *jōruri* is extremely difficult to write to perfection. . . . The *jōruri*, while it deals with matters as they are, sometimes also describes things which have no existence save in art. The lack of expression on the dolls' faces has to be compensated for by dialogue of a particularly expressive nature."

Again he says: "Art lies in the shadowy frontiers between reality and unreality. Art appears unreal, but it is not unreality; art has the appearance of reality, but it is not reality. The worth of art lies between reality and unreality. Painting and sculpture are arts because, while they aim at depicting real things, they contain something unreal. Even Yōkihi [1] was not without some defect in her person and were she painted as she actually was the result might contain some displeasing element. The same is true of drama; while aiming at reality it nevertheless contains something contrary to the nature of reality. This is what art is and this art

[1] The most beautiful Chinese woman that has ever lived.

delights us." The reader will be struck if he compares Chikamatsu's words " Art lies in the shadowy frontiers between reality and unreality " with Goethe's famous saying " Art is art only because it is not nature ".

I will close this consideration by quoting a passage from Dr. Tsubo-uchi : " Chikamatsu was at pains to produce spectacular as well as auditory effects. He also observed the relations between drama and samisen and between drama and puppet. Those whose desire it is to form a just estimate of him should not regard his plays as compositions for the study, but should consider their value to the ear and their effect upon the eye. Indeed, the appeal to the eye and the appeal to the ear, these are his constant preoccupations."

So far as the chanter's art is concerned, a picturesque rhythm and suitable melody of language are naturally of prime importance. Half the identity and distinction of Chikamatsu's work lies in the perfection of his language. His rhetoric, which matures to its finest point every element of melody and variety inherent in the Japanese tongue, is amazing. His sentences, although for the most part in verse, are a highly skilful union of classical and colloquial styles. Alliteration, metaphor, simile, personification, an imperceptible modulation of the last word or words of a dialogue into song, frequent use of related words, pivot words and pillow words, nay, of all the varieties of word-play, a delightfully easy introduction of classical songs, poems and Chinese couplets, Confucianist sayings, Buddhist hymns, lovely passages from nō plays, folk-songs, maxims and proverbs— all these graces combine to make his sentences perfect gems of expression. It should, nevertheless, be remarked that the frequent sacrifice of sense to sound for the sake of euphony, amounts to a failing in our poet. His beautiful language is often enlivened with wit and humour, but he sometimes abuses his employment of these resources. Even in the middle of a pathetic passage he is liable to introduce humorous vulgarities which rudely dispel the illusion engendered in the intellectual reader. Objection is also taken to his occasional indulgence in obscene language, which, nevertheless, seems to have been very far from lessening the interest taken in his pieces by the audiences of his day. It speaks greatly for his level - headedness in writing that, although his dramas are for the most part in verse, they yet remain quite intelligible even to the uncultured. That the shopkeepers and merchants of Osaka should have fully enjoyed the poetic interest in the verse - narratives of his new plays the first night of their appearance, as we know they did, is a notable fact.

The fondness for playing upon words, often held up against Shakespeare as a weakness in his earlier works, constitutes in Chikamatsu's drama his most beautiful characteristic. Every line almost of his poetic narratives acquires an unusual power for the initiate by this subtlety. It should be ever remembered that the play upon words is the most important rhetorical resource of Japanese classics, and in particular of old Japanese poetry. The elimination of such pivot words and puns from the text of the old Japanese poems would reduce them to mere flatness. It should be added that the pun, which in English almost always produces a ludicrous effect, is used in classical Japanese in nearly every case as a means to euphony and beauty. The truth is that the term " pun " does not give an exact notion of the use of play upon words in Japanese classics. And Chikamatsu is the greatest master of these embellishments. " The use of pivot words," says Mr. Arthur Waley, " is not in itself a decoration more artificial than rhyme, and I cannot agree with those European writers to whom this device appears puerile and degraded. Each language must use such embellishments as suit its

D

genius. It would be impossible to render these pivot words into English."

In a word, Chikamatsu is a hierarch of rhetoric. A writer of the olden days pronounces him " a god of writing " and another " a dragon among men ". By " dragon " is meant a demigod, not a rapacious monster; among the Japanese the dragon is regarded as a sacred being. No correct estimate of his plays can be formed without an appreciation of their musical elements, which it is unfortunately almost impossible to render into English, save by an English Chikamatsu with a thorough knowledge of Japanese.

It is a matter for regret that, owing to the exclusion policy steadfastly pursued by the Tokugawa Shogunate, Japan was isolated from international currents of civilization during two centuries. For her the Renaissance did not exist, Columbus had not discovered America, Shakespeare had not sung, and the *Novum Organum* and the *Principia* had never been written. I made use above of the phrase " Chikamatsu's extensive learning ", but his range of knowledge did not actually exceed the bounds of Shintoism, Buddhism, Confucianism,[1] and the Chinese and Japanese classics. As far as he was concerned, European history and literature and the world's science and philosophy were non-existent. Had he lived in a milieu in which the scientific spirit was active and if he had been able to draw upon those stores of knowledge which remained inaccessible to him, Chikamatsu, with his imagination, his descriptive powers, and his many-sided genius, might have achieved even more substantial triumphs.

---

[1] It is true that Buddhism and the Chinese classics contain something like European philosophies; but these metaphysical speculations were generally neglected by Japanese priests and scholars.

IX

CHIKAMATSU'S CONTEMPORARIES AND THE SUBSEQUENT
HISTORY OF THE PUPPET PLAY

We have seen how Toyotaké Wakatayū, with Ki-no-Kaion, an able writer, as his playwright, in 1702 established a marionette theatre, called the Toyotaké-za in the same quarter as the Takémoto-za.

Kaion, a native of Sakai, a thriving city near Osaka, was born in 1663 and was thus ten years junior to Chikamatsu. His father and older brother were poets and he himself, like Chikamatsu, served in his youth as a Buddhist priest, returning later to the outer world in order to study medicine. Subsequently he followed the medical profession and resided in Osaka. His leisure hours he spent in taking lessons in Japanese classics from Keichū, a Buddhist priest noted for his ascetic life and profound knowledge of Japanese literature. Gradually Kaion drifted into literary work, to become at last a puppet dramatist.

From the year 1702, when he became connected with the Toyotaké-za, till his retirement in 1723, he wrote one drama after another. To accentuate his competition with Chikamatsu, he often had the audacity to choose for his plays topics almost identical with those of his rival. For instance, when Chikamatsu brought out *The Love Suicide at Sonézaki*, first performed in 1703, Kaion produced during the following year *O-Shichi, the Greengrocer's Daughter*. *The Emperor Yōmei* and *The Courier for Hades*, Kaion countered with *The Pine-Tree at Soné* and *O-Somé, the Oil-merchant's Daughter*. That the Toyotaké-za could hold its own with the Takémoto-za must be largely ascribed to the merits of Kaion's dramas;

nevertheless, in imagination and descriptive power he is no match for Chikamatsu. Among his forty dramas the palm is usually awarded to *O-Shichi, the Greengrocer's Daughter, The Three Kamakura Shoguns* and *Two Waist-Bands for Love Suicide ;* for my part, however, *Ono-no-Komachi's New Year Gift* seems to me as good as any of them and far more interesting to modern readers. He died in 1742 at the age of seventy-nine.

Kaion was succeeded by Nishizawa Ippū, an Osaka bookseller (1665–1731), who wrote twelve pieces in collaboration with Yasuda Abun and Namiki Sōsuké, for it was about this period that the custom originated of two or three, and sometimes even four or five, authors collaborating upon one drama. To this custom, which became more and more prevalent among subsequent writers, we may impute a serious defect of such pieces—the lack of unity in plot.

Ippū's best work *The Story of Hōjō Jirai* (1726), although it was an adaptation of Chikamatsu's *A Hundred Beauties,* was accorded such a hearty reception that there were many who pronounced it as good as *The Battles of Kokusenya.*

Namiki Sōsuké (1694–1750), after Kaion the Toyotaké-za playwright with the most considerable reputation, wrote more than twenty pieces in collaboration with three or four other writers. Among his best works are *Nasuno Yoichi's Exploit in the Western Sea, Karukaya the Priest's Souvenir from Tsukushi* and *The Battle of Ichi-no-Tani.* When Sōsuké died in September, 1750, at the age of fifty-six, he had outlined the plot, and written the first three acts, of this last piece, which runs to five long acts. Asada Itchō and four other pupils wrote the remainder, and the drama was performed in December, 1756. Even to-day *The Battle of Ichi-no-Tani* is so popular that one or two acts of it are often performed at regular theatres. Sōsuké had many able pupils and his style so influenced subsequent dramatists that many of them assumed his surname Namiki.

Several other authors wrote for the Toyotaké-za, but they are not worthy of notice in the present volume.

The successor of Chikamatsu, as playwright for the Také-moto-za, was Takéda Izumo (1691–1756), son of the proprietor of an Osaka marionette theatre. His maiden effort, *Prince Daitō's Scarlet Armour*, which appeared in 1723 while Chikamatsu was still alive, was written by him in collaboration with Matsuda Bunkōdō, and was revised by his master Chikamatsu. It was Izumo, in fact, who set the example of collaboration adopted by subsequent writers. His style of composition in no way bears comparison with that of Chikamatsu, yet his plays mark an advance upon his master's in technique and interest of plot. Among more than thirty works of his, in addition to the piece mentioned above, *The One Thousand Cherry-Trees*, *Sugawara's Secrets of Calligraphy* and *The Treasury of Loyal Retainers* are worthy of note. *Sugawara's Secrets of Calligraphy* is a five-act historical play founded on the fortunes of Sugawara Michizané, a celebrated ninth century statesman, now worshipped as the god of penmanship. Izumo had the assistance of two other authors in writing it. So successful did it prove in performance that it enjoyed a run of sixty-five nights. Its fourth act *The Terakoya* or "The Village School", which exhibits a striking illustration of loyalty, the alpha and omega of Japanese knighthood, is so popular with the public that it has been acted at regular theatres times beyond number. If my memory serves me, this act was played years ago in New York and some other American cities by American actors, under the title *Bushido*. More famous still is *The Treasury of Loyal Retainers*, a version of the well-known story of "The Forty-Seven Ronins", a very long play running to eleven acts. A large number of plays (more than sixty, it is said), have been written on this subject, the authors including Chikamatsu, Sōsuké and Hanji, but this piece alone holds the boards. Until quite recently it was indeed such a favourite with the public, that any regular theatre, in the event of its audiences falling off, could recapture its patrons by performing one or two acts of this drama.

Matsuda Bunkōdō, who collaborated with Izumo in *Prince Daitō's Scarlet Armour*, was also the author of twenty other plays, the best of which are *Ki-ichi Hōgen and the Three Volumes on Tactics* and *The Battle of Dan-no-ura*. The majority of these works, however, were written in collaboration with Miyoshi Shōraku and another writer.

Shōraku, who was an Osaka physician, took lessons from Izumo and, as a dramatist, collaborated in the production of some fifty pieces, of which the best is *Mount Imosé*. Both Shōraku and Bunkōdō were playwrights for the Takémoto-za.

Another writer for the same theatre, Chikamatsu Hanji (1724–1783), who called himself Chikamatsu because he belonged to the Chikamatsu school, collaborated with two or three other writers, in fifty-four pieces. His best works are *The Twenty-four Dutiful Sons of Japan*,[1] *The Banner Worth One Thousand Ryō*, and *Hisamatsu and O-somé*, a Japanese "Romeo and Juliet", the last so popular that it still holds the boards at regular theatres.

Chikamatsu Tokusō (1753–1810), pupil of Hanji, wrote many pieces for the Takémoto-za. His best are *The Flowers at Uéno and a Stone Monument of Honour* and *The Miracle at Hakoné : A Cripple's Revenge*. About 1804 he wrote a *kabuki* play entitled *Miss Morning Glory's Diary*, and in 1850

---

[1] The title of *The Twenty-four Dutiful Sons of Japan* was suggested by the title of a famous Chinese book by Kwaku Kyogyō called *Twenty-four Dutiful Sons*, although in the Japanese play only one dutiful son is to be found among the principal characters. Among the honoured number are Mōsō and the Emperor Shun the Great.

another author appropriated it and wrote the famous puppet play *The True Story of Miss Morning Glory*. This play has made myriads of our countrymen suffer and rejoice over the adventures of its heroine Miyuki; but strangely enough, the author's real name has never been discovered, although his pseudonym "Yamada Kagashi", which means "a scare-crow in a mountain rice-field", is known to us.

Chikamatsu Yanagi, yet another author, wrote six plays, of which *The Exploits of Taikō*, first performed at a small marionette theatre in Osaka in the year 1799, continues to be such a favourite with our countrymen that its tenth act is often revived at our regular theatres.

The puppet performances, which at the opening of the eighteenth century, when Chikamatsu commenced to work as playwright for Gidayū, had begun to overshadow the regular theatres, slowly increased in public favour as the regular theatre declined. Both the Takémoto-za and the Toyotaké-za reached the zenith of their prosperity toward the middle of the same century, while Takéda Izumo and Namiki Sōsuké were writing for them. Thereafter, both theatres slowly lost their hold on the multitude, until to-wards the end of the century, they had to close their doors. The centre of marionette theatricals then shifted to Yedo, where they flourished until towards the middle of the nineteenth century, after which Yedo saw no more of them.

Early in the eighteenth century, and subsequently, many Osaka *jōruri* chanters and puppeteers migrated to Yedo; the pieces they played, however, were all compositions by Osaka writers. Toyotaké Hizen-no-Jō, a famous *jōruri* chanter, established a marionette theatre named Hizen-za in Yedo, where another great chanter, Satsuma Geki, set up a rival theatre called Geki-za or Satsuma-za. For several years following their establishment it was the custom of these theatres to invite Osaka chanters to perform pieces by Osaka writers. About 1770, however, they took to performing pieces by Yedo dramatists.

Hiraga Gennai (1729–1779), whose pseudonym was " Fukuchi Kigai ", was the greatest of the Yedo puppet dramatists. The eldest son of a minor samurai of Shido-ura in Sanuki Province, this ambitious youth bestowed his birthright on his brother and betook himself to Nagasaki, where he studied the Dutch language, botany and physics. Later, in Yedo, he studied Chinese and Japanese classics. He had extraordinary ability and was responsible for several industrial inventions, which unfortunately he could find no one to patronize. To work off his discontent he took to writing humorous essays and puppet plays. His best play *The Miracle at the Ferry of Yaguchi*, given at the Hizen-za in 1770, was very successful, and its fourth act, which relates the adventures of Nitta Yoshiminé at the ferry of Yaguchi, is still frequently performed at regular theatres. In 1779 Gennai went mad, killed a man and was thrown into prison, where he soon fell ill and died.

The following are the most noteworthy plays of other Yedo authors : *The Vendetta at Shiga* (1776) by Kinokami Tarō ; *The Town-Bred Weeping Cherry* (1777) by Kinokami Tarō and Tatsuda Benji ; *The Amorous Girl's Old Hachijō* (1778) by Matsuda Kwanshi and Yoshida Sumimaru ; *The Old Colour-Prints of Kagamiyama* (1782) by Yō Yōtai ; *The Famous Hagi-Tree at Sendai* (1785) by Matsuda Kwanshi, Takahashi Mohei and Yoshida Sumimaru ; *The Story of Shiraishi* (1787) by Utei Emba and Kinokami Tarō. *The True Story of Miss Morning Glory*, performed, as mentioned above, at Yedo in 1850, and *The Clouds of Flowers at the Dawn of Sakura* by Toyoshima Gyokuwaken and a collaborator, performed at Yedo in 1853, were the last puppet-plays ever written.

While the Takémoto-za and the Toyotaké-za enjoyed prosperity in Osaka, there were one or two small marionette theatres in Kyoto, and now and again the Osaka troupes visited Kyoto and the chief cities and towns in the neighbouring provinces.

A century and a half sufficed to witness the rise, apogee and fall of the marionette theatres. Probably more than one reason can be put forward to account for their melancholy fate. We may observe for instance that none of the later dramatists and performers attained the æsthetic eminence of their predecessors. In the meanwhile the regular theatre steadily advanced in costume, setting, acting, music and technique, and above and beyond all employed its actors to perform the best of the puppet-plays, for at that period there were no laws of copyright. Naturally enough the public, which had so greatly fancied the puppet play, gradually forsook the inanimate dolls and almost entirely transferred its patronage to the performances of living actors whose countenances could express the many shades of emotion. None the less, though puppet plays, as such, ceased to be performed, many of the best puppet plays were kept alive by the actors who interpreted them at the regular theatres and proved rather more popular than plays written for the *kabuki* theatre.[1] It was in fact the puppets, and not the puppet plays, of which the public had wearied.

X

PRESENT CONDITION OF PUPPETRY—TWO TYPES OF PUPPET

To-day marionette performances are occasionally given in Tokyo by two skilful puppeteers, Yūki Magosaburō and Yoshida Kunigorō. They have, however, no theatre of

---

[1] For further information on this subject the reader is referred to the first part of section eleven : The Regular Theatre of New Japan.

their own and attract only a few spectators. In Osaka there is a marionette theatre called the Bunraku-za—the only theatre of its kind in Japan—which is said to have been established by an amateur Awaji chanter named Uĕmura Bunrakuken, about a hundred years ago. This theatre, in which skilful chanters and puppeteers give performances almost all the year round, is reckoned among the especial attractions of the city.

The puppets are of two kinds : little and great puppets. The little puppets are not more than one foot high and are operated from above by strings, assumed to be invisible. The great puppets are large figures at least two-thirds life-size. Their appearance is very realistic, mimicry of nature being carried in them to the minutest detail, so that when operated by skilful puppeteers to the accompaniment of able chanters they have for the enchanted spectator all the appearance of human beings. Their mechanism is exceed-ingly elaborate : they have hands in which each joint of each finger is articulated, eyes which move from side to side, eyebrows which ascend in anger or surprise, a mouth which opens or closes. Their costumes are of rich silk or brocade, profusely embroidered and often jewelled. These puppets are held upright from behind and are operated by numerous strings. Each puppet requires one puppeteer in chief and two, sometimes three, assistants. The chief puppeteer moves the head and right hand ; one assistant moves the left hand and the other assistant the legs. The puppeteers work " on-stage " in full view of the audience, the puppets being placed before them. The chief puppeteer is generally very gaily apparelled, but the assistants wear black hoods and robes to render themselves inconspicuous. All the puppeteers wear high clogs to give them the extra height necessary to the holding of the figures upright.

It is probable that the little puppets were introduced

THE HERO OF *KAGÉKIYO AND HIS DAUGHTER* MANIPULATED
BY MR. YEIZŌ YOSHIDA

A SCENE FROM *THE RECENT AFFRAY AT THE DRY RIVER BED.* MR. MAGOSABURŌ
YŪKI'S PUPPETS OPERATED FROM ABOVE WITH STRINGS.

from abroad sometime during the Tokugawa Period. They were used by itinerant puppet showmen and *jōruri* singers, and by puppeteers at variety halls, in the old days. They are now used by the troupe of Yūki Magosaburō, while the Bunraku-za and Yoshida Kunigorō use the great puppets. The great puppets were much used in the theatres of the old days, and we may consider them the characteristic Japanese puppets.

Several centuries before the puppet play arose, puppet makers were in the habit of presenting the Imperial Court with their figures and receiving titles of honour. At a later date, when puppet performances became the rage, these titles were no longer conferred on puppet makers, but on puppeteers. Still later, when *jōruri* chanters attained a higher status than the puppeteers, the honours fell to them in their turn. Thus, Takémoto Gidayū received the title of Chikugo-no-Jō, or Vice-Lord of Chikugo Province. From this usage, the modern custom of *jōruri* chanters, samisen players, puppeteers, and even girl chanters wearing *kataginu* and *hakama* or " a cape and trousers ", the full dress of samurai, would seem to have originated.

XI

THE REGULAR THEATRE OF NEW JAPAN

The most important of all plays performed in the regular theatre of to-day are the puppet plays treated by living actors. As the accompaniment of rhythmical chanting and of samisen music exactly suits the Japanese taste, and the sentiments to be found in these dramas appeal to the psychology of the masses, and above all since these plays possess a remarkable literary value, the puppet play remains highly appreciated and is frequently played all over the country. The most representative are Chikamatsu Monzaémon's *The Love Suicide at Amijima* and *The Courier for Hades ; The Exploits of Taikō* by Chikamatsu Yanagi ; Takéda Izumo's *Sugawara's Secrets of Calligraphy* and *The Treasury of Loyal Retainers ;* and *The True Story of Miss Morning Glory* by Yamada Kagashi.

Next in general favour are the classical *kabuki* plays, and of these the public accords the heartiest welcome to historical and domestic plays written in the last years of the eighteenth century, the best of which are *The Temple-Gate and Paulownia Flowers, Yosaburō and O-Tomi, Suzugamori Forest* and *Benten Kozō*. The other variety of *kabuki* drama, *shosagoto*, or *buyōgeki* (dance-plays) as they are more generally known to-day, has recently grown remarkably in esteem, the most typical being *The Maiden at the Dōjōji Temple, Shakkyō Bridge, The Barrier Gate, Hōkaibō* and *The Kanjinchō*.

Toward the close of the nineteenth century a group of amateurs began to put on the stage realistic plays portraying the current life of New Japan. These plays are generally dramatizations of the masterpieces of living novelists and are known as " plays of the new school ". They were acted with success for some years, but, since the dramatists are not of first-class ability, and despite the fact that certain of the actors attained considerable skill, they have now fallen in public estimation. The best known are *The Cuckoo*, a dramatization of Rokwa Tokutomi's novel of the same title, and *Foster Sisters* by Yūhō Kikuchi.

In recent years there has arisen a new school of *kabuki* playwrights, a school which discards the conventions of the classical school and endeavours to adapt itself to the needs of modern audiences. Their plays have no musical accompaniment and admit little exaggeration of action. They thus

MR. SHŌCHŌ

MR. SHŌCHŌ AS *O-SOMÉ*, THE HEROINE OF *THE LOVE SUICIDE AT TORIBÉYAMA*, A *KABUKI* PLAY, BY MR. KIDŌ OKAMOTO

MR. UTAÉMON AS *HANAKO* IN *THE MAIDEN AT THE DŌJŌJI TEMPLE*

possess scarcely any of the characteristics of *kabuki* plays ; none the less their subject-matter is always the life of Old Japan. They find a warm welcome with modern audiences who are tired of the conventionalism of the classical school. The pioneer of this school is Shōyō Tsubo-uchi, famous as a translator of Shakespeare, among whose works *A Paulownia Leaf* is the best known. The most successful writer of the movement is Kidō Okamoto, author of more than one hundred pieces, the best of which are *The Tragedy at Shūzenji, The Origin of Saké, Chōbei of Ogurusu* and *Lady Hosokawa.* Among other playwrights of this school, Shōyō Matsui, Shikō Yamazaki and Roppuku Nukada call for mention.

What for want of a better name may be called Japanese modern dramas are a decidedly new phenomenon. At first they were regarded simply as dramas for the study, but through the efforts of Kanya Morita, Ennosuké Ichikawa and certain other ambitious young actors who have success-fully staged them, they have won a still increasing share of public approval. Among writers of modern drama Kichizō Nakamura, Sané-atsu Mushakōji, Masao Kumé, author of *The Origin of Jizoism*, and Kwan Kikuchi, author of *The Housetop Madman,* are held in high esteem.

Translations and adaptations of European dramas once enjoyed a considerable vogue and are nowadays occasionally played. They have exercised a great influence upon the younger generation of dramatists and are, in fact, the proto-types of Japanese modern dramas.

This summary would not be complete without mention of two little opera houses, one in Tokyo and the other in the vicinity of Osaka, where translations of European operas and original pieces by native composers are performed. To the younger generation, which has a real taste for European music, these operas need no recommendation.

The following table approximately displays the relative frequency of performance of the above types of plays :—

(a) Puppet-plays performed by living actors   .   35 per cent.
(b) Classical *kabuki* plays   .   .   .   .   35 ,,   ,,
(c) Plays of the new school   .   .   .   .   10 ,,   ,,
(d) New *kabuki* plays   .   .   .   .   .   10 ,,   ,,
(e) Japanese modern dramas.   .   .   .   5 ,,   ,,
(f) Translations and adaptations of European
        dramas and operas   .   .   .   .   5 ,,   ,,

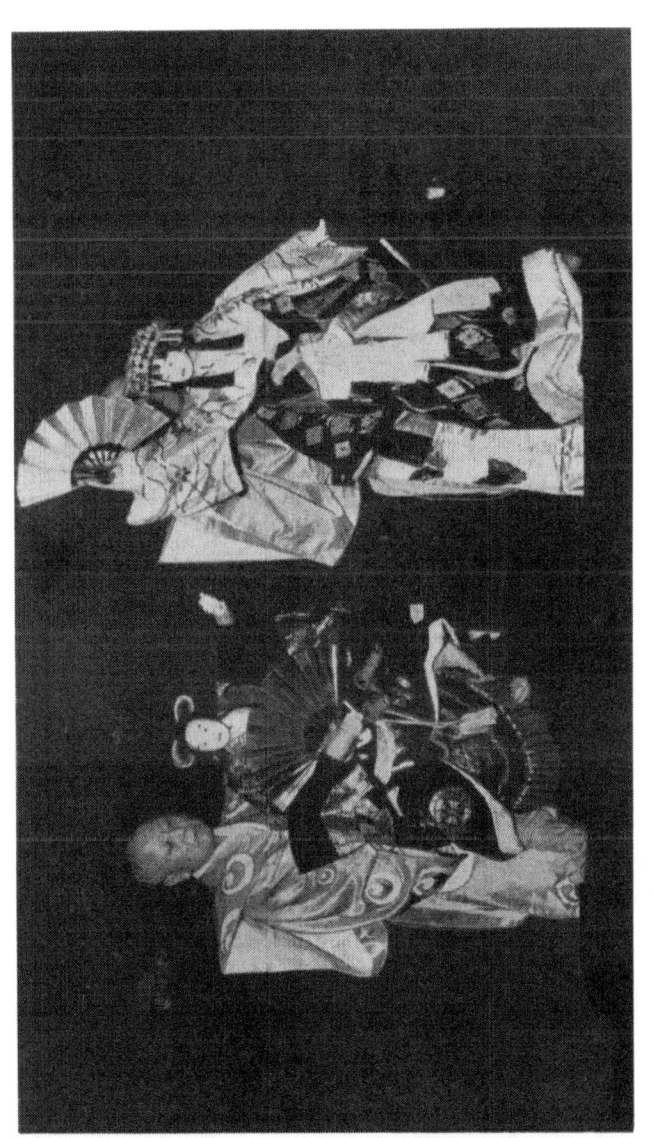

A SCENE FROM *THE ONE THOUSAND CHERRY-TREES*

[*face p.* 62

A SCENE FROM *THE FAMOUS HAGI-TREE AT SENDAI*

A SCENE FROM *O-SHICHI, THE GREENGROCER'S DAUGHTER*

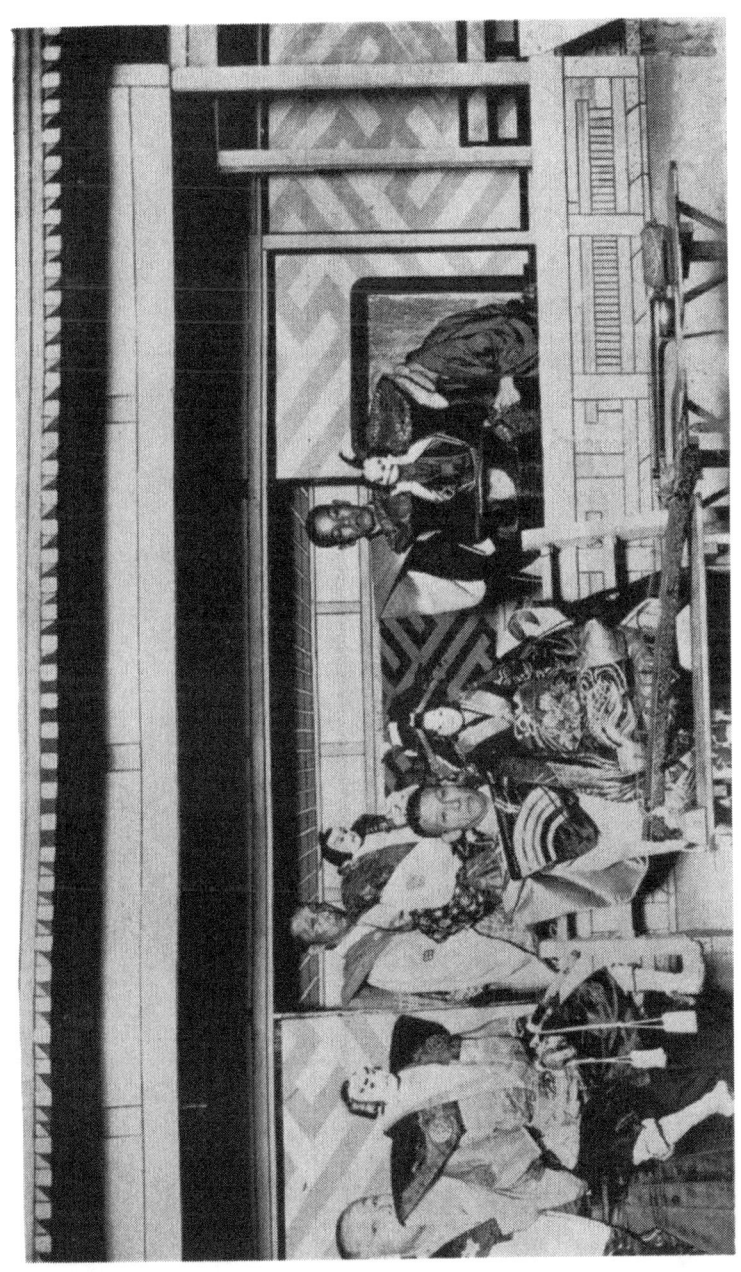

A SCENE FROM *THE BATTLE OF DAN-NO-URA*, A PUPPET PLAY

A SCENE FROM *THE GORGEOUSLY COLOURED FAN OF THE GIRL*, A PUPPET PLAY BY
CHIKAMATSU HANJI

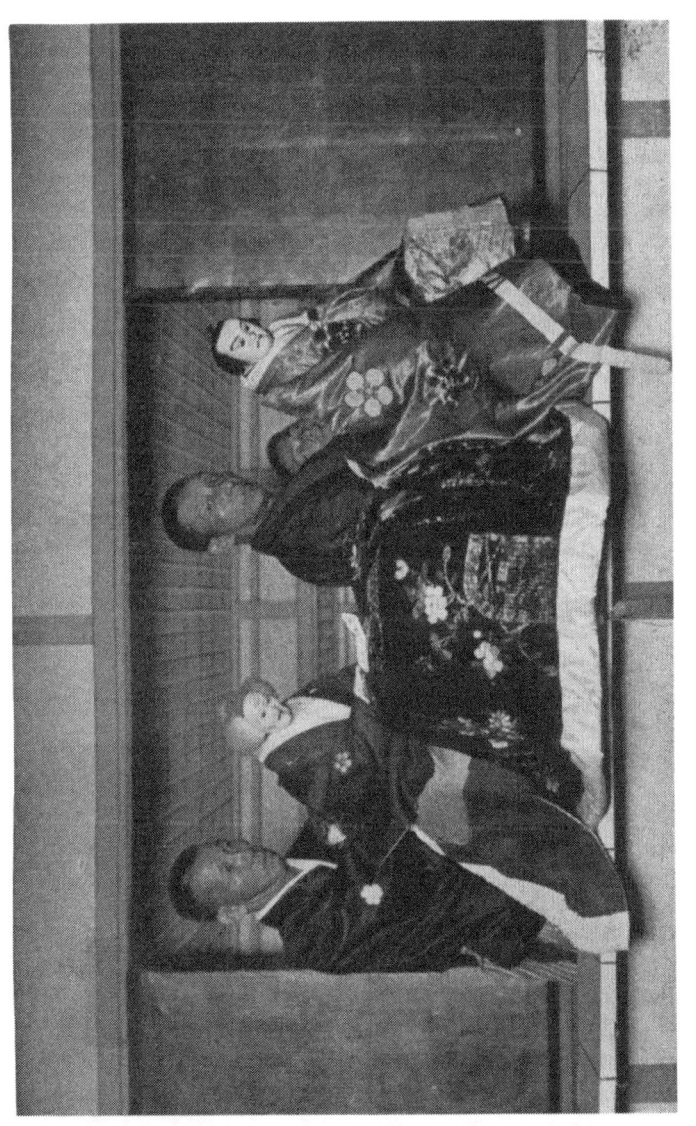

A SCENE FROM *THE EXPLOITS OF TAIKŌ*

A SCENE FROM *THE OLD COLOUR PRINTS AT KAGAMIYAMA*

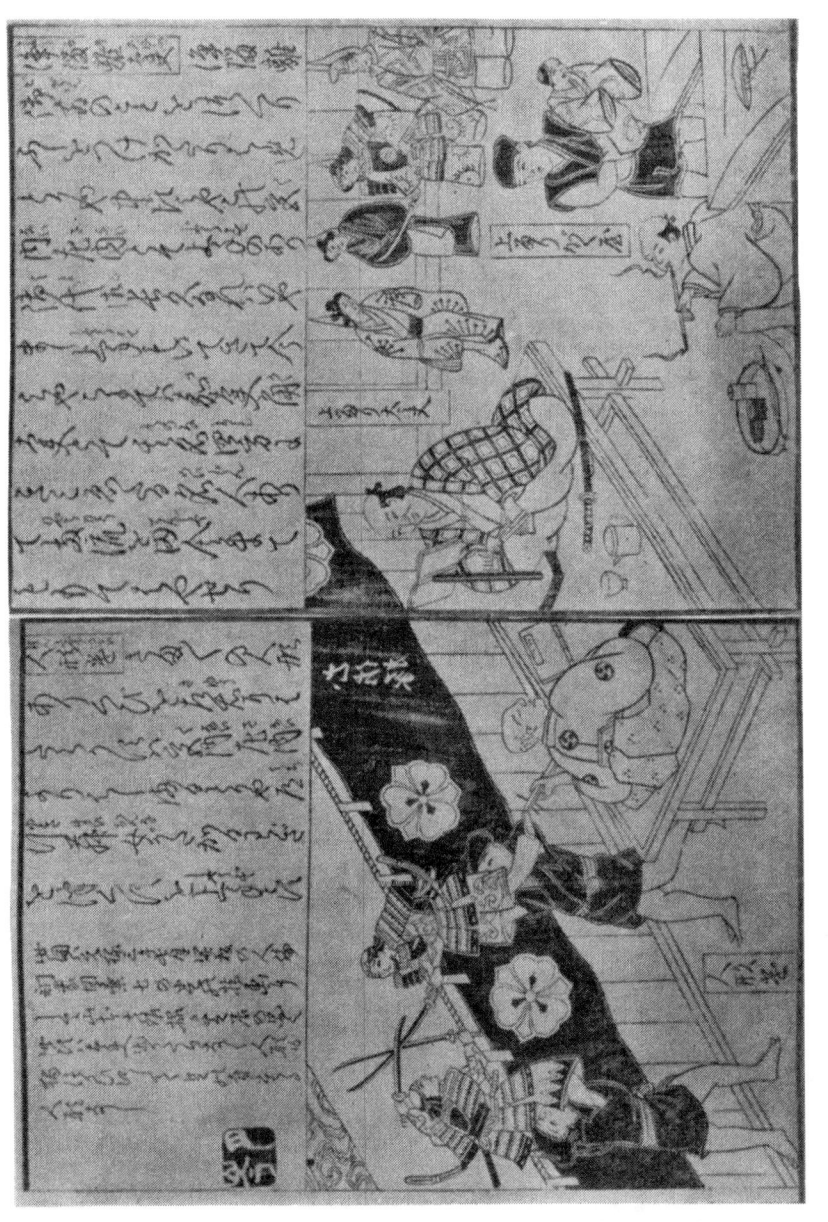

A PUPPET PERFORMANCE IN OLDEN DAYS—BEHIND THE SCENES

From an illustration in *The Jinrin-Kummō Zué*, published in July, 1690 (the third year of Genroku)

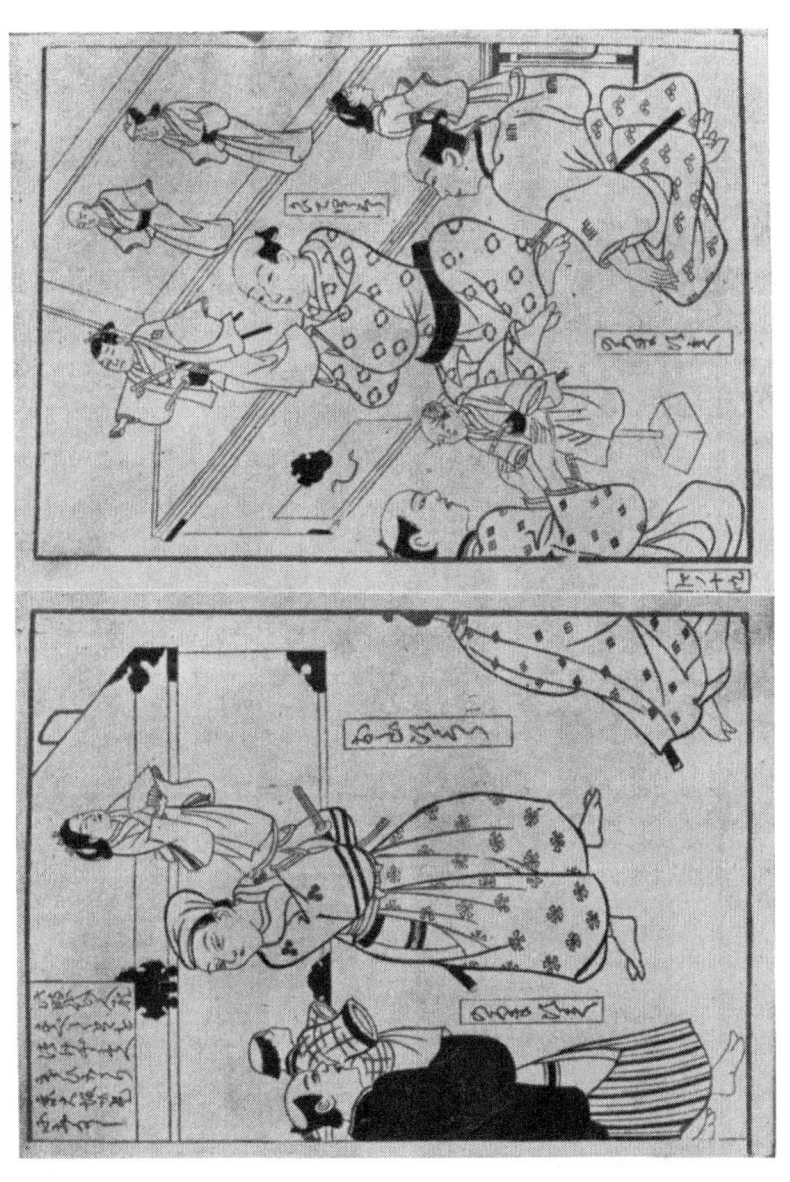

A PUPPET PERFORMANCE IN OLDEN DAYS—BEHIND THE SCENES

From an illustration in an old book, *The Seikyoku Ruisan*

Notice that these puppets have no legs and are manipulated by one operator.

BEHIND THE PUPPET STAGE—MR. MAGOSABURŌ YUKI'S PUPPETS MANIPULATED
BY STRINGS FROM ABOVE

THE FAMOUS HAGI-TREE AT SENDAI, PRODUCED AT THE BUNRAKU-ZA

THE EIGHT CAMPS, A PUPPET PLAY BY NAKAMURA GYOGAN, PRODUCED AT THE
BUNRAKU-ZA

.

THE STORY OF TWO BUTTERFLIES, BY TAKÉDA IZUMO, PRODUCED AT THE
BUNRAKU-ZA

FIG. 13

A SCENE FROM *THE FORTY-SEVEN RONINS*

THE ALMANAC OF LOVE
(*Koi Hakké Hashiragoyomi*)

THE ALMANAC OF LOVE

(*Koi Hakké Hashiragoyomi*)

I

SINCE early morning of this, the first of November in the first year of Jōkyō (A.D. 1684), all had been animation and merriment in the house of Ishun the *daikyōji*,[1] publisher of almanacs, living at Karasumaru, a fashionable quarter of Kyoto, the Imperial capital. A stranger might, indeed, have mistaken this day for New Year's Day. Such, however, was not the case : to-day was merely the great day on which it was the firm's wont to commence the distribution to subscribers of the almanac for the ensuing year. Ishun, visiting the Imperial Court, the Princes of the Blood and court nobles, that he might present new almanacs, had accepted refreshments to such a tune that, drunk and still wearing full dress, he now slumbered in the sitting-room. Sukéyemon the head clerk, the pillar of the family, a man accustomed to exercise as much authority as his master and mistress, devoted himself despite the happy occasion to fussing and finding fault with all and sundry, while his underlings wrapped up the presentation almanacs and packed them for despatch to the provincial subscribers.

[1] The *kyōji* or *kyōji-ya* is now a sort of paper-hanger, but in days gone by he made Buddhist scripture-rolls, picture-scrolls and so forth. The *daikyōji* or chief *kyōji* worked for the Imperial Court, but the publication of the almanac was his principal occupation. He ranked between the samurai and the tradesman, belonging to the same class as the physician, and, as was the case with the samurai, he was exempt from taxes.

" So the master's asleep ! " Sukéyemon remarked sourly.
" Well, he's scarcely to be blamed perhaps, being away at our
patrons' since daylight. Where's that lazybones Mohei got to?
I mean to visit our patrons in his stead just as soon as he
shows his face. I'll wait no longer. If I don't hurry, this
most important job of presenting the almanacs to our fine
patrons will be delayed. Why, O-San Sama," he cried
impatiently as he caught sight of Ishun's pretty young wife
toying with the cat, " is this the time to be playing with a
cat, for all the world as if you were her ladyship ? Please be
so good as to remember that all your relatives will be here to
offer us their congratulations on this day according to custom.
What, Tama," so did he abuse the maid, " you too idling ?
Be so good as to make haste and sweep out the little parlour
in the courtyard, and, when that's done, you can kindle a
fire in the kotatsu,[1] and after that set out the backgammon
and chequer-boards, and after that set water in the wash
basin and set out new towels, and after that put live charcoal
in the tobacco trays, and after that clean the bowls and spread
the table, oh, and yes, get your supper before the guests
come. Now then, there's plenty to do : hurry up. Why,
even the cat is an idler—mews loud enough, but as for catching
a rat ! Good for nothing but trotting after the gentlemen of
her own colour, squeezing through the fence and scampering
over the roofs. Now Kyūzō, take up this box of almanacs
and follow me. There'll be tips to be had at some of our
patrons' houses but don't run away with the idea that you're
going to be in pocket over it. Anything of that sort will be
deducted in advance from your pay, that you may be bound.
I thought I'd let you know."

---

[1] The kotatsu is a fireplace in the floor. A wooden frame shaped like a box is
placed over this, the frame itself being covered with a large, thick quilt, which
confines the warmth. The body is thrust under the quilt while the user of the
kotatsu lies or squats upon the mats, which of course are never soiled by shoes or
geta (wooden clogs resembling the cothurnae of Greek tragedy).

Satisfied at having given a taste of his tongue to all concerned, not excluding the unwitting tabby, Sukéyemon hurried away, accompanied by Kyūzō.

O-San and the maid exchanged disgusted glances.

"That's a nice way to talk, O-Tama, isn't it? What would he lose by speaking gently as Mohei does? He's a well-meaning man at bottom I daresay, but his forbidding face doesn't help his talk. I think he'd make a very nice husband, eh? D'you fancy him? Give me the word and I'll play middleman."

"O Madam," rejoined the maid, not without a frown, "how can you? Indeed I'd rather be butted by a regular bull than marry such a man! Now Mohei San, the clerk, is quite the gentleman. A soft way of speaking he has, kind he is and pulls no angry faces. She'd be a lucky girl who should marry such a man."

O-San was reminded of her own married life. She uttered a brief sigh. "True, very true," she returned. "'It's the same for cats and kings'; 'birds of a feather flock together'. Take our pussy now. The tortoise-shell tom from the perfumer's next door has a gentle way with him and woos in a pretty voice. That's the sort of tom I'd like poor pussy to have. But over the way at the dyer's there's a gray tom, an ugly beast that it positively hurts one to look at, and he calls our puss from up the roof in the voice of a savage, no better than if he were driving a horse. A horrid beast. Now listen to me, pussy, you mustn't flirt—d'you hear?—with such a cat. If he makes dishonourable advances, pussy, you must treat him as a lady should. Give in to him and you're done for. If you want a mate I'll find you one myself. Think of that, dear pussy!"

O-San embraced the cat, which mewed softly. At that moment several tom-cats gave vent to amorous plaints without. Puss endeavoured to extricate herself.

" Wicked puss ! Hush ! What a caterwauling ! What's the good of such a number ? You're a flirt and no mistake. One's enough for any woman. Be careful or you'll find yourself in hot water. Have you no sense of decency ? "

O-San clutched the cat—but in vain. The creature struggled, scratched her mistress' hand and was off.

" You bad cat, you're looking for trouble, are you ? "

So saying, O-San ran off in pursuit of the cat. O-Tama was about to follow her when Ishun abruptly awoke and clasped her from behind. " Pretty puss, I've got you ! "

And he began to pay her attentions after a style of his own ; but, struggling to shake him off, she cried :—

" Stop it ! Whenever you get half a chance you cuddle me. Please let go or I'll tell my mistress and make her pinch you till you're black and blue all over."

" Let you go—not I ! A jealous woman's as common as flies in midsummer. That won't frighten me. What if I do turn blue or even black ; that's nothing to me for your sake, you hard-hearted little thing. Night after night haven't I been coming to your room, yet you've never given me a single ' yes '. Well, it's going to be different this evening, eh O-Tama ? "

Ishun tightened his hold.

" Please yourself. But I tell you I'll call my mistress."

Nor did she hesitate to do so, " O-San Sama ! O-San Sama ! "

The wretch was taken aback. At this moment there was heard a knock at the front door. O-San's aged mother had called to offer her congratulations. An offering of a basket of fish preceded the arrival of her palanquin.

" There ! If that confounded hag of a mother-in-law of mine hasn't come ! " Ishun retreated to the inner room.

A moment later the palanquin reached the porch. Stepping forth, the dame was greeted by O-San.

" Welcome, mother ! Isn't father with you ? "

" No, he's laid up at home with a slight cold. I congratulate you, my daughter, on this happy occasion. Ishun Dono is well pleased with the way his business is doing, eh ? "

" Thank you, mother. My man's come back not quite himself on account of the *saké* served him in honour of the occasion at his illustrious patrons'. He's asleep at present in the back parlour. Come mother, let's go in."

The palanquin bearers and the two maids attendant on the old woman being dismissed, mother and daughter joyfully entered.

Now the above-mentioned clerk Mohei was a gentle, good-tempered, young fellow. Of modest disposition, kindly toward all and especially toward his fellow clerks, he was regarded with affection. And now it was that, accompanied by a servant, he returned tipsy and fatigued from the distribution of almanacs that had commenced at dawn.

" What a round, Shichisuké ! You must be tired. Go and rest. My master and mistress' relatives will certainly come to call by and by. I'll keep my *hakama* [1] on and smoke and try and get sober before they arrive." He sat down, lit up and was leisurely smoking when O-San called to him from the inner sitting-room. He tapped out his pipe and presented himself respectfully before his mistress.

" I am sorry, Mohei, to trouble you when you have just got in tired, but I have got something important over which I would like your help. Please come nearer me."

Mohei sat down near her. His mistress spoke timidly under her breath. " The fact is, Mohei, my father's got into a scrape and I want to consult you about it. I am sorry to have to say it but this is what has happened. Being hard up, my father mortgaged his house and grounds the year

---

[1] A ceremonial flowing garment worn over ordinary clothes, extending from the waist almost to the ankle, and covering each leg separately.

before last for four hundred and fifty *ryō* under the joint signature of his principal neighbours. Last spring, finding himself once more in difficulties, he again mortgaged the house and grounds, this time for one hundred and twenty *ryō*, and of course in secret without the knowledge of his neighbours. And now the first creditor, having got some wind of the truth, has suddenly notified the authorities in father's district, demanding that father either give up his house or repay the money by the third of this month, otherwise the first creditor says he'll bring an action against him. Poor father! He persists that he doesn't much fear the lawsuit or doesn't even mind giving up the house and grounds, but he can't stand the ignominy of having his secret disclosed. For you see, should the truth come out that he's mortgaged the same house to two parties it would be all up with his honour as a man of business. The very thought of it, I hear, has reduced him to tears. Fortunately we have induced certain persons to act as mediators and they have arranged that the matter be settled by the payment of an interest of thirty *ryō* by the third of the month. Not without a great deal of difficulty father has managed to raise fifteen *ryō*, but as to the remaining fifteen there is most unfortunately no prospect, no matter what he does. Of course I know that if I were to tell my husband he would forthwith help us out of the trouble. But I am not to breathe a syllable to him ; for my father, with the obstinacy and pride of the aged, will have it that if he ask his son-in-law for a loan his beloved daughter will be placed in an awkward position. If again I turn to Sukéyemon for help he's sure to go and blab the matter to my husband and pull a long face about it at the same time. If that happens my husband will take it as no end of an insult and that will make matters worse than ever. I know for a fact that a sum of about thirty *ryō* is due to father from a Court nobleman at the end of this month. So the money's only wanted for three weeks. Save you, I have nobody to ask assistance of. Do you think you could be so very kind as somehow to raise this fifteen *ryō* and relieve my parents of their trouble ? Think of the pity of it ! I wouldn't let my parents suffer over such a trifling matter if I were a man. How hard on them it is that I was born a woman ! What a curse this womanhood is ! I appeal to your sympathy, Mohei."

O-San, who had the heart of a man in the body of a woman and whose regard for her parents was profound, spoke in tones of deep concern.

" Can my lady be as faint-hearted as all that ? " returned the sympathetic and loyal-hearted Mohei, in whose being the *saké* had not ceased to exert its exhilarant influence. " A sum, of one thousand *ryō* say, might well worry you, but why speak with such anxiety of a miserable sum like that ? You see, my master often tells me to take his seal [1] when I go to a wholesale merchant to get a bill of exchange for thirty or forty *ryō* accommodated. You only want the money for three weeks. Be easy in your mind, madam. I'll raise you fifteen *ryō* without fail to-day. If I do play false for a little while—what of that ? I shall not be committing theft. I am only going to make a temporary use of my master's seal. A parent's dishonour is a child's dishonour, and a father-in-law's dishonour is a son-in-law's dishonour. So in helping your father out of this mess I'm virtually serving both my master and mistress, aren't I ? Please be quite easy in your mind about it, madam."

" I'm indeed glad to hear you say that, Mohei. I haven't appealed to you in vain. Let me tell mother and put her at her ease. Remember I entirely depend on you."

---

[1] In olden times both seals and signatures were used to authenticate documents. But the seals were by far the most important, signatures often being written, strange to say, by others than the parties concerned.

It was with a happy countenance that O-San went within.

" I might well do such a thing," Mohei ruminated, " were it only for a friend. How much more then can I do it for my mistress' sake ! Though the deed may in itself be wrong my conscience is clear enough."

Emboldened by these reflections, he stealthily produced his master's purse from its receptacle and, taking out the seal, affixed its mark upon a blank sheet of paper with the intention of thereafter inscribing the due words and figures. Meanwhile, all unknown to him, Sukéyemon, returned home, was watching him from behind his back.

" What on earth are you at, Mohei ? " he cried sharply.

Mohei started, but, quickly regaining his presence of mind, answered in desperation :—

" It's you Sukéyemon, is it ? Surely it's the height of ill-luck that I should be caught by you ! This is the real truth. Needing about fifteen *ryō* I was by way of borrowing it in my master's name. I can surely repay it in the course of this month. Can't you see your way to overlooking the matter for three weeks ? . . . A heartless man you must be that doesn't turn a hair even at the idea of a friend's head being cut off ! So be it. I am prepared for any chastisement. Bind or kill me, whichever suits you best."

" And why not, pray, you thief ? Hullo there, come here a minute. Hi ! master, hi ! "

At this startling summons the whole household assembled.

" Look there, master," cried Sukéyemon, " look at that thief who has stolen your seal and affixed it to a blank page. How are we to tell what he'll do to-morrow if that's the way he behaves to-day ? A blackguard like that will betray his master and ruin the business. You should bind him and deliver him to his surety."

O-San and her mother turned pale. Ishun was struck

with amazement. " What meanness, Mohei ! " he exclaimed.
" And I have always considered you an honest man incapable
of misconduct. Leaving as I do my household management
and business dealings to both of you it may of course sometimes happen that pressure of circumstance causes you to use
my seal unbeknown to me. But since this time Mohei has
seen fit to try and use it without even Sukéyemon's knowledge
it stands to reason he must have been intending some piece
of crookedness. Now Mohei, come, what's made you steal
my seal ? Sukéyemon, make him confess his secret."

" You're too easy-going," cried the impatient Sukéyemon.
And seizing the apparent scoundrel by the hair he dealt him
blow upon blow with clenched fist.

" Come, confess, you rascal," he roared, gazing malignly
into the young man's face, who, his torn hair in his eyes,
resentfully made answer :—

" Go on, punch me, kick me. It's unpardonably wrong of
me to have secretly used my master's seal, I know it. But
so far I have never visited a tea-house. I don't know how
to play cards. I am quite as well dressed as most men of
my station. I am not married and haven't any children
dependent on me. Then why should I do such a dirty trick
on my own account ? However, I don't intend to explain
why I did it ; no, not though I should be beaten to a pulp.
O-San Sama and you, madam, I'll never forgive you if you
intercede on my behalf. I tell you, Sukéyemon, that if
heaven should speak for me and disclose my secret I could
return your blows with double interest till you fell down
and begged pardon on your knees. What an infuriating
position ! "

He ground his teeth, he wept.

" Dear, dear," said Ishun, bewildered, " a fellow that has
so faithfully served me for twenty years without a slip can't
have suddenly turned into a rogue. You must have some-

thing to say in your defence, Mohei.   Come, speak up, plead for yourself."

But the determined clerk made no answer.   Tama the maid, whose heart had long been so set upon Mohei that she would have died for him, kneeled before her master.

" It's all my fault, master," she said, " and not Mohei's. This is the truth : my uncle and surety, Bairyū, living at Okazaki and who is a poverty-stricken samurai out of employment, wrote to me saying he would kill himself because he couldn't repay a debt of eight *ryō*.   To save him from such an act I have asked Mohei San to lend me that sum.   It's his sympathy for me has induced him to do what he's done. Humbly I ask you to forgive him, my master."

At this saving plea O-San and her mother heaved a sigh of relief.

" Bravely spoken, Tama," exclaimed O-San, " what a fine honest confession !   You see, husband dear, Mohei has done this wrong all on another person's account.   Don't you think his motive is truly praiseworthy ?   To-day too is a joyful day, won't you please pardon him ?   I beg of you to grant my request."

" And I too," chimed in O-San's mother.

With clasped hands both women supplicated Ishun, but to no purpose.   He forthwith flew into a passion due to jealousy of and hatred against the young pair.

" So you're both carrying on, are you ? " he roared. " You will both please be good enough to remember that a *daikyōji* isn't an ordinary tradesman but at the Imperial Court enjoys the privileges of a samurai.   How can I forgive Mohei such a crime as the theft of his master's seal and of carrying on an intrigue, if you please, in the household of a true samurai ?   It's getting dark now and accordingly I'll wait till to-morrow morning before summoning his surety and getting him properly tried.   Hi !   You !   Conduct Mohei to the upstairs room of the empty house next door and mount guard on the ground floor. See to it that you keep your eyes and ears open."

O-San and O-San's mother, overcome with mortification and regret at Mohei's sacrifice, were still wondering whether the best course wouldn't be to reveal the secret when the servants seized the clerk. Mohei suffered himself to be led away without further protest.

Ishun addressed himself to his mother-in-law :—

" Since O-San may feel lonely without you, will you please to stop the night here ? I think I shall call on your husband to ask after his health. I shall acquaint him with what has happened and ask his advice. My hood, O-San, if you please. One moment, Sukéyemon : it will be late before I get home. See that they all turn in early ; shut the gate and be careful of fire. Light me a lantern, Denkichi ; Shichisuké, you will come with me ; as for the rest of you, keep an eye on that empty house next door lest Mohei make off."

Upon this he departed, taking the servant with him. Sukéyemon, having observed each of these injunctions, retired to his room.

.   .   .   .   .   .

The midnight bell had long since tolled in the far-off temple. The night was absolutely still. O-San, sitting up, brooded over this day's doings. Something struck her and, attired but as she was in her night-dress, she made her way to Tama's quarters, a corner of the tea-room next the kitchen. Softly she pushed aside the screen about the maid's bed and found Tama sitting up lost in thought.

" So it's you, madam, is it ? " said the maid, giving her a wondering glance. " I presume that, since you've deigned to come to my poor bed after midnight, you must have something important to tell me. Is that it ? "

" Still awake and sitting up ? I've come to express my heartfelt thanks to you. Mohei's trouble is all my fault. I wonder how you came to know about it. Indeed it's too good of you to have taken all the blame and helped me out of the difficulty. You were my sister perhaps in a previous life. I shan't forget your favour to my dying day."

O-San burst into tears.

" But madam, madam, I don't deserve your thanks. I didn't do it for you but for myself."

" No, no, that's not the reason. Why should you have pleaded for Mohei without knowing the circumstances ? "

" No wonder you should think I did it for you. I am sorry to have to confess it, but the truth is I am—I am— up to the ears in love with Mohei San. For two years I have done all I could to attract him, but to no purpose. Despite his looks he is stubborn and unsympathetic. He says that while he's in service he'll never put his arm round a woman or even so much as look in her face. Never has he spoken a kind word to me. Because of all this my love for him turned to hatred and I couldn't find a good word for him when, un- expectedly enough, there came this trouble of his to-day. At first I thought him well served for his treatment of me. But in a few moments I saw the unreasonableness of my resent- ment. Sympathy took the place of hatred. I determined to turn his trouble to account if so be I might win his heart. I told a fine tale and pleaded on his behalf. Yet for all that I can't help wondering whether he'll have any feeling for me or not. Imagine how I feel, madam. What's more, I'm sorry to say I have another secret to soil your ears with," she continued tearfully. " I regret to have to call your husband by such a nasty name and you must excuse my rudeness in doing so, but Ishun Sama is a mean, contemptible seducer. His cruelty to Mohei San is all due to jealousy. The fact is he's so infatuated with me that whenever he gets a chance he attempts to mishandle me and tugs me by the sleeve. Then he will whisper to me coaxingly, ' Leave my service, Tama. I'll set you up in secret somewhere. I'll look after your folks in the country. I'll buy you dresses and give you money. Yes, anything and everything you may want.' He hangs round me day and night behind your back and worries me to death with his nasty suggestions. So far I have kept the secret from you for fear of domestic upheavals. Every evening you know he goes out until late and kills time in listening to gossip at some neighbour or other's. Then, when everything's quiet, he steals upstairs through the menservants' rooms, from there creeps over the roof and, slipping down the skylight rope, makes for this room here. What a nuisance all this is! Every time he makes a visit I tell him angrily what a plague he is and that I can't stand his dirty tricks. ' If you don't get out immediately ' I say to him, ' I'll peach on you to O-San Sama and what's more I'll tell the police! ' He feels the rebuke and slinks off crestfallen. Then, pretending to have just come home, cries, ' Hullo, I have just got back! ' and enters your bedroom. Think what a comical and odious figure he cuts! Naturally under these circumstances he was consumed with jealousy when I stood up for Mohei this afternoon. Yes, there's no doubt jealousy was at the bottom of it. He'll come stealing into my room again to-night, I'll be bound, so I've stayed up awake like this without undressing properly, determined to scream when he appears. No wonder you should feel annoyed and grieved. It makes me shiver to think of his nasty goings-on."

" What a sensible, strong-willed woman you are! " exclaimed O-San with a sigh followed by tears. " What a perfect beast that Ishun Dono is! Of course a man often loves another woman than his wife, but it makes me furious to think of the insult he offers me. I can't bear it. . . .

Well, I've a favour to ask of you. Let us exchange places to-night. Please let me sleep here. If Ishun Dono calls according to his wont I'll suffer him to woo and woo in darkness. I'll make him believe that I'm you and that you are yielding to him. I'll sleep with him till daybreak and then revile him to my heart's content in the presence of my mother and the whole house. Now will you please let me put on your night-dress."

" You are welcome to it, madam, but I fear you will be cold in a cotton night-dress, you who are used to silk."

" You needn't think that. It's a common saying that in the old days the flames of a certain woman's jealousy made the water in her pail boil. I'm so consumed with jealousy and hate that the cold is nothing to me. Now Tama, will you please go to my bed and allow me to remain here in yours."

" With pleasure. We must hurry. Good night, madam."

Tama replaced the screen, blew out the light and vanished in the darkness.

Meanwhile Mohei, who had so guiltlessly disgraced himself out of loyalty to his mistress, had fallen into a reverie.

" Poor Tama," he thought to himself, " how good it was of her to have shielded me like that instead of resenting my repeated and heartless rebuffs ! How generously has she returned good for evil ! I am ashamed of my hard-heartedness. Executed I may be, but I must visit her once before my end and do my best to repay her kindness."

Thus he resolved and, drawing over his head a hood which left only his eyes exposed, stole out of the upper room and made his way to the roof of the main house. Foot by foot, with bated breath, fearful lest he be discovered and captured for a thief, he crept forward on all fours. More than once he narrowly missed slipping off the shingle roof, wet as it was with rain and mist. After much difficulty he reached the skylight and peered down into the kitchen. He could make out nothing, so dark it was down there. At length, he seized the skylight rope and slid down it. Arrived, he stole stealthily forward, feeling his way with his hands upon the walls and pillars until he found himself in the maid's room. He knocked gently on the screen, quivering with apprehension. At this O-San's heart beat fast, but, mastering herself, she feigned sleep. Gently and slowly Mohei pushed aside the screen and putting both hands on the quilt softly shook the sleeper. O-San pretended to have just awakened, not without surprise, and feeling his crêpe hood took him for her husband and nodded recognition. Mohei expressed his extreme gratitude for the maid's kindness not by words but by gestures. Again and again he thanked her with tears. The woman took his hands and suffered him to enter her bed. Thus they passed some time together to each other's great content when they were aroused by a shrill crowing, repeated knocks upon the front door and the sound of a voice announcing, " Hi ! There ! The master is back."

O-San burst into a cold perspiration.

" Hullo ! Hullo there ! " cried another voice, which could not by any possible means be mistaken for any but Ishun's, " I have come back ! Open the door." Sukéyemon awoke and grumbling, " Fast asleep everyone of them ", appeared lantern in hand to open the door.

What was the consternation of the couple in bed at discovering by the passing light the mistake they had made

" What ! Is it O-San Sama ? "

" What ! Are you Mohei ? "

II

Near Kyoto in a village called Okazaki stood two fine villas belonging to persons of wealth and between them an old thatched cottage. Contrasted with the other buildings this hut appeared as mean as a sparrow between two peacocks. From its eaves a paper lantern hung, painted with the sign, " Akamatsu Bairyū, a reciter of the Taiheiki ".[1] This Bairyū, a samurai out of employment, was Tama's uncle and her guarantee.

One evening, when Bairyū's recitation was done, his audience dispersed by twos and threes eulogizing his performance as they went.

" It's worth the money and more ! " exclaimed one of them. " He's close upon seventy I should say. What dignity in his person and what power in his interpretation ! When he recited with gestures an account of Wada bravely fighting at the battle of Minatogawa he looked the hero himself, didn't he ? Let us come again to-morrow evening. Good night, all."

" Good night."

" Good night."

Hardly had they departed when Sukéyemon made his appearance behind a palanquin. He made as if to open the door, crying, " Is Bairyū San at home ? " But the door was locked.

" Locked up so early ? What's the point of locking it at all ? There's devil a thing to steal ! "

With this sneer he loudly rapped on the door.

" That's a pretty noise ! " exclaimed the reciter. " Who's there ? No one in this house is deaf. If it's recitation you come for kindly be so good as to call to-morrow evening."

" I've no wish to hear you recite. I am Sukéyemon, clerk of Ishun the *daikyōji*, and I come on urgent business. Open the door at once."

Once more he hammered on the door.

---

[1] *The Taiheiki* or " Record of Great Peace ", entirely contrary to what its title suggests, is the chronicle of one of the most disturbed periods in Japanese history (A.D. 1181–1368). So popular was it in the old days that there sprang up at Yedo and Kyoto a special class of persons who made a living by reciting it.

" You're in a great hurry. Can't you wait till I come ? "

Reluctantly enough Bairyū opened the door and stepped forth. A partially bald, grizzled, big, old man, dressed in paper dishabille with a long sword at his side.

" Now Sukéyemon Dono," he said bluntly, " What's your business, knocking me up at this time of night ? "

" What business ? Why, several times during the last few days we've sent for you about this affair of Tama's, but on one pretext or another you have refused to put in an appearance, now haven't you ? Where do you think we can find in all Japan another surety like you, eh ? You will kindly be good enough to lend an ear, my old friend. At daybreak on the second my master returned home at the very moment when Mohei the clerk saw fit to have the audacity to elope with Ishun's wife O-San Sama. In fact we learned it precisely then. On looking into the matter we found that the lovers had slept in O-Tama's room while she remained in madam's. O-Tama had in fact acted as confidante and for this she can scarcely escape punishment. Since you are her uncle and her surety I have brought her in this palanquin to put her in your keeping until madam and Mohei are hunted out. Please to remember that if the couple are crucified she will surely be beheaded. You will now take charge of her. Now my men, carry that palanquin indoors."

At this the coolies made as if, muddy-legged though they were and none too clean in body, to carry the palanquin into the house. Bairyū's indignation knew no bounds. Seizing the pole of the palanquin he exclaimed, " That's a nice way to behave," and forced it back a few yards. " I'd have you keep in mind," he said, " that this is my castle for all that it's a mean cottage and a rented house. Yes, I tell you, a castle it is and a castle as great as the castle of Chihaya, that proved impregnable, yes, even to sixty thousand troops from Rokuhara. How dare you bid these scabby coolies break

F

into my castle ? Strictly speaking of course I ought not as a samurai to have put my niece out to service with a trades-man, but unfortunately Tama is an orphan and I, in whose care she is, am a reciter of *The Taiheiki* and poor enough at that. I haven't the means to buy Tama pretty dresses and put her out as a maid of honour to a nobleman's family. The *daikyōji* is of course a tradesman, but unlike an ordinary tradesman, it falls to him to publish the almanac, which is, in a manner of speaking, a mirror all the year round even with the Emperor and the Ministers of State. Moreover this almanac, I'd have you know, is an accurate record of the sun and moon, so that in serving the *daikyōji* one is serving the deities of the sun and moon. That's why I sent my niece into his service. In my own province I served its lord and received payment. True, I am now out of employment as a samurai, but for all that I am a samurai. Know then that there are ceremonies proper to dealings between gentle-men. Therefore, if you want to deliver Tama, deliver her up with the ceremony proper."

He spoke with a force and fluency worthy of his profession.

" Enough of such threats. Sukéyemon is not the man to be afraid of a samurai. Well, I will deliver the girl with ceremony."

Sukéyemon dragged Tama, bound hand and foot, from the palanquin. Poor girl ! She was bathed in tears.

" I am truly ashamed of myself, uncle."

So saying she once more burst into tears. Saddened by the sight the stout-hearted old man became silent with grief and rage.

" Sukéyemon San," said Tama resentfully, " every ques-tion has two sides. O-San Sama and Mohei San, having fled together, it may be impossible to plead their innocence. The real cause of this trouble, as you very well know, is in

Ishun Sama's evil ways and your jealousy and wickedness, Sukéyemon. You were wildly in love with O-San Sama. You fancied yourself as her lover. I am very well aware that you won over my fellow maid O-Kaya by plenty of presents, asking her to bring about a secret meeting between you and madam. Many a time I all but informed my master of your evil purposes, but each time just refrained. Such a thing would, I thought, lead to your utter ruin, bad as you were. I took it to be enough if through my vigilance O-San Sama might be preserved from guilt. With this in my mind day and night I waited upon her so constantly that O-Kaya couldn't find a chance to tell her of your unlawful love. I remember O-Kaya casting a look of hate toward me and burning a billet-doux of yours in secret. From sheer malice and treachery at your disappointment you gave Ishun Sama an exaggerated account of what happened the other night and this serious trouble is the result. But for my good nature and restraint you would have been crucified and O-Kaya beheaded. Whenever I began to plead for my mistress and Mohei you twisted the truth round and prevented me speaking further. Alas! My forbearance has proved my own undoing! Sukéyemon, you are a devil in human shape!" Once more she relapsed into tears and fell prostrate.

"Nonsense, you crazy girl! Take notice, Bairyū San, I have now placed Tama in your charge."

Sukéyemon was making as if to depart when Bairyū, springing upon him from behind, took him by the throat.

"What are you up to now?" demanded the clerk in a fright.

"What am I up to? Pray, why have you bound Tama for all the world as if she'd been taken up by a policeman? I'd have you call to mind that it's against the law for a mere tradesman to bind anybody. Much more so to bind anybody policeman fashion. It's perfectly within my power to hale you before a magistrate and get you a sharp sentence, but if you apologize and unbind Tama I will pardon you. Will you do so, you scoundrel, or do you wish to see the inside of the law-courts ? "

The old samurai gripped the young man's throat.

" Ouch ! Ouch ! I think there's no harm in binding O-Tama like a prisoner. The *daikyōji*, you know, is different from an ordinary tradesman—he is, after a manner of speaking, in the service of the Imperial Court. If you wish her unbound you can unbind her yourself."

" Silence ! Such a thing has never been heard, from the days of old till now, as to bind a person put in one's charge. But since you know such a lot about it kindly be so good as to enlighten me as to who has issued a law permitting tradesmen in the service of the Imperial Court to bind a person as a prisoner and when was it issued ? I can take any steps I wish with a person who breaks the law. Here's a present for you, you villain ! "

Bairyū pulled out the pole from the palanquin and belaboured Sukéyemon with a right good will.

" You brute ! " Sukéyemon whimpered, almost battered out of breath. " You dare to take a stick to Sukéyemon ! "

" I have indeed. Which is worse—my giving you a drubbing or your having bound O-Tama as if she were a prisoner ? Let's go to law about it. You come along with me, Sukéyemon."

So saying he endeavoured to propel him forward.

" Have it your own way then," faltered Sukéyemon. " Give me a moment and I'll unbind her."

Bairyū released Sukéyemon who however made no sign of fulfilling his pledge.

" Well, why don't you unbind her now ? D'you want another taste of the stick ? "

At this threat Sukéyemon unbound the maid sulkily

enough, saying, " Take notice, she is in your charge now.
I'll be off and report the matter to the head man of this
village. Remember that if you should let her out of your
sight a minute your head and body will part company and
so will Tama's."

" That'll do now."

Bairyū contented himself with dealing the younger man
a cuff or two over the head with his fist, led Tama into the
house, shut the door and locked it.

The coolies, somewhat crestfallen on Sukéyemon's account,
said, " I fear you've been damaged, sir, you'd better ride
back in the palanquin."

" Thank you," replied the sufferer, nursing his cheek.
" This sort of thing hasn't happened to me before. But such
a thing is scarcely to be wondered at for the almanac says
that this place is likely to be unlucky this year as far as I
am concerned. And there's no getting past the almanac as
you observe."

He stepped into the palanquin and the party set out at a
smart pace.

.   .   .   .   .   .

O-San and Mohei, who had never previously loved each
other either waking or dreaming, had been driven by the
caprice of fortune into a dream-like love and had run away
as if in a dream. Impossible to make any preparations for
so unexpected a journey, Mohei's slender purse contained
but three pieces of silver. Under these circumstances O-San
disposed of certain trifles of apparel, and the unfortunate pair
travelled onwards without any particular goal, in constant
dread of pursuers and of the police. Nara and Sakai were
reached. There they turned about and retraced their way
to Ōtsu and Fushimi. Forsaken, as it seemed, alike by the

gods and Buddha, by relations and by friends, they found their hearts bowed down by grief. Walking together they would covertly gaze at one another, blush and stifle their tears.

Now through the village of Okazaki the couple took their way.

" Ah ! Mohei San," said O-San between her sobs, " now we are in such plight that sunset to-day or sunrise to-morrow shall behold us no more ; the delight of life has gone from me. Nevertheless Tama's fate is yet a matter of concern to me and how I long to see my parents. However hard I endeavour to renounce this idea I cannot achieve it."

" Even so do I feel, madam. I also long to see your parents who were so kind to me. I see we are now at Okazaki, O-Tama's native place. That house on which the paper lantern hangs is her uncle's abode. Indeed I have guided you here from no other reason than to visit him for news of your parents and O-Tama. It were rash however to enter without learning somewhat of what goes forward within."

Standing at the door of the house they listened. O-Tama's voice was audible, but the sense of what she spoke indecipherable for tears. The uncle's voice was heard :—

" This volume is the twenty-first of *The Taiheiki* which I recite nightly. The story concerns Kōno Moronao, chief counsellor of the Shogun Taka-uji. Kōno Moronao fell in love with the beautiful wife of Yenya Hangwan, a warrior of high rank, and in consequence has left an evil reputation. As a result of this love affair the unfortunate Yenya was murdered. The cause of all this trouble was a maid of honour attendant on Yenya's wife who acted as a go-between. Now, though O-San Sama and Mohei Dono may not always have been lovers, it's beyond all question that they have run away together. Therefore, should you happen to meet them anywhere or if they should chance to come hither,

[face p. 86

A SCENE FROM *THE ALMANAC OF LOVE*. *O-San*, painted by Toyokuni (Ichiyōsai), *Mohei*, by Toyokuni (Kōchōrō)

From a colour print by the two Toyokunis.

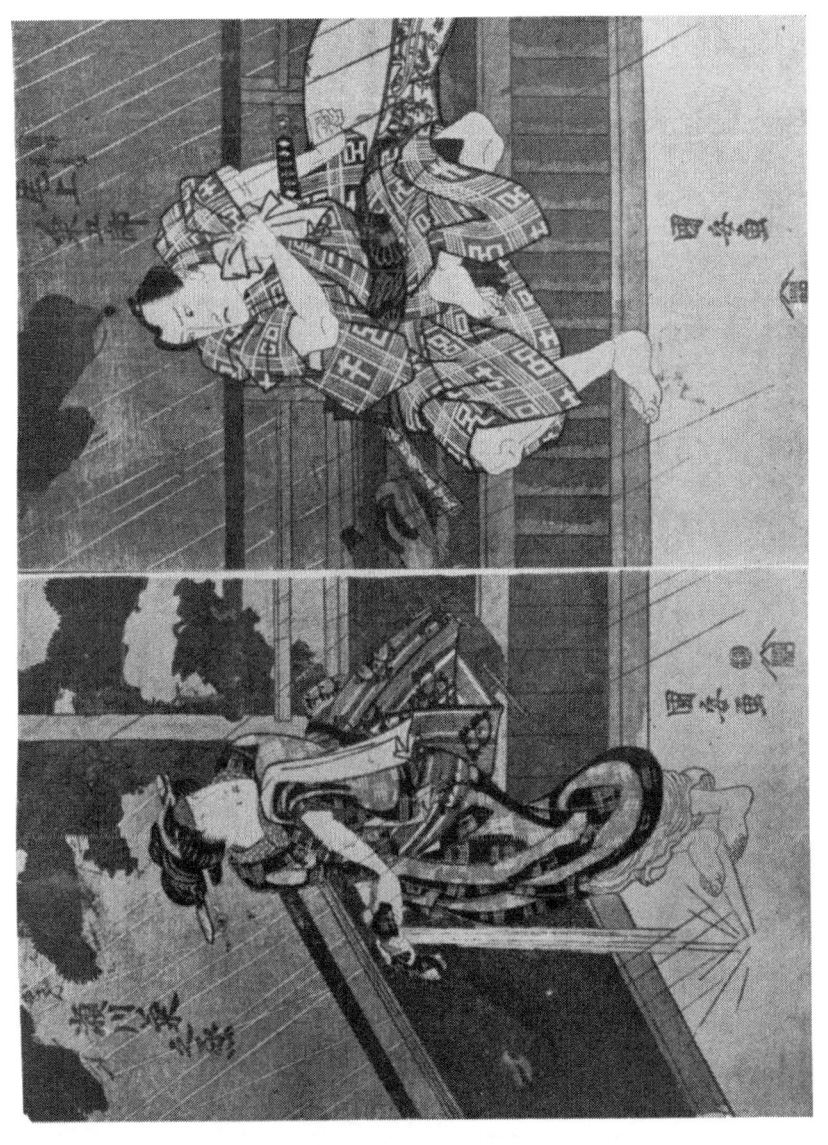

A SCENE FROM *THE ALMANAC OF LOVE*, PLAYED BY CELEBRATED ACTORS OF
OLDEN DAYS

From a colour print by Kuniyasu

do not speak to them but turn your face away. I know my words may sound harsh, but I don't wish you to be harsh. It is for their sake I say it. If it should become generally known that those two, already branded as lovers and you, suspected to be their go-between, have met together, you may be perfectly sure people will say, ' They are foxes of the same earth, just as we thought. There can be no doubt since they meet together that O-San and Mohei are lovers and Tama is their go-between.' If such a rumour should get about their punishment could but become the heavier. Think over this. Your seeming harshness will but prove to their good in the end. As this affair has already caused you the humiliation of being bound and put in my charge, so you may expect such punishment as falls to their lot. I charge you, therefore, though you may be beheaded or suffer the loss of a limb or be used as a subject on which to test the sharpness of a new blade, never to show cowardice, but to take thought to yourself that you fall a noble victim to your mistress. Remember you are the niece of a samurai : be brave to the last, my dear.''

O-Tama's voice followed. Though it was not strong it tokened a firm resolution.

" Have no fear on that score, uncle, I am quite prepared for death. Yet in this wide world we are but two—an uncle and a niece. How lonely you will feel when I am dead. Ah ! That I could know what Mohei San is this moment doing ! How grieved I feel for O-San Sama's sake ! Where, I wonder, is she now and what has become of her ? Knowing what an honest but chicken-hearted woman she is I can well imagine her grief and pain.''

" It's natural enough you should so feel. For my part I can well imagine the great grief of her parents.''

Uncle and niece mingled their tears.

O-San and Mohei, listening without, dared not give themselves away, but, contenting themselves with peeping through the chinks of the door, gave way to tears like the subdued sound of winter crickets.

Inseparable is the bond of affinity between parent and child. At this very moment O-San's parents, Dōjun and his aged wife, chanced to pass by. The old couple had been overwhelmed with shame at the news of their daughter's elopement. Afraid of meeting their neighbours in broad daylight, they chose night-time for their errands. This evening, accompanied by a little maid, they were walking to their family temple at Kurodani. The moon had not yet risen. As they were about to pass the cottage the sound of fugitives sobbing reached their ears. Mechanically they stopped to listen.

" Who can it be ? " said Dōjun, peering into the darkness.

Ere the old woman could make answer Mohei caught sight of Dōjun by the light of the lantern and, turning to O-San, exclaimed, " See, it's your father ! "

O-San, overjoyed, ran to her parent and embraced him, exclaiming, " Father, father ! "

He shook her off.

" Father ! Not I ! I would not be called father by one as guilty as you." He lifted his cane to strike at her, but instantly the old woman blew out the flame in the lantern and shielded her daughter with her sleeve.

" Oh ! Grandpapa," she intervened, " please pardon her."

" Alas, my life in the other world is doomed," mourned the old man. " O-San being our only daughter, we hoped to have chosen a husband for her and made her succeed to the family estate. But alas ! during the last few years many of my customers in the provinces have failed to pay their dues and I have been reduced to such narrow circumstances as to be obliged to mortgage my house. Were she to succeed to the family estate she would, as things are at present, be the loser. Pondering over this I resigned myself to our family relinquishing its name at my death and gave O-San in marriage to Ishun Dono. This I did out of sheer affection and sympathy for her. As for Ishun Dono's family, it was good enough to sympathize with me and declared it needed neither bridal outfit nor marriage portion. That family had a high opinion of the qualities of our line and concluded O-San must be possessed of a like virtue. Accordingly no dowry was asked but that of her pure soul. Oh! The pity of it! Before anyone was aware, the soul of an animal took the place of her soul. Observe the wild ducks and the mandarin ducks on the pond, or the swallows nestling under the eaves. With them one male pairs alone with one female, such is the rule of all creatures. What female, with the exception of the bitch and the tabby, bears different coloured children to different fathers? And my daughter—Oh! My daughter! Can it be that she was born a dog or that I have brought her up to be a cat? Not one word would I speak to such an unclean beast. So much from my point of view—but now the mischief is done O-San ought to hide in the depths of the mountain that she may escape pursuit as long as may be. Thoughtless indeed it is of her thus to linger anywhere near Kyoto. Is it her wish to be arrested and led in open shame through the streets branded as an adulteress? Does she desire that her body be pierced with the spear of the executioner— her body for which we had such care? Whether she is alive or come to her death I don't care a fig—I neither sigh nor weep over either event. But it grieves me to see grandmama weep."

Once more the old couple abandoned themselves to tears. Mohei cast himself at their feet.

"Mother dear," said O-San, clutching her mother by the sleeve, "we were never guilty of a deliberate intrigue, but

the caprices of chance drove us to a seeming sin and in consequence the infamy of a supposed misconduct attaches to
us throughout the capital. It is now no longer possible to
prove our innocence. Grieved am I indeed for father's
sorrow and mother's grief, yet we must account ourselves
lucky in having met you before taking our journey to the
world beyond. To that world I shall take the memory of
father's kind words. Now that I have seen you I can leave
this world without regret. Yes, I shall be without regret,
even though the next minute find me caught in the web of
fate and though I be fastened upon a cross and pierced with
spears."

"Do not say that," cried her father shuddering. "We
are all anxiety that you should escape crucifixion."

Once more he wept. O-San's mother produced a purse
from her rosary bag.

"I give you all there is in this," she said, "poor girl, you
must feel the cold for I see you have disposed of some of
your garments. You can use this to renew your wardrobe.
I should advise you to escape notice by leaving this neighbourhood with all possible speed and in a palanquin. Spare
us the knowledge of your death."

"Thank you, mother," returned O-San, accepting the
purse with gratitude. "You are quite right, I have sold my
light blue under-dress. But this upper-dress, bearing upon
it the design of a heron standing still among the rushes, the
present you made me last autumn, I shall wear till the last
moment as a memento. Don't be troubled about my clothes,
mother, I am past feeling cold now. So long as we do not
fall ill we can beg our way. This money I will keep for
funeral expenses."

"Alas," her mother replied, "again you speak of death!"

At length Mohei found his tongue. He addressed the
aged pair :—

" To you it may seem unmanly and shameless that I should still cling to life after committing so great a sin, but my only motive is to find some way or other of saving O-San Sama's life. Will you please take her home with you. Once I am assured of her safety I will assume all the blame and meet execution alone. Consider the matter, I pray you."

Once more he wept, clasping his hands.

" What nonsense is this you are talking ! " O-San scornfully exclaimed. " Were it possible for me to remain unpunished both could remain unpunished. Although the happening was unintentional it is a fact that I, a married woman, slept with you. Though I were reborn a woman with a different face yet would it be impossible for me to rid myself of this stigma. I fear you have lost your judgment, Mohei."

" You are right, O-San Sama. Hark ! Surely that is the sound of vehicles passing along the street of Sanjō. Day will break ere long. I have no special place of refuge in view, but let us make at all events for my native place Kaibara in the province of Tamba. Come, O-San Sama, bid farewell to your parents."

O-San hesitated. Her parents were unwilling to let her go, fearful lest this might be an everlasting farewell. Till this moment the moon had not arisen and since they could not clearly descry each other they might more readily have overcome the pain of separation. Now, however, the moon illumined their faces and rendered that separation the more difficult. Almost they hated the moon.

" Ah, father," cried the dame, " for all that a sick man's pulse may be gone we yet know they continue to give him medicine, trusting to a lucky chance. Our only daughter, our most precious possession, may at any moment be discovered and put to death by the authorities. If this should happen how can we leave her to her fate ? Let us three therefore remain in each other's company until the worst befall and let us die together, parent and child. That is my plan."

" No," replied her husband. " True it is that an apparently mortal disease has sometimes been known to be cured by skilful treatment or miraculous potions. And even a man whose heart has ceased to beat is suffered to repose for twenty-four hours undisturbed before he is given up as dead. But this most fatal of all diseases, violation of the national laws, is beyond the farthest art of the great physicians of China, India and Japan. Only one hope remains—to beg forgiveness of Ishun in humility upon our knees. When O-San is arrested and faces her last moments let me bow my grey head to the earth in supplication to the authorities for her life or in entreaty to permit me to die in her stead. For the present it were best if we parted from each other, for thus we shall best benefit O-San. Did it become known that we were sheltering you, the deed could but become an offence to Ishun who cannot forgive you even if he would. Whereas, if it gets about that O-San is deserted, even by her parents and her household, and is undergoing all kinds of misfortunes, Ishun's sympathy may be excited. Do not remember it against me, O-San, that I have called you hard names, likening you to a cat or a dog. There is neither god nor Buddha to whom I do not make supplication for your sake. Every morning, old man of seventy years of age though I am, I purify myself in icy water that I may be in more fit condition to worship sun, moon and stars. Thus doing, all my bones seem to freeze, but, thinking how my suffering can be nothing to the agonies you must experience when crucified, I fortify myself and address those deities the more fervently. Nor do I consider those prayers will be of none avail. Have a care of O-San, Mohei, lest she fall ill. See, I have fifteen *ryō* which I have borrowed from the priest of the temple at

Kurodani as part of the interest of the mortgage on my house. As things are now I have no further care for public reputation and shall accordingly deliver up my house to my creditors. I have therefore no longer need of the money which I ought in truth to return to the priest. I cannot therefore either give it you nor can you accept it if I make the offer. Nevertheless, suppose an old gentleman named Dōjun, being under the influence of great emotion and blinded with tears, should happen to let it fall out of sheer absence of mind "—here he dropped the money upon the ground—" Why, then one may suppose that you, O-San, would not be incapable of picking it up. Neither the powers of this world or the other ever punish the pickers up of un-considered trifles. Now, mother, we must home." The old couple took two or three steps forward. Mohei and O-San burst into tears. She picked up the money and held it to her forehead, exclaiming, " What generosity ! What love ! O father, mother, I am overwhelmed." The old man, per-mitting himself one backward glance, answered, " Say no more, my darling. Farewell," and made as if to proceed. His wife stopped him and, did she show signs of going forward, he in turn stayed her. Thus did the poor fond fools linger. O-San and Mohei, equally reluctant to take the path appointed them, climbed a neighbouring mound that they might follow the old couple with their eyes. Then did the moon, casting their twin shadows and the shadows of Bairyū's two clothes-poles beneath which they stood, project upon the white of the cottage wall in hideous silhouette the figures of twain crucified.

" Look there ! Look there ! " cried the mother aghast. " See the figures of two crucified ! "

" No, what are they but shadows ? Heavy am I, for how can I but take this for a sign that their pardon is beyond even the succour of the gods ! "

Again they wept bitterly, whereon the cottage door softly opened and O-Tama's head appeared, casting a dismal shadow on the outer wall.

" See ! " cried the old woman.

" How dejected a head ! " cried Dōjun.

They stood momentarily stupefied while O-San and O-Tama gazed on each other in recognition.

" Is it O-Tama ? "

" Do I see O-San Sama ? "

The aged couple, recovering from their stupor, made off with a final farewell. Hardly had their adieus been uttered when the lesser bell of the temple at Kurodani tolled *Shōmetsu-metsui* (appearance and disappearance—both illusions), to be shortly followed by the peal that announces the dawn known as *Jakumetsu-iraku* (Nirvana turning to true joy), sounds such as appeared prophetic of the final destiny of the young lovers.

III

In the province of Tamba, among the mountains, spring, sweet with flowers and loud with bird-song, was come. From the snow of winter, already thawing beneath the warmth of the breeze, a mist ascended, to hang its curtains above the fields and along the flanks of the hills. No more did the icicles glitter like swords from the angles of the eaves. Glens were musical with the universal voice of many waters released.

At Kaibara, an out-of-the-way little town, a troupe of *manzai* (strolling comic dancers) made their appearance and the pulse of their tabors seemed to possess something of the joyful abandon of the running streams.

Dancing before a cottage door they sang :—

> All upon New Year's Day
> The springs unfrozen play,
> Green burgeoneth bud and spray;
>   Hurrah for the Happy New Year!
> Ten good deeds does the Emperor do,
> Nine only can the wise gods do,
> The third day brings Ebisu,
> Under whose kindly care
> The merchant and his ware
> Prosper right well and fair.
>   Hurrah for the Happy New Year!
> Then in the city streets,
> Where mart with mart competes,
> What welcome our eye greets:
> See in the fisher's store
> Bass, sea-bream, "Johnny Dore."
> And—heaven knows what more;
> Near by turnip and bean,
> Plump pumpkin and radish lean,
> Red peppers and peppers green;
>   Hurrah for the Happy New Year!
> With gold and silver hoard
> Is the merchant's chest now stored,
> Joy gladdeneth house and board;
> In family unison
> Grandad and his son's son
> Alike now share the fun :
>   Hurrah for the Happy New Year!

" Thanks for your good wishes. Here is a hundred *mon* [1] for you with the prayer that my father and mother may live to be each a hundred years old and in good health."

The speaker, a beautiful young woman, offered the dancers the alms wrapped in a piece of paper and set upon a tray. The leader of the dancers received the offering with thanks, at the same time curiously scrutinizing the donor's face.

" Ah, madam, how are you ? This is indeed a pleasant surprise."

" Your meaning ? I have no friend among the *manzai*."

" There's no reason why you should recognize us, but how can we forget you, madam ? You are the lady of Mr. Ishun

---

[1] The smallest coin, made of bronze, with a hole in the centre for a string.

the *daikyōji* at Karasumaru, Kyoto, are you not ? Every
year when New Year's Day came round we danced in your
courtyard while you were pleased to look on us from your
parlour where you sat on a splendid cushion attended by
your waiting maids. That was you, wasn't it, madam ?
You used to like the Rice-Planting tune. Shall we dance it
now, madam ? ''

O-San was taken aback.

" Those are sharp eyes of yours," said she. " I must have
seen you every year and yet I don't remember you personally.
. . . I ask you to be so good as to tell nobody that I am here.
The fact is my father, owing to a business failure, retired and
took up residence in this town some months ago. I myself
came here recently to inquire after his health and my mother's.
For a particular reason, with which I won't bother you
now, I thought it best to report myself to the head man of
this town as a light-o'-love from Shimabara, Kyoto, who had
been bought out by her lover. If anybody should question
you concerning me, please say I am a lady of easy virtue you
used to know at Shimabara, and when you visit the capital
please don't talk of me, but keep my presence here a dead
secret. Let me offer you something more."

O-San took some fifty further *mon* off the string of cash
and gave it to the dancer.

" A thousand thanks, madam. We shall go up to Kyoto
in two or three days and during our visit call at your house
and take a friendly cup with Sukéyemon Sama and your
other clerks, according to our annual custom. I'll inform
them that you are in good health, madam."

The dancers were about to make off when O-San called
them back.

" Oh ! And this too, gentlemen. May I beg you never
to mention my name before the people of Karasumaru.
Somewhat fearful I am lest my name should escape your lips

when the *saké* has done its work. I therefore beg of you, give up this idea of going to Karasumaru this year. The following New Year I hope to be back at Kyoto, when we will celebrate the occasion together. I wish I could offer you some *saké* here and now, but unfortunately we are out of it at present. Will you use this to drink with when and where you choose ? ''

She slipped two or three pieces of silver as hush-money into the leader's hand.

" A thousand thanks, madam. Depend upon it we won't mention you anywhere. Such a sum makes us more drunk than any *saké* can. Again a thousand thanks."

The dancers departed, rejoicing over their luck.

O-San was yet immersed in a brown study, pondering a thousand things, when Mohei returned, pale and crestfallen.

" How glad I am to see you back, Mohei San," she hastened to say. " It is but a few minutes ago since the *manzai* that used to call on us every year in Kyoto were here. They were much surprised to see me and asked me how I came to be here. I concealed my consternation and told them a cock-and-bull story. However, I feel we can hardly remain here, for not even here are we safe."

Mohei, no less panic-stricken, made answer :—

" In great danger we are indeed. I have but this moment learned that Ishun Sama, Sukéyemon, and all the other clerks have halted from their pursuit of us in the next village. I don't wonder at it. ' Both heaven and earth ' as the proverb says ' know all about it '. Beside the *manzai*, many chestnut sellers and hawkers of firewood from Tamba who occasionally visit Kyoto must have noted us, and it is probably from their lips that our enemies have heard of our movements. Moreover two palanquin bearers went by just now, carrying visitors to the hot springs of Tajima Province, and let drop some unpleasant details, saying, ' O-San, the wife of the

G

daikyōji, is known to be hiding in the mountains of Tamba and despatches from the authorities at Kyoto to this effect have reached the bailiff's office in this town. We have carried an officer post-haste these five miles from Oinosaka Hill, searching for O-San's whereabouts.' They said they were paid no less than ten *ryō* for the job."

"Our hours then are numbered," exclaimed O-San. A shudder shook her frame.

"Well, I am prepared for it. But how my parents will grieve at the news ! That alone worries me. Since it is my duty as my parents' daughter to prolong my life every hour I can, let us leave the town during the coming night."

"That will be best. Of the money your father so kindly gave us we have spent but three *ryō*. There is therefore twelve *ryō* yet remaining which I have put in charge of Sukésaku, the owner of this house. Thinking that it would be better to die with that money, the symbol of your father's affection, in our hands, than leave it as treasure to another man, I have this moment called on Sukésaku to ask him to return it. He said he'd bring it presently. We had best make our way somehow or other to Miyazu in Tango Province, where a relative of mine is living. But in the event of ill-luck overtaking us before we reach the spot, I beg of you, as I have often begged before, to resign yourself to the ordinances of fate. It grieves me to think that your precious life may come to be lost through any doings of mine."

Mohei appeared much dejected.

"Once more you repeat yourself. Remember what we suffer now was preordained from the beginning of the world. I am therefore resigned to it, but none the less cannot refrain from constantly thinking of my parents. For Ishun Sama I also grieve, who has been my companion from childhood up. I nurse a desire to prove to him our absolute innocence before we die."

So saying, O-San wept bitterly. Sukésaku entered abruptly.

" Shinroku San," [1] he said brusquely, " I thought it a pity to let your money remain idle in my coffer and have accordingly lent it out on interest for your benefit. I cannot therefore return it to you forthwith. Please allow me one or two days' grace. You're a reckless man. Give up, my dear fellow, your foolish project of wasting more money after redeeming such a light-o'-love as this."

" Nay, Sukésaku San," broke in O-San, assuming the manner and language of those amongst whom she gave herself out to be numbered, " 'tis not my lover but myself who needs the money. A woman who has ' gone gay ', why, the more patrons she has the more showy must her style of life be. This means that she gets into debt and has a poor time of it in consequence. A sum I borrowed from one of my former patrons is due to-night. If I fail to repay it at this the proper time I shall cut a poor figure. Shinroku San, you see, has been disinherited by his father, the Osaka millionaire, purely on my account ; none the less we expect to be reconciled ere long. When that reconciliation takes place and he returns to Osaka be sure to call for his assistance if you need it at any hour of the day or night. He can accommodate you with any sum you please, a thousand *ryō* if you like, why, ten thousand if necessary—I speak the truth, sir—and that without asking any interest." She turned to Mohei. " You could do that, couldn't you, dear ? "

" Certainly," replied Mohei. " I regret to be such a trouble to you, Sukésaku, but will you please do your best to return me the money to-night."

" Why, then I will do so. I had no notion of your urgent need. I won't fail to bring the money between four o'clock

---

[1] Mohei had taken this name, pretending to be a millionaire's son eloped with his sweetheart, a light-o'-love from Shimabara.

and nightfall.   You two will make sure to be at home, won't you, for I shall need a written receipt."

" Why not ?   We shall not stir."

Sukésaku departed in haste.

" How skilfully you deceived Sukésaku.   Your frequent play-going has not been without its results I see.   If we set out directly we receive the money and walk as fast as we can we should be able easily to cover some seventeen or eighteen miles in the course of the night.   The priest of the Monju Temple near Miyazu is a relative of my mother's.   If we ask him to shelter us he can scarcely refuse.   Come, let us make ready."   As they made their preparations the sound of arms and of heavy footsteps drew near.   O-San listened intently.

" What's that ? "

" Heaven protect us !   I fear Sukésaku has undone us. We can no longer escape.   Do not play the coward."

" I am quite prepared.   Have no fears."

A moment later several officers appeared, Sukésaku guiding them.   No sooner did they spy the pair than, crying out, " Consider yourselves our prisoners ; we arrest you in the name of the authorities," they rushed forward, flourishing maces and cords.

Mohei, not a whit daunted, stepped forward and said :—

" Quietly, sirs, I offer no resistance.   I am a tradesman and bear no arms—as you see—not even a dagger.   True it is I have practised *jū-jutsu* [1] from boyhood up and therefore can if need be throw half a dozen officers and more, for all that my arms are so slender.   But resist you I will not, for this trouble arises from my master's resentment.   Were I to resist you it would be tantamount to resisting my master. As for my companion here, I could proffer you irrefutable proof of her innocence, but I will not do so.   If your charge be adultery, please make that charge and bind us."

---

[1] An art of self-defence.

The officers, once more crying, "Consider yourselves our prisoners," closed in upon the young pair and tightly bound them. Neither offered any resistance or showed the least fear. The officers were struck with admiration at their heroic bearing.

"How mean a peasant," O-San exclaimed, fixing her eye on Sukésaku. "Out of what depth of base avarice have you betrayed us!"

She turned to the officers. "One moment please. The truth is, sirs, we have lodged twelve *ryō* in this man's charge. We prisoners have no need of money, but that sum is a symbol of my father's profound love toward me. I beseech you, sirs, extort it from this man and have it sent to the priest of the temple of Kurodani, of whom my father is a debtor." Scarcely had she thus spoken when Sukésaku roared :—

"The jade! I never borrowed a penny of her! Quite the contrary. I let this house to you for some fifty days for which you owe me about five *ryō*, representing the house-rent and the price of rice and *miso*.[1] It's sheer cozenage to suggest that you have entrusted me with twelve *ryō*." At this Mohei, bound as he was, rose to his feet and dealt the villain such a kick as to send him sprawling.

"To what end should we lie to such a wretch about so paltry a sum? If you covet it so badly why then we make it yours. When you get to Hell's house be sure to have the money about you, then you can spin a yarn to King Yama as to how you were a Midas in this world."

So saying, Mohei dealt Sukésaku another sound kick or two and resumed his seat with some composure.

Then it was that Sukéyemon, who had been observing the scene, rushed forward. Turning to the officers he said respectfully :—

"Sirs, I am cousin of this informer, Sukésaku, and head

---

[1] Bean paste.

clerk of Ishun the *daikyōji* of Kyoto and my name is Sukéyemon. Accept my thanks for the trouble you have been at
in effecting the arrest of O-San and Mohei. My master and
I rejoice at the glad news. Our desire is to carry the prisoners
home to Kyoto. Will you be so good, sirs, as to deliver them
up to us ? "

" A saucy fellow," rapped out the chief of the officers,
" to demand the delivery of the prisoners ! Keep in mind
that we haven't arrested them on your account, but on the
order of the authorities in Kyoto, whither we are forthwith
to carry them, there to be placed in gaol. They are prisoners
of particular importance and are to be the subject of a careful
examination. Offer any more impertinence and you will
very soon find yourself a prisoner too."

Sukéyemon, abashed and not a little scared, withdrew.

A palanquin, borne in great haste, appeared, from the
recesses of which there stepped out no other than the old man
Akamatsu Bairyū, having in his hand a closed wooden box.
He made obeisance to the officers and began :—

" Sirs, my name is Akamatsu Bairyū and I am uncle and
surety to O-Tama, a maid of Ishun the *daikyōji*. I beg
to assure you these prisoners are not guilty of adultery.
Some misconstruction of my niece's hasty talk and an overhasty jealousy have caused O-San and Mohei most unjustly
to be considered as adulterers. My little fool of a niece
was alone to blame. That she might make atonement for
her great fault I have killed her and brought her head here in
this box. I humbly beseech you, sirs, to save the lives of
these innocent prisoners."

Bairyū uncovered the box. Within reposed O-Tama's
head, the eyelids lowered as if in slumber. A murmur of
horror escaped the prisoners, then, averting their eyes, both
burst into tears. The chief of the officers bent a compassionate glance upon Bairyū.

" A rash deed have you done, old man ! Know that the prisoners' guilt has not yet been clearly established. It was our intention to carry them for examination at Kyoto and to summon your niece as witness. Under such procedure all would become clear and all three of them might possibly be found innocent. But, forasmuch as you have seen fit thoughtlessly to slay the witness, what evidence have we that can stand them in good stead ? I grieve to have to say it, but their punishment is settled. To Kyoto must they go, there to suffer execution. Officers, make ready to convey the prisoners."

" As you will, sir."

The henchmen, taking up the ends of the cords, ordered the prisoners to stand up.

Bairyū stamped and raged in vain :—

" Rash and thoughtless have I been ! All in vain have you perished, Tama. Seventy summers have I seen and, having seen them, made the greatest blunder of my life. Shame overcomes me, but if I despatch myself as token of atonement a mere laughing-stock should I be. Where may I find me an enemy ? "—here he caught sight of Sukéyemon— " Sukéyemon, none fitter. You I will slay that, charged with murder, I may be executed with this poor couple."

In a flash the old samurai had drawn his blade and fallen upon Sukéyemon, who, cut about the face, ran hither and thither, dripping blood.

" Nothing but the head itself will suffice me."

Bairyū made at him, but the constables stepped between, crying, " Enough, no murder ! "

" Let me get at him ! Let me get at him ! If it be murder it has a purpose."

Vainly he struggled to free himself, the waning strength of an old man borne down by the strength of many.

O-San and Mohei, tightly bound, were seated upon

separate horses and the procession started for the execution ground in the suburbs of Kyoto. The horses that bore the prisoners were, no less than all other living creatures, doomed sooner or later to the land of shadow, but to that pair of prisoners, whose last moments were so rapidly approaching, it seemed that they alone were vanishing from the world. Slowly as the horses ambled, too swiftly, all too swiftly were they felt to proceed by those who momentarily neared their lasting home. Nineteen summers had one and but twenty-five the other, from whose eyes, wistfully gazing upon the frosts that starred the path, the hot tears fell like drops of dew down their cheeks and upon their saddles. Passers-by and guardians alike were moved at their sorrowful faces and dejected figures.

" Listen, Mohei San," said O-San timidly, her little voice nigh broken, " What grief is mine that for my foolish jealousy's sake you, who are guilty in no wise, should have come to be branded as an adulterer. Very grieved am I for your sake and beg your forgiveness."

Mohei lifted his head a little.

" Not so should you speak, O-San Sama," Mohei made answer, scarce able to speak for tears. " Whether I be burned by fire or the water take me, I am resigned to my doom. Yes, I am utterly prepared for the worst, but, that I may be spared the agonies of the life to come, I make prayer to Amida Buddha in my heart. Do you pray too."

" I thank you. So will I."

At length the slow and dreary journey, across the mountains, down the ravines and over the plains, drew to its close. Lo ! Afar off glittered through the bitter boughs of winter a ghastly flashing : the naked spears of executioners. When this reality came home to the prisoners a shudder seized them. For all their resolution a low murmur escaped their lips. Gazing upon each other they wept bitterly, the tears falling even upon the manes of the horses. Through the tops of the pine-grove whistled the frore wind of evening, scattering upon them a handful of snowflakes. Numbed were the prisoners' hands and upon their sleeves the tears were frozen.

Reverie of intense melancholy fell upon the prisoners, and thinking upon their natures,[1] each was downcast. Might not O-San's " metal-nature " signify that it was ordained she must perish by a blade ? Might not Mohei's " earth-nature " prefigure a doom consequent upon a former life that early he should be buried in the earth ? Her maid's name " O-Tama " or " Bead ", what could it have been but an omen that, like a bead of dew O-Tama should perish early ? Short as O-San and O-Tama's relationship as mistress and maid had been in this world, now might they enjoy companionship in Hades. Ere long the party found themselves upon a level road and approaching the execution ground. A throng of spectators noisily discussed the prisoners. Dōjun and his spouse, with difficulty making their way through the crowd, prostrated themselves in tearful entreaty before the officers. " Sirs, our daughter's crime is dire, nevertheless most humbly we beseech you, favour her with mercy. For her sake we fear neither crucifixion nor decapitation. We here beseech you that you grant our earnest request, which is that you kill us as substitutes for her. Do this and save our dearest daughter's life. Ah ! O-San, poor daughter ! "

Weeping, the pair clung to O-San as she was lifted from the horse. The henchmen drove them away.

The fatal moment was all but come, when, like a messenger of the gods, the priest Tōgan of the temple of Kurodani suddenly appeared.

" Permit me, sirs, to make an attempt to save the lives

---

[1] Every individual is superstitiously considered to have a distinctive nature belonging to one of the five categories ; wood, fire, earth, metal and water.

of O-San and Mohei.   Refuse a priest's request for mercy and damned you must be eternally."

So saying, he endeavoured to shelter the prisoners behind his flowing sleeves.   This Tōgan was a celebrated priest who enjoyed great influence with the authorities of the capital. None the less the chief of the officers made angry answer :—

" Not so, your reverence, you overleap yourself in seeking to save the lives of criminals whose sentence has already been pronounced.   It is not your affair."

But for all that the priest persisted.

" Grant me these lives.   Guilty though they may be, were I to take them for my disciples, who knows but that they might find such a path as would release them from the burden of sin.   Suffer me, sirs, to save their lives in this world, whatever be their lot in the next.   Saved them I have, yes, I see they are pardoned ! "

At this assertion a cry of exultation suddenly arose from the sympathetic crowd.   It goes without saying that the old couple were beside themselves with joy and gratitude.

Thus were saved O-San and Mohei.

This joyful tale, even as the *daikyōji*'s almanac, came to be repeated year after year and is thus handed down to this very day.

A SCENE FROM *SUGAWARA'S SECRETS OF CALLIGRAPHY*
From a colour print by Kunichika

[face p. 106

A SCENE FROM *YASAKU'S SUICIDE WITH A SICKLE*

FISHMONGER GOROBEI IN *FELLOW-PASSENGERS' TALKS ABOUT THE VENDETTA*, PLAYED BY KŌSHIRŌ THE FOURTH
From a picture by Sharaku

A SCENE FROM *THE SOGA BROTHERS' BOWS BENT TO THE FULL*, A *KABUKI* PLAY,
BY TSURUYA NAMBOKU, PERFORMED BY FAMOUS ACTORS OF OLD JAPAN

From a colour print by Kunisada (Gototei)

FAIR LADIES
AT A GAME OF POEM-CARDS

(Kaoyo Utagaruta)

FAIR LADIES AT A GAME OF POEM-CARDS

(*Kaoyo Utagaruta*)

I

DURING the reign of the Emperor Takakura, eighty-eighth emperor, it was Kiyomori, the Prime Minister, and his clan the Taira who in reality steered the ship of state and achieved the zenith of their prosperity. His son and heir, Shigémori, Lord Keeper of the Privy Seal, celebrated throughout Japan for his wisdom and virtue, for literary accomplishments and military proficiency, was an object of love and veneration among the warriors of the two greatest military houses, the Taira and the Minamoto. Among courtiers and court nobles he was also held in esteem, inasmuch as he was elder brother of the merciful and sagacious Empress Kenrei-Mon-in, mother of the Crown Prince shortly destined to become the Emperor Antoku.

On September the ninth, the Feast of the Chrysanthemum, of the first year of Yōwa (A.D. 1181), Lady Tonasé, chief lady-in-waiting, was despatched by the Empress as messenger to Shigémori. The warrior nobleman, having accorded her a hearty welcome, requested her to reveal her message.

" Permit me to congratulate your lordship upon this happy occasion," began Lady Tonasé. " Since the chrysanthemums are now in full bloom, Her Imperial Majesty graciously deems that the maple leaves upon the mountains must be at their best and accordingly desires to view them. It is therefore her Imperial pleasure that your lordship should order a mushroom picking party to be held upon Mount Kita [1] according to annual custom."

" Your message delights me, my lady," replied Shigémori. " I had intended to transmit precisely this suggestion to Her Majesty. Pray tell Her Majesty that the mushroom picking party will take place on the twelfth and the moon viewing party on the thirteenth, and that I beg Her Majesty to prolong her visit upon the mountain for two or three days after the parties are over."

" The invitation gives me pleasure," returned the Imperial messenger. " I can well imagine what delight that will cause Her Majesty. The younger ladies-in-waiting, nay, even the more elderly such as myself, always look forward with great pleasure to the two annual Imperial picnics, the flower viewing in spring and the maple-leaf viewing in autumn. Now I must hasten to return and report your lordship's kindly answer to my Imperial mistress. Well can I imagine the scarlet brocade upon the trees and the sweet music of the field insects. Since we have had fine weather for several days now the moon is sure to be bright and beautiful. We should all enjoy ourselves exceedingly. I heartily thank your lordship's samurai in advance for the trouble they will be at in making the appropriate arrangements. I beg to take leave of your lordship."

Her ceremonial speech ended, she returned to the Imperial palace.

Shigémori summoned his retainers, Morihisa, Moritsugu and Takiguchi [2] and thus addressed them :—" The Imperial

---

[1] A mountain north of Kyoto or Miyako (the capital), as it was called in ancient times. At this period the Imperial Court was situate in Kyoto.

[2] His full name was Saitō Takiguchi Yorikata. Takiguchi is his official title as warrior in the guard of the *Seiryōden*, an Imperial palace. He is however better known by this title than by the name Yorikata.

mushroom picking party is to be given on the twelfth. You must do your utmost, as is your wont each year, in the matter of escorting Her Imperial Majesty, in sweeping the mountain, and in building the temporary Imperial pavilion. Furthermore, Her Majesty being a great lover of song-birds, you are to place in front of the pavilion for her entertainment a large and beautiful cage containing many song-birds of the four seasons. I hear that the titmouse [1] recently presented to me by Lord Kadowaki can perform several feats at suggestions of the hand, such for instance as passing through rings and drawing water. It were a somewhat childish thing in me to make much ado about such a bird ; I therefore wish to make a present of it to Her Majesty. Takiguchi, this errand shall be yours. Make ready." With these words Shigémori entered the inner apartment.

Takiguchi was an extremely handsome youth of barely nineteen, a fitting envoy for such a task. He promptly trimmed himself up and set out for the Imperial palace accompanied by a henchman who carried the precious bird in a cage.

Now that the date for the mushroom picking party had been announced, the maids-of-honour impatiently awaited the day, not so much for the pleasure of the picnic as for the opportunities afforded of seeing young samurai. For the samurai and men-servants in the palace of the Empress were all men above sixty.

There were to be found among these court ladies two damsels in particular, exceedingly beautiful, named Yokobué and Karumo, both great favourites with the Empress on account of their personal grace, intelligence and sweetness of disposition. Their comrades too felt for them real affection. This day it was Yokobué's turn to serve as usher. She was

---

[1] The Japanese name is *yamagara*. It is known to science as Sittiparus Varius Varius.

on duty in the chamber. The other young ladies were gathered in the same chamber and were chattering merrily.

" Yokobué Dono," said one of them, " let us hope that on the occasion of the mushroom picking party we get plenty of chances to see handsome young samurai. I can't help wondering who will accompany Lord Shigémori on that day. What young men of the Taira clan will there be ? What fun it will be if there are handsome young men among the attendants ! But if it unfortunately turns out that only such warriors as the ferocious, woman-hating Lord of Noto should appear, a very poor time of it we shall get."

" Have no fear on that score," Karumo took up the tale. " Tastes differ. Lord Tsunémasa is commonly held to be the most handsome of the clan of Taira, but he is such a precocious boy that his voice broke at fourteen. Such a trifler too ! I don't fancy him. Lord Atsumori is a simple-minded, lovable creature, but I fear he is already engaged to a certain lady. Master Moritsugu's younger brother, Yoshitsugu Dono, is a kind-hearted, lovable man I've no doubt, but that scorpion of a brother of his is so strict about his behaviour that not a girl can get near him. How can a woman choose her comrade for life when this is the case ? We can but leave the matter to providence."

" I don't agree with you," said Yakumo and O-Hana simultaneously. " If we leave the matter entirely to providence it is probable that she will provide us with such boorish warriors as Kagékiyo or Gorōbyōé. How could one live a happy life with such a person as that ? Master Morihisa certainly played a very pretty tune on the lute at last year's mushroom picnic on Mount Kita, but what an effeminate fellow he is ! The gallant who suits the taste of everybody, high and low alike, the paragon of men, he is surely Master Saitō Takiguchi Yorikata. Don't you agree with me, Yokobué Dono ? "

Yokobué met this banter with, " I don't share the opinion of any of you, my friends. You talk as if Master Takiguchi were the only handsome man in existence. He's handsome enough in all faith ; nobody can call him ill-favoured ; but such a person is always too conceited about his own good looks and usually spoilt and ill-natured into the bargain. I tell you I positively dislike him."

But this assertion only provoked an immediate burst of laughter.

" What a liar ! " everyone cried. " The hypocrite ! Nobody blames Karumo Dono who frankly states she thinks Master Yoshitsugu is the sort of man one could love. We hate such dishonesty in Yokobué Dono. You are loud in your protestations of dislike for Master Yorikata, but your tenderness of heart did not escape us when you were good enough to mend a burst seam of his *hakama*[1] and we all know how you kissed its gusset at the football[2] match at Lord Shigémori's house the other day. What's more you carried to your lips with obvious pleasure a towel with which he had wiped his mouth. And yet you dare to declare that you positively dislike him ! What a little liar ! Make a clean breast of it, Yokobué Dono ! Confess ! If you don't we'll untie your *obi* as a punishment and strip you to the skin. Come, girls, let's do it now ! "

" Please forgive me ! "

" Tickle her ! " cried the girls, laughing. " Pinch her ! "

It was at this moment that Takiguchi arrived before the

---

[1] A ceremonial flowing garment worn over ordinary clothes, extending from the waist almost to the ankle, and covering each leg separately.

[2] Football was one of the stock court amusements. Needless to say it had little in common with that organized form of refined savagery which we find in the west to-day. It was a stately game, played in a costume of which the voluminous trousers formed not the least important item. We are informed that this diversion has been revived of late. The pleasure of this pastime is however we believe the prerogative of the elect.

porch and announced, " Saitō Takiguchi, a messenger from Lord Shigémori, desires to see the lady usher."

At this announcement the girls were overcome with merriment and excitement.

" Speak of angels——" one of them whispered, laughing. " Your beloved's come, Yokobué Dono ! "

" Dear Yokobué," said another, " you're in luck to-day, being usher."

" I can never hope to be a *yokobué*,[1] but I desire to be a *shakuhachi* [2] and to be set to the mouth of that *takiguchi*." [3]

" I should like to bring him tea."

They stole toward the paper doors of the porch and peeped through.

" I'd like to bite those lovely cheeks," one whispered.

" I'd like to be held so hard in his arms that I'd die."

The chatterboxes were startled to hear the voice of the chief lady of the court crying, not without asperity, " Girls, Her Majesty summons you ! Her Majesty has clapped her hands several times. It's very thoughtless of you that not one of you is in attendance on Her Majesty."

" Gracious me ! That old thunderstorm of a hag is blowing up again. Hurry, lest the lightning strike you ! "

The girls precipitated themselves into the inner apartments.

Yokobué, who had longed for Takiguchi, opened the doors. Her heart was violently beating. The words she pronounced were tremulous.

" Welcome, sir messenger."

Takiguchi, who had pined for the girl, was transported to

---

[1] The girl's name Yokobué means literally ' a bamboo flute ', a flute of nearly the same shape as the modern European flute. One end is closed and the player blows with the mouth through a lateral hole.

[2] A *shakuhachi* resembles the ancient and mediæval European flute. The player blows through a mouth-piece at the upper end.

[3] Takiguchi means literally " the mouth of a waterfall ", *i.e.* " the crest of the fall ".

see her before him. For a moment he was struck speechless. It was with an effort that he controlled himself sufficiently to say a moment later, " I beg to declare to you my errand. My Lord Shigémori orders me to announce that Her Imperial Majesty be requested to set out early in the morning of the day after to-morrow that she may visit Mount Kita."

His attitude underwent an abrupt change.

" I think and think of you till dawn breaks. All night I am awake thinking of you, so that I never meet you in dreams. By daylight your figure floats continually before me and comes before me and my duties. Passionately I long for you and most of all toward evening. A warrior ought never to shed tears, no, not even once between birth and the grave. Little befits it him to do so. And yet from morn to evening I find tears in my eyes. Can you guess who makes me weep ? What nonsense I have been talking ! Please forgive me ! Well, as I was saying, this titmouse performs several tricks at suggestions made by the hand. She can pass through rings and draw water. Her name therefore is ' The Wonder of the Capital '. Lord Shigémori begs respectfully to present this bird to Her Majesty since he knows her to be a great lover of song-birds. Now, my pretty "—he addressed the bird —" do some tricks for the entertainment of the lady usher."

So saying Takiguchi made some passes with his hand, whereupon the little bird threw several somersaults round and round the perch—*hira-hira-hira, kuru-kuru-kuru.* Next the bird nimbly threaded the first, second, third, fourth and fifth rings. Now she hopped to the well and, seizing the rope with her beak, lifted the bucket and drew the water. This operation she repeated again and again—*shiton, shiton, shiton.*

" Oh, Yokobué Dono," said Takiguchi, not without

significant glances, "I have improvised an ode on this dear little creature.   Please listen :—

> 'The very titmouse hops through rings,
> Draws water if my will so be;
> I would that you would draw my heart
> And through great trials come to me.'

If it's not asking you too much, would you be kind enough to make an ode in reply ? "

Yokobué, so much entranced that she had noticed neither the bird nor Takiguchi's message, drew close to him, murmuring, "A delightful verse, dear Takiguchi ; "—she fell into a brown study, then her face brightened as if with a happy thought—"here is my reply," she said.

> "The walnut which the titmouse loves
> Lies fallen in the dingle, where
> Scarlet the autumn maples burn
> And you, my love, may find it there."

"You suggest that we meet secretly in the glen on Mount Kita at the mushroom hunting ? "

"Exactly."

"I thank you.   I shall not fail."

They drew nearer and embraced so passionately that they tilted the cage, which fell on its side.   The bird's food and water rolled out, the rings lost their form.   Panic-stricken, Takiguchi hurriedly opened the door of the cage, inserted both his hands and endeavoured to right the damage.   But as fast as he pulled one piece straight another would go out of shape.   Now he turned the cage upside down, now he laid it on its side, while the frightened bird struggled, flutter-flutter.   In his confusion Takiguchi ignored for a moment or two the fact that the cage door was open.   With a glad twitter the little prisoner escaped.   Frantic with despair, the pair pursued the bird hither and thither around the garden.   Takiguchi waved his hand, crying, "Come, my

pretty ! "—at which the titmouse somersaulted in the air
two or three times, then, rejoicing in her freedom, sped away
across the sky. Takiguchi and Yokobué stood watching
the bird with a vacant stare. They were at their wits' end.
They followed the bird with their eyes.

Kaga-no-Gunji Morotaka, police superintendent of the
Empress' palace, younger brother to Lady Tonasé and a
haughty, heartless old samurai who tyrannized over his subordinates, hearing of the occurrence, rushed out. To Takiguchi
he did not vouchsafe a single word of greeting ; Yokobué he
seized by the arm. " Hussy ! " he roared, bending upon her
a withering glance. " Do you think this palace is a tea-house
or a brothel ? Even in the Emperor's palace certain rules
of etiquette are observed in the conduct of messenger and
usher. How much more then are they and must they be
observed here, where almost every office, high and low, is
occupied by a woman. Despite the eye I have been keeping
on you, you have managed to behave with indecency, nay,
the word indecent does not adequately describe your conduct.
What is more, you have been so careless as to cause the escape
of this precious bird. With these misdeeds to answer for
how can you live on shamelessly and dare to show your face
before people ? Were you a samurai I could apportion you
a certain heavy punishment for these serious offences. Since,
however, you are a woman, I sentence you to imprisonment.
Now, my men, bind Yokobué and be quick about it."

Takiguchi stepped forward and excitedly intervened.

" No, no, Morotaka Dono, Yokobué is not to blame. I
am entirely responsible for this mishap. I am resolved to
commit *seppuku* [1] as apology. I cannot however allow
what you said just now to pass unchallenged. What was
your meaning when you said, ' Were you a samurai I could

---

[1] *Seppuku* (*harakiri*) signifies self-dispatch.

assign to you a certain heavy punishment ' ? I am a samurai ; tell me what punishment you propose for me."

" You are overexcited. I never meant such punishment for you. Don't take what I said amiss. If any samurai under my command were guilty of such impropriety I could forthwith order him to be bound, decapitated and his head to be exposed. You, however, are a retainer of Lord Shigémori ; therefore, though you should flirt with a maid-of-honour, pluck the titmouse's feathers, roast and eat it, whatever you might do would be of no consequence to me. If you care to commit *seppuku*, however, you are perfectly at liberty to do so. It would make no difference to the fate of Yokobué. Now, my men, why delay ? Bind her at once and cast her into prison."

The desperate girl defied him.

" Morotaka Dono, blame yourself before you blame others. There is not one of us to whom you, superintendent as you are, have not written notes. What explanation have you for this foulness ? "

Takiguchi laid his hand upon his sword.

" Morotaka," he cried, " I have no option but to believe Yokobué's charge. If it be indeed the law to bind a samurai and behead him for such offences, I, retainer of Lord Shigémori, will begin with you. Prepare yourself, you old fool ! "

He rushed upon Morotaka, but the latter leapt back.

" Bind me if you can ! " he replied.

None could tell what the outcome might be. Maids and henchmen, struck with terror, could but look at them with anxiety and fear.

At this juncture a voice was heard saying, " See that the quarrel is stopped." It was none other than the Empress, who had been informed of the incident and now stepped out on to the verandah. Upon which the maids cried all together, " It is Her Majesty's pleasure that you stop quarrelling ! "

Both samurai instantaneously stopped and bowed their heads in respect.

" I cannot but consider," said the Empress, " that the report is false which accuses Yokobué of impropriety. If any of my maids were guilty of impropriety the blame would be upon Morotaka who is their superintendent. That Takiguchi has let the titmouse escape is no offence at all. Every time he gave the bird food and water he had to open the door of the cage. Is it to be wondered at that the caged bird longs for the blue sky and hungers for an opportunity to escape ? Luckily enough the titmouse alighted in the inner garden and I myself have caught her and put her in the *fusege*.[1] I learn that a large cage containing song-birds is to be ready for my diversion on Mount Kita. Takiguchi, tell Lord Shigémori that I will place the titmouse among the other birds and display her to his lordship. Yokobué and Takiguchi, be of good cheer about that bird. Girls, entertain Takiguchi with *saké* and give him refreshment. Be of good courage, Takiguchi, and present Lord Shigémori with my hearty thanks for his precious gift."

At these kindly words Takiguchi and Yokobué reverentially bowed their heads and gave way to tears of gratitude. Morotaka made a wry face and ground his teeth in mortification.

" And Morotaka," continued the Empress, turning her eyes upon him, " you are most strictly to command all under your authority never to say a word of what has happened to-day. Should they, in spite of your injunctions, mention this matter, it is you who will be held answerable for it."

Having thus spoken to the relief and satisfaction of all present save the old samurai, the Empress withdrew.

The day of the picnic at last arrived. Shigémori, as host,

---

[1] A bamboo frame resembling an inverted basket, upon which ladies' dresses were hung that they might be perfumed with sweet incense burned within the folds.

had done all in his power to make the Imperial visit a success. On Mount Kita had been built a temporary pavilion beautifully thatched with scarlet maple leaves. In front of this was set a large cage containing hundreds of pretty birds, such as nightingales, wagtails, robins, parrots, tits and ducks. Their fine plumage shone brilliantly in the gold of the afternoon sun. They flitted hither and thither uttering sweet notes. The Empress and her retinue had that morning been escorted thither by a large number of Shigémori's retainers.

The Empress stepped down, advanced to the cage and contemplated the birds with seeming interest. Need attention be drawn to the fact that the titmouse presented by Shigémori was not to be found among them? The Empress had pretended that she had caught the bird in order to cover the fault of Takiguchi and his sweetheart.

" My Lord," said the Empress after a while, " I thank you for your kindness in diverting me with the sight of these beautiful birds. True, I enjoy the sight of them exceedingly, but even more joy will be mine at setting these birds free. It is said that even such little birds as these have the same Buddhist nature as ourselves. Permit me to set them at liberty."

So saying she opened the doors of the cage and let the birds escape. The little creatures, uttering cries of happiness, flew out and soared far away into the blue sky. Shigémori who, like his sister, was of a compassionate nature, was struck with admiration.

" This is a real *Hōjōé!* " [1] he exclaimed. " I cannot but admire Your Majesty's benevolence. Your Majesty would do well to view the maple leaves and search for mushrooms to-morrow. Let us retire early this evening in order to

---

[1] On August 15th (lunar calendar) it is the custom to release many caged birds before the shrine of Hachiman, the God of War, in Kyoto. This is called *Hōjōé.*

enjoy the sound of the deer's cries in the stillness of the night."

So saying, both retired into the pavilion.

The night was far advanced ; all was still. The mountain sides were obscure, for the thickets obstructed the brightness of the moonlight.

Yoshitsugu, a retainer of Shigémori and younger brother of Moritsugu, referred to above, had stolen from his post and was now standing, head and face swathed in a kerchief, by the hedge of the Imperial pavilion, the place of the assignation made between himself and his sweetheart Karumo, maid-of-honour. There was a love of long standing between them. Passionately had they desired to meet in secret ; they had sworn to avail themselves of to-night's opportunity. Yokobué, who likewise had promised to meet her lover by stealth this night, arose when all her companions had fallen asleep. Now wearing a *katsugi* [1] she stepped down to the hedge. She beckoned to the man in disguise. He advanced toward her readily enough. They conversed in nods and gestures and were in such a state of joyful excitement that they did not trouble to verify each other's identity. The young samurai lifted the damsel on to his back. In this manner their faces remained undisclosed to one another. The young samurai set out with a light heart toward the glen.

As for Karumo, intending to keep her word with Yoshitsugu, she stole out, also wearing a *katsugi*, at a moment when the position of the moon in the sky declared that midnight had passed. Now she awaited her lover's arrival. Takiguchi, with a kerchief about his head and face, emerged from the darkness intending to meet Yokobué. The expectant

---

[1] The *katsugi* or *kazuki* was a large flowing coat worn over the head and reaching down to the waist, so that it served as a veil. In days of old, ladies of high birth wore it when walking-out.

Karumo, as was only natural, mistook him for her sweetheart. She beckoned to him. Nor did Takiguchi harbour any doubts as to her identity. Hurriedly he hoisted her on to his back and hastened toward the glen. Presently the passionate lover found himself on the bank of a rivulet, along which he walked awhile, when, to his surprise, he overtook another man also with a woman on his back, toiling up-stream. Each was equally scared and tried to avoid being seen by the other, but since they were colleagues by daylight it was not long before they recognized each other.

" Is it Takiguchi ? "

" Yoshitsugu, is it ? "

" You're in for luck, I too am enjoying myself. Ha ! Ha ! "

" Let us keep our sweet secrets to ourselves."

With that they parted and each hurried on his particular way. But the girls on their backs remarked to each other, " It would seem we have got mixed up. Are you not Yokobué Dono ? "

" Is it Karumo Dono ? "

" Eh ? Have we got the wrong girls ? " said one of the samurai. " We are a couple of fools ! "

The two samurai lowered their lovely burdens. Each man removed his kerchief and each girl her veil. The four, to their vast surprise, realized the mistake that had been made. All burst out laughing.

" It would appear we have been overhasty ! Had we not realized our mistake until a little later there is no knowing what might not have happened. We're lucky ! Let each return his charge to the other none the worse."

They wandered no further. Each pair settled down in a chosen spot and enjoyed moments of supreme happiness.

At this moment a considerable body of men carrying sticks and paper lanterns appeared upon the further hillside. These lanterns bore upon them a crest which turned out to be none other than the butterfly of Morotaka, police superintendent of the Empress' court.

" Heaven defend us ! " cried the samurai. " If our secret is detected by that fellow it will prove our ruin. Sweet ladies, do you think you could climb up the valley and find your way safely to the pavilion ? "

" Of course. For love's sake we would be ready to tread upon sword-blades. As for you, samurai, make haste and save yourselves."

Hastily bidding their lovers farewell the girls summoned up courage and hand in hand made their way up the glen. A happy thought came to Takiguchi in the shape of a plan to detain Morotaka in the wood sufficiently long to give the girls time to make good their return in his absence. He assumed Yokobué's *katsugi* that he might appear like a woman. So disguised, he waited near Yoshitsugu for Morotaka's coming.

Having searched here and there and all to no purpose, Morotaka cried, " No wonder Karumo and Yokobué are missing ! I know who their seducers are ! See, over there are some figures, down by the rivulet. Don't let them escape."

No sooner had he spoken than Morotaka and his followers swooped upon the erstwhile lovers and surrounded Yoshitsugu.

" Aha ! " cried Morotaka in triumph. " So Yoshitsugu is the man, is he ? Arrest him."

" An unjust charge ! " cried Yoshitsugu, as if in confusion. " I came here but a few minutes ago to view the maple leaves by moonlight. That's the exact truth ; I am not guilty of any such crime as seduction."

Hardly had he spoken when the superintendent roared, " No further lies, you rogue ! That figure over there is

Karumo, I'll be bound. It's two years now since my heart was set on her. Had she yielded to my wishes I intended to ask Her Majesty to bestow her on me as wife. It appears that I have wooed her day and night to no purpose, because of her attachment to you. I have long suspected the cause. You are a criminal who corrupts the morals of court ladies. Why, you're as good as the lover of my would-be wife ! That woman standing there is an adulteress."

Morotaka rushed upon the supposed Karumo and snatched away the veil. What was his astonishment and fear to behold himself confronted by Takiguchi who glowered upon him, hand laid upon sword-hilt. But he recovered his presence of mind.

" If you're here," he said brusquely, " Yokobué must be hereabouts. You must have scented the danger and concealed her. Well, I shall inquire into this matter later. Let us return, my men."

Morotaka beat a retreat ; but Yoshitsugu and Takiguchi made haste to intercept him in a threatening fashion.

" There's no ' later on ' about it, you old fool," they said. " We want justice here and now. Do you think you can make off with impunity, after snatching a veil from one samurai and seeing fit to call the other a seducer of women ? You can't behave with us as you behave when you lord it over the Empress's court and thunder at the maids-of-honour. Just you try to return to the pavilion without first explaining those insults and you'll find, if these swords can speak, that you'll have no legs to walk on ! "

" Calm yourselves, sirs," replied Morotaka, not without trepidation. " It is Yokobué and Karumo whom I call corrupters of morals. As their superintendent it is my duty to inquire into every particular of these happenings, but with you I have nothing to do. If my words offend you I pray your forgiveness and throw myself upon your generosity."

" Sir Superintendent," returned Takiguchi provocatively, " but a few minutes ago you confessed that during the last few years your heart has been set upon Karumo and that you have wooed her day and night. Who then is her seducer if it isn't you ? As you yourself were good enough to remark at court the other day, such an offender as yourself richly deserves to be bound and decapitated. Now, Yoshitsugu, bind this fellow ! I'll behead him. His retainers too we will chasten. See that they don't escape."

At this threat Morotaka's henchmen threw down their sticks and lanterns and ran for their lives.

" How mercilessly you have argued me down ! " cried the deserted Morotaka. " But you wait ! I'll show you how I'll be revenged on Yokobué and Karumo ! "

So saying, he precipitantly took to his heels.

The two samurai burst into uproarious laughter ; then they made their way back to the pavilion at their leisure.

II

Takiguchi's father, Katsuyori, was an old samurai with a record of long service under Shigémori and Shigémori's father, Kiyomori. He had abandoned the profession of arms, had shaved his head, hoary with the snows of seventy winters, and, having assumed the sacerdotal [1] name of Sairai and having donned a *henzan* (clerical robe), now led a life of abstinence and devotion and made it his daily task to visit the family temple that he might worship Buddha.

One day Sairai, producing an *eboshi* [2] and a beautiful *kariginu*,[3] summoned his son Takiguchi and spoke as follows :

---

[1] Priests' names differ from laymen's names. Samurai in ancient times were generally Buddhists and on retirement were often wont to assume clerical names and lead a life of devotion.

[2] A kind of cap.   [3] A robe affected by early warriors.

" These articles were the gift of Lord Shigémori to me many years ago on the occasion of a grand banquet to the ministers of state. I wore them and, in company with my colleagues, received the guests. I make them yours. As heir of our house, you are to wear them on public occasions. Up to now I have not heard any reports, favourable or unfavourable, concerning the manner in which you discharge your duties. Tell me how you stand in the graces of your lord ? "

" My dear father," respectfully returned Takiguchi, " albeit my ability is small, I stand, thanks to your influence, higher in his lordship's favour than any of my comrades. Such pleasure does this give me that I serve his lordship with all the loyalty of which I am capable and attend to my duties with the utmost diligence. Furthermore, Her Imperial Majesty is pleased to regard me with a special favour, so that I am entrusted with all messages to Her Majesty's court. Thus, upon the occasion of the recent picnic upon Mount Kita, I often had the honour of being summoned to Her Imperial presence for this purpose or that. Also I was made much of by the maids-of-honour and my colleagues. Under these circumstances I am not without hopes that, thanks to his lordship's authority and your influence, I may shortly receive promotion."

Hardly had he uttered these words when Sairai glowered upon him and roared, " Silence, silence ! Listen to me, you brazen-faced boy ! In your foolishness you are bold enough to suppose that I have no knowledge of your behaviour. Forasmuch as I have retired from the world I have no particular business with it, but waking or dreaming I never cease to consider your well-being. Indeed, I give more thought to that than to my future happiness. I am ever all ears to pick up any rumour, good or bad, concerning you. You need not therefore presume to suppose that your movements escape me. I know very well how infatuated you

are with a maid-of-honour named Yokobué. You made such
a fool of yourself flirting with her that you let the titmouse,
intended for the Empress, escape. For that you were severely
reprimanded by the superintendent Morotaka, who sentenced
you to a heavy punishment from which Her Majesty's mercy
alone released you. That ignominious news came to my
ears the very day of the incident itself. As if this mishap
were not sufficient warning, you shamelessly misconducted
yourself, as I hear, under cover of night with Yokobué on
the occasion of the Imperial picnic on Mount Kita. Caught
in the act by Morotaka, notwithstanding the multitude of
your shortcomings, you yet managed to turn the tables upon
your accuser. What behaviour! What audacity! Even I
in my retirement have heard the circumstances. That it
should have reached my ears is a sure sign that the story is
common property, and what the general public knows must
of course have reached the ears of the mighty Lord Shigémori.
You must know that Lord Shigémori is the wisest man alive
and, albeit his lordship does not let his feelings show in his
countenance, yet one can hardly doubt but that his lordship
has given you up as a good-for-nothing. Without the protection of his lordship our house is bound sooner or later to
come to ruin. I grieve for this. You must know how true
the story is better than any one else. The report goes abroad
that your boon companion, Yoshitsugu, like you was carrying
on an affair with a maid-of-honour. Her name is Karumo
and she is pregnant by him. It is further asserted that his
brother, Moritsugu, keeps him confined to his house on the
score of pretended sickness. If I follow his example and
confine or disown you, our house, since I have no other son,
will become extinct. How can I on your account suffer our
house to come to extinction? Our house which, for generation after generation, has served in vassalage the great
family of Taira. It had been my hope to continue my life

in comfortable seclusion on the pension graciously bestowed upon me by my lord and to have devoted my remaining years to the attainment of spiritual enlightenment and to prayer, that I may live happily in the Pure Land with your dear mother. Alas! Your behaviour has entirely undone my hopes; nay, your sins will bring us to hell. Undutiful wretch!"—he burst into warm tears—" but what good can come of reviling a devil? From to-day on I return to my secular life and once again serve Lord Shigémori as warrior. I am no longer Sairai but Katsuyori! My seven long years of abstinence and devotion are now at an end!"

With these words he slipped from off him the clerical robe and assumed the *eboshi* and the *kariginu*. Takiguchi, over-whelmed by tears, clung to him exclaiming, " Not so, father! I declare to you that I will once for all give up my love. I will start a new life and serve my lord to the best of my ability. Pray forgive my errors, father."

The old man pushed him aside.

" A father may well forgive you, but how can we apologize to my lord and to the world at large? I hardly see how you can remain in your present position." He rose to his feet and took both his swords in his hand.

" Listen, my men," he cried with an air of determination, " make yourselves ready to follow me! Saitō Katsuyori is once again about to serve Lord Shigémori as a warrior!"

With that he entered the inner chamber. Takiguchi was at his wits' end. His sobbing was followed by a melancholy reverie. At length he roused himself, slapped his thigh and thus communed with his spirit: " That's how it stands, is it? My tears are vain. The reproaches of my father are reasonable, but what is done is done. Nothing will be gained by weeping over a past error. I must do something to atone for my fault. Should I attain to spiritual rebirth my wise and compassionate lord would pardon me and my past would be wiped out. But ah, what shame it is to think how I have stood in the way of my father's spiritual enlightenment and of the peace of my mother's soul! That is indeed a greater sin than the Eight Crimes, the Five Crimes and the Ten Evils rolled in one.[1] Well, let me follow the example of Mongaku, who took to the priesthood in consequence of the great love he bore a lady and in time was enabled to lead all his relations to the Pure Land. Life is after all but a dream; reputation and infamy illusions; hatred and compassion but reflections quivering upon the water. Let me hope that my mistake in love will prove but a first step upon the path of spiritual enlightenment. Yokobué will doubtless grieve at my resolution. But she will offer up prayers to meet me and I too will pray for future happiness until such a time as we two are again joined together in the Pure Land. Now is the time for me to make my resolution " —he drew his dirk, cut off his queue and, reverently taking up his father's clerical robe, slipped it over his clothes—" I thank you, father, for your kindly hint. My living father, my dead mother, my sweetheart and I—do we not all aim at attaining a new life in the lotus flower![2] Namu Amida Buddha." He prepared himself for a journey, then stole out to find his way to some Buddhist temple.

Karumo, having repeatedly met her lover in secret, now found herself, to her great mortification, pregnant. The scandal had spread beyond court circles. Very much ashamed of herself, she again and again begged dismissal, but Morotaka prevented her discharge. She remained in her chamber; her comrades were strictly forbidden to pay her visits of sympathy; two or three maids were permitted

[1] Takiguchi refers to the catalogue of crimes and evils found in Buddhist scriptures.

[2] By this he means, of course, a rebirth in paradise, the lotus, the sacred flower of Buddhism, being the symbol of Paradise.

to serve her. Under such circumstances the girl's heart was heavy with shame and grief ; her tears fell without ceasing.

One day Morotaka, followed by his retainer Iwamura Gengo and by servants bearing a palanquin, intruded upon her in her room.

" Karumo," said he, assuming a severe air, " this is indeed licentious conduct of yours, that you, a woman in the Imperial service, should over and over again have stolen out of the strictly guarded palace gate to a clandestine meeting until at last you have become great with child. You presume too much in begging for your mere dismissal after the committal of such grave offences. You will have heard, I am sure, that your lover Yoshitsugu is confined to his room by his brother's command. As to your own offence, forasmuch as you are in the Imperial service, the laws require that you be heavily punished. But for all that, my heart, which has been set on you all these years, remains the same toward you as before the event. Come, will you not change your mind and, mindful of all my notes to you, tell me in one word that you are mine ? Pronounce the word and I will at once take you to my residence. You shall become my wife and be honoured as such, and this palanquin shall be your bridal palanquin. If, however, you answer ' no ', this palanquin shall be a prisoner's palanquin. Answer ' yes ' or ' no ' promptly. Remember that this pressure I put upon you is entirely because I am enamoured of you."

The old satyr, who had spoken in a coaxing tone, now concluded and cast sheep's eyes toward the lady.

" It is very kind of you," answered Karumo with a forced smile, " not only not to hate me, though my offence is heavy, but to offer to take me to yourself as your lady. Many thanks for your attentions ; I am minded to become your wife, but I very much fear me that Yoshitsugu will hardly give his consent. What would you do should he refuse ? "

" Have no fears on that score. No difficulty would be experienced in disposing of that fellow on the pretext of an Imperial order. Well then, we may consider the bargain struck. Be happy, my girl."

" Shall I arrange for a discreet abortion or may I give birth to my child, sir ? "

" An arrangement of that sort is apt to be dangerous to the mother, so I won't have it A child is indeed a somewhat unacceptable remembrance of an unfortunate episode ; but for my sweet girl's sake I would have it enjoy an easy and natural birth. And if it be a boy I will adopt it as my son and heir."

" There's the rub, sir. This child is Yoshitsugu's son. When he grows up and discovers you are his father's murderer I hardly see how he can fail to plan your death. What would you do then ? "

" Oh, kill the young devil. Don't worry about that ! "

He had hardly answered when Karumo angrily broke in.

" Do you indeed deem me such a nerveless kind of woman as would be contented to remain the wife of the murderer of her sweetheart and child ? The devil take you ! Love is everything with a real man or woman. For its sweet sake one takes no care for one's life. It was not because I wished to escape death or preserve my name untarnished that I sought dismissal. My object was, the displeasure of Yoshitsugu's brother being known to me, to visit Yoshitsugu and share his fate. Were I a woman forsaken by all the Gods and by Buddha, were I, I say, such a woman, I might consent to be your wife. Nothing however is further from my present intentions. Most willingly would I forfeit my life for my sweet love's sake. Wreak your vengeance on me, you rascal ! Take your fill of it ! My only grief is to imagine with what severity you may visit yourself upon Yoshitsugu, doing so under the pretence of an Imperial order. Mean and merciless man that you are ! Do you think you can live for ever ? Everyone is doomed to die once. Do you imagine there is no future world ? That divine justice knows no way to retribution ? If you think so, you are but a thoughtless shallow-pate."

With such reproaches the luckless girl sought to overwhelm him until at last she sank to the floor, weeping the bitterest tears. These many insults had their effect upon Morotaka, who flew into a tremendous passion.

" Iwamura Gengo ! " he cried. " This wench's reckoning is made up. Away with her to Funaoka-Yama and do with her as I bade you ! "

" I will, my lord."

Gengo gripped the damsel by one arm and by the hair, forced her face down toward the floor and thrust her into the palanquin. Her maids, in tears, did their best to prevent this, but Gengo, either pushing them aside or kicking them down, motioned to the servants to carry the palanquin away to Funaoka-Yama. He himself headed the little procession.

Takiguchi had sought refuge in the Ōjōin, a Buddhist temple in the farthest corner of the lonely country district of Saga, which lies many miles west of the capital. He entered the priesthood, assumed the sacerdotal name of Saishun, but soon found the temple was too near the capital for him to be able to apply himself wholly to the life of devotion. Tidings of what passed in the capital occasionally reached his ear and disturbed his quiet study of the scriptures. He therefore resolved to go to the great monastery of Kōyasan,[1] one of the holiest spots in Japan, and which is at a great distance from the capital ; but though he had resolved upon

[1] This monastery was founded about eleven centuries ago by Kōbō Daishi, the most famous of all Japanese Buddhist saints. It is the headquarters of the Shingon sect of Buddhists.

this change, he still lingered in the Ōjōin and nightly visited cemeteries in the neighbourhood of the capital. In these cemeteries it was his practice loudly to chant prayers, striking with a stick at the same time upon a small bell that hung about his neck. This he did by way of bidding an eternal farewell to his birthplace and by way of praying for the peace of his dead mother's spirit and his father's future bliss.

One evening Takiguchi found himself in such a cemetery at Funaoka-Yama. He prayed at all the new made graves in succession. Here the smoke from one cremation died away ; yonder arose the smoke from another—both smokes symbolizing the uncertainty of human life   He who had been left behind by one who had already taken the journey of the spirit, now, in his turn, left behind another fellow-traveller who would follow him the next day. Takiguchi found himself pleased in reflecting that he had become a priest praying for the departed. Again he sounded his bell, fervently praying the while, " Namu Amida ! Namu Amida ! Namu Amida Buddha ! Show thy mercy upon all creatures. May all aspire to Buddhahood. Amen."

At that moment a warrior appeared accompanied by some soldiers who bore a palanquin. The warrior glanced hither and thither about the burial-ground, then, selecting a spot overshadowed by a tall pine-tree, ordered the palanquin to be set down.

" Another dead person," Takiguchi thought to himself. " Poor soul—already hastening on the journey to Hades. But sooner or later one and all are bound to follow him." And, unnoticed, he murmured a prayer for the supposed deceased.

The soldiers dragged the occupant forth from the palanquin. To Takiguchi's great astonishment it proved not a corpse but a damsel of noble appearance.

All agog to know what was about to happen, our hero

hid himself behind a tombstone. Iwamura Gengo, for it was none but he, cried, " Now, Karumo, face your last moment ! Once your head falls all is over. It is my master Lord Morotaka's pleasure that you be beheaded at once, but it seems to me a distinct pity that this should occur. Come, can't you see how cruel it is to let the child now in your womb be slain along with you, thus suffering it not to see the light ? Neither living nor dead can you expect to meet your sweetheart again, so as far as that matter is concerned there is nothing to choose between them. But if you consent to become Lord Morotaka's lady there is not one of us who will not regard you with the respect due to you as our mistress. Ponder the question well before you answer."

" A saucy fellow ! You will remember I refused to answer even your master—why should I change my mind ? Don't disturb my preparations for the future life by provoking me at the last moment, but cut off my head and be quick about it."

" A stiff-necked woman ! Die then ! "

Gengo drew his sword and took station behind her, but, before his blade could flash down, Takiguchi rushed forward and shielded Karumo.

" One moment, sir ! "

" Out, fool of a priest ! Do you dare plead for this girl's life ? No, that's impossible."

" That is not my meaning, sir. I am a priest who nightly visits these cemeteries to pray for the dead. You are, it would appear, about to kill this woman for some grave offence. ' Sin reaps its reward ' ; that is inevitable. But you have said the woman is pregnant. Are you going to slay the guiltless with the guilty ? What do you think can be your reward for such a deed ? We do not know the child's age, but as many months as it has lived will it have patron Gods and Buddhas. Queen Maya's [1] Scripture runs, that the wrath of such patrons and Gods descends upon the infanticide, who will presently be seized with an incurable disease or perish by the sword, cut off before a year is out. Nevertheless it is sometimes necessary for a warrior to kill a pregnant woman. In such a case he can divert the divine wrath from his head by the triple repetition of a mystic formula before he commits the deed. There's nothing for it apparently but to slay this poor girl; but, inasmuch as I am acquainted with the formula, it would be wanton cruelty on my part not to try and save you from such punishment. Of a truth I feel very sorry for you and that is the reason why I have momentarily stayed your hand."

" Are these things true ? " exclaimed Gengo, overcome by surprise and fear. " I never dreamed of such things. A thousand thanks to you, kind and reverend sir. If it's not asking too much of you, would you please be so good as to teach me the formula ? "

" I learned this formula after three weeks' practice of religious austerities and it is one of my greatest secrets; but I can hardly refuse to instruct you in it when it is a case of sudden death for you if I do not. Be sure, however, never to teach it to others."

Having thus cautioned him, Takiguchi whispered in the warrior's ear, " *Riken sokuzé Mida-gō* (The title of Amida is a sharp sword to cut off thy sins with) *Isshō shōnen zaikaijo* [2] (If thou once sayest ' Namu Amida ' thou shalt be absolved from all thy sins). Repeat this formula thrice before you kill this woman and no evil shall come to you after the deed. Should evil fall on you, however small, I will make atonement for it."

" Dear me ! How hard the formula is ! I shall never be

---

[1] The mother of Sakya Muni, the founder of Buddhism.

[2] These Buddhist expressions in the Chinese tongue are as unintelligible to most laymen as are Latin expressions to uncultured Europeans.

able to learn it. Isn't there a shorter form?—one easier to learn?"

"Hand me your sword. I'll enchant its blade by repeating the formula over it. And that will be as good as if you repeated the formula itself."

"Excellent! Please be so good as to enchant my sword for me."

So saying, Gengo, without the least misgiving, handed the delighted Takiguchi the drawn sword.

"Well, sir," said Takiguchi sarcastically, "I observe that after all you won't need the formula or any other thing of that kind; for since the girl is now not going to be killed neither retribution nor curse will fall upon you."

"Impostor of a priest!" roared Gengo, flying into a great rage. "Was this all a trick to rob me of my sword? How can I suffer you to remain in possession of that sword? What a fool you are to lose your life in the senseless attempt to save the life of a sinner! Prepare to die!"

He sprang at Takiguchi. Takiguchi dodged.

"Come, come," he cried, "it's unreasonable of you, a mere layman, to try and recover what has come into a priest's possession. I will now proceed to take this girl too "—he placed his hand upon Karumo's—" Taste the sharpness of Amida's sword!"

With these words he lifted the sword.

"Insolent priest!" cried Gengo and the soldiers and precipitated themselves upon him. Hither and thither Takiguchi whirled the blade. His adversaries, finding themselves no match for him, were not long in taking to their heels. Gengo, however, eager to recover his sword, ambushed himself behind a large tombstone. Presently the soldiers returned and attacked Takiguchi from right and left simultaneously. Again Takiguchi whirled the blade with such dexterity that, as he advanced upon them, they were at last reduced to

standing at bay against the tombstone. Takiguchi pressed
them and suddenly the tombstone, heavy as it was, toppled
over upon the hidden Gengo and crushed him to death.
The panic-stricken soldiers sought safety in flight. Takiguchi returned to the girl.

" Can you recognize me, Karumo Dono ? "

" Can I believe that you are Master Takiguchi ? A
thousand thanks to you. But for your assistance I should
by now be dead ; but I cannot suppress my surprise at
finding you a priest."

" We will speak of such things at leisure. Here we should
linger no further." Takiguchi hoisted the girl on his back and
hurried away.

III

Shigémori, Lord Keeper of the Privy Seal, who was Leniency
and Sympathy incarnate, not only refused to sit in judgment
upon the misbehaviour of Yoshitsugu and Takiguchi, but
even went so far as to feign perfect ignorance of the scandal.
Among his retainers, and among his younger warriors in
particular, the affair was a subject of frequent gossip. " Poor
soul ! " Takiguchi's friends whispered, " Takiguchi, led
astray by the wanton Yoshitsugu, has come to ruin. Yoshitsugu is the cause of all his troubles." While those who
sympathized with Yoshitsugu murmured, " Yoshitsugu,
through keeping company with the lecherous Takiguchi, has
earned a bad name for himself. A man is known by the
company he keeps, good or bad. Yoshitsugu's brother,
Moritsugu, has also lost in reputation on account of Takiguchi. Moritsugu's anguish is sure sooner or later to give rise
to a quarrel between him and Takiguchi's father, Katsuyori."

Subject to this tittle-tattle, which rose whenever and wherever Shigémori's retainers were gathered together, Katsuyori and Moritsugu became little by little estranged, to such an extent that at last a hidden feud arose between them. One day Moritsugu came to duty in the drawing-room of Shigémori's palace and was there greeted by those young samurai who sympathized with his brother. They saluted him with enthusiasm.

" Master Moritsugu, we are delighted to see you. It grieves us to hear of your brother's lot. We young men are apt to be led into youthful follies by bad companions. We wish to say how deeply we sympathize with you and your brother."

" Many thanks for your sympathy, my friends, but you are misinformed. The truth is, Yoshitsugu is seriously ill."

Hardly had Moritsugu seated himself when Katsuyori, who as ill luck would have it happened to be his appointed comrade on duty for this day, appeared. He wore an *eboshi* (official head-gear) pressed down to the eyes to conceal his shaven head. Takiguchi's friends gave him a hearty welcome.

" We hear your son, Takiguchi Dono, has forsaken the world. What a pity ! But it is always one's friends who lead one to fame or to ruin and, as the Chinese proverb runs, ' To such as possesses three good friends, three bad Dame Fortune also sends.' He's a lucky man who never meets either a bad friend or a whirlwind We can well imagine how you feel towards your former friend."

Katsuyori made his salute to Moritsugu, then, like the haughty old samurai he was, took a seat higher than Moritsugu's.

" How now ! Priest Sairai ! " exclaimed the indignant Moritsugu, " I can't but think your aged eyes fail to recognize me. Know then that I am Moritsugu. You have taken the wrong seat. Take a lower."

" Eh ? " replied Katsuyori in scorn   " Believe me, my
aged eyes don't fail to recognize my colleague's face.   Albeit
you are not yet well on in years, your memory seems to fail
you with regrettable ease.   Kindly recall to yourself that
you are of the Fifth Grade in court rank, while I am of the
Fourth.   There is therefore nothing incorrect in my sitting
above you.   A very forgetful person evidently !   A few drops
of medicine might indeed be efficacious in restoring your
health and memory."

" Insolent dotard ! Take a lower seat and be quick about
it, or I will pull you down to a lower.   And if I resort to
force your hat may slip off and your shiny pate appear, to
your shame and humiliation.   Perhaps you would prefer
that, eh ? "

So saying, Moritsugu pressed against the old warrior.

" So you despise me because of my old age ?   Seize me
by the arm if you choose.   What new-fangled notion of
etiquette is it that requires a samurai of the Fourth Grade
to sit below another of the Fifth ?   Where is the authority
enables you to insist upon it ?   Come, give me a reason, you
green boy ! "

" You're in your dotage all right," returned Moritsugu,
in no whit discomposed.   " Fourth Grade, Coarse [1] Grade !
True you are of the Fourth Grade, but aren't you also a lay-
brother and consequently out of office and service ?   In
point of fact it's your son Takiguchi's turn to be on duty,
but there are those that say that, ashamed of his past bad
behaviour and consequent ill reputation, he has seen fit to
forsake the ways of the wicked world.   It is as well that he

---

[1] The pun made in scorn by Moritsugu is scarcely to be rendered in English.
I have merely indicated something that implies a similarity in sound ; this similarity being associated with an idea that would be offensive.   What our ingenious
author says is, " Shii no kashi no " or " The Pasania (a kind of oak) or the oak."
The word " Shii " means either " Fourth Grade " or this variety of oak ; and
kashi means " oak ".

has done so. Had he remained in office, any young samurai who might have continued as his friends and colleagues could only have followed his bad example and shared his degradation. Takiguchi's punishment, however, depends upon the pleasure of our lord, and whether he will be ordered to commit suicide or will be beheaded none can tell. I understand that, acting on the supposition that your son's forsaking of the world saved him from punishment, you have returned to secular life and are once more in his lordship's service. To-day I meet you in your second service for the first time. You see there has been no change in our turns of service for some considerable time and to-day Takiguchi and I are to be on duty together. You appear then to-day as Takiguchi's substitute. Now I, Moritsugu, am of the Fifth Grade, while Takiguchi is of the Sixth ; and I have never sat below your son. Accordingly you, as his substitute, should sit below me. If I am wrong pray correct me at once."

" So ! " sneered Katsuyori. " No more cavilling, please, about the ordering of our seats. You would seem to blame me for having permitted Takiguchi to forsake the world sooner than await our lord's punishment, but, if it be our lord's pleasure to have him recalled for self-slaughter or for decapitation, I can so call him back. Since when has it become impossible to punish one who has forsaken the world ? As for your brother, Yoshitsugu, is it not everyone's secret that you have confined him to your house, alleging illness, the better in your cowardice to cover up the ill name his bad behaviour has earned him. It is as well that you have done so. Were such a man as he allowed to remain in office, the young samurai, his friends and colleagues, would be bound to follow his bad example and this would lead to their utter degradation. But were our lord, out of his great mercy, to employ him again without first punishing him, you would, I suppose, have the unblushing impudence to

permit him to return to service among the other samurai.
No man of honour of course could do such a thing, but we
all know that, as the saying goes, the scarlet-faced ape laughs
at the golden [1] face of the Lord Buddha when he marks the
difference in their complexions ! "

" Well, well. And another saying goes, the crab who
walks sideways laughs at the man who walks forward."

" And the green persimmon, so they say, laughs at the
sweet persimmon in the beak of the crow."

" And the man crucified head downward, so I've heard,
dies of laughing at an exposed head because it's set forsooth
below his feet." [2]

" You seem to speak from experience."

" You perhaps have never seen steel ? Shall I let you
have a taste of it ? "

" Do you think you can do that ? "

" Why not ? I will oblige you this minute if you wish it."

The excited couple prepared to draw their swords and
forthwith all the other samurai, taking sides, assumed defiant
attitudes. A period of breathless suspense followed. It was
broken by the startling announcement that a messenger
from the Empress had this moment arrived. A moment
later Shigémori made his appearance and seated himself on
the dais. All kneeled reverently. Morotaka, for it was he,
addressed Lord Shigémori.

" I beg to deliver my message to your lordship. Recently
two court ladies, named respectively Yokobué and Karumo,
indulged themselves with Takiguchi and Yoshitsugu. This
has occasioned great scandal and disaffection at court.
Furthermore, Karumo became pregnant and could no longer
remain in service. Her Imperial Majesty, grievously offended

---

[1] That is of course the face of a golden image of Buddha.

[2] In cases of such crucifixion the cross was very tall, while the wooden frame
on which the head of a criminal was exposed was much lower.

with her, ordered me to put a period to her existence. Finding it impossible to disobey the Imperial command, I ordered the damsel to be taken to Funaoka-Yama for execution. Her decapitation was imminent when an unknown stranger, suddenly falling upon my retainer, Iwamura Gengo the executioner, murdered him and carried the prisoner whither none knows. It can hardly be doubted that the rogue in question is Karumo's lover Yoshitsugu. This heinous crime, by which the law has been set at naught and the Imperial will flouted, has much incensed Her Majesty. She requires that Yoshitsugu be instantly executed. Yokobué is to be beheaded at court. Her Majesty will let your lordship know later on the arrangements made for this ceremony. Allow me to repeat once more that it is Her Majesty's pleasure that Yoshitsugu be forthwith beheaded."

" An infamous order ! " exclaimed Shigémori after a brief silence. " The like of which has never been heard of before. Izumi Shikibu indulged herself with Hirai-no-Yasumasa and later with Tachibana-no-Michisada, by whom she became the mother of Koshikibu, the poetess. There are the cases too of Akazomé Emon and Nakano Kwampaku ; also of Murasaki Shikibu with Nishinomiya-no-Sadaijin. All the above affairs took place while the ladies were in the Imperial service and yet Jōtō-Mon-in, the Empress then reigning, inflicted upon them no punishment whatever. Thus, not only were these ladies spared any disgrace, but have left behind them undying names as authoresses. With these precedents before my eyes, I cannot but deem the present Imperial order of an excessive severity. Surely, Morotaka, you and your sister Lady Tonasé must have joined in remonstrating with Her Majesty ? "

" Yes, my lord, my sister and I again and again importuned our Imperial mistress, but with no result. Since Her Majesty is your lordship's sister and comes of a military family she ordains everything according to the manners and customs of the military classes."

" There you err. The Imperial order is contrary to the rules of the military class. I would draw your attention to the fact that the executioner Gengo, in having Karumo carried off, did not act according to the manners that obtain among warriors. Do you suppose that the strict guard kept over a criminal with drawn spears and naked halberds is merely an arrangement made for the safety of the condemned ? Is it not also to fend off any violence that may be indulged in by his comrades and relatives ? It appears to me to have been an uncommon piece of carelessness on his part that Gengo should not only have permitted his prisoner to be snatched from him, but also to have suffered the loss of his own life. The corpse of so foolish a warrior should undoubtedly be crucified ; his relatives should be punished ; and you, his lord, required to commit suicide. Such is the rule of the military classes. The Imperial order is against the law inasmuch as it is neither in accordance with the rule of the military class nor with that of the court. To me it appears quite unreasonable ; but Her Majesty's pleasure is no less binding than His Majesty's order. Yoshitsugu shall therefore be beheaded during the course of the day. Moritsugu, order your brother to come here ! Now, Morotaka, so Yokobué is to be executed at court, eh ? Who is to be her executioner ? I feel nervous about the matter. Should she be carried off, even as Karumo was, I can well imagine what a scandal would arise at court. You will return therefore to Her Majesty and inform her that I shall send an inspector [1] and an executioner. Such is Shigémori's reply to

---

[1] An officer called *kenshi*, that is a man who acts as sheriff or witness of an execution or a harakiri.

(See Redesdale's *Tales of Old Japan*, appendix A, page 285, edition of 1910) : Ceremonies observed at the harakiri of a Hatamoto, petty noble of the Shogun's court.

the Imperial order. And by the way, now I'm on the subject of love affairs, I hear there is a samurai—his name escapes me at this moment—who has written notes to a court lady and who now, out of jealousy caused by her rejection of his suit, is attempting to avenge himself upon her and her lover. There is a villain if you like ! If he does not submit himself to punishment by you let me know, Morotaka, for I would have you know that it is my intention to have him heavily punished."

Cowed by these words, Morotaka could but murmur, " Yes, yes, my lord." A cold perspiration bathed his body. He made a bewildered bow, then, stumbling over the skirt of his *hakama* and slipping on the mats, precipitantly withdrew.

Luckless Yoshitsugu ! Promptly obeying his brother's urgent summons, never dreaming of the doom in store for him, he dressed himself completely albeit his hair remained in an unpresentable condition. He hastened to Shigémori's mansion and presented himself at the hall of reception. Moritsugu said to him, " His lordship's order is that you leave your two swords here and go round to the *shirasu*." [1]

Instantly the frightful truth flashed upon the mind of the young samurai, but he smiled as he answered, " Certainly, sir." His composed air as he removed his swords showed that he was prepared for the worst.

" A pattern of knighthood," murmured all the samurai present. Their eyes glistened with tears of admiration.

Shigémori bent his gaze upon the young man and said kindly enough, " I am delighted to see you, Yoshitsugu, but I greatly regret that I must tell you that Her Imperial Majesty, in her displeasure at your misbehaviour, has ordered that you be at once beheaded. Know therefore that there is no hope of reprieve. Alas, my poor friend ! Since you have served me from your childhood with all possible

---

[1] Inner courtyard wherein a criminal was condemned and executed.

faithfulness I very much wish that I could at least permit you to commit self-dispatch,[1] but I cannot act in a manner contrary to Her Majesty's pleasure. By reason however of the sympathy and love that a lord feels toward his retainer, I will slay you with my own hands.[2] Therefore bid farewell to your brother and your colleagues and quickly make your way round to the inner courtyard."

So saying Shigémori rose and went within.

Yoshitsugu looked round the company and thus addressed them: "My brother and my friends, pray listen to me a moment. I wish to record the shame my misbehaviour causes me and for which I richly deserve capital punishment. Yet, shamed though I am, I deem myself fortunate in that I am to be slain by His Excellency Lord Shigémori, who is at once my own liege lord and the wisest personage in all Japan. Moreover his lordship saw fit to address some words of gracious consolation and compassion to me, which are indeed of more comfort to me than the ministrations of a holy priest. Dearly do I wish to live on in this world that, if the need arose, I might fight to the death in defence of his lordship, so to requite his favours toward me. It is the consideration of such an interest that alone worries me on the eve of my death. Farewell, farewell, my dearest brother and my most honourable friends."

Having spoken these few words he made his way toward the inner courtyard. Every warrior present, both his friends and those who had aforetime entertained no feeling for him—and his brother who was already completely resigned to his condemnation—everyone of them was moved to silent tears.

---

[1] Condemnation to *harakiri* or self-dispatch was looked upon as a privilege in that it was far less humiliating than decapitation by an executioner.

[2] It was considered much more honourable for a samurai to be slain by his own lord than by an executioner.

K

After a brief space Moritsugu exclaimed, casting the while a scornful glance at Katsuyori, " I am a glad man ! Had Yoshitsugu forsaken the world, not only would he have missed being favoured with his lordship's comfort and the privilege of dying at his honourable hands, but he would have suffered the humiliation of having his shaven head cut from his body by a nameless soldier. My brother's manner of death is truly worthy of a warrior."

At this moment Morihisa, the chief retainer of Shigémori, emerged from the inner apartments carrying two head-boxes in his hand.

" Here, Katsuyori," he said with an air of authority, " his lordship has slain Yoshitsugu and has placed his head in this box, which has been sealed. Your orders are to take this box to the court, to break the seal, to examine the head and to display it to Her Imperial Majesty. When you have done this, you are to decapitate Yokobué, place her head in this box and bring it back. You, Moritsugu, are ordered to act as inspector at her execution. You are both to proceed at once upon your errand."

" His lordship shall be promptly obeyed," answered Katsuyori respectfully.

He took up the two boxes and rose to his feet. Moritsugu also rose.

" Katsuyori," said he, " dare you accept the order ? Can you really be going to examine my brother's head and decapitate Yokobué ? "

" Why not ? Dare you not act as inspector ? "

" Of course, I certainly intend to. And I would have you know that if your manner of head examination and of decapitation is in any way faulty I shall not fail to report it to his lordship. You understand ? "

" I do indeed. And if you are at fault as sheriff, I in my turn will not fail to take notice of it. You understand ? "

" Yes. We have given each other our words. Don't forget that. Come with me."

" Go before me."

The two samurai, glaring upon each other, proceeded on their way. They resembled two hardy pine-trees growing on a rugged rock, the one old and the other young, which struggle with one another in the storm.

Under the early winter twilight, rain mixed with hail was falling. From the boughs of the trees in the gardens of the Empress' palace the scarlet embroidery of the leaves had been loosened ; already the chrysanthemums had faded ; the crickets shrilled sadly. That the tedium caused by the weary atmosphere might be shaken off, the Empress thus addressed her maids-of-honour : " Backgammon does not hold my interest since the die does not fall as I wish. *Hentsugi* [1] is so difficult ; *kaiawasé* [2] chills our hands ; what do you say to a game of poem-cards,[3] my girls ? "

" A merry game, Your Majesty. Quick, let's play it ! "

The young girls promptly seated themselves, produced the cards and spread them on the mats. So engaged, they chattered blithely and glanced about in all directions. Not so Yokobué—who, all melancholy, pined for her lover—for she had continued in service despite the fact that her sleeves were forever wet with her tears. The Empress, in her mercy,

---

[1] A game in which Chinese characters have a prominent place.

[2] A game played with a number of clam shells. Roughly speaking, what constitutes this game is the picking up and fitting together of the two respective sides of the shells from those which have been scattered about. The insides of the shells are painted with coloured illustrations of the fifty-four scenes of *The Story of Genji*, the greatest work of classical fiction.

[3] The pack contains one hundred poem-cards, each inscribed with the latter half of one of the odes in the famous anthology *Hyakunin Isshu* or " Single Verses by an Hundred Poets ". The game is played as follows : the reader reads the first half of the odes and the players endeavour to pick up the corresponding halves. The skill of course consists in knowing the poems by heart and quickly recognizing the characters.

had extended her sympathy and tenderness to the damsel and had even comforted her with kind words. Observing Yokobué's mood and touched by it, the Empress had a happy idea. " Somehow," she said to the party, " I feel that I would prefer not to take part in the game, but to be merely the reader. I think you will find an increased interest in the game if you practise a sort of divination by the poems you pick up, a divination to inform you whether your wishes are to become facts or no. If I were you I would put up an inward petition to the gods of poetry to grant that you have your favourite cards in your hand. Well, are you ready ? I am going to read the first lines. This is Semi Maru's poem : [1]

> 'The stranger who has travelled far,
> The friend with welcome smile,
> All sorts of men who come and go'

I would have Yokobué get the last half of this. Don't let the others pick up this card, my dear. Look sharp ! "

" I must get it, I must get it," Yokobué thought to her-self " It runs :

> 'Meet at this mountain stile,—
> They meet and rest awhile.'

And it seems to suggest our happy reunion."

Eagerly she sought the card, her heart beating violently with hope and fear. But Kozakura, another girl, too quick for her, picked it up to the disappointment of both the Empress and Yokobué.

" Come, this is the Minister Fujiwara-no-Sanékata's poem :

> 'Though love, like blisters made from leaves [2]
> Grown on Mount Ibuki
> Torments me more than I can say,'"

---

[1] The translations of these odes are from " A Hundred Verses from Old Japan " by Mr. William N. Porter to whom my hearty acknowledgments are due.

[2] The artemisia plant (or mugwort) is used in Japan for cauterizing ; a conical wad of the leaves is placed on the spot, lit at the top, and allowed to burn down to the skin ; this produces a blister, and is extremely painful. Mount Ibuki is famous for its artemisia.

Hardly had the Empress read when Izayoi picked up the card and read :

> " ' My lady shall not see
> How she is paining me.'

This poem does not apply to my case. I'm certain nobody pines for me."

" But we are not so sure ! " cried the other girls, laughing.

" Now Lady Isé's poem :

> ' The double cherry-trees which grew
> At Nara in past days
> Now beautify this palace, and '

The last lines symbolize good fortune and happiness. Now Yokobué ! "

" Thank you, Your Majesty," responded Yokobué. But Ukon, flurrying her, picked the card up and read :

> " ' Their blossoms all ablaze
> Perfume the royal ways.'

That's lucky ! " she exclaimed. " The poem must mean that the clothes I am going to receive at the year-end will be as beautiful as these cherry-blossoms."

" The next is the poem by the Mother of the Minister of State :

> ' How difficult it is for men
> Not to forget the past ! ' "

" At least I can't fail to pick one up ! " cried Yokobué excitedly. She took up the card and read mechanically :

> " ' I fear my husband's love for me
> Is disappearing fast ;
> This day must be my last.'

Oh, I hate this ! " she exclaimed regretfully. " What a luckless omen ! "

" Here, girls, is the poem by the Mother of Udaishō Michitsuna :

> ' Throughout the long and dreary night
> I lie awake and moan ; ' "

The bewildered Yokobué again picked up the correct card. It read :

> "How desolate my chamber feels,
> How weary I have grown
> Of being left alone."

The exactness of this description was too much for her ; she burst into sobs.

"The High Priest Gyōson sings :

> 'In lonely solitude I dwell,
> No human face I see ;'

I myself will take up this one."

With this the Empress took up the card and read :

> "'And so we two must sympathize,
> O, mountain cherry-tree ;
> I have no friend but thee.'

Don't say 'I have no friend but thee ', Yokobué," continued the Empress, gazing with kindness into the girl's face, " for you see you have a sympathetic friend in me."

Yokobué wept in joy and gratitude.

" Come, girls, be quick. Kakinomoto-no-Hitomaru's poem :

> 'Long is the mountain pheasant's tail
> That curves down in its flight ;'"

Another girl picked up the card which read :

> "But longer still it seems to me,
> Left in my lonely plight,
> Is this unending night."

" Don't be despondent, girl," said the Empress in a soothing tone. " I will not long permit you to be left in solitude. Now, girls, Prince Kentoku's poem :

> 'I dare not hope my lady-love
> Will smile on me again ;'

It's Kohagi, I'll be bound, who has picked up the last half :

> 'She knows no pity and my life
> I care not to retain
> Since all my prayers are vain.'

You are still only fourteen. Never put yourself in such a position as may cause you to exclaim, ' My life I care not to retain.' The Imperial adviser Yakamochi's poem :

> 'When on the Magpies' Bridge I see
> The Hoar-frost King has cast
> His sparkling mantle, well I know ' "

" Heaven ! " said Kojijū, smiling, as she took up the latter lines :

> " ' The night is nearly past,
> Daylight approaches fast.'

Even now I feel drowsy enough over my nightly vigil. How much more drowsy I should feel if I had to watch till daylight came ! "

" The retired Emperor Sutoku's poem :

> ' The rock divides the flood in two,
> Both streams with might and main
> Go tumbling down the waterfall,'

How interesting this poem is ! The second half reads :

> ' But well I know the twain
> Will soon unite again.'

Suggestive surely of the successful attainment of every desire. Can't you see it ? Look, look, it's there ! "

So saying the Empress glanced at Yokobué. The grateful girl, pushing some of her comrades aside, picked up the card.

" I have it ! "

Overjoyed at this happy omen, she pressed the card to her breast, and the Empress showed the delight with which she read the girl's feelings.

At this moment an aged lady of the court entered and

announced that Superintendent Morotaka would shortly be present, having come on some urgent matter which required a personal interview with the Empress.

" Indeed ? " said the Empress, amazed. " Why doesn't he speak through Lady Tonasé ? What can be the matter, I wonder. Now, Yokobué, hide yourself under this awhile "— she bade the girl lie down and concealed her under the *fuségo* —" don't speak, not a sound."

Then she spread a silk garment over the *fuségo*, drew it close to her back and was sitting at her ease when, a little later, Morotaka presented himself wearing an assumed air of dejection.

" I regret to have to inform Your Majesty that a melancholy message has arrived from His Excellency Lord Shigémori. His Excellency, having heard that Karumo has been discharged on account of her pregnancy caused by a love affair with Yoshitsugu, has seen fit to slay Yoshitsugu with his own hands and has ordered Katsuyori to bring Yoshitsugu's head hither to display it to Your Majesty. The old messenger is now waiting with it. Furthermore, His Excellency wishes to declare that he is of the opinion that Takiguchi deserves the same fate, yet, inasmuch as he has forsaken the world and his present whereabouts are unknown, His Excellency considers that Yokobué should be decapitated in his stead. ' If Her Majesty refuses to deliver Yokobué '—such were the words His Excellency spoke to Katsuyori—' it will be your duty to hunt out and behead Takiguchi, but do your utmost to prevail upon Her Majesty to deliver up Yokobué, then decapitate her and bring her head to me.' Acting on these orders, Katsuyori and Moritsugu are at hand in respective capacities of executioner and sheriff ; they await Your Majesty's pleasure at the middle gate. This is indeed in my opinion a cruel punishment and one unworthy of His Excellency, but against it there is no remedy. I venture to assert that Your Majesty had better yield to His Excellency's wish and permit them to behead Yokobué. Poor girl! She has served Your Majesty so faithfully; I am saddened at the thought."

He let fall a few crocodile tears. For a while the Empress was speechless with astonishment. Yokobué, struck with terror and grief, closed her mouth with her sleeve lest she should utter a cry. The tears ran down her face. " It grieves me to have to say such a thing of my brother," exclaimed the Empress, " but verily I believe Lord Shigémori must be out of his senses. To indulge the passion of love with a married person is extremely wicked and Sakya Muni counsels us against it. Sincere love, however, is the root of faithfulness and in the sacred art of poesy love is considered as the most important of themes. In days of old the court noble Ariwara-no-Narihira carried on an intrigue with a virgin princess who was at that time purifying herself for the priesthood at the great Isé Shrine ; and albeit his conduct was brought to light, yet was he acquitted because of his fame as a poet. This precedent clearly displays to us that the punishment meted out by Lord Shigémori is not in accordance with the rules that regulate the lives of court nobles. The celebrated authoresses Izumi Shikibu, Koshikibu, Murasaki Shikibu and Akazomé Emon again took lovers to themselves while in the Imperial service ; yet Generals Yorimitsu and Yorinobu, the actual rulers in those days, did not punish them. The proposed execution of Yokobué therefore cannot be in accordance with the rules regulating the life of the military classes. Whatever her misbehaviour, how is it possible for me to suffer Yokobué to be killed, who has served me with all diligence and loyalty ? I and Yokobué, as mistress and maid, are tied with the Karma relations of the three existences.[1] On no account will I consent to her execution, nay, even though I run the risk of losing my rank

---

[1] That is the past, the present and the future life.

as Empress and my very life by so doing."—She put her hand behind her back and took a firm hold of Yokobué's fingers—" Morotaka, from to-day henceforth you would do well to consider me as Yokobué's sister or her mother. Never will I permit my daughter to be slain or my sister to be beheaded. Sympathize with me and be so good as to plead with Lord Shigémori on her behalf."

Overwhelmed with gratitude and writhing with anxiety, Yokobué reverently pressed the Empress' hand to her forehead. Morotaka, however, remained unmoved.

"I fear, Your Majesty," he returned, "that the executioner and the sheriff, who have come hither for a definite purpose, will not be readily persuaded to depart. Shall I tell them that, as Yokobué's death is against the will of Your Majesty, they are to hunt out Takiguchi and decapitate him ? "

'Twas with difficulty that Yokobué restrained herself. She made as if to emerge from her hiding-place, but the Empress, covering her face with her flowing sleeve, looked back and signed to the girl to do no such thing. The girl drew herself up on her knees and whispered in the Empress' ear between her sobs, "I beg Your Majesty's pardon for seeming to reject your mercy, but Morotaka Dono says that if my life is spared my sweetheart's will be taken. May I ask Your Majesty to deliver me up and thus save Takiguchi from death ? "

A brief silence ensued ; then the Empress said to Morotaka, "I understand that it is Lord Shigémori's will that either Yokobué or Takiguchi shall be slain ; very well. You tell me that two warriors have come, one as executioner and one as sheriff. Now, girls, bid the two warriors enter the neighbouring chamber, as I have something to impart to them from behind the lowered blind.[1] You, too, Morotaka, are to listen to me."

[1] In ancient days it was the custom for the Emperor and Empress to address people of the inferior ranks from behind a blind.

The Empress wiped away her tears, then took her position on a low seat and in a posture full of dignity behind a bamboo blind.   Beauty, awe and majesty emanated from her countenance and bearing.   Presently the warriors were announced. The Empress' voice was clearly heard.

" Welcome, both of you.   Albeit Lord Shigémori is my elder brother, yet he is now my subject.   Despite the fact that he occupies the exalted position of Lord Keeper of the Privy Seal, he has with his own hands beheaded Yoshitsugu. I cannot but think he is bereft of his senses.   I count it an outrageous thing moreover that he should have dispatched persons of brutal office to the court.   Is it nothing to him that he should desecrate the Imperial Palace with bloodshed ? How can I suffer that poor girl Yokobué, who has tended me from her youth up, cruelly to perish by the executioner's sword ?   Albeit a woman, I was born of a ' family of bow and arrow ' and am the daughter of Lord Kiyomori, a Prime Minister.   I have not learnt how to deal death in battle, but there is no reason why I should not be able to perform the office of beheading another person.   I will myself behead Yokobué and display her head to the sheriff.   Moritsugu— that is your name, isn't it ?—if you are proficient in the duties proper to a sheriff you will carefully examine the head and report on it to Lord Shigémori.   When I have performed the deed I, in my turn, will inspect Yoshitsugu's head.   Yokobué, I would do everything and anything in my power, but it is evident that my efforts are unavailing.   Step forth therefore and prepare for death."

The bright, keen eyes of the Empress glistened with tears. Yokobué revealed herself and prostrated herself before her Imperial mistress.

" Most gracious Majesty," she sobbed, " your benevolence is higher than Mount Shumi and deeper than the ocean, but to pollute your honourable hands with my blood, that is impossible ! Divine punishment would visit itself upon me ; I should bring disgrace on myself in the next world. I beg one more boon of Your Majesty—let me die by the executioner's sword. I will not complain of the mode of execution, however severe. It is my hope that I shall be able to meet my sweetheart in the life to come. I grieve to part from Your Majesty, whose benevolence is so overwhelming that, were I to be reborn seven times into this world, I could scarcely hope to find another mistress of a like benevolence. Permit me to die at the hands of the executioner."

" No, I cannot permit the maid who is dearest to me to be slain by a warrior. Reconcile yourself to dying by the edge of my sword."

The Empress tucked up her skirts and, taking her sword from the sword-rack, tucked it under her left arm, saying, " Come with me, my girl, you shall meet your death in one of the inner chambers."

She departed quietly and composedly. Yokobué followed her. All those present, and particularly Katsuyori and Moritsugu, were smitten by awe and pain at what seemed her wrath and at the melancholy they read upon her countenance

" Katsuyori Dono," remarked Moritsugu in tones of reconciliation, " have you noticed that the views of Her Majesty upon the subject of Yokobué and my brother would seem entirely contrary to what was asserted to be her first command ? Have you observed how Her Majesty and Lord Shigémori seem to find fault with each other ? Does not this seem strange ? I am certain that some wicked wretch is deceiving both of them. Our mutual hostility is a private matter and the affairs of Takiguchi and Yoshitsugu are matters of but small public importance. An estrangement, nay, a discord between Her Majesty and Lord Shigémori, however, were an affair of grave concern which might lead to public disturbance. Let us therefore make our peace and bend our joint powers to inquiring into the matter."

" Certainly," nodded Katsuyori, " that is precisely my thought too. First of all let us consider our friendship restored, then let us take note of everybody and keep a sharp lookout."

The two warriors exchanged significant glances, then sternly looked about them. Morotaka, who all this while had been ill at ease, could no longer contain himself.

" Ugh ! I have a fit of lumbago, my loins ache ; I can bear the pain no longer. Pray excuse me, sirs. Be so good as to apologize to Her Majesty for my taking my leave now. Ugh ! There again ! Good-bye, sirs."

With a wry face and holding his sides, Morotaka took himself off. The eyes of the two warriors followed his retreating figure not without wonder.

" I consider it very suspicious," both exclaimed, " that this fellow, who is the superintendent of this palace, should remove himself on an occasion like this which is one of greatest importance, merely offering a pretext of sudden illness."

Hardly had they spoken when Lady Tonasé appeared, head-box in hand.

" Good-evening, sirs," said she as she sat herself down. " Her Majesty has beheaded Yokobué and has placed her head in this box which, as you see, she has sealed. Her Majesty orders me to receive Yoshitsugu's head from you and, when I have done so, to deliver Yokobué's head to you."

Katsuyori bowed his head respectfully and, unsealing the box he had brought, removed its lid. With what wonder did not all three behold within, not Yoshitsugu's head, but a queue and a stone as make-weight. Then Lady Tonasé, in her turn, cut the seal from her box with her dagger and so disclosed the contents. Lo and behold ! these consisted merely of a bamboo flute cut in two at the mouthpiece and, as make-weight, some earth! All three were dumbfounded. After some rumination Katsuyori exclaimed, "It is above the privilege accorded a man of my rank and station to remark it, but what wise persons Her Majesty and Lord Shigémori are! I am filled with awe and reverence at the boundless benevolence displayed and at the precisely same measure each has taken without pre-arrangement between them. Had his lordship slain Yoshitsugu he could not have spared Karumo's life; it has therefore pleased his lordship graciously to spare Yoshitsugu by cutting off this queue of his and so making a priest of him. By entering the priesthood a man disconnects himself with the secular world, for he who has taken to himself a Buddhist name is, after a manner of speaking, a dead man. This make-weight of a stone is a symbol of the tomb; thus one may say his lordship has slain Yoshitsugu. This is a merciful measure and in accordance with the Buddhist doctrine that ' the bad shall be saved in the same hour as the good.' Her Majesty is apparently of the same mind. Had Her Majesty beheaded Yokobué, how could Takiguchi have survived? The *yokobué* or flute is a wonderful instrument, possessing miraculous notes and a soul of its own. By cutting this flute in twain and covering it with earth Her Majesty signifies that Yokobué, being dismissed, is as it were no more in this world. Thus, two of them being saved from death, it follows that the four of them are saved and how great will be the joy and gratitude of their parents, brothers, sisters, other relatives and friends. It would appear that a life-granting measure, such as has here been taken by Lord Shigémori and Her Majesty, is a more pious deed than prayers offered by a million priests for æons. Boundless is their benevolence! Oh, Moritsugu, how can we repay this great favour shown us in sparing the lives of your brother and his would-be wife and of my son and his would-be wife? The mercy, the benevolence of it!"

The lion-hearted heroes grasped each other's hands and were speechless, choked by tears of gratitude. Lady Tonasé was also moved to tears.

" I am ashamed, sirs," she said, " for at the bottom of this affair there is a great knave. I need not specify his name. Now that my parents are no more, the love I bear my brother is like the love of a mother for her son. Alas, to know him for the man he is ! How can his wickedness fail to attract the notice of Her Majesty and of Lord Shigémori, both being so wise and sagacious ? I cannot but think that they will judge me his accomplice. I am prepared for that, though by the Gods and Buddha I have had no hand in the matter. I fear however that their suspicions will not be allayed, even after I am dead. Pray sympathize with me, sirs."

A melancholy silence ensued. At length Katsuyori spoke softly.

" You have our hearty sympathy, lady. Everyone has a mind of his own. A parent cannot know what is in a child's mind and the mind of a brother is unknown to his sister. We can very well understand that you are a perfect stranger to your brother's intentions. A mirror reflects an object exactly as an object appears. Gaze in a mirror with distorted features and a distorted face will look back at you ; gaze at it with a placid face and a placid face will greet you. The same is true of Her Majesty : behave innocently and sincerely toward Her Majesty and your reflection will be the same in Her Majesty's mental mirror."

They exchanged head-boxes. The warriors bade her a polite farewell and went their way.

IV

Luckless Yokobué! For a considerable period she had led a sequestered life at Kwazan, nigh the capital, though not a day passed without her pining for Takiguchi. At length her passionate longing induced her to undertake a journey in quest of her sweetheart. Having assumed travelling garb and veiled her face with a sedge hat, she set out one morning before daybreak. She bade a sad farewell to her hermitage and wearily trudged the narrow roads through the rice-fields.

As she plodded on she beheld, far away to the south, the scarlet maple leaves upon Mount Inari, which the poetess Izumi Shikibu immortalized in a love-poem. Her fancy wandered to the village of Fukakusa, situated below the mountain, famous for its connection with the court noble Fukakusa-no-Shōshō, who died a tragic death because of the power of his love for the beautiful poetess Komachi. As, crossing the Kamo River, she came to the street of Gojō, she beheld pass by many flower-sellers' carts on which reposed mountains of flowers sparkling with morning dew. At sight of them the love-sick maiden could not but associate them with the ox-cart in which the hero of *The Story of Genji* visits the daughter of a peasant living in this neighbourhood. Before she reached the village of Saga, the retreat of numerous recluses, she had to pass through many villages and forests and cross certain streams. Their very names were significant to her, either of hope or fear.

At Saga she found so many hermitages in the glens and on the hill-tops that she knew not at which to call in inquiry after her sweetheart. In this quandary she addressed a peasant girl who was going home from the garden where she had been gathering vegetables.

" Somewhere hereabouts lives a young samurai of the capital who has turned priest. Pray tell me which is his hut?"

" Hm! A young samurai is it, who's a priest? Let me see, which can it be? Father Nensai was a huntsman. Father Dōkin [1] was a—shall I say a Dorking cock? Father Dōsai it cannot be, for he has removed to Nara. I have it!—some time ago a young samurai of the Taira family shaved his head at the Ōjōin Temple yonder. Follow this lane and you will find his hermitage easily enough. Listen, you can hear the sound of prayers in his cell."

Having said this the girl made off. The joy of Yokobué knew no bounds. Beyond doubt the young priest must be her Takiguchi. She ran along the lane and soon reached the cottage, from within which sounded the bell accompanying prayers. It was with a beating heart that she lifted her hand and knocked upon the garden gate and fence.

" I want to speak to you, sir! Please unlock the door; please open the gate."

" As you will," replied a gruff voice.

The next moment there appeared within the fence a shabbily attired man with a shaven head, of about forty years of age.

" My mistake," he said, leering, " I thought it was the woman bringing rice for to-morrow. Here comes an excellent meal for the night-time; I'd have you know, my pretty girl, that the priest here is a young man, but he was a samurai once and behaves himself very strictly. However skittishly forward you may be with him, let me warn you he will in no-wise do even so much as to uncover your dish. No, not he, never! As for me, I too abstain from flesh to-day and to-morrow, but if it's only a matter of a small consideration, call again the day after to-morrow."

---

[1] There is, in the original, a pun which I have reproduced to the best of my ability.

L

" Nonsense ! What do you mean ? I know very well he is a man of strong will ; but if we meet he will recognize me. Pray be so good as just to tell him, sir."

" You're his friend then ? You might have told me so earlier. Wait a moment." So saying he ran into the cell. Yokobué, following him with her eyes, said to herself, " Taki-guchi Sama was wont to say that he had a favourite sandal-carrier ; this fellow should be he. What a loyal servant to have entered the priesthood with his master ! How admirable ! "

The shaven henchman ran out crying, " Oh, terrible, terrible ! Are you waiting still, girl ? What a fright I got ! When I told my master of your coming he glared at me with eyes like saucers and roared at me, ' Have I ever invited in a girl or woman since I retired here ? In the first place I am short of money. You lecher ! Whenever you come across a woman you dilly-dally with her. I am tired of such an idiot ! Never come on such an errand again ! ' And when he had said this he beat me again and again about the head with a bell hammer. Be off, girl ! "

" Indeed, he did right in taking amiss what I said. I am sorry to put you to further trouble, but be so kind as to inform him that I come from Her Majesty's court. Your master will then understand."

" No, no," he said sourly, shaking his head with vehemence, " let there be no tattle about Her Majesty's court.[1] He never will give ear to any mention of silk coat [1] or petticoat.[1] If I go and speak to him I shall get another knock. Terrible, terrible ! "

" You seem to have recently shaved your head. I expect you feel cold about the head ? I should like to present you with a hood, but I haven't got one, so allow me to offer you this."

---

[1] These are more untranslatable puns.

Yokobué proffered him a cloth wrapper, then threw it over the fence. The fellow seized it joyfully enough.

" Thank you, girl. This is expensive crêpe I see, and the lining red silk. I can use it as a hood. Wasn't there something wrapped up in it ? "

" Yes, it contained money which I gave to beggars on my way here, but next time I come I will bring you anything you want. I suppose you have nose-paper ? "

" Yes, I have such things. What would do better—you understand ? "

" I understand. I shan't fail to bring it. Will you please grant my request ? "

" Very well then."

Once more he rushed into the hermitage.

" None are so frank and simple-minded as people of the lower classes," she said. " He is indeed love's messenger on my behalf. I think I will stay at this hut to-night and talk with my sweetheart all night long."

An ecstasy possessed her. She trembled on tiptoe. But it was a crestfallen messenger of love who returned a moment or two later.

" Well, what did he say ? Quick ! "

" All for nothing. He refuses to see you. He merely rapped out with an oath, ' A friend, eh ! No friend if it's a female. I wouldn't cross the road to speak with a bitch or a hen much less with a woman.' I'm sorry, my girl I fear you've given me a crêpe wrapper in vain."

He disappeared into the hut again. Yokobué's disappointment was so deep that she was quite confounded. She sank to the ground and wept bitterly. " What change in him ! Three years we pined for each other. Three years may seem a short space of time, but when told day by day they amount to more than a thousand days and nights. For so many days and nights did he and I pine for each other. Once we had achieved intimacy, what trouble and difficulty was ours, managing to meet in secret ! We vowed to each other that we would become husband and wife through seven existences to come and now he even refuses to see me."

She clung to the gate-post and cried bitterly, but no one came to comfort her.

" It is an idle complaint that I make. Now that I am forsaken by my belovèd, to what purpose do I live on ? What are the bright moon and the beautiful flowers to me ? I will drown myself in yonder stream and in Hades enjoy gazing at the reflection of my lover as it comes and goes upon the river." Having come to this melancholy resolve, the girl hurried toward the " Plover's Pool." [1]

The serving-man turned priest caught sight of her and was astonished.

" Master ! The girl is going to drown herself. See, see ! She is running toward the river."

The startled priest rushed out, wrenched open the outer gate and, running to the girl, seized her in his arms.

" Takiguchi Sama, is it ? " she exclaimed as she embraced him.

" No, I am not Takiguchi."

" Don't lie to me, dear."

She clung to him but he gently freed himself.

" Is it Yokobué Dono ? "

" Are you Yoshitsugu Sama ? I feel sad. My life was spared through Her Majesty's mercy ; since when I have lived on in hopes of meeting Takiguchi Dono. Alas, my hope is frustrated. Pray kill me, Yoshitsugu Sama."

She seized Yoshitsugu's sleeve and wept bitterly.

" Don't be so cast down," said Yoshitsugu, himself almost in tears. " I too was graciously pardoned by my liege lord, since when I have become a priest. I have not been able,

---

[1] The name of the deepest part of the stream.

however, to free myself from worldly passions, so that I never cease from remembering my belovèd Karumo. Beholding your grief, I can well imagine how passionately she is longing after me. Even in this life we four are separated by fate from one another, so that there seems even less hope that we may be able to ' live together in one lotus blossom in the Pure Land.' But since Takiguchi and Karumo, both of whom are pining for us, cannot have gone to the furthest provinces, let us set out in quest of them. The proverb says, ' Desire finds its way even through a rock ' ; sooner or later what we wish will be accomplished. Be of good heart, Yokobué Dono. In this world a priest has no fixed place of stay ; I can therefore start at any moment. Buddha is one and the same all over the world. Everywhere and anywhere Buddha can be found. I therefore need not take leave of the Buddha in my shrine. Hold yourself ready to depart, Yokobué Dono."

On that Yoshitsugu made over the hermitage to his serving-man turned priest, bade the fellow farewell and departed with the girl.

Like a mandarin duck separated from its drake and a cock pheasant parted from its hen, the pair wandered hither and thither, weeping inwardly, but comforting each other as week after week went by without the achievement of any special destination.

Late one winter's afternoon they found themselves trudging along a mountain path in the district of Shiga. Snow was falling thick and fast. A freezing wind from Mount Hiei howled through the snow-crusted trees. The sufferings she had endured upon the long journey had told upon Yokobué. Recently she had grown weaker and now the bitter weather tried her so hard that she seemed scarcely able to take another step.

" Take heart of grace, Yokobué. Have no fears on account

of your weakness. I am sure you will soon be able to meet Takiguchi."

" Thank you—for—your—kind—words."

So benumbed were her lips that these words proceeded from them but brokenly.

" Naturally you are tired," returned Yoshitsugu. " It was very much my idea to beg two or three nights' lodging for your health's good, but unfortunately it is near the year's end and every house consequently is busy, and in any event nobody would give lodging to a priest and a young woman. We have slept in the open air now no less than a hundred nights—a hard time this must have been for you who have led an easy and comfortable life at court from your childhood up. You have my sympathy. About a mile further on lies the village of Shiga. I will certainly ask them, at the very first house we come on, to give us lodging for the night. Please try to walk on."

Thus urged, Yokobué did her best to obey, but so weak and benumbed were her legs that she tottered and fell down in the snow.

" What a helpless creature I am ! " she exclaimed. " Indeed your kindness overwhelms me. You are searching for your love, yet, despite your sufferings, you have fended every care from me for a long while. You have kindly tended a dying woman without any sign of impatience, despite the heavy snow-storm sweeping this strange country-side and without taking thought to your own discomfort at all. Surely you must have been my father or brother in a former existence ; in nowise can I consider you a mere friend. I was lucky in coming across you, but I begin to wonder why I have been so long unable to meet Takiguchi with whom I exchanged vows of fidelity. I fear my hapless lot may be a divine counterpoise to the undeserved benevolence Her Majesty showed towards me. By my own anguish I can well imagine

Karumo Dono's pain. Five [1] long years have passed since she was with child and yet you have not met each other. A hard lot hers! I heartily sympathize with you in your agony. It grieves me much to have put you to such trouble when you are already weighed down by your own troubles, but there is no help for it. My anguish and this snow-storm seem to rob me of my breath ; I feel dizzy ; I think I shall scarcely live until the morrow. My hours are num-bered. I have not even strength enough to pray to Buddha. Aid me to pray, that I be suffered to be reborn in the lotus flower in the Pure Land with Takiguchi." She found difficulty in breathing and seemed on the point of death. Yoshitsugu, himself grief-stricken and much fatigued, spoke somewhat sternly to encourage his sick companion.

" This is spiritless of you, Yokobué. If your sympathy really extends even to Karumo, why do you not take heart and venture not only through the snow but also through fire to find Takiguchi and then to search for Karumo in his com-pany and mine ? You appear a somewhat helpless woman."

He aided her to her feet.

The exhausted Yokobué exclaimed, " I am ashamed of my helplessness and selfishness ; I ask pardon of you."

She leaned upon Yoshitsugu's arm. They continued on through the dusk by the light of the snow itself. When they had toiled a little further through the falling snow they were overjoyed to descry, far ahead, a cottage lit by a hearth fire. They stumbled to it and, peeping through the chinks of the paper door, caught sight of a flame drowsily wavering before the images of the " Three Deities of Welcome." [2] They saw

---

[1] The statement that five years had elapsed since Karumo's pregnancy does not seem to tally with the statement that Yoshitsugu had recently become a priest. Our author displays a singular lack of explicitness as to where Yokobué and Yoshitsugu had spent these years.

[2] These deities are Amida, Kwannon and Seishi and they guide the souls of the dead to paradise.

too an intelligent-looking boy of five to six summers feeding with firewood the hearth, whereon a kettle was boiling. Hope brightened in them. Yoshitsugu slightly opened the door.

" I say, little sir ? "

" Who is it ? " said the child on tiptoe. " What do you want ? "

" We are travellers who have lost our way in the snow ; there are but two of us. Please allow us to rest in that corner till day breaks."

" I'm sorry," replied the boy, with an innocent but firm air, " but the priest of this house has given me orders never to open the door in his absence. I therefore can't allow you in."

" You are right to refuse, as 'tis the time of the year when every house must be guarded against thieves. But see—my companion is a woman who is sick. We are neither of us such as steal. I beg your pardon for using such phrases as are used to grown-ups, but it would be a work of great mercy to give us a lodging. We will apologize to your master. Again I say, do be so good as to grant our request."

" No, I can't."

" Then will you permit us a drink of the water that is boiling there ? "

" That is not water but medicine. The first infusion[1] is not yet made."

" There's somebody sick here then ? Who is it ? "

" My mother. She's long been ill. She lies abed behind that screen day and night. The priest cooks the morning and evening meals.[2] This evening he has gone down to the village hard by, to get mother's medicine."

" In that case, though the priest be absent, you will still

---

[1] In former days internal medicines were decoctions prepared from medicinal herbs and tree-roots that had been subjected to prolonged boiling in water. This process of boiling was often repeated two or three times.

[2] In those days Buddhist priests had two meals a day only, one at morning and one at night.

be able to ask your mother to give us a night's lodging. Please be so kind, little sir."

" No, no.   The priest takes every care of my mother.   He says I am never to let in anybody, whomsoever they may be, in his absence, for fear mother should be carried away.   I can't allow you in."

" Kaméwaka," called a woman's thin voice from behind the screen, " there are travellers asking for lodging, aren't there ? They must be cold in this weather.   The priest will soon be back, so call them in quick."

" No, mother," said the boy stubbornly, " the priest told me never to open the door, even to our friends.   I'll just go down and fetch him."

So saying, he took from the wall a large hat of bamboo sheaths, placed it on his head and set out through the heavy snow.

" Well," Yoshitsugu said to himself, " it's only natural a priest should hide his wife.   I suppose he calls this son of his a pupil.   While the boy's away let me steal in with Yokobué and let us warm ourselves by the fire.   Ah, no.   If the priest is offended we shall get no lodging to-night ; let us be patient a little longer."

He laid his hat and the girl's on Yokobué where she lay in the snow and, shivering with cold himself, endeavoured to warm her in his arms.   Thickly fell the snow upon their hats. Night wore on.   When he shook himself the snowflakes fell off him like goose feathers ; the icicles hanging from the sleeves of both of them tinkled like tiny bells.

" Hey, travellers ! " cried a youthful voice.   " The priest is back."

Priest and child appeared out of the darkness.

" Are you the folk asking for lodging ? "

" I am, sir.   What, you're Takiguchi, aren't you ? "

" Yoshitsugu !   A strange reunion indeed !   Before anything else let me return to you my precious charges. This is your son from whom you parted when he was yet in his mother's womb. Karumo Dono ! ' "

Karumo made her appearance. She was overjoyed.

" My dear Yoshitsugu, this is our son."

" My dear father ! "

The three embraced each other, gazing happily from face to face. All were speechless with joy.

After a brief pause Yoshitsugu said to his friend, " As for me, I have brought you a splendid present ; here is your Yokobué Dono."

" I thank you for your friendship."

Takiguchi shook his sweetheart, crying, " Yokobué ! My dear Yokobué ! " But answer came there none.

He shook the snow from the girl. He clasped her in his arms. In vain ! To their consternation she showed no sign of life. He forced open her clenched teeth and blew a restorative into her mouth, but to no purpose. Pulse and life had completely fled. Takiguchi, grief-stricken, held her on his knees and warmed her body by pressing her to his naked breast.

" Oh, Yokobué, how unlucky our love is ! " he exclaimed with sobs. " These five long years have we pined for each other and suffered hardships indescribable for each other's sake. And now you have died without enjoying a single day of complete wifehood. How sad it is that you came all unwittingly to your own beloved's door and were frozen to death in the snow when all the while a cheerful fire was burning within ! Oh, Yokobué, if you really love me, let me hear the single word ' My dear ' from your lips ! "

Yoshitsugu and Karumo, also in tears, assisted in lifting Yokobué's body up to the hearth, where they warmed it with great care and tenderness. No signs of revival appeared. Karumo, between her sobs, opened her amulet case, saying,

" Here I have a precious incense named ' The King of Medicines ' and it is said to be possessed of miraculous powers. It is a portion of a present from the Chinese Emperor to the Emperor Goshirakawa, who gave it to Her Majesty. Her Majesty graciously bestowed it on Yokobué Dono and myself as a token of the relationship between mistress and servant extending to the next world. It is my trust that the odour of this incense will restore Yokobué to life. I will therefore burn it."

No sooner did she begin to burn the incense than a sweet odour filled the air and, wonder of wonders, Yokobué's body instantly recovered its warmth and pulse and her face its colour. She gave a sigh and opened her eyes. Then she cried, " Is it Takiguchi Sama ?   I am overjoyed to see you ! " She was again a beautiful woman in sound health. The others were filled with amaze and joy.

" When my spirit had all but fled and I seemed to be half in a dream, I smelled the sweet odour of precious incense and heard Her Majesty's voice crying, ' Yokobué ! Yokobué ! ' The next instant my dream dissolved and I came to my senses. Great is Her Majesty's goodness ! "

All of them spent a happy night, merrily talking of what each had experienced during those five weary years.

V

When the full extent of Morotaka's roguery and calumny became known, it was evident that he deserved death ; but, for the sake of his sister Lady Tonasé and because the quality of mercy is the foundational principle of government, his punishment was reduced to banishment from the Imperial city. He found it difficult to keep body and soul together and so formed a gang with the villains Genkurō and Muzō, relatives of his retainer Iwamura Gengo, slain at Funaoka-yama. They roamed the neighbourhood of Karasaki, on Lake Biwa, eking out a living by swindling, highway robbery. burglary, blackmail and the like, as chance and opportunity served.

One day Morotaka whispered to his subordinates, " To-day there should be many visitors to the Shrine of the God Sannō in this place. See, there is a boat adrift yonder! Genkurō will pretend to be her boatman, will give passage to some of the worshippers and rob them when you have rowed out some distance. In the Hall of Worship in the Myōjin Shrine the priest leaves his hat and robe. Muzō will wear them, pretend to be the priest and appropriate the offertory and the money paid for the ' Twelve Lights '. I, for my part, will prowl the highway and pick the pockets of absent-minded travellers. Come, let us set about our jobs."

They parted on their respective enterprises.

Presently Lady Tonasé, in a palanquin, accompanied by a few attendants, arrived under the Giant Pine-Tree at Karasaki. She had come to the town of Ōtsu, as proxy for the Empress, for a week's worship at the Shrine of Sannō and of Myōjin. She alighted from her carriage, glanced about and said to her attendants, " See whether the priest Sandayū is now in the shrine."

Muzō, having donned the priest's robe, made his appearance.

" Honoured lady," said he, " I am Sandayū's father. I may take orders for the Sacred Dance or the Twelve Lights as well as he."

" Are you Sandayū's father ? Sandayū must be sixty and you look younger."

Muzō was confused. " No, no. I said Sandayū was my father. My name is Nidayū."

" So you are his son ? Come nearer."

The rogue perforce advanced.

" I have the honour," continued the lady, " of doing proxy to Her Imperial Majesty. Sandayū may have told you that the young court ladies, Yokobué and Karumo, were discharged some years ago on account of their love affairs. Her Majesty has taken pity on them and, a report having come to her ears that they are living a miserable life hereabouts with their lovers, Takiguchi and Yoshitsugu, Her Majesty has commanded me to find them and bring them back to the capital. With this purpose in my mind I have journeyed hither and am now putting up in Ōtsu in order to pray here to the Gods Sannō and Myōjin for guidance as to their whereabouts. I intended worship of a week and have already spent five days in prayer. I beg you to pray to the God to let me have news of their whereabouts."

So saying, she worshipped the deity with her whole heart and soul.

Morotaka who, unnoticed, had played the eavesdropper, suddenly rushed upon her, seized her by the nape and drew her down on her back.

" What villainy ! " the frightened woman cried. " Who does this deed ? "

" Let not the villain escape ! "

So cried her henchmen ; and the palanquin bearers instantly hemmed him in.

" Maggots ! Touch me if you dare ! Hi ! Comrades ! Knock the old woman down and strip her of her garments."

Genkurō jumped from the boat and cut at the servants. Muzō, who had also rushed to the scene, drew and flourished his weapon. The terrified, cowardly servants precipitantly took to their heels, crying, " Robbery in broad daylight ! Highwaymen ! Help ! Help ! "

" So it is you, wild beast and brother ! " exclaimed Lady

Tonasé. " You who gave so much trouble to Her Majesty, you who wronged so many, you who, for these crimes, were about to be put to death ! To whom do you think you owe it that your head still remains upon your shoulders ? Partly it is due to me, but also largely to the benevolence of Her Majesty. You ought immediately to have become a priest, that you might atone for your crime. A cursèd wretch, reduced to such a condition, do you not even yet repent of your crime ? What shame this is ! "

" Pah ! If I had repented I should not have come to this pass. Since we are relations I spare your life. I know your purse is full ; you have, I am sure, three or four *ryō* about you. Come, hand it to me at once. If you don't I will kill you."

He forced her head to the ground as he spoke.

" A base villain ! " said the lady. " You say you mean to kill me if I don't give you my money ! Naturally I would not grudge even thousands of *ryō* as the price of the redemption of my life. What should a chief court lady have money about her for ? Kill me if you choose."

" Aha ! I see you have no money on you. Your money must be in your inn at Ōtsu. You are not to stir till I fetch it."

He produced a cord, bound her cruelly and thrust her into the palanquin.

" Come along with me and be quick about it, comrades. Since she says she's to stop here for a week she must have brought plenty of gold and silver coins with her. Think of the special booty there will be—her chests, her fine clothes, her bed-trappings ! "

They ran off highly pleased.

They had scarcely taken themselves off when Yoshitsugu with his wife and son appeared. They had spent many days at the temple praying the God Myōjin to restore Yoshitsugu to his former situation as a retainer to Shigémori. They now proceeded to the shrine and, bowing their heads and clapping their hands, prayed with great fervour. While they were absorbed in their devotions a voice was heard insistently crying, " Karumo Dono ! Yoshitsugu Sama ! " The surprised couple glanced backward.

" The cry comes from that palanquin, I believe."

" Yes, you're right. It is from the palanquin. Dear Karumo Dono, please come to me ! "

Karumo rushed to the palanquin and slid open the door.

" Is it Lady Tonasé ? Why, how's this ! How did you get into such a state ? "

She lifted the old woman out and loosened the cord. Tonasé thanked her and, restraining her tears, said, " Where are Takiguchi and Yokobué ? I have come here as Her Majesty's proxy to pray for guidance as to your whereabouts. In point of fact Her Majesty orders me to find you and bring you and your friends back to the capital. A few minutes ago, as I was worshipping the God, that villainous brother of mine, who had been banished and who appears to have turned robber, seized and bound me in the fashion you found me in just now. He will shortly return. Before he returns, let us set out together to the capital."

" Have no fear," laughed Yoshitsugu, " nothing will happen to you now that I am with you. Takiguchi and Yokobué will presently be here to worship. Abide here a while. Karumo, you will hide in this palanquin and when Morotaka returns you will say to him, ' I am forsaken by that heartless monster Yoshitsugu.' Appeal to his sympathy and coax him into going aboard that boat. I will pretend to be the boatman. I have a plan for his chastisement."

" Certainly," returned Karumo, entering the palanquin. " I will do my best, dear husband. But be careful of yourself."

" Have no fears for me."

Yoshitsugu took his child in his arms and embarked with Tonasé. He hid them both in the bottom of the boat and, assuming a straw rain-coat and a sedge hat, sat down and feigned a doze. Morotaka presently returned, exuding perspiration.

" Sister," cried he, striking the palanquin, " they would deliver us nothing at your inn without a note from you. We cannot break into your rooms in broad daylight. You will please write a note demanding the delivery of your money and clothes. Be quick about it ! "

No response.

" What next ! " he cried, and, tearing the blind from the carriage, was amazed to find Karumo within.

" Oh ! " said she, assuming a bashful air. " I am ashamed to meet you in this plight, Morotaka Sama. I regret to have to tell you that I have been unkindly forsaken, as a just punishment for my flat refusal of your kind proposal, by that brute Yoshitsugu. Enraged by my jealousy, he swears that he will drown me in this lake. I have managed with great difficulty to escape and have hidden in this unoccupied palanquin. I trust that, though it be but half of what formerly obtained, your affection for me still exists ? "

" Has my sister fled then ? But I wouldn't exchange you for a thousand sisters. How unkind of you to say ' half my former affection ' ! Truly my love has grown an hundred-fold since then. Make your mind easy ; under my protection you are now in no danger. You're even handsomer than when I last saw you. I am madly in love with you ! I would die for you, my dearest girl ! "

So saying, he embraced her.

" Don't ! People might see us. What do you say to hiring yonder boat and spending cosy and pleasant hours in the offing, away from the eyes of common folk ? "

" Aha ! You've improved in wits as well as looks. Hello, my man ! I thought it was merely a boat adrift, but it's yours, boatman, is it? Row us over to Ishiyama, will you?"

" With pleasure, sir. I saw in a glance you were lovers. I shan't be wanting any fare. Come, get aboard."

" Thank you. This really is, as the saying goes, a boat that arrives just when one wants to cross over."

The old rascal was making as if to embark with Karumo, when Yoshitsugu exclaimed, " It's dangerous for two to try and get on board simultaneously ; one at a time, please ; the girl first."

He took Karumo in his arms and placed her in the boat, then, seizing the oar, to Morotaka's vast surprise and anger, rowed out into the lake. A moment later the boat was a hundred yards from the shore.

" Slave-trader ! Robber ! " roared the villain. Frantic with despair he waded into the shallows. Yoshitsugu, doffing his coat of straw and his sedge hat, disclosed himself to the astonished Morotaka.

" Has divine punishment sealed your eyes, you villain ? " he cried. " Know then that I am Yoshitsugu ! It is I have sheltered Lady Tonasé. My advice to you is that you kill yourself instead of continuing to lead a dishonourable life."

Lady Tonasé and Yoshitsugu's son appeared.

" Ah ! That I should have been duped ! Were this water a hundred or a thousand fathoms deep, yet would I wade out ;o your boat and capsize it ! "

With these words Morotaka tucked up his skirt and rolled up his sleeves for action ; but at this moment Takiguchi and Yokobué came on the scene. Takiguchi rushed at him, knocked him down on to the beach and kneeled upon him, while Yokobué beat his head and pinched his legs. The villain writhed. " A shame it is," he cried, " to have been brought down by a greenhorn of a boy ! "

" Don't kill him ! " Yoshitsugu shouted. " It would be wrong for us to kill one whose life Their Imperial Majesties

M

have graciously seen fit to spare. Let us lie in wait for his comrades and kill them."

He rowed to the beach, jumped ashore, trussed the old knave up hand and foot, thrust a handful of straw into his mouth, wound a kerchief round his face and threw him into the palanquin. The party then hid behind the shrine.

Presently Muzō and Genkurō, both out of breath, returned at a run.

" Can't find our boss anywhere ! And a pretty poor time we've been having ! We owe it all to this old hag too ; let us finish her."

They approached the palanquin on both sides and thrust their swords again and again through the blinds.

" She mayn't have any money, but I daresay we can find something or other hidden in her bosom."

They dragged the corpse out. Great was their consternation to find themselves gazing upon the bloody body of their chief.

" Muzō, beware ! " exclaimed Genkurō, alarmed. " Takiguchi or Yoshitsugu must be about."

" A good guess, villains ! " cried the two heroes, rushing from hiding. " You see Yoshitsugu *and* Takiguchi before you ! "

Mighty strokes fell upon the frightened rascals. The villains were held down, stabbed to death.

At this moment Saitō Katsuyori and Etchū Moritsugu appeared.

" Listen, Takiguchi and Yoshitsugu ! " they cried. " We bring you a written order from Lord Shigémori, restoring you to your former situations and fiefs."

The joy and gratitude of both couples knew no bounds and the whole company wept for delight over their happy reunion after five years of weary separation.

TWO SCENES FROM *THE TREASURY OF THE LOYAL RETAINERS*

From a colour print by Toyokuni

[face p. 178

A SCENE FROM COLOUR PRINTS, *THE NOTED PRODUCTS OF YEDO, A KABUKI* PLAY BY
NAKAWA TOKUSUKÉ

From a colour print by Kunichika

THE DESIRE FOR REVENGE REALIZED BY NAKAWA KAMÉSUKÉ, PLAYED BY
FAMOUS ACTORS OF OLD JAPAN

From a colour print by Toyokuni

A SCENE FROM THE MAIDEN AT THE DŌJŌJI TEMPLE

From a colour print by Kunichika

THE COURIER FOR HADES

(Meido no Hikyaku)

THE COURIER FOR HADES

(*Meido no Hikyaku*)

I

In Awajimachi, a thriving street in the heart of the city
of Osaka, stood a post-distributing office which enjoyed
a good reputation and was called Kaméya. Day and
night the entire establishment busied itself putting up and
untying packets, collecting and distributing letters and entering up accounts. A brisk interchange was carried on with
all parts of Japan. Thousands of *ryō* passed through the
office every day for all the world as if coins of gold and silver
had taken to themselves wings. Four years previous to
the opening of our story Chūbei, a young man of four and
twenty, had been adopted as heir by the elderly widow
Myōkan and was now master of the house. The son of a rich
farmer in the province of Yamato, he had brought with him a
considerable sum of money which had formed as it were a
portion. Thanks to the guardianship of Myōkan the young
man was now thoroughly versed in all the ramifications of the
business, to such an extent in fact that he had several times
been to Yedo in connection with the affairs of this business.
In the tea ceremony he was an adept. He was no mean
composer of *haiku* [1] odes. He could play a good game of
chess or backgammon, wrote a graceful style of calligraphy

---

[1] The shortest form of Japanese verse, consisting of seventeen syllables.

and could down his few glasses of *saké* [1] with the best.　For the rest, Chūbei was an uncommonly handsome young man and one who exhibited a certain grace of deportment but rarely observed in a country-bred youth.　It was now some time since he had taken to visiting the pleasure quarter of Shimmachi.　Every evening, as soon as it turned dark, he bent his steps thither, having first carefully evaded the eye of his foster-mother.

Late one afternoon, when the couriers had returned from their errands and letters were being franked, an attendant of a *yashiki* [2] samurai, a constant customer, made his appearance.

" Is Chūbei at home ? "

" So it is Jinnai Sama, is it ? " inquired one of the clerks courteously.　" Chūbei himself is out, but should you want something sent down to Yedo be so good as to give me instructions.　Now, maids, bring the honoured guest some tea."

" It's nothing to be sent down," returned the henchman, knitting his brows.　" We have received a letter from our young master staying at Yedo.　I will read it you."　He opened and read as follows : " ' I will send you three hundred *ryō* by the post of the second of next month.　The money will await you at the post-distributing office Kaméya on the ninth or tenth of next month.　You are requested to arrange the matter I told you of the other day.　I enclose a receipt which you are to hand over to Kaméya when you receive the remittance.'　So runs his letter.　But as the money hasn't reached us yet we can't carry out his instructions.　Why are you so behindhand ? "

" Your reproaches are well-founded, sir.　But prolonged

---

[1] Moderate drinking, or perhaps we may say immoderate drinking, was at this period considered, as indeed it was considered in England in the eighteenth century, one of the properest accomplishments of a gentleman.

[2] Every clan had a granary establishment in Osaka, that the clan might sell the tribute rice collected from farmers.　Such establishments were known as *kura-yashiki*, or more simply as *yashiki*.

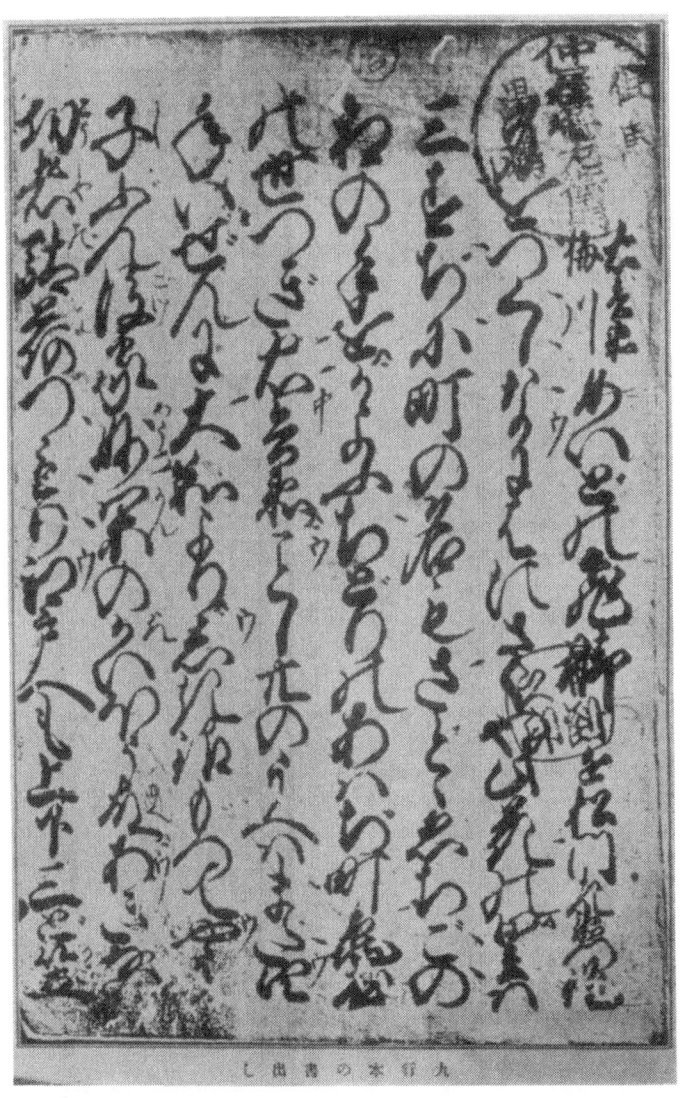

FAC-SIMILE OF A MANUSCRIPT OF *THE COURIER FOR HADES*, USED BY THE *JŌRURI* CHANTERS OF THE AUTHOR'S DAY

rains have swollen the rivers and the couriers are consequently delayed. Not only has your money not arrived, but we ourselves are suffering pecuniary loss. Suppose robbers make off with some thousands of *ryō* or the couriers yield to a sudden temptation, yet you need not be troubled. The guild of the eighteen post-houses will reimburse you and you will suffer not the least loss."

No sooner had he spoken these words than the messenger answered haughtily, " That goes without saying. You needn't stress that aspect. Mind this, however, should our master suffer loss, Chūbei's head will not remain long on his shoulders. I have come, as I told you just now, because your delay prevents the satisfactory conclusion of our master's affair. Be so good as immediately to send a courier to meet those from Yedo and bring us the money with all possible despatch."

He spoke in a dubious [1] dialect and with an arrogance guaranteed by the authority of his sword, ornamented with dubious silver, then strutted away. Hardly had he turned his back when a second messenger arrived.

" I come as messenger," he announced haughtily, " from Tambaya Hachiémon at Nakanoshima. My master has received notice of a remittance from the wholesale rice merchant at Kobunachō, Yedo, but has not yet received the money from you. He wrote to you the other day, but as yet you have deigned to make no answer. Then he sent you a special messenger, but on this pretext or that you evaded making a reply. My master is curious as to when you will send him the money. He therefore commands me to spare no pains to obtain the money from you to-day. I will give you this note in exchange for the money. Come, hand it over."

---

[1] The original contains a piece of word-play. The " dubious dialect " means the man makes use of a curious provincial dialect ; " dubious silver " means that that which had the appearance of silver may in reality have been lead.

The loyal-hearted chief clerk, Ihei, replied composedly :

" Now, sir, you do not mean to say that Hachiémon Sama sends us as peremptory a message as all that ! Surely you must know our firm always holds in trust thousands of *ryō* belonging to other people and is at home anywhere on the three hundred mile route between Osaka and Yedo. Your master is not our sole customer. Naturally enough delay in the delivery of remittances occasionally occurs. My master may return at any moment. When he does so we will send you a reply. Pray do not make such an ado about so small a sum as fifty *ryō*."

Subdued by so summary a reply the messenger departed quietly. Myōkan, the widow, had overheard the above colloquy. Now, reluctantly enough, she left the *kotatsu* [1] and came to the office. Wonderingly she looked at the clerks.

" How can this be ? " she said. " It's ten days and more ago that Hachiémon Sama's money arrived. Why didn't Chūbei deliver it, I wonder. I have heard you pressed for remittances two or three times this morning. Now, never since the days of my dead husband has this Kaméya been dunned for a penny. It's never given trouble to the guild and indeed has got a name for itself as a model among the eighteen post-houses. Chūbei's manner has been strange of late. Perhaps some of you have noticed it ? The new-comers among you may not be aware of it, but he is not my true son. He is the only son of a rich farmer named Katsuki Magoémon of Ninokuchimura, a village in the province of Yamato. His father, who had lost his first wife, very much feared that the ill terms obtaining between Chūbei and his step-

---

[1] The *kotatsu* is a fireplace in the floor. A wooden frame shaped like a box is placed over this, the frame itself being covered with a large, thick quilt which confines the warmth. The body is thrust under the quilt while the user of the fireplace lies or squats upon the mats, which of course are never soiled by shoes or *geta* (wooden clogs resembling the cothurnae of Greek tragedy).

mother might drive Chūbei to a vicious life and therefore gave him to me as heir to this house. I have so far no fault to find with his manner of keeping house and his management of the business. I have however noticed that of late he is always restless and cannot attend as seriously as he might to business. I have wished very much to advise him, but have feared that he might regard me, a foster-mother, with much the same feelings he might a step-mother. Hoping that silence on my part may shame him out of his present mode of conduct, I refrain from lecturing him, but none the less I watch his behaviour. Before I could realize it Chūbei has grown so wasteful that he blows his nose with two or three expensive paper handkerchiefs at a time. My dead husband used to say, ' A fellow who wastes handkerchiefs is a ne'er-do-well.' When Chūbei goes out he takes three quires of paper handkerchiefs with him and when he gets in he hasn't a sheet. I wonder how often he blows his nose. Even though he is young and healthy, if he keeps on blowing his nose at that rate he will become sick."

Grumbling after this manner the old woman withdrew, whereon the clerks and shop-boys, taking pity on her, re-marked, " We hope our master will soon be back."

The sun was sinking. Soon the office closed.

Chūbei, who had been to the pleasure quarter to enjoy sweet [1] moments with his sweetheart Umégawa, returned as fast as his legs would carry him, his heart surcharged with sorrow and anxiety concerning the shifts necessitated by the cost of his pleasures and weighed down by the fear of his foster-mother. A few steps from the door he halted, overcome with anxiety as to how he might have fared at home should Myōkan have got knowledge of any duns calling in his absence. Still he waited, hoping that one or other of his work-people would come out, from whom he might learn what had chanced.

[1] This is intended to be a word-play.

He peeped through the chinks of the closed door and observed the kitchen-maid O-Man about to go on a visit to a wine-shop. She was an unobliging woman ; he would not get his information for nothing. He was still cudgelling his brains how to get round her when she stepped out all but on top of him. He took her firmly by the hand that held the wine-keg, whereon she cried, " Why, it's my master ! "

" Quiet, my dear. I love you, and, as they say, ' the man in whose heart love finds place will surely show it in his face.' You noticed my manner toward you, didn't you ? What a heartless creature you are to trouble me with those love-compelling looks of yours. Why not kill me straight out and have done with it ! "

So saying, he made haste to embrace her with warmth, but she shook him off. " You're a pretty liar ! Don't I perfectly well know you visit Shimmachi every day and flirt with pretty girls ! Why should you cast a single glance at such a woman as myself ? What a liar you are ! "

" It's the truth," he returned, hastily embracing her again. " What have I to gain by telling you a lie ? It's the truth I'm telling you."

" If you are speaking the truth, will you come to my room to-night ? "

" Why not indeed ? Thank you very much. By the by, there's something I want to know."

" It'll be cosy listening to your questions in my room. Don't fail to come. I'll get ready and wait for you. Good-bye till to-night."

So saying, she freed herself and ran off in a high good-humour. Baulked in his scheme, he stood blankly staring, when his eye was arrested by a man hurriedly approaching from the north. Alas ! it was Hachiémon of Nakanoshima. Did they meet, trouble were sure to arise. To avoid him he turned eastward, but the other cried, " Chūbei, don't you attempt to give me the slip."

" Hachiémon, I haven't seen you for a long time. Yesterday, to-day, nay the day before yesterday I intended to send you a messenger, but something or other caused a delay. The weather's turned very chilly, hasn't it ? How is your father's lumbago and your mother's toothache ? You smell of *saké* ; don't drink too much. I'll send you a messenger early to-morrow. I know where there's a little lady [1] waiting for you ; let's go on the spree one of these days, my dear chap."

" Enough," said Hachiémon gruffly. " I am not the fellow to be taken in by fair speeches. Isn't conducting a posthouse your business ? Why don't you send me the remittance of fifty *ryō* from Yedo ? I can stand three or four days' delay, but I'll have you know that more than ten days have now passed. Friendship's friendship and business is business. You charge a high price and your service should be on a par with it. To-day I sent a messenger to your office and some clerk or other of yours took upon himself to make him a sharp reply. Do you deal that way with all your customers ? Are you having a little fun at Hachiémon's expense ? You should remember I am known as ' the Boss ' in Kitahama, Utsubo, Nakanoshima and Temma. If you're pleased to make fun of me, please do so, but you're going to pay me that money to-day, or would you like me to report the matter to your guild ? First of all, however, I am going to make a point of seeing your mother."

Hachiémon made as if to step in, but Chūbei intercepted him.

" My dear friend," he whispered, " pray forgive me. I most humbly crave your pardon. Be so good as to listen to one word of pleading, I beseech you."

---

[1] A courtesan in Shimmachi is meant.

" Fair words butter no parsnips," said Hachiémon with a stern look. " You may be able to get round Umégawa but you can't get round a man. If you have something real to say, say it at once."

" Should my mother overhear your words, even my death couldn't save my face. Please speak more softly, my dear friend. Do me this favour, if for once only." He burst into tears. " The truth is your money arrived a fortnight ago, but, as you are aware, Umégawa's guest from the country rivalled me owing to his possessing money. All I have is a wretched sum of two or three *ryō* which I lay my hands on when my mother and the clerks are not looking. Driven into a corner by my rival I was in despair on learning, to my great astonishment, that a conference concerning her ransom had already been held and that the bargain was about to be concluded. Umégawa was as much overwhelmed with grief as myself. We resolved upon double suicide. We laid the sword to our throats, but—it seemed our doom was not yet come—circumstances prevented our death. That night we separated in tears and on the following day, the twelfth of the month, your Yedo remittance arrived. Scarcely knowing what I did, I placed it in my bosom and, as in a trance, ran at full speed to Shimmachi. I argued and argued with Umégawa's master until I prevailed upon him to break his contract with the guest from the country and to consent to my ransoming her. I handed him the fifty *ryō* as earnest and succeeded in securing my sweetheart. For all this I am indebted to you, my good friend, and morning and evening I do you homage on this account. Of late, however, I have reflected that our friendship is no excuse for my embezzlement of your money. At the very moment when your demand overtook me I was regretting the deed and have been obliged to tell lie after lie so that even the first excuse I gave you was a lie. Quite naturally you give no credence to anything I now

THE COURIER FOR HADES   189

say, but in three or four days at latest other remittances are bound to arrive. I will make every effort to pay you the money. You shall not lose a *sen* through me. Were you to think of Chūbei as a man, you could not but be angry ; I beg you, however, to tell yourself that you have given a dog its life, and so bring yourself to forgive me. Is it to be wondered that there are capital offenders when you consider circumstances such as mine ? Should you press upon me now, no resource would be mine but theft. How does a man come to say the things I am saying now ? Harder is it for me to speak this than to swallow a sword ! Have pity on me."

Chūbei gave way to tears and Hachiémon, who in the ordinary course of events would have matched himself against an ogre, gave way to tears also.

" You have made a very clean breast of what it must have been hard to confess. Tambaya Hachiémon is a man. I pardon you and grant you grace. Do your best to pay me."

" Thank you," said Chūbei, shedding further tears as he fell on his knees, " I have had five [1] parents, two fathers and three mothers, but the kindness of Hachiémon exceeds theirs. Never shall I forget your kindness."

" If such be your feelings I am satisfied. Well, we may be observed. We shall meet again."

Hachiémon was about to make off when the old woman's voice was heard within : [2]

" Is that Hachiémon Sama ? Ask him in, Chūbei."

The hesitating Chūbei was perforce obliged to step within doors with his friend.

" Good evening, sir," said the old lady. Innocence and

---

[1] *Hachi* of " Hachiémon " means eight. This is a play upon numerals. When Chūbei says he has had five parents he reckons as follows : by two fathers he means his real father and his foster-father ; by three mothers he means his real mother, his step-mother and his foster-mother.

[2] The doors of a Japanese house in elder times were a lattice frame covered with thin paper. The conversation between persons without was thus often audible to persons within.

uprightness of heart spoke in her voice. " It's natural enough that you should have sent a messenger and that you should now visit us in person. Come, my son, you know that this gentleman's money has been here over ten days. Why this delay ? Rack your brains honestly. If the package is delayed, the post-house can give no aid. What are you about ? Come, hand the money to Hachiémon Sama at once."

Her words put Chūbei in a quandary. Hachiémon came to his aid.

" Do not put yourself out, madam. Such a sum as fifty or sixty *ryō* makes no difference whatever to Hachiémon's purse. As I am even now on my way to Nagabori, I will call in again to-morrow or———"

" Certainly not. When we have your precious money in our keeping we cannot sleep at night for anxiety. Come, Chūbei, hand over the money at once." Thus urged, Chūbei made answer, " As you will, mother," and entered the closet. He looked round bewildered, but there was no money to lay his hands on. To keep up the deceit he turned the key in the lock of the *todana* or locker, empty as it was. At the squeak of the wards he sweat for very shame. Beside himself with despair he prayed the Gods to disclose to him some device. " Thanks be to the Gods," he murmured, " here is a *binmizu-iré* [1] in this comb box. My tutelary deity must be helping me." Thrice he reverentially held the little vessel to his forehead, then, deftly wrapping it in excellent paper, inscribed upon the exterior in bold, black strokes the words " Fifty gold *ryō*." Returning to the office he addressed Hachiémon.

" Here's your money, Hachiémon Dono. You see I pay you on the spot, trusting that you will see your way out of your generosity to set my mother at ease. Pray receive it in the

---

[1] A small earthen vessel for holding water, the water being used in combing the hair. Its elliptical form somewhat resembles in shape several *koban* or gold coins piled upon one another.

spirit in which it is given and reassure my mother. You needn't open the packet. Content yourself with feeling it and making sure of the amount. I am sure you will consent to this composition, as I."

" Assuredly," returned Hachiémon, receiving the package. " Am I not Tambaya Hachiémon ? Of course I make no objection. You see, madam, I am in sure receipt of the Yedo remittance. When you visit the Fudō Temple call at my place."

He made as if to depart. All unsuspecting the old woman returned :

" Now, Chūbei, it's customary to take a receipt in exchange for a remittance. If Hachiémon Dono has brought no receipt, please ask him for caution's sake to write out a line."

" Certainly," answered Chūbei, not without a significant glance towards his friend. " Though mother can't read or write, please pen a line for form's sake."

" As you will," returned Hachiémon, " I'll write one."

He wrote at random as his ready wit dictated :

" I am *not* in receipt of fifty *ryō* in gold. According to your suggestion, which I accept, I agree to have a spree with you some evening in the pleasure quarter at your expense. Whenever you feel like making merry, I shall be yours to command. I swear to the truth of the aforesaid by the *binmizu-iré*. Signed, Tambaya Hachiémon."

He handed the paper to Chūbei and with a brief " Good evening to you both," made off.

The good-natured mother, not entertaining the least suspicion of the deception practised upon her, was well satisfied with the paper. Mother and son sat down anxiously to await the mail from Yedo. The night wore on. At length the tinkle of horse-bells was heard, shortly followed by a loud voice crying, " Ho ! there ! The packet has arrived ! Open the doors ! " Alertly the coolies carried in the wicker baskets.

Chūbei and the old woman were in high spirits. " Good luck has come back to us," cried the delighted old woman. " Fortune should shine on us next year as well. Give *saké* and tobacco to the drivers."

Chūbei and the clerks busied themselves counting up the packets and entering them in the books. An air of merriment hung about the house. None the less, the chief clerk Ihei remarked sulkily to the courier in charge, " Jinnai Dono of the *yashiki* at Dōjima was here this afternoon. A remittance of three hundred *ryō* ought to have arrived on the ninth, according to him. He had received an early notice to that effect and wanted to know why we made such a delay in the delivery. He made a great noise about it and went off in a huff. Have you that remittance with you ? Make haste and tell me."

" I have it about me, I'll be bound. It is an urgent matter and you must deliver it during the course of the night. I have brought several remittances, totalling eight hundred *ryō* altogether."

The man counted out the jingling money. Chūbei's spirits rose.

" Put the silver in the inner go-down and the gold in the *todana*. I'll take the three hundred *ryō* in gold, mother, to the *yashiki* forthwith. Now, my men, as we've got other people's money in our keeping, make haste to close the doors and put yourselves on guard. Keep a careful lookout for fire. I shall be back late, but as I shall go by palanquin you need not be nervous. Take supper and go to bed early."

He pocketed the money and stepped out into the frost-ribbed street. His intention was to walk northward, but his legs according to their wont carried him farther and farther south until he came to Koméya-chō. " What ? Am I not to visit the *yashiki* at Dōjima ? What ails me ? Am I possessed by a fox ? " He retraced a few steps, but halted.

CHŪBEI, THE HERO OF THE COURIER FOR HADES.

[face p. 192

" Let me see, I came here by no means of my own accord. Surely it must be because my tutelary deity in person compels me to Umégawa because she must want to see me on some important business. I will pay her a short visit." He turned south again. " No, I must not. I should be tempted to spend the money there. That's dangerous. Shall I give up the idea of the visit ? . . . or shall I go ? Yes, I must go."

After a few moments' struggle he turned his steps toward Shimmachi with an air of resolution like a missioned spirit, we may say like a very courier for Hades.

II

When the moon climbs clear and high
" Come, come," the wanton crows do cry
And hark, O hark,
When the night is deep and dark
Still wantonly the hid fowls cry
" Come, come."

Wanton crows indeed were the visitors to the pleasure quarter of Shimmachi. All the year round the sweet zephyr of love breathed through the streets of this neighbourhood.

Love and compassion are born of one seed. The " plum-blossom " [1] and " pine-tree " are fragrant and beautiful, but about them hangs an air of unapproachability and dignity. Their sisters of more lowly estate are more approachable and more readily arouse feelings of compassion and this compassion often transforms itself into sincere love.

The tea-house Echigoya was a sort of club attended by these lower [2] grade courtesans, who would indeed have liked to have bridges built between it and their respective houses.

[1] Nicknames of the higher grade courtesans.
[2] The licensed courtesans of Osaka, Kyoto and Yedo were divided into four grades.

Since the keeper of this tea-house was a woman, the girls called at the house more readily and unbosomed to her their secrets.   Thus the streams of love within their hearts found an outlet within the walls of this house.

Chūbei's sweetheart, Umégawa, was among those who called there, to the neglect, be it added, of her guests at other tea-houses.   On this particular night she had deserted her country guest at the Shimaya and was now making a call at the Echigoya.

" Good evening, madam.   That brazen-faced bumpkin of mine has been vexing me all day at the Shimaya and so I've found myself a headache.   Isn't Chūbei San here yet ?   I've called just to have a sight of your face, madam."

" You're welcome.   Listen, there are several girls amusing themselves in the upstairs room, having a good time before being invited out by their guests.   They are playing *ken* [1] and drinking.   Won't you come up and join them ?   Some of your friends are there."

The two women stole upstairs and peeped into the room. The company was entirely composed of girls and a bottle of *saké* was being heated in a kettle set over the brazier   The players cried gaily, " *Romasé !   Tōrai !   Sanna !* [2]   See it's a draw ! "

" *Hama !* [2] *Sankyū !   Gō !   Ryū !   Sumui !*   You're beaten, Narutosé San.   You can take a cup of *saké* and I hope you enjoy it."

" Aha, there's Umégawa San.   You're just in time. You're a good hand at *ken*.   I've been beaten by Chiyotosé San all the evening.   I'm quite put out.   Please come and revenge me.   Have some *saké* first."

" No, thank you.   I detest *saké* and I don't care to play

---

[1] A game played with the hands—a kind of mora. The loser has to drink a cup of *saké* as forfeit.

[2] Corrupt Chinese expressions probably indicative of numbers. The game is said to have been introduced from China early in Japanese history.

ken. I'd rather have you weep with me over my present situation. To-day at the Shimaya my guest from the country tormented me about my ransom. He got me into a corner. I lost my temper and hated him. He was, however, the first to make an offer of ransom. He did so before Chūbei San and it was only through the most determined efforts of my master that Chūbei San was enabled to supplant him. Chūbei San paid a certain sum as earnest money, the payment of the remainder being allowed to stand over until to-day. But he is, you know, an adopted heir and thus cannot have a free hand in domestic affairs and moreover he carries on an onerous business between Osaka and Yedo. He deals with the samurai of the granary establishments and with prominent merchants. I am therefore all the more afraid some unexpected circumstances may intervene that will give my country guest the chance he desires to ransom me. If such should happen folks would say, ' Umégawa, being a lower grade courtesan, was lured by gold and basely forsook her lover.' How then could I show my face before Kamon San and my other friends ? I feel that to save my honour I might do well to put an end to my life. But what would Chūbei San do without me ? Pray, what shall I do ? Dear friends, pray sympathize with me."

At these sad words all the girls present bethought them of their own sad lot and gave way to tears.

" How sad we are ! " said one of them after a pause. " Let us cheer up and hold a *jōruri* [1] recitation. *Kaburo*,[2] just go and bring Takémoto Tanomo [3] Sama."

" He is out," broke in another. " Just now I went out to buy a cosmetic and happened to hear that he had called

---

[1] Properly speaking *jōruri* is a general term for the *gidayū* (puppet drama) and several kinds of popular epic song. But in Chikamatsu's days, as indeed to-day, *jōruri* was often used in the sense of *gidayū*.

[2] A little girl attendant on a courtesan.

[3] A famous *jōruri* reciter who lived in the immediate vicinity of the pleasure quarter of Shimmachi.

at the tea-house Ōgiya on his way back from the theatre,
but being his pupil I can recite after his manner. Listen to
me, my friends. Now play the samisen." She recited to the
accompaniment of the samisen :

" It is said that the courtesan is not faithful, but those who
say this do not speak true. This is a saying of the ignorant,
of those who know nothing of her life. The truth and the
untruth are originally one and the same. For instance,
however loyally a girl devotes herself to her lover, yes, even
at the risk of her life, should he for some while not visit her and
no communication come from him, yet she, in her condition of
servitude, cannot call upon him however she may pine after
him. Under such circumstances she is at length compelled
to suffer herself to be ransomed by some other guest and so her
plighted word proves false. On the other hand, if a guest
whom a courtesan treated with a false warmth simply for
business purposes repeats his visit time and again till she at last
consents to wed him, all her first lies turn out to be truths.
Thus in the world of love there is neither truth nor untruth,
since only the existence of affinities gives rise to truthfulness.
How often indeed does it happen that a courtesan pines and
pines for her lover for so long that she at last gives him up in
despair ! In such a case the man cannot but resent her
seeming indifference and her inconstancy. Yet to blame her
were unreasonable." [1]

The recitation ended, some of the girls exclaimed, " Such
resentment cannot be helped. At any rate we cannot help
but love. To have lovers is, I daresay, a chronic habit
among women of the quarter." The love-sick girls fell into
a melancholy mood.

Tambaya Hachiémon, who had but that moment entered
the pleasure quarter, chanced to overhear the recitation and
the ensuing chat.

---

[1] A paragraph from a puppet drama entitled *The Yūkun Sanzésō* or " A
Courtesan's Three Existences " by the author.

" Pretty girls' voices that I know ! Is madam in ? "

He entered the lower room and seizing a broom struck the ceiling a loud rat-tat, crying, " What chitter-chatter for a man to overhear ! What kind of two-legged creature is it you girls long for ? If it's lonely you're feeling in the absence of your lovers, I give notice that here is a man perfectly willing to make a little offer of himself, though of course he mayn't be quite to your exacting tastes."

" Come," called Umégawa, ignorant who the newcomer might be, " it's natural enough that we should want to see our dears, isn't it ? If you feel jealous come and vent your jealousy on us. Whom do you think it is, madam, down-stairs ? "

" You need have no fears. It's Hachiémon Sama of Nakanoshima."

Umégawa started.

" Ah, madam," she hastily whispered, " I wouldn't for the world see that man." She addressed the others. " Go down-stairs all of you. Don't on any account tell I'm here. Promise you never will."

" Never," they answered, and went down to the lower room.

" Chiyotosé Sama ! Narutosé Sama ! " exclaimed Hachié-mon. " What a bevy of beauties ! I hear Umégawa Dono left the Shimaya early this evening ; and Chūbei it seems isn't here yet. One moment, madam. Ladies and *kaburo*, one step nearer "—then continuing in an undertone—" I have something secret to tell you about Chūbei."

" What can be the matter ! Pray tell us quick."

Thus said the women, none the less fearful lest some evil report of her lover be heard by Umégawa. At this precise moment Chūbei, bosom and heart alike icy cold with the weight of three hundred golden *ryō* and the sharpness of the night air, reached the entrance of the Echigoya. He peeped in. Great was his surprise to see Hachiémon sitting cross-legged in gossip concerning his affairs. Chūbei stiffened against the door-post. Overhead Umégawa crouched down perfectly still to listen. The unsuspecting Hachiémon began to speak : " You might imagine from the things that I am going to say about Chūbei that I hate and am jealous of him. But the real truth is that I am very anxious about his future. It's true, of course, that he always holds in trust one or two thousand *ryō* belonging to other people and that these sums lodge temporarily under his roof. But his property—his house, grounds and furniture—all these are worth no more than two hundred and fifty *ryō* at the utmost. His father in Yamato is said to be a man of great wealth, but when we consider that he gave his son to the Kaméya, it seems more reasonable to infer that he must be a petty farmer. I will confess that I myself spend, as young men will, at least fifteen *ryō* a year at tea-houses. But Chūbei's case is quite a different matter : he spends above his means. Apparently he has lost his head over Umégawa, for it seems he has been paying her continual visits since May last, and this as a rival to that countryman who visits the Shimaya. It is said that not very long ago some kind of an arrangement concerning her ransom was come to ; and I understand that Chūbei has already paid fifty *ryō* as earnest money of the whole price amounting in all to one hundred and sixty *ryō*. As a consequence he has failed in the payment of several remittances and has been obliged to utter downright falsehoods. He is in great difficulties. If Umégawa, who probably has some debts, is to be ransomed at once, it means that Chūbei must raise at least two hundred and fifty *ryō*. He cannot, however, expect the sum to fall in a shower from the sky or to bubble up from the ground. No course is left open to him but theft. Where do you suppose that earnest money of fifty *ryō* came from ? He made use, if you please, of a remittance of mine from Yedo. Ignorant

of this fact I called at the post-distributing house for its payment. His foster-mother—poor woman!—who knew the
money had arrived, urged Chūbei to deliver it to me. Guess
now, girls, in what sort of gold coin he paid me?"

Hachiémon produced a small packet.

"What's the difference between this and fifty *ryō*? Let
me show you a scurvy trick."

So saying, he tore open the paper and displayed the
crockery water-holder. Mistress and courtesans recoiled in
open-mouthed astonishment. Overhead, Umégawa pressed
her face to the mat and wept in silence.

Outside the quick-tempered Chūbei reflected, "The devil!
What a malignant backbiter! How mercilessly he betrays
me to those snobbish girls. And what for?—all on account
of a paltry sum of fifty *ryō*. If Umégawa should hear of this
she will die of shame. Enough of this, you scoundrel! Let
me draw fifty from the three hundred *ryō* in my bosom, cast it
in your teeth and say all I have in me to say to save my face
and Umégawa's. Ah, no, no—I must not—a samurai's
money—a particularly urgent remittance. I can't be rash
now—I can't, I can't. I simply must control myself."

Again and again did he thrust his hand into his bosom and
wrench it forth again, anguished and self-divided young man
that he was; while Hachiémon, never dreaming that Chūbei
listened, held up the water-holder and continued his discourse:

"Such a vessel cost some eighteen *mon* However low
the price of gold has sunk, never since the age of the Emperor
Jimmu [1] has fifty *ryō* in gold been exchanged for eighteen *mon*.
If so he acts to his friend, you can well imagine how he cheats
strangers. The time will come, and that time perhaps is
not so very far off, when he will turn cutpurse, then take to
burglary and finally do murder! I cannot but feel for him.
Sunk as he is, neither his mother's disowning him nor the

---

[1] The first Japanese Emperor, founder of the Empire.

remonstrance of Sakya, or the prayers of Dharma could induce him to turn over a new leaf; nay, even the personal admonition of Prince Shōtoku [1] could not prevail upon him now. Such being the circumstances I ask you to be so good as to spread this report of mine throughout this neighbourhood and to do your best to prevent him visiting the tea-houses. I would have you tell Umégawa Dono this. Induce her to break with him and get her ransomed forthwith by the countryman. Such a debauchee as Chūbei often brings about double suicide or steals courtesans' dresses or does something worse, and his punishment is to be exposed with one of his sidelocks shaven [2] at the great gate of the pleasure quarter, to the dishonour, alas! of his friends and relatives. Chūbei is indeed a fool. If any of you chance to feel any compassion for him don't permit him to call."

Umégawa had heard it all. Now she broke anew into sobs of grief, sympathy and despair. " Oh, for a sharp instrument," she wailed, lying at full length in her agony, " a bare bodkin! Let me bite off my tongue and so die! "

The company below-stairs, guessing her feelings, were overcome with compassion. " Unhappy Umégawa! " Thus did they reflect. " How well we can imagine what she feels. How much is she to be pitied." The very maids, cooks and little *kaburo* melted into tears of sympathy.

Chūbei, unable longer to restrain himself, rushed in and, crouching down, bent over Hachiémon's lap.

" Here, Hachiémon Dono," he exclaimed with rancour, " you call yourself a gentleman and this is your attitude! How well your deeds match your words! Well do they say, ' Three men make a public '. [3] Permit me to thank you

---

[1] A son of the Emperor Yōmei (572–621), the Constantine of Japanese Buddhism.

[2] Such was the punishment meted out by private citizens at pleasure quarters in the feudal period.

[3] A proverb.

for cataloguing my property before such a company. You will recall that before I handed you this water-holder I asked you as man to man to accept it that my mother might be set at ease. Yet you babble the matter abroad in the pleasure quarter to the injury of my reputation. And this you do because you are afraid that I will not pay you the fifty *ryō* or—stop !—can it be that you are bribed by the guest at the Shimaya into talking against me to Umégawa, thus winning her over to him ? Enough of that ! You need not be nervous : Chūbei will not lose a friend either fifty or a hundred *ryō*. Now, Hachiémon Sama, good Hachiémon, see me pay you the money. Return me the bill."

He produced the packet of coins and was about to untie it when Hachiémon interrupted him.

" One moment, Chūbei. Don't be a fool. I know your character well. I know no advice will have any effect on you. It has been my care therefore to request these people to shut the door on you whenever you might appear. For so it has seemed to me and so alone could your nature undergo a change and you become a right-minded man. My intentions, believe me, have been honourable. Had I entertained any apprehensions about my fifty *ryō* I should have declared them in your mother's presence. To reassure your mother, unable as she was to read and write, I wrote a comical paper. Was Hachiémon, even in this, unkind ? The money you hold now amounts to three hundred *ryō*, doesn't it ? So large a sum can't be your own property. It's somebody else's re-mittance, I'll be bound Were you to ' inflict a wound ' [1] on that sum, you couldn't settle the difference by a water-holder, as you have done with Hachiémon. Or do you mean to make up this difference with your head ? If you have all this time to excite yourself in, you would do better to spend it

[1] Waste.

paying the money, for at present you are behaving like a feather-pated fool."

This well-intentioned lecture infuriated Chūbei all the more.

" Enough of your hypocritical benevolence ! So you think this money belongs to somebody else, do you ? I haven't three hundred *ryō*, haven't I, eh ? Since you are good enough to put yourself to the trouble of estimating the worth of my property in the presence of this sort of company, it seems that I am the more to pay you your money to save myself in their eyes."

He tore open the packet and counted out ten, twenty . . . thirty . . . fifty *ryō* and wrapped it in paper.

" Here is proof," he cried, " that Kaméya Chūbei is not a robber. Take it ! " And he cast the money into Hachiémon's face.

" That's a polite way to act ! " returned Hachiémon, not without asperity. And he handed the money back. " Oblige me by saying ' many thanks ' and pay it me politely."

" And why should I thank you, traitor ? " Once more he cast the money at his antagonist. Hachiémon cast it back at him and so their quarrel continued.

Umégawa, half blinded by tears, ran down the staircase.

" I have heard all," she said. " Hachiémon Sama was in the right. On my knees I beg you, Hachiémon, to forgive my Chūbei San. For my sake, Hachiémon San ! " She turned toward her lover. " My poor Chūbei San," she cried, " Why are you so much excited ? Don't you know that those who visit the pleasure quarter, even rich men, often find themselves short of money. That kind of dishonour is here no real dishonour. But if you spend another man's money without the faintest prospect of being able to repay him, you will be arrested and find yourself in prison. Such an eventuality as that, not even you would compare with the present unpleasant predicament, and not only would it be in

MR. GANJIRŌ AS *CHŪBEI*

" He tore open the packet, counted out fifty *ryō* and wrapped it in paper."

[*face. p* 202

itself a disgrace to you, but what do you think could be its outcome for Umégawa? Pray calm yourself, apologize to Hachiémon Sama, put the money together again and immediately pay it to its owner. I know you wouldn't have me go into another's hands and I myself do not wish to go. For your sake I am prepared to brave the worst. I have two more years of servitude, but to support you I would, if need be, undergo any hardship and undertake anything, howsoever hard. Never will I let you suffer. Pray quiet yourself, you that have grown so reckless and all through my own doing. Know that, since I am the cause of your rashness, I feel both grateful to you and sorry for you. Can't you see that?"

She wept afresh and the tears, falling on to the gold coins, appeared like dewdrops falling upon yellow roses. The bewildered Chūbei resolved upon one last random and desperate fling.

" Silence, my dear. Do you take me for a fool? Have no fears about this money. As Hachiémon will remember, this is the gold I brought from Yamato when I was adopted as heir to the Kaméya. It was taken care of for the time being and I have received it back in order to redeem you. Now, madam "—he addressed the mistress of the house— " up to date I have paid Umégawa's master fifty *ryō* as earnest money. Here are one hundred and ten *ryō*, making in all one hundred and sixty *ryō*, the price of Umégawa's ransom. Please hand this money to her master. This sum of forty is for several things I bought and for which you presented the bill the other day. This five *ryō* is for the *yarité*.[1] I should say that the charges for my invitations to Umégawa since September amount to about fifteen *ryō*, but since the exact reckoning may be a trouble to you cross out the account and let us call it twenty *ryō*. This ten *ryō* is

---

[1] A maid at a tea-house who makes arrangements between courtesans and guests.

your gratuity. Let me thank you in advance for your trouble. Rin, Tama, Gohei, one *ryō* to each of you. Here now, take it."

So saying, Chūbei distributed gold coins with the utmost freedom. A Crœsus for the nonce even as Rosei [1] in his dream.

" Come, madam," he concluded, " pray lose no time in making such arrangements as are necessary that Umégawa may be able to leave with me to-night. Pray make haste."

" Very good, sir," returned the delighted mistress. " Poor one day, rich the next. It's queer how it goes with money. Why do folks worry about it, there's no need to despair. Umégawa, my girl, you feel happy I'll be bound. Well, now I shall have to hurry off to call on your master and since I shall be carrying a large sum do you, Rin and Tama, come with me."

And taking the two maids with her she hurried out.

" I don't believe Chūbei speaks true," said Hachiémon doubtfully, " inasmuch as he distributes money even when he doesn't owe it, I can't very well refuse to accept what is due to me. Chūbei, I acknowledge the receipt of fifty *ryō*. I return you the note. Umégawa Dono, you are fortunate to find such a handsome man as husband. I bid you good night, all of you."

And placing the money in his bosom Hachiémon took himself off.

" It is time for us to go home. Accept our congratulations, Umégawa Sama."

The girls made off to their respective houses.

" Why is madam so late ? " Chūbei inquired fretfully. " Go and hurry them, Gohei."

---

[1] Tradition avers that an ambitious young man named Rosei who lived in China once dreamed that he lived in extravagance and attained to eighty years of age.

" I am afraid you'll have to wait a short time longer, sir. In order to get a courtesan redeemed, even when a settlement has been come to with her master, the seals upon the contracts must be cancelled by the director of this quarter and a pass for the gate be signed by the manager for the current month. Until this is done she cannot step beyond the great gate, so pray wait a moment longer, sir."

" But won't you hurry them up ? " He cast another *ryō* to the man. " Please do your best."

" Very well, sir." Responsive to the golden spur, the servant ran out.

" Now, my girl, make ready at once," Chūbei urged his bride-to-be. " In what disorder you are ! Rearrange your *obi*." [1]

" Why in such a hurry, Chūbei San ? This being the greatest occasion in my life, please allow me to exchange cups of farewell with my friends and to take a leisurely leave of each and all."

Her innocent, joyous countenance provoked him to a flood of tears. He clung to her sobbing.

" Innocent creature, those gold coins were an urgent remittance to a samurai connected with a granary establishment at Dōjima. I perfectly well knew that to scatter them as I did was to compass my own ruin. I did my utmost to control myself, but seeing your beloved self the victim of indignities among your friends and guessing the mortification you must feel and experiencing a sudden and overwhelming impulse to relieve you of it, hardly knowing what I was doing, I put my hand to the money. Having once done that it was no longer possible for me, a man, to leave the deed half done. Pray resign yourself to fate. Hachiémon's expression plainly declared that he intended to proceed to my mother. It can be but a question of a short space ere the eighteen post-

---

[1] An *obi* is a broad, stiff sash, tied at the back.

houses secure a warrant for my arrest. Let us face the abyss :
will you fly with me ? "

Umégawa trembled like an aspen.

" Have courage," she returned in a voice choked with
tears. " Haven't I often talked with you of such an emer-
gency ? Why do you fear death ? I should be more than
satisfied to die with you. I can die with you even now and
that willingly. Let us prepare for the last act."

" Of course. Do you imagine I could have done anything
so reckless had I not been prepared to die at any moment ?
But let us try to live as long as may be and thus keep in each
other's company as long as possible   Remember death is the
last evil."

" Yes, let us enjoy each other's company in this world as
long as may be. You had best hide yourself lest your pursuers
arrive as well they may at any moment now." She pushed
him behind a screen. " I have left my precious amulet in my
chest-of-drawers : indeed I need it now."

" No amulet, however powerful, can save us from the
consequences of so ill a deed. Since we must die ere long,
let us pray for the peace of each other's soul after death."
So saying he thrust his face above the screen.

" Ah, horror ! Don't, don't ! I dare not say what you
resemble." [1]

Clinging against the screen she wept bitterly.

It was at this moment that the mistress and her maids
returned.

" You can set yourself at rest, sir. All is now settled.
The pass for the gate has been sent round to the western
entrance, that being the nearest way to your home."

The young pair trembled. " We thank you. Farewell,
farewell."

---

[1] She hints that his face above the screen has for her the appearance, being so
thrust up, of the exposed head of an executed criminal.

" You look chilled. Will you have a drink, sir ? "

" No, thank you. I can't drink now."

" I am glad you are ransomed, Umégawa Sama, but at the same time I am very much loth to part with you. I feel somehow saddened. I couldn't tire of saying such things even for *a thousand days (sennichi)*."

" Oh, do not say *sennichi*." [1]

At cockcrow the passionate pair, leaving the pleasure quarter, proceeded hand in hand as fast as might be toward Chūbei's native village in the province of Yamato.

III

The Lovers' Journey in a Double Palanquin

The passionate pair's sweet and peaceful dream, dyed with the green and red of Umégawa's bed-chamber, had been suddenly and mercilessly broken. That courage which they had often displayed in their secret midnight meetings was now of no avail. On leaving the pleasure quarter they took refuge in a double palanquin and hurried on their way. Sitting face to face there was nothing between them but a small *kotatsu* [2] or fire-box and the fires of love more served to keep warm their chilly feet than this. Chūbei's hair, which had been left uncombed since yesterday, became dishevelled. Umégawa tidied it with her tear-frozen hand. The snug atmosphere in the palanquin brought to their minds the comfortable nights spent in her small, cosy chamber, but the hot, red fire in the box had now turned white as the morning

---

[1] The Japanese for " a thousand days," *sennichi*, reminded the pair of the execution ground Sennichi-Mayé in the suburbs of Osaka.

[2] A small wooden box of fire is called a *kotatsu* no less than the fireplace in the floor covered by a large quilt.

frost. Since still a little space was wanting to daybreak they lifted the blind. Their attention was caught by a small pine-tree shuddering in the chilly blast and this put them in mind of a *kaburo* tormented by a *yarité*. The sight of it, giving rise to " the remembering of happier things," moved them to tears. After they had given themselves up to grief awhile they consoled each other by observing that their sitting together in a palanquin was like " Living together in a lotus-flower," [1] prophesied in Buddhist scriptures.

The morning mists, resembling the thin smoke from the *hiyoku-giséru* [2] which they were smoking, had cleared. A breeze was billowing over the young wheat. A farmer lingered about his field. Fearful lest he might approach and request them for fire to light his pipe with, the couple alighted from the palanquin, paid the bearers liberally and began to walk. Before a small temple by the roadside they worshipped, and, gazing backward beheld, walking along another road, many visitors to the temple of the God Aizen. These were young actors and persons connected with the tea-house business who went up to intercede on behalf of the prosperity of their avocations. Having started before dawn they carried unlighted lanterns. Umégawa looked with longing upon the crests painted on the paper of the lanterns, crests familiar enough to her eye. One lantern in particular arrested her attention. It bore the character " Tsuchiya," the name of the bordel in which she had lived and her own crest paired with the crest of the house. This unlit lantern, flameless though it was, blazed in her heart and illumined for her all her past joys and sorrows.

Umégawa shivered as she realized that their lives were tending downward to extinction, even as the taper gutters.

---

[1] A Buddhist saying signifying the living together happily in paradise of husband and wife or of lovers.

[2] A pair of long bamboo tobacco pipes having a single bowl. This pipe was intended for lovers and was formerly to be found in pleasure quarters.

She thought too of the darkness of Hades and, weeping, averred that she was desirous of carrying with them to Hades a lantern figured with her crest to illumine that dim road to darkness.

Forasmuch as they traversed an unfamiliar route, guided only by the answers of wayfarers, they made but little progress. When they found themselves at Hirano the sky was overcast : sleet mingled with hail began to fall. Since they were wearing *setta* [1] upon bare feet they were the more chilled. A lass of about seventeen, who was plucking herbs in a field at the back of the farmer's house, made her way back to the house and called in the young man standing by the door, and it seemed to them that she was saying, " Come in, my lad, out of the cold. We shall be warm enough within." The young fugitives smiled wanly upon each other at the discovery that every nook of the country was a little world of love. Chūbei, walking through the thin snowflakes as they fluttered about in the breeze, with pleasure remembered how one snowy morning on his way back from the tea-house at Shimmachi, Umégawa in a gay night-gown had accompanied him to the great gate of the quarter. What an innocent, simple-hearted girl she had been in those days ! Since then the clear stuff of her heart had been dyed ever deeper with love. Then it had been light blue, now it was utter black, colour of midnight. Unspeakable pity and regret rose in his mind. Calling to mind how often they had taken the names of many Gods and Buddhas in vain when plighting vows of fidelity, he told himself that perhaps their present fate was allotted them in retribution, and with agony asserted that he would shoulder Umégawa's share of the punishment. Continuing their dreary journey in talk with each other upon such things, many a time were they startled by the sudden clatter of birds' wings or by the keening of the wind. The very crows,

---

[1] Leather-soled sandals.

noisily cawing in Tonda forest, seemed to mock at the foolish-ness of the way they had taken.   Beneath Mount Katsuragi they remembered the legend of Hitokotonushi, God of that mountain, how he hid himself while the light was abroad and worked only at night ; and remembering this they grieved that they themselves had become even as bats fearing the light of day.   As they traversed a narrow pass, they felt that no defile was narrower than their way in the world, which way they themselves had gone about to make so narrow.

Thus did the luckless pair pick their way over the stones of passes, plod over plains, creep between mountains, thread townships and hamlets and so drew near their destination.

Meanwhile the police had busied themselves upon the track of the culprit, a particular search being made in the neigh-bouring provinces.   Yamato, Chūbei's native province, was especially singled out for narrow search by the authorities and by persons connected with the eighteen post-houses, who, disguised as pilgrims, ragmen, pedlars and strolling singers, spied at every door.   Certain of them, tricked out as amé-[1] vendors complete with peep-shows, enticed children into the telling of every stranger's movements.   So came it that the couple's lot was that of fish in a net, or birds in a trap.

At the end of a wearisome journey of over twenty days and after spending their last penny, the fugitives reached Nino-kuchi-Mura, Chūbei's native village.

" Here, O-Umé," [2] whispered Chūbei, " is the place where I was born, in which I lived till I was twenty.   Never as far as I can recall have I seen so many traders and travellers in the village at the year-end ; no, nor even in spring.   I cannot help suspecting that man over there, and surely those two or three men standing at the outskirts of the village are in

---

[1] A viscid, tenacious sweet made of barley.

[2] Umégawa's name as Chūbei's wife. A courtesan possesses a professional name and this differs from her ordinary name.

disguise. Alas ! I have a presentiment. My father Magoémon's house stands about half a mile further up ; but for
a long time past I have not written to him, and besides, the
woman is my step-mother." He turned toward a straw-
thatched hut by the roadside. " This is my father's tenant,
the farmer Chūzaburō's house. Since my boyhood he has
been my great friend. He is a reliable man ; let us visit him."

The couple opened the door of the house and stepped in.

" Is Chūzaburō Dono in ? I haven't seen him for a long
time."

The woman within was cooking. " Who may you be ? "
she demanded. " Chūzaburō Dono is away. He has been
up at the village headman's since this morning."

" Chūzaburō Dono had no wife. May I ask who you
are ? "

" Well, I married into this house three years ago and I know
none of my husband's old friends. I'll be thinking you are
both Osaka folk, aren't you ? I have heard tell my husband's
master Magoémon's son—Chūbei Dono they called him—went
to Osaka as an adopted son. I am hearing he bought a
curzon [1] and Sir Governor has commanded a search. Magoémon Dono long ago ceased to have any truck with him and
so he is not answerable, I'll be reckoning, for the lad's mis-
doings. But still, as they are father and child, the affair
worries the old gaffer a deal. My man, being an old friend
of Chūbei Dono, is anxious about his safety. He is keeping
an eye open for fear the lad should wander in these parts and
get caught. The headman has sent to see him. The whole
village, spite of it being the end of the year, is all of a pother
over this ' curzon ' affair. Every day almost they hold
meetings at the headman's. A regular bad lot, that
' curzon '."

<hr />

[1] She is so illiterate that she doesn't know what *keisei* or " courtesan " is,
hence her mispronunciation *keisen*, which the translator and reviser have done
their best to render comprehensible.

Chūbei was disconcerted at the bluntness of her speech, but he answered composedly enough :

" Indeed ?   Well, the affair's a subject of talk all over Osaka as well.   My wife and I are by way of making a pilgrimage to the Great Shrine in Isé Province ; and we have come this way round on purpose to see your husband whom I am very anxious to see.   Will you be so good as to fetch him from the headman's, as I should like a brief interview with him.   Don't tell him, however, that we come from Osaka."

" Are you in such a hurry ?   I will fetch him.   I ought to tell you that a holy priest of the capital has now come to the temple at Kamata-Mura where everyday he preaches.   It is quite within the bounds of possibility that my husband has gone on from the headman's to the temple.   Please be so good as to keep the fire alight under the soup caldron while I'm away."

She made off with sleeves tucked up.   Umégawa promptly shut the door and fastened the latch.

" We are among enemies.   Is there any danger, do you think, in this house ? "

" Have no fear, my dear.   Chūzaburō is a type of chivalrous man rarely to be found among farmers.   I will beg a night's lodging of him.   What though I perish here— there will at least be some satisfaction to die at home among my own people, and did we come to be buried here, the village in which the grave of my real mother is to be found, it would be possible for me to have you and her meet in the next world as daughter-in-law and mother-in-law."

" How happy I should be !   But my mother lives at Rokujō in the capital.   I feel sure that the authorities must have recently gone to examine her.   I wonder what has become of her, and she poor soul always suffering so from giddiness in the head.   How much I should like to have a glimpse of her before I die."

" Naturally, my dear. And I too wish to meet your mother as son-in-law." Since no strange eye was upon them, such as might know them for what they were, the couple embraced passionately, the tears showering [1] upon their sleeves. At this moment a shower beat against the lattice of bamboo. " Hark ! It's raining ! " they exclaimed with one voice, and slightly opening the window's paper panel, they cast their eyes along the narrow path through the paddy-field. Several persons were hurrying toward the temple. Their umbrellas were held aslant against the rain which came hurrying behind them.

" There's not one I don't know," said Chūbei. " The foremost is Sukésaburō of Taruibata, one of the leading men of this neighbourhood. That old woman is the old mother of Den, the hunchbacked porter ; she is a great woman for tea drinking. That other old man used never to be able to make both ends meet. When he found he couldn't pay his land tax, he sold his girl to Shimabara in the capital ; fortunately she was redeemed by a man with any amount of money and became his wife. His son-in-law saw to it that the old fellow was provided for, so now he lives in comfort, the owner of two go-downs and a dozen acres of rice. I, too, have redeemed you, but it grieves me to think what trouble and grief I have brought your mother. The next old man is Tōjibei of Tsurukaké, who ate a quart and a half of boiled rice on his eighty-eighth birthday. He is now ninety-five. The bald [2] head following him is the cure-all [2] Dōan. He did for my mother with his treatment and so I count him my mortal enemy. Oh, look, look ! There is my father ! "

---

[1] A play upon words here.

[2] In the old days physicians shaved their heads. What Chūbei says is : " That bald head who follows him is the acupuncturator Dōan. My mother was killed by his needle ". In old days acupuncture was extensively practised in Japan. See Basil Hall Chamberlain's " Things Japanese ".

" Is that really Magoémon Sama, in a *kataginu* [1] of coarse silk ? Oh, his eyes are just your eyes ! "

" Ah, that parent and child, so alike in face, cannot meet face to face in public ! How he has aged ! How unsteady his steps are ! " Chūbei clasped his hands together. " This is my last farewell to you, father."

" Dear father-in-law," murmured Umégawa, " this is the first and last time I shall set eyes upon you. I am your daughter-in-law. My husband and I may be killed at any moment. When you have attained to your hundredth year, may you and I meet in the next world."

Through eyes half blinded by tears they watched the aged Magoémon pass by on feeble steps. His feet in their heavy clogs faltered. How slow, how dragging his pace ! The old man had all but passed the door of the hut when he slipped upon a frozen puddle at the footpath's edge ; the strap of his clog snapped ; and he fell with a thud into the miry field. " Poor father ! " Chūbei involuntarily exclaimed and writhed with anguish, but having regard for his present position dared not step out to his aid. Umégawa, however, rushed out ; helped him out of the field ; wrung the water from his clothing and rubbed his knees and waist with her hands, as she said in kindly tones, " I am sorry, old gentleman. Don't you have pain anywhere ? I shall wash your feet and mend your clog-strap, Tell me anything you want without hesitation."

" Thank you for your attention. Fortunately I am in no way hurt. You're a very considerate young woman. You show me more sympathy than even a daughter-in-law would. Although a man may visit the temple for worship, if his heart "—the old gentleman pointed at his breast—" is hard, all the worship in the world won't help him, A kindly person like yourself, though, is not far from the Kingdom of Heaven. Please wipe your hands. Luckily there's some straw here

[1] A form of cape.

THE COURIER FOR HADES, PLAYED BY CELEBRATED ACTORS OF OLDEN DAYS

From a colour print by Toyokuni

"Don't trouble, sir, I have good paper myself.
Allow me to make a string of it for you."

[*face p.* 214

and I have some paper. So I'll twist myself a strap with them."
So saying he produced a few sheets of paper from his bosom.

"Don't trouble, sir, I have good paper myself. Allow me
to make a string of it for you."

Her manner of tearing a paper handkerchief [1] struck the
old man with amaze. "You are evidently a stranger in these
parts," he said, narrowly regarding her. "May I ask who
you are and why you put yourself to such trouble about me?"

"I'm a—traveller," returned the girl, her heart beginning
to beat. "The fact is, my father-in-law is just about your
age and has much your appearance. In serving you I don't
feel as if I were serving a stranger. It's a daughter-in-law's
duty, you know, to tend an old father-in-law when he's in
trouble and therefore it's a pleasure for me if I can be of any
service to you. I am sure my husband would be pleased that
I should do so. Permit me to take your paper in exchange
for mine. I'll give it to my husband and make him carry it
about as a momento of one who looks so like his father."

She received his paper and slipped it into her sleeve and
then, despite her utmost efforts, burst into tears. Her words,
her manner, her looks proclaimed the truth to Magoémon.
He was overcome with emotion; tears streamed from his
eyes. After a pause he said:

"Hum . . . so you're kind to me because I resemble
your father-in-law, eh? Well, that both pleases me and
makes me angry. You see, I happen to have disinherited my
son—better not ask why—and I sent him away to Osaka
as an heir by adoption. Possessed by some devil or other he
recently took it into his head to spend a large sum of money
belonging to another and then run away. An official search
is now being conducted for him in this neighbourhood and I
am now, as you may well imagine, in great trouble of spirit

---

[1] A courtesan's manner of tearing a handkerchief has something distinctive
about it.

about him and all on account of my daughter-in-law to be. Perhaps it's foolish of me to acknowledge it, but my feelings can be expressed exactly by the proverb which says, ' One doesn't so much hate the son who is a thief as the officer who arrests him.' Since we are no longer father and son it makes no difference to me whether he does right or wrong, but none the less, think of my joy if I should hear folks saying, ' Chūbei's an intelligent, shrewd and diligent young man and what's more he's made a fortune. Magoémon must be an old fool to have disinherited such a son.' And so you can imagine what my feelings will be when presently he is hunted out and arrested and I hear people say, ' Magoémon did well and is lucky to have disinherited his son at the right moment.' I cannot help being very anxious as to his fate. I pray the Lord Buddha, may he let me die as soon as may be, before my boy comes to the place of execution. That is my prayer and I never lie to the Lord Buddha.''

He prostrated himself and wept loudly. Thereupon Umégawa could not refrain from further tears and Chūbei, at the window, wrung his hands.

" Blood is thicker than water,'' continued the old man, brushing away his tears. '' I suppose it's human nature that, however close the affection between intimate friends may be, it can never be so great as between father and son, although the son be disowned. Why, before he set about embezzling another's money, didn't he write secretly to me that he was in love with such and such a courtesan and wanted money for her ransom ? If he had done so—he is my real son, you know, and a motherless son at that—why, I'd have sold even the field intended for my support when I retired from life, rather than have him bound as a criminal. But now that the report of his crime has caused his foster-mother pain and occasioned another person financial loss and trouble, how can I call him my son and give him lodging even for a night ?

All this is his own doing. I've no doubt but he suffers a great deal himself and certainly he causes his wife to suffer too. He is a fugitive in the wide world. He must conceal himself from his friends and acquaintances, yes, and from his very relatives, and sooner or later is bound to die a miserable death. That sort of disgraceful position is not the life he was born to. I think he is a despicable fellow and yet I cannot help but love him."

Once more he gave way to bitterest tears. At last, though yet weeping, he took a silver coin from his purse and handing it to the girl, resumed :

" I happened to have this money about me. I intended it as a contribution to the building fund of the Temple of Naniwa. I give it you, not because I take you to be my ' daughter-in-law,' but as a token of my gratitude for the kindness you showed me just now. If you wander hereabouts, you are bound to be arrested, having the likeness you have to the offender, and the same is even truer of your husband. I therefore advise you both to betake yourselves to the Gosé highway, with this money to speed you on your way, and make off as quick as may be. Ah, that I might have but a glimpse of your husband's face, even though I didn't speak with him ! No, no ! If I should do so I should sin against society, but oh, let me know when he is in hiding, safe and sound. Let me know the glad news of his final safety. Goodbye, girl."

He took a few steps, then returned and softly inquired, " Do you think there is any harm in meeting him ? "

" Harm ? How can anybody know of it ? Do meet him, father."

" No," said Magoémon, breaking into renewed sobs, " I cannot wrong his adopted mother in Osaka. Will you please insist on him making his escape while he can, lest he die before I ? "

In tears the old man made off, again and again gazing back over his shoulder. When he was no longer in sight the couple prostrated themselves and took their fill of tears. Chūzaburō's wife returned, drenched with rain.

" I am sorry to have kept you waiting so long. My man went on to the temple direct from the headman's and so I couldn't get a sight of him. The rain is clearing ; I hope he'll soon be back."

At this moment Chūzaburō appeared, running. He arrived out of breath.

" I am pleased to see you, Chūbei Sama. Your father has just told me all about you. I know, too, that spies have come up from Osaka and an official search is in progress by order of Sir Governor. Found amid swords in the day-time your doom is sealed. I don't know whether they have wind of you, but they have suddenly begun a house-to-house search. They are now at your father's. Next they will come to mine. Your poor old father, frantic with despair, bade me tell you to escape quickly. You are now ' in the jaws of the crocodile.' Come, come, lose not a minute, but escape along the back road to the Gosé highway over the mountains."

At these words the pair were panic-stricken. Chūzaburō's wife, who had not a notion of what was in process, exclaimed, " Shall I escape with them ? "

" Don't talk nonsense." Chūzaburō pushed her away and rapidly tricked out the fugitives as persons of the farmer class, by placing old sedge hats upon their heads and old straw rain-coats upon their shoulders.

" My friend," said Chūbei, " we shall never forget your kindness even in death."

The two stole away in haste. No sooner had Chūzaburō heaved a sigh of relief than constables, guided by the headman and a local magistrate, rushed into the house by both back and front entrances, and, searching everywhere, rolled up the straw mats, broke the hurdles, prised open the coffer and inspected the rice-chest and ash-bag.

" This house is too small for them to find any place of hiding. They cannot be here. Let us search the paths through the fields."

The officials and constables made their way through the tea-garden and vegetable fields. Magoémon appeared, barefoot.

" How is it, Chūzaburō ? Tell me quick, are they all right or not ? "

" Have no fear, sir. I have so managed that both have made good their escape."

" Thanks be to Heaven! This is the Lord Buddha's favour ! Let us at once visit the temple and offer up thanksgiving. How glad I am ! How glad ! "

They were preparing to depart when a knot of persons, gathered at a short distance, suddenly cried, " Kaméya Chūbei and Umégawa of Tsuchiya have been arrested ! " A moment later the constables returned, convoying the young lovers, now bound with cords.

Magoémon swooned at the sight. His spirit all but passed from his body. Umégawa wept bitterly.

" Listen all of you ! " cried Chūbei. " I have done wrong and I am quite prepared for death. I beseech you to pray for me when my soul shall have quitted this body." He turned to the guard. " Sirs," he said, " my father's agony strikes me to the heart and will torture my soul in Hades. For mercy's sake, cover my face."

A sympathetic officer blinded him with a scarf, as the devil is blinded in blindman's buff.

What further fate was theirs tongue need not recite. Suffice to say their names remain upon the roll of those whom passion has made its prey.

HISAMATSU AND O-SOMÉ PRODUCED AT THE BUNRAKU-ZA.

MR. TSUDAYŪ, A FAMOUS *JŌRURI* CHANTER, MAKING HIMSELF
READY FOR THE STAGE

HIYOSHIMARU AND THE YOUNG CHERRY-TREE, BY CHIKAMATSU HANJI, PERFORMED AT THE BUNRAKU-ZA

PUPPETS OF OLDEN DAYS

From an illustration in an old book, the *Seikyoku Ruisan*.

No. 4

THE LOVE SUICIDE AT AMIJIMA

(*Shinjū Ten-no-Amijima*)

THE LOVE SUICIDE AT AMIJIMA

(*Shinjū Ten-no-Amijima*)

I

So long as it remains true that " the ocean cannot be emptied with a tiny *shijimi* [1] shell " [2] so long may we say love will exert its dominion over the human heart ; and well may Sonézaki-Shinchi, the quarter of light-o'-loves in Osaka, be called an ocean of love, and it does not seem mere chance that the river running by the quarter is called Shijimi.

The early winter's evening at Sonézaki-Shinchi glimmered, softly illumined by the inscribed lanterns of the tea-houses. Through the thronged streets young rakes were strolling, singing folk-songs as they went, reciting fragments of puppet dramas or imitating famous actors at their dialogues. From the upper room of many a tea-house floated the gay plucking of *samisen*, and so witching was the music as to entice certain of the frequenters of the district to visit the courtesans. Others, who had donned disguise, more freely to enjoy the merry atmosphere of the streets, being detected by the tea-house maids, were beguiled into visiting this or that house.

The bridges spanning the Shijimi River are named " Plum-Blossom " and " Cherry-Blossom " ; and in this district, among the numerous girls, no less lovely than these flowers, was a damsel of supreme beauty named Koharu of the brothel Kinokuni-ya.

Escorted by Sugi, her maid, she was even now about to

---

[1] A kind of corbicula.　　　　　　　　[2] A proverb.

pass a lantern hung out as a sign, pondering the while who would be her patron this coming night, when another of the sisterhood, on the way back to her master's brothel, halted beside her.

" Ah ! Koharu Sama," she said, " I haven't seen you for a long time nor heard from you.   How much thinner you have grown !   You are unwell perhaps ?   A certain ittle bird told me your master is very particular as to whom you entertain on account of your love for Jihei Sama and that it isn't often you're allowed to be invited out to other tea houses ; while another little bird tells me you have been ransomed by Tahei Sama and are off with him into the country to Itami.   Which is true ? "

" Sh !   My dear friend, don't mention Itami.   I hate the name.   Poor Jihei Sama !   He and I are not particularly close, but that braggart of a Tahei has put about a rumour concerning us, so that all my patrons have forsaken me, and my master, who lays all this at Jihei's door, keeps him away from me and I cannot even write to him.   Oddly enough I am being sent to-night on the command of a samurai to the tea- house Kawachi-ya.   Making my way thither, as I now am, I am very nervous of encountering that wretch Tahei.   It's as if I had a mortal enemy seeking to avenge himself upon me.   Hist !   Do you make him out over there ? "

" Perhaps.   You had best hide yourself.   See—a strolling singer [1] approaches, reciting something comical, and among the listening crowd there's a young man with his hair dressed in the fashionable style and who seems to be well pleased with himself.   It is Tahei Sama, I'll be bound.   See—they're coming this way."

---

[1] The Japanese name is *namaida-bōzu*. The *namaida-bōzu* was a strolling singer dressed in the style of a Buddhist priest. He recited fragments of puppet drama or folk-songs, accompanying himself on a tiny bell which he struck with a little stick. His recitations concluded with the repetition of " Namaida " which is a comical modification of the Buddhist invocation " Namu Amida Buddha ".

In less time than it takes to tell, the singer, garbed in a large fantastic hood and a black robe, came up followed by a crowd, reciting the while after a comic style and to the accompaniment of a tiny bell :——

> "'The Han-Kwai[1] style of breaking
> The castle gate is commonplace.
> Thus does a Japanese do!'
> With this he broke the bar,
> Leaped over the entanglements,
> Uryōko knocked down, and Saryōko,
> And quickly broke into the castle.[2]
> Namaida! Namaida! Namaida!

> 'He wandered and wandered
> In quest of his dear Matsuyama:
> No shadow of her could he find.
> Then when his grief turned his wits
> All day he laughed and wept,
> Until at length exhausted
> He stretched him on the turf.
> What misery! Oh, what a plight![3]
> Namaida! Namaida! Namaida!

> '*Ei! Ei! Ei! Ei!*
> The dyer Tokubei's heart
> Was deeply dyed with love for Fusa.
> So large was his property
> That even dye could not wash it off.[4]
> Namaida! Namaida! Namaida!'"

" My good fellow," said Koharu's attendant Sugi, " such doleful ballading of deaths for love is poor hearing. Here at Sonézaki, I am glad to say, such things have ceased to be heard of. Won't you give us the *michiyuki* [5] of Kokusenya ? "

---

[1] A famous Chinese hero.

[2] A paragraph of *The Battles of Kokusenya*, a puppet-play by the author, enjoying such popularity with the Osaka people that any paragraph of it was of interest to them.

[3] A paragraph from a puppet-play entitled *The Madness of Wankyū.*

[4] A portion of a comic song based on *The Love Suicide at the Kasané-Izutsu*, a puppet-play by the author. The song is also by the author.

[5] The narrative of the journey of the hero or heroine or both in a puppet-play. It is a description both epical and lyrical and generally forms the most beautiful paragraph of the play.

She proffered a coin. The singer looked at it and murmured :

> "Pooh ! It doesn't pay to make a long tour
> To China three *sen*[1] (thousand) miles away,
> For the sum of one or two *sen !*
> Oh ! It doesn't pay ! Oh ! It doesn't pay !"

The singer made off.

Koharu, parting from her friend, deftly threaded the throng
and hastened into the Kawachi-ya.

" You are quickly here, Koharu Sama," said the mistress
of the tea-house gaily. " I haven't set eyes on you for a long
time. I am indeed delighted to see you, my dear Koharu
Sama, my dearest Koharu Sama."

" Hush, madame ! Please don't repeat my name so loud
lest it carry without the door, for the hateful Ri Tōten [2]
himself is there. Please be quiet, dear madame."

But it was too late. Tahei and two other young men
suddenly entered.

" Koharu Dono," said Tahei with a sardonic smile, " let
me hasten to thank you for bestowing on me the good name
of Ri Tōten. Gentlemen, this is the Koharu Dono who, as
I told you, is known for her warm-heartedness and generous
treatment of her guests. Please hasten to make her acquaintance. It is not beyond dreaming that she may soon enough
become my wife or—who knows ?—shortly be ransomed by
my rival Jihei."

With these words he approached her haughtily.

" What nonsense ! " said she indignantly, drawing away
from him. " Jihei Sama is a stranger to me. If it does you
credit to give him a bad name be as diligent as you please in
this, but don't let me hear such nonsense."

---

[1] *Sen* means either " thousand " or " a small sum of money ". The passage
contains a play upon the words. Most of the scenes in *The Battles of Kokusenya*
are laid in China, in olden times said to be three thousand miles away from Japan.

[2] A villain in the play *The Battles of Kokusenya*.

" Even though you mayn't want to hear it," said Tahei, drawing closer once more, " I'll put you in the way of hearing it none the less, with the jingling of gold coins. You are indeed a lucky woman, Koharu Dono, to be loved by Jihei, of all the numberless men of Osaka, a nice little paper-dealer—the father of two children, whose wife is his cousin and whose father-in-law is his aunt's husband. Alas! His business is in such a poor way that he can hardly make two ends meet at the end of the quarter. And yet he proposes to pay a ransom of two hundred *ryō* for you. Bah! It's an impossibility! I, on the other hand, have neither wife nor children, nor father-in-law nor parents and no uncles to lean on me. I am widely known as ' Bondless Tahei '. True, I am no match at boasting in the pleasure quarter for that fellow Jihei; but you observe I am by no means lacking in riches and in that respect I have the better of him. Indeed, as far as money goes, I am anybody's master. I am sure Koharu's guest to-night is Jihei, but madame, I will take his place. ' Bondless Tahei ' will possess Koharu Dono to-night. Well, a drink, madame."

" Keep a watch on your tongue," said the proprietress bluntly. " To-night's guest is a samurai and he will be here shortly. Will you please be so good as to take your spree elsewhere."

" Madame," replied Tahei with a laugh, " samurai and tradesmen alike are your guests, whether they wear swords or no. No samurai can wear as many as five or six swords; two suffice him. To-night I will invite Koharu Dono and her samurai into the bargain. However much you try to avoid me, Koharu Dono, you cannot help meeting me—for we are closely related by affinity. I owe this meeting with you to the strolling singer. Miraculous is the efficacy of prayer made to Amida Buddha. So let me make my prayer. And do you listen."

Then, striking with a tobacco pipe on the fire pan of the tobacco tray by way of accompaniment, he cried aloud in imitation of the strolling singer :

> "*Ei! Ei! Ei! Ei!*
> The paper-dealer Jihei
> Is infatuated with Koharu;
> And his property has become
> As thin as rice-paper
> And thinner than toilet-paper.
> Jihei is worthless as waste-paper
> Which is not good enough
> Even to blow the nose with.
> Namaida! Namaida! Namaida!"

At that moment someone stealthily peeped in at the entrance, the face being largely concealed by a muffler and the low brim of his *amigasa* or braided hat.   Catching sight of this apparition Tahei mocked :

" Aha !   Here is Toilet-paper !   What a pretty disguise ! Pray step in, Waste-paper.   Coward, are you afraid of my Namaida prayer to Amida Buddha ? "   With these words he dragged the man into the room.   Profound was his surprise and fear when the newcomer proved to be a two-sworded samurai, who glared upon him with a savage expression. Tahei, speechless, ejaculated " Ah ! "   But, hurriedly composing himself, resumed :

" Now, Koharu Dono, I am only a tradesman and have never worn a sword, but it's not beyond possibility that the glint of gold coins in my coffer may outshine any sword. Presumptuous is it in a mere toilet-paper seller, with a capital as thin as rice-paper, to attempt to vie with ' Bondless Tahei.'   If I take a stroll between Cherry-Blossom Bridge and Nakamachi Street I should be able to put my foot on Waste-paper somewhere thereabouts.   Let us be off, friends."

Tahei and his companions made off haughtily enough.

To avoid a scene in the pleasure quarter the samurai was compelled to accept this affront.   Stung to the quick by these

MR. JAKUÉMON

MR. JAKUÉMON AS *KOHARU*

[*face p.* 228

vilifications of her lover, Koharu, lost in thought, did not greet her new guest. Sugi ran in, cast a hurried look about and exclaimed :

" When I escorted Koharu Sama here just now her guest had not arrived, so I went back, but no sooner was I home than I was severely rebuked for not inspecting the guest. Pardon my rudeness, sir."

Forcing up the samurai's hat she narrowly scanned his face.

" Well, it's not he, not he. There's no occasion for nervousness. Have a pleasant time, Koharu Sama, with this gentleman. Good-bye, madame. I will return later."

She departed in haste. The serious samurai was much displeased.

" What behaviour," he grumbled. " Did the maid think me a tea-caddy or a tea-cup that she examined my face as a connoisseur does a curio ? Understand, madame, that at our official residence entrance and exit are closely watched, even by day, and notice must be given to the officer in charge if one intends stopping out even one night that he may enter it in his book. Despite such strict regulations I have contrived a pretext to pay this call unaccompanied by my servant this night—that I may meet Koharu Dono, the famous courtesan, whom I have so longed after. Not long ago I was here and arranged with you for this interview, wasn't I ? And, Koharu Dono, how eagerly I have expected that you would deign to let me enjoy myself with you to-night. Deep is my disappointment. You have not favoured me either with a pleasant smile or a word of greeting, but all the while have been gazing downwards as if counting the money in your bosom. I fear your neck must ache. Madame, no gentleman comes to a tea-house to attend a woman in childbirth ! "

" Your reproaches are justified," pleaded the mistress, " I do not wonder you consider Koharu's attitude strange. The fact is she has a particularly intimate guest named

Kamiya [1] Jihei Sama. Day and night he paid her visits so that no other patron could have access to her, until at last all have been scattered like autumn leaves overtaken by storm. When relations reach such a pitch things can't but turn out badly. Koharu Sama's master has no patience with these passionate lovers and so, according to the usual proceeding in such cases, all her guests have to undergo scrutiny to make sure that Jihei Sama is not one of them. That's the reason for her low spirits, sir."

She turned to the girl.

" As mistress of this tea-house, Koharu Sama, I must ask you to do your best to entertain your guest. Come, take a cup and make merry with the gentleman. Now, be good, Koharu Sama."

The girl made no answer, but, lifting a tearful face, abruptly inquired :

" Is it true, Sir Knight, that one who dies in the ' Ten Nights ' [2] shall go to paradise ? "

" How should I know such a thing ? You had best ask the priest of your family temple."

" You are right. I have another question to ask you. Which is the more painful method of suicide, by the knife or the rope ? "

" How should I know ? " replied the samurai disgustedly. " I have never cut my throat. What a question ! And what a disagreeable young person ! "

" Come, Koharu Sama, what a way to greet a new guest ! Come, cheer up, my girl. Well, well, I wonder when my hus-

---

[1] " Kamiya " signifies " paper-dealer ", but in feudal Japan tradesmen, among whom the luxury of surnames was unknown, often used such professional titles as surnames.

[2] The period from the 6th to the 15th of October (by the lunar calendar) is known among Buddhists as the *Jūya* or " Ten Nights " and they have a saying :—Such as in the Ten Nights dies finds the way to paradise. During these days pious Buddhists make special visits to their family temples where they hold prayer meetings.

band will be back. I'll be off and fetch him to prepare a feast for you. Be good enough to excuse me a while, sir."

The mistress sought the street.

The crescent moon by this time neared the horizon ; the clouds were lifting ; and the passers-by were few.

Kamiya Jihei, proprietor of a paper shop at Temma, no great distance off the pleasure quarter, becoming infatuated with Koharu, had neglected his business and given way to a life of dissipation. The passionate pair, prevented from meeting each other, falling into a state of desperation, had secretly exchanged letters vowing suicide together upon the first renewal of their meetings. Night after night had Jihei, heavily disguised, wandered the streets of Sonézaki Shinchi. This night he again made his appearance in the quiet streets. Having his face half covered with a kerchief and a short sword at his side, he was now walking stealthily, a far-away expression upon his face. At a chop-house he learned that Koharu was even now at the Kawachi-ya with a samurai guest. It seemed to him his opportunity was come at last. He hastened to the front of the tea-house and peeping through the lattice beheld Koharu sitting in the inner room [1] and opposite her a samurai about whose face was bound a muffler. He observed the samurai's chin move, but the voice was inaudible, and scanning Koharu's profile, illuminated by the lamp-light, Jihei said to himself, " How thin the poor girl has grown ! She thinks of nothing but me. How I wish I could whisper to her that I am here and should like to elope with her. How I long to let her know of my coming ! How I long to call her by name ! " Overcome by his emotion he clung to the lattice and gave way to tears. Within, the samurai gave a prodigious yawn and remarked, " It's poor fun tending

---

[1] Even in winter it often happens that the paper doors of the tea-house are left open, with the result that the interiors of both the front and the inner rooms on the ground floor are visible from outside the lattice.

a love-sick maiden. Since the street seems to be quiet I'll go to the front room and divert myself looking at the sign-lantern. Come with me, girl."

With these words he entered the front room bringing Koharu with him. Jihei, startled, stooped and hid himself in the shadow of the wall beneath the lattice that he might hear their talk.

" Now, Koharu Dono," said the samurai softly in amiable tones, " I judge from your manner and speech that you are resolved to commit suicide with this lover Jihei of whom madame has spoken. I am right, am I not ? Neither kind advice nor reason can gain the ear of one possessed by the God of Death ; nothing however could be more foolish than your intention. Your lover's relatives would not resent his rashness, but all their hatred and reproach would be heaped on you. Your dead face moreover would be exposed to the public gaze. That is a great disgrace. I don't know whether your parents are alive or no. If living you may be sure that your undutifulness towards them would bring down upon you Heaven's punishment. Not only would you be unable to fare hand in hand with your lover toward paradise, but even such a journey to hell would be forbidden. Albeit I meet you this evening for the first time it is impossible for me as a samurai to refrain from taking some action to rescue you from such a humiliating death. I am sure it is a matter of money. Well, I can accommodate you with five or ten *ryō* if that will prevent your death. And I will swear to secrecy by Tenshō Daijin and Hachiman and on the honour of a samurai. Pray confide all your secrets to me."

" How kind you are, sir," Koharu responded, clasping her hands, " how grateful I feel ! Your kind offer supported by an oath makes me weep for gratitude. You have exactly hit the mark : I have, as you guess, taken a vow to die with Jihei Sama. Owing to my master, we are prevented from seeing

A SCENE FROM *THE LOVE SUICIDE AT AMIJIMA*

From a colour print by the two Toyokunis. *Jihei* by Toyokuni (Kōchōrō). *Koharu* by Toyokuni
(Ichiyōsai)

" Jihei unsheathed his sword, and, making a pass for Koharu's side, thrust it through the lattice."

each other and Jihei Sama's circumstances do not permit of him ransoming me at present, while his rival, a rich man, is arranging for my ransom. Out of despair, then, he begged of me to die with him and I was forced to say ' Yes, I will die '. I promised him to seize the first opportunity to steal out and to join him in his journey to Hades. I am indeed due to die any day at any moment. My mother, whose only support I am, is living miserably in the slums. At my death she is likely to become a beggar and may eventually die the death of a dog. Thinking of her fate sorrow overcomes me. Moreover I have but one life. You may think me an insincere woman, but to tell the truth I am anxious to escape death if possible. I beseech you, sir, to do something to save me from death."

At this the samurai nodded his head and fell into deep thought. As for Jihei, her unexpected confession amazed him beyond measure. Beside himself with anger, " Was all she said a lie ? " he asked himself. " What rage I feel ! Two long years have I been bewitched. Fox ! Badger ! Shall I rush in and strike her ? Or shall I revile her to my heart's content ? "

He ground his teeth and gave way to tears of mortification.

Within doors Koharu spoke through her tears :—

" I have a cowardly request to make you, sir. Will you be so good as to come to see me frequently from now on till about March next, so as to be in Jihei's way whenever he comes with intent to die with me. I hope that while the tragic hour is thus delayed my relations with him will come to a natural end and both be thus saved from death. I wonder now why I was inclined to vow to die with him. I deeply regret it."

Thus speaking she wept, leaning on the samurai's bosom.

" I comply with your request and I have an idea. There is a draught and people may see us."

So saying he shut the paper doors behind the lattice *bata-bata*. Jihei flew into a frenzy of passion. Oh! The woman was a thing for sale! Cheap goods! He had been infatuated with a mere light-fingered wanton. Should it be point or edge? Even now their faces were silhouetted on the paper doors. Oh! To beat her, to trample her down! What were they plotting? They nodded each to each; one worshipped the other; they whispered and made low exclamations. Unavailing was Jihei's effort to control himself. He was now past all holding. He unsheathed his sword—an excellent blade by Seki-no-Magoroku—and, making a pass for Koharu's side, thrust it through the lattice. The couple started, but no injury was done for they were sitting out of reach. The samurai immediately sprang forward, seized the would-be assassin's hands, drew them in and in a trice tied them with the cord of his sword fast to the post of the lattice.

" Koharu," said he, " make no ado. Don't peep out."

At this juncture the proprietor and his wife returned, to halt amazed at the scene.

" What's the matter, sir ? "

" Nothing's the matter   This fellow barbarously thrust in a drawn sword through the paper doors. So I have tied his hands to the post. I have a plan in my head. Let him alone lest we gather spectators. Come with me, Koharu, let us repose together."

She answered " Yes, sir," but the sword being one familiar to her eyes her spirit received a wound from the blade which had failed to pierce her side.

" You see," she pleaded gently, " drunken folk often misbehave themselves like that when in the pleasure quarter. So I think, Kawachi-ya San, we had best let him go unpunished, hadn't we ? "

" No, indeed," said the samurai, " leave the matter to me Let us go in. This way, Koharu."

They entered the inner room. The more Jihei struggled, the more the cord tightened about his wrists. Realizing to the full the bitterness of his plight he gave way to tears of mortification. Tahei, returning from a stroll, caught sight of him.

" If I am not mistaken that's Jihei standing at the lattice of the Kawachi-ya. I'll trip him up."

He seized Jihei by the collar and shook him.

" Do you call out, you coward ? So you're tied, are you ? Aha ! I have it ! You're a thief ! You're a pickpocket ! "— he drubbed him with a closed fist—" burglar ! A face for a pike ! "—he kicked him—" Hi ! Kamiya Jihei has been thieving and someone has tied him up here ! "

Upon this a crowd collected. The samurai rushed out. " Are you the fellow," he cried, " who called this man a thief ? Come, tell me what Jihei has stolen ? " He seized Tahei and thrust his face to the ground. Whenever Tahei struggled to rise he pressed him down again and holding him thus in a firm grip cried : " Come, Jihei, stamp on this fellow and revenge yourself." So saying he thrust his captive down to Jihei's feet. Tied up as he was Jihei trampled upon the prostrate form. At length, covered with dirt, Tahei rose and glared upon the crowd. " Lookers-on, you have suffered me to be maltreated, but I have taken note of every face and I'll have you know I shall not fail to take revenge upon each one of you."

Thus he spoke and then took to his heels. The crowd burst out laughing. " He gets trampled on and yet he clacks his tongue like that ! Let's throw him from the bridge. Drown him ! He shan't get off ! " The crowd pursued him pell-mell. The samurai advanced on Jihei, untied the cord, removed his own muffler and uncovered his face.

" What ! " exclaimed Jihei astonished. " Is it my brother Magoémon Dono ? Shame overcomes me."

He sat down on the ground and wept bitterly. Koharu

ran out of the house. " Are you really Jihei Sama's elder brother ? " she cried.

Abruptly Jihei rose to his feet to seize the girl by the breast of her dress. " Beast ! Fox ! I'd rather trample on you than Tahei." So saying he raised his leg, but Magoémon stopped him.

" How can you ? " he cried reproachfully. " Your foolishness is a source of never-ending trouble. I hope you now see that it is the business of a courtesan to cozen folks. At first sight I saw into the bottom of this girl's heart. Blockhead that you are to have been unable to look into the heart of a woman whom you have visited day and night for more than two years. Why don't you stamp on your own stupid wits instead of on Koharu ? The pity of it—you, Jihei, are close on thirty and a father of two children, your son and daughter, Kantarō and O-Sué, six and four years old. And in spite of this you have given yourself up to dissipation night and day, blind to the fast dwindling of your fortune and in despite of my well-intentioned advice. Your wife's father is your aunt's husband, your mother-in-law is your aunt, as good as a real mother to you, and your wife O-San is a cousin of mine, thus all the members of your family are closely related by blood. At the meetings of our relatives they talk of nothing but your everlasting visits to the pleasure quarter. Your poor aunt ! Her husband, Gozaémon Dono, an unamiable old-fashioned fellow, got hot about you. ' My beloved daughter,' he said, ' is shamefully treated by my wife's nephew. I'll take O-San back and make him notorious throughout Temma.' But your aunt pleaded for you and has taken such pains to cover up the tale of your misdeeds that she is almost ill. You're an ungrateful cad, bound for illluck, if only by reason of punishment for your ingratitude. Under the present circumstances, unless steps be taken, your house will come to ruin. To save your family from such misfortunes and to reassure our aunt I thought I ought first to sound Koharu as to her intentions. I therefore arranged with the proprietor for this night's visit and have thus been able to ascertain the cause of all your anguish. It seems natural enough in you perhaps to desert wife and children for the sake of such a warm-hearted, truthful bit of goods. You have done very well, Jihei. Thanks to a wise brother, Koya [1] Magoémon, a merchant of some reputation, has been compelled to disguise himself as a two-sworded samurai and play the fool like a minor actor. I might well be taken for a person in fancy dress at a carnival or for a madman. I don't know what to do with these swords. My heart is hot both with anger and with a sense of the ridiculous."

He ground his teeth and frowned, with difficulty repressing tears. Meanwhile Koharu continued sobbing and all she could find to say was, " You are quite right, sir, you are quite right."

Jihei patted the ground in sign of indignation. "Pardon me, brother, oh, pardon me ! The pity of it !—These long years have I been eaten up with regard for this old badger and have neglected my family and relatives. I grieve that, cozened by this thief of a Koharu, I have wasted my property. This very moment do I give her up once and for all. Never will I set foot again in this neighbourhood. Listen, you badger, you fox, you thief, you ! Here's proof that I give you up "—he produced an amulet case from his bosom— " here are the written vows you have made me, one at the beginning of every month these three years : twenty-nine altogether. Once I restore these papers I owe you neither love nor sympathy. Take these back, you harlot ! "—he threw the papers toward her—" Take back, brother, in exchange, the written vows I have made her, count them up

---

[1] " Koya " means " flour-merchant ", but is here used as a surname.

and burn them yourself. Come now, girl, hand them over to my brother."

" As you will, Jihei Sama."

With tears the girl handed over her amulet case to Magoé-mon, who took the papers out and counted them. " One, two, three, four . . . ten . . . twenty-nine. The number is correct. Ah, here's a letter in a woman's hand. Whose can it be ? " He was making as if to open it when Koharu endeavoured to stop him saying, " That's an important letter which I can't let you see." He pushed her aside and scrutinized the superscription by the light of the lamp. To his amaze the address read : " To Koharu Sama from Kamiya O-San." However, he pocketed the missive conclusively enough.

" Koharu, a little while back I swore by the honour of a samurai. Now let me take an oath on the honour of a merchant that I will show this letter to nobody, not even to my wife. I will read it in private and afterward I will burn it with the other papers. Rest assured I will not break this oath."

" Thank you, sir," she returned, sinking to the ground, " my honour is preserved."

" Your honour ? Stuff and nonsense ! Come, brother, I won't look on her a minute longer. Let us away. Great is my regret and mortification. I can control myself no longer. Let me place my foot upon the hussy's face if but once only." Jihei advanced and stamped upon the ground. " A thousand pities ! This very moment with my foot I bid an everlasting farewell to all the love and affection I have spent upon you these three years." He kicked her on the forehead. She gave a cry of pain. The brothers sorrowfully departed. Touching was the gaze wherewith Koharu followed them. Was she crafty and false of heart or a truthful, warm-hearted woman ? Whatever her true nature was it was bound up in a mysterious letter from O-San, Jihei's wife.

A SCENE FROM *THE LOVE SUICIDE AT AMIJIMA*
MR. GANJIRŌ AS *JIHEI*   MR. JAKUÉMON AS *KOHARU*

II

Jihei's house and paper shop, in a thriving street by the Tenjin [1] Shrine at Temma, was a business of old standing, and despite the master's long neglect of business it yet retained some appearance of prosperity—a prosperity entirely due to the efforts of his wife, O-San, ever busy about deals with customers and the management of household affairs. At present Jihei was dozing at the *kotatsu* [2] in the sitting-room.   O-San set a bed screen by him to shut out the draught. Beyond the window visitors, come to the Buddhist temple to celebrate the Ten Nights, were seen passing.

" The evening is drawing in," O-San said to herself, not without concern.   " Supper-time is already come.   I wonder what Tama, my maid, whom I sent on an errand to Ichino-kawa, is doing ?   Why hasn't that idiot of a Sangorō come back ?   The wind is chill.   My children must be feeling cold. Doesn't he know now is the time O-Sué wants her milk ? What an idiot !   I shall surely lose patience."

" Mama," said her son running in, " I have come home alone."

" Is that you, Kantarō ?   I am glad to see you back. What are O-Sué and Sangorō doing, my darling ? "

" We played at the shrine.   O-Sué cried hard for milk."

" That's natural enough.   Your hands and feet are stiff as wood.   Warm yourself at the *kotatsu* by which your

---

[1] A famous shrine dedicated to the great minister and scholar, Sugawara-no-Michizané, or Kwan Shōjō, who, a victim of calumny, was in A.D. 901 degraded to the post of Vice-President of Dazaifu or Governor-Generalship of the island of Kyūshū and died in exile two years later.   Throughout Japan he is worshipped as the God of Calligraphy.   It is almost always the custom to plant a plum-tree near his temple since this was his favourite tree.   Tradition avers that the most beautiful plum-tree in his garden at Kyoto flew after him to Dazaifu.

[2] A fireplace in the floor covered with a large thick quilt.

father is sleeping. What shall I do with that idiot of a Sangorō ? "

Impatiently she ran out to the shop, only to meet Sangorō lazily returning without his charge.

" Come, you idiot, where have you left baby ? "

" Let me see now. I must have let her drop somewhere. Somebody's probably picked her up. Shall I go back and have a look for her ? "

" Alas ! " O-San cried angrily. " If my darling is hurt I'll beat you to death."

At this moment the maid Tama returned carrying the baby on her back. " Poor baby ! " she exclaimed. " I found her crying at the cross-roads, madame. Sangorō, if you are going to take care of the baby you must do so properly."

" My darling," said the mother caressing her child, " how much you must have wanted your milk ! "

She took the little one to the *kotatsu* where she suckled it, saying :—" Well, Tama, let the idiot have [1] it, so that he will long remember it."

" No, madame, we have had enough already, thank you," said Sangorō jocosely. " Just now I let each of the children have a couple of sweet oranges and I myself had five."

The women smiled grimly.

" Chattering with this idiot I have almost forgotten the more important matter, but I just now saw Magoémon Sama and your mother approaching from the west."

" Are they indeed coming ? If so I ought to wake my husband. Now, my dear, wake up. My mother and your brother are approaching, so Tama says. Should they find you, a merchant, dozing in the daytime—and the days as short as they are now—they would be vexed again for certain."

" All right." Jihei rose, hurried to the shop and, seating himself at the desk, pretended to be very busy reckoning

---

[1] This and the following speech contain an untranslatable play on words.

MR. GANJIRŌ AS *JIHEI*   MR. FUKUSUKÉ (OSAKA) AS *O-SAN*

" O-San wonderingly approached him and, putting aside the quilt, found him weeping so
bitterly that the tears rained thickly upon the pillow."

MR. FUKUSUKÉ (OSAKA)

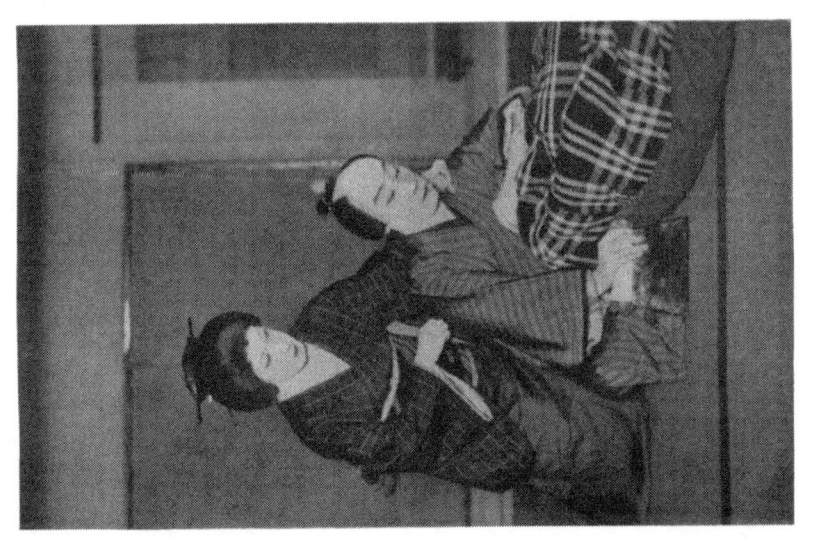

MR. FUKUSUKÉ (OSAKA) AS O-SAN (left)

on the abacus and in consulting the book beside it. " Ten divided by two is five ; nine by three is three ; six by three is two ; . . . er, seven times eight is. . . ."

The fifty-six-year-old [1] aunt and Magoémon stepped in.

" Ah, aunt and brother," Jihei greeted them, looking up from the abacus, " pray step in. I have just begun making up a pressing account. Pardon me if I finish it. Four times nine is thirty-six ; three times six is eighteen, and two over. Now, you two, Kantarō and O-Sué, grandmama and uncle have come. Bring the tobacco tray. Three times one is three (san). Here, O-San, bring tea." [2]

" By no means ! " exclaimed the mother-in-law bluntly. " The object of our call is not to drink tea or to smoke tobacco. Now, O-San, young as you are, you are the mother of two children. It is not enough for you to be merely good-natured. A husband's evil courses are undoubtedly traceable to a wife's want of care. When losses compel a man and wife to part, the man is not alone to blame. You must keep wide awake."

" How mistaken you are ! " said Magoémon. " The sly fellow who deceives even his brother wouldn't take advice from a wife. Yai,[3] Jihei, how shamelessly you have deceived me ! In my presence the other day you returned the courtesan her written vows and now, before ten days are out, you are proposing to ransom her. Good-for-nothing ! This very moment you are totting up Koharu's debts. Stop it ! "

So saying he snatched the abacus from Jihei's hands and flung it into the yard.

" The charge is unjust," Jihei pleaded. " Since last we met I haven't crossed the threshold of my house except to call

---

[1] The full flavour of this joke is but with difficulty appreciable in English.

[2] This speech is replete with verbal humours such as must produce their effect upon the stage, being dependent rather upon the situation and the motions of Jihei, hesitant between his abacus and his visitors, than upon the written page.

[3] A Japanese exclamation of reproach.

twice at the wholesale dealer's at Imabashi and to pay one visit to the Tenjin Shrine. I haven't even called that old badger to mind, much less thought of ransoming her."

" Who is going to swallow that ? " inquired the mother-in-law excitedly. " At the Ten Nights' prayer meeting last night the congregation talked of nothing else. The rumour ran that a *daijin* [1] at Temma who has particularly close relations with a courtesan named Koharu of the tea-house Kinokuni-ya at Sonézaki has supplanted all other patrons and proposes to ransom her to-day or to-morrow. So the rumour ran, and they added, ' What a lot of money there must be even in these hard times and what fools there are in the world.' This piece of gossip indeed occupied the whole evening. My husband, Gozaémon Dono, to whose ear the name of the woman sounded only too familiar, was extremely mortified to hear it. When he got home in a high state of excitement, he said ' The silly *daijin* at Temma can be none other than that villain Jihei. Though my wife's nephew, he is no kin to me. My daughter means more to me than he does. A fool bent upon ransoming a tea-house woman is quite capable of selling his wife to a tea-house. So, before he sells O-San's dresses, I must go and bring her and her belongings back. There is not a moment to lose.' With those words he was half-way out of the house. But I stopped him and soothed him down saying, ' Don't be overhasty, my dear. I think we can better manage the matter quietly, after assuring ourselves as to the truth of the rumour.' That is the reason of our call. I rejoiced to hear Magoémon say ' The Jihei of to-day is not the Jihei of yesterday. He has broken with Sonézaki and most certainly turned over a new leaf ' ; but no sooner did I get the good news than his con-

[1] A rich man who spends extravagantly in the pleasure quarter is called a *daijin.* A *daijin* signifies literally " a great spender ". Etymologically the word is probably originated from another word of the same pronunciation meaning " a minister of state ".

fidence proved to be ill-founded.   What an evil spirit is yours
indeed ! Your poor father, my elder brother, admonished
me on his deathbed saying, ' Sister dear, take care of Jihei,
who is both son-in-law and nephew to you.'   His words still
ring in my ears, but your viciousness is a stumbling-block to
my carrying out his dying instructions.   It is a thing that
grieves me to the core."

She sank her face upon her hands and wept tears of the
bitterest resentment.

" Aha ! " said Jihei, clapping his hands.   " The Koharu
talked of is undoubtedly the Koharu in question, but the
daijin who proposes to ransom her, that's a different matter.
It must be that ' Bondless Tahei,' who, you remember, behaved so outrageously the other night and whom I trampled
on.   The fellow has neither wife nor family.   He can draw
money freely from his native place Itami, and, but for my
rivalry, he would long ago have ransomed her.   Happy to
find his opportunity come at last, I'm sure it's he who has
arranged for her ransom.   At all events I have nothing to do
with the matter."

At this O-San recovered her good humour.

" Good-natured woman I may be, mother," she said, " but
that's no reason why I should side with my husband ransoming
a tea-house woman.   It's the real truth he is speaking ; of
that I feel sure."

These assurances set both aunt and nephew so much at ease
that they clapped their hands for joy.

" I am relieved to hear you, Jihei," said the aunt, " but
about such matters one cannot be too careful.   To dispel any
remaining doubts that my husband may retain I should like
to have it in the form of a sworn statement.   Do you
consent ? "

" Most certainly.   I am ready to write a thousand such."

" I rejoice to hear you say so," said Magoémon, producing

a sheet of paper from his bosom. " You see, this is *Kumano-Goō* [1] paper, I bought it on the way here. Please write your statement upon it."

Jihei took the paper and forthwith wrote down a vow to the effect that he had broken with and given up Koharu, and that, should his vow prove false, might he be punished by the Gods Bonten and Taishaku, by the Four Great Elements [2] and by all the other Gods and all the Buddhas. This he signed and sealed with blood drawn from his forefinger and then handed it to his brother.

" Thank you, mother and brother," cried O-San joyfully, " now I am indeed reassured. This is the first time my husband has ever written such a solemn undertaking since we had children. You should both of you be happy."

" Excellent, my daughter. Thus resolved, Jihei is sure henceforth to behave steadily and his business consequently to prosper. It is solely for Jihei's good and for the sake of the grandchildren that his relatives put themselves out about him. Let us be off now, Magoémon, for I should like to get home as soon as possible to reassure my husband. Good-bye, O-San, take good care of the children. Now the weather is cold you don't want them to catch a chill. Surely this happy settlement is due to our Ten Nights' prayers to Buddha. Let me make a prayer of thanksgiving now. Namu Amida Buddha."

The pair made off, cheerful enough in the bliss of ignorance.

No sooner had he seen them off the premises than Jihei retraced his steps. No sooner recrossed the threshold than,

---

[1] In early days the Kumano Shrine of Kumano in the province of Kii produced sacred papers for the writing of solemn vows. One side of such a paper was blank, the other side bore the sacred seal. On the seal were represented many sacred crows, messengers of the Kumano God—hence the paper's name *Kumano Goō no Muragarasu*, that is " The Village Crows of Bull-King (another name for Buddha) at Kumano." The papers were on sale throughout Japan.

[2] Earth, water, fire and wind ; which, according to a Buddhist scripture, are the elements of all things.

ying down at the *kotatsu*, he dived under the quilt. Alas !
Had he not yet forgotten Sonézaki ? O-San wonderingly
approached him and, putting aside the quilt, found him
weeping so bitterly that the tears rained thickly upon the
pillow. She raised him to a sitting posture against the frame
of the *kotatsu*. " It is too much," she said gazing intently
into his face. " If you are so reluctant to part from her why
write a vow ? Since the midmost day of the Boar,[1] in October
the year before last, when we lay down here together to
celebrate the opening of the *kotatsu*, you have left my bed
solitary. That is two years ago. Is there an ogre or
serpent in my bosom that you should treat me thus ? Only
through my brother-in-law and mother's mediation have
you been restored to me, and I was looking forward to
talking with you to-night in bed. But alas ! my expectations
have already vanished in a moment. How cruel and cold-
hearted you are ! If you regret her as much as all that you
may weep and weep as much as you choose. May your tears
flow down the Shijimi River and Koharu drink them, heartless wretch that you are ! "

So saying she clung to him with lowered face and commenced to wail.

" Don't cry, O-San dear," said Jihei wiping away his tears.
" If the tears of sorrow came out of the eye and the tears of
mortification out of the ear you might see into my mind
without my pleading ; but all tears coming out of the eye
and being of the same colour it is only natural that you
should not see into my mind. I have no longing after that
woman, that beast in human form. You remember my
enemy, ' Bondless Tahei,' who had lots of money but neither
wife nor family and some time ago was bent upon ransoming
Koharu ? She rejected his offer and vowed to me, ' Have no
fears, my dear ; should our relations be severed so that I

---

[1] There are in a month three days of the Boar : O-San means the second day.

couldn't wed you, I would none the less refuse to be ransomed by Tahei ; and should my master hand me over to him for money I would kill myself.'   Over and over again she repeated this vow to me, yet see how it is, ten days have barely passed ere she consents to being ransomed by Tahei.   My heart no longer yearns after that beast of a woman, but, for all that, the slanderous Tahei is sure to spread the story all over Osaka, ' Reduced to beggary, Jihei couldn't afford to ransom Koharu,' thus humiliating me and discrediting me with the wholesale dealers.   This thought allows me no peace ; I am thrown into a passion by it.   The tears I shed now are more than mere hot tears or tears of blood, they are as of red-hot iron.''

He sank upon his face and burst into bitter tears.   O-San was astonished.   A thought came to her.

" If this be so, Koharu will kill herself.''

" No, ah, no.   Though clever you are as a respectable wife, you know nothing of people in her station of life.   Why should such a liar kill herself ?   She would be more likely to cauterize herself with moxa and take medicine for her health.''

" You do not know her.   I intended to keep the truth from you to my life's end, but now, fearing lest concealment should lead to such a tragedy, I will disclose my secret. Koharu Dono has not an atom of untruthfulness in her.   It was through a trick of mine that you and Koharu were induced to break with each other.   When I saw that you had lost your head about her and were likely to commit suicide with her, I was overcome with grief.   In desperation I wrote to her, beseeching her to sympathize with me and break with you, even at the cost of her love, and thus save you from so rash an act.   Touched by my prayer she returned me a kind letter saying, that though you were her dearest lover, more precious to her than life, yet her sense of duty toward me and her sympathy compelled her to give you up.   See, I carry her letter in the amulet case.   Why suppose that such a woman should break her vow and shamelessly wed Tahei ?   Woman is a constant creature and will not readily change her mind. Koharu will surely kill herself.   She will die.   How terrible ! Come now, save her from death !   You must, my husband."

" Then a letter from an unknown woman," returned the astonished Jihei, " which my brother found among the written vows restored me by Koharu, was the note you had written her. That must be so, mustn't it ?   If so, Koharu must die."

" Die she must.   The pity of it !   Should she die my duty toward her would be unfulfilled.   Please go and stop her."

Bitterly weeping she clung to Jihei.

" So be it . . . but what shall I do ?   It will mean that I must pay at least half her ransom as earnest money.   In order to ensure that Koharu live on in this world it is necessary forthwith to pay one hundred and fifty *ryō*.   Could I raise so much to-day ?   No, not though I be soundly beaten."

" You exaggerate.   If that amount be sufficient nothing can be easier."   Opening a small drawer of the *tansu* [1] she produced a bag and shook a packet out of it.   Jihei took it up and said wonderingly, " That's money ; as much as eighty *ryō*.   How have you raised this ? "

" I will tell you some other time.   This money was intended for the settlement of the paper account, due on the seventeenth.   You can, however, use it for this affair.   Be at your ease about the account ; I will consult with your brother and manage somehow."

She now turned to the large drawers and produced her own and the children's garments—some fifteen sets of beautiful silk clothes containing her best finery—and wrapped them in a *furoshiki*. [2]

" I think you could raise at least seventy *ryō* on these

---

[1] A chest of drawers.
[2] A square piece of cloth used to wrap a parcel in.

clothes. I and the children can get along without finery; but with a man public esteem is everything. So I ask you to take this money and to raise the rest on these clothes, and thus save Koharu from death and keep up your reputation against Tahei."

Jihei, who all this time had been sobbing face to earth, said, "When I have prevented her death by paying the earnest money and thus ransoming her, shall I keep her outside the house? For if I admit her to this house what will you do?"

Before this unlooked-for interrogation O-San was at her wit's end. "Well, we must see. Perhaps I will turn nurse to our children, kitchen-maid or an *inkyo*." [1] She burst into a sudden wail and sat down.

"Ah, no, that's impossible. Even though I should not be visited by my parents' chastisement, Heaven's chastisement and the Buddha's and the Gods' chastisement, yet the chastisement of the knowledge of what I inflicted on you would suffice to make my future life unhappy. I beg your forgiveness, dear wife."

He stretched his hands toward O-San.

"That is too much. Why should you supplicate me? A wife should do everything in her power for her husband. I have pawned almost all my clothes to meet the bills of the wholesale paper merchants so that my *tansu* is now empty, but I do not regret it. The Koharu affair is urgent. You have no time to lose. Come, make haste and change your clothes and be off with a pleasant smile. Make haste now."

His wife assisting him, Jihei dressed himself in fine silk clothes and assumed a sword of medium length ornamented with gold which none but God could tell would be stained with the blood of Koharu this very night. Accompanied by Sangorō carrying the package of clothes upon his back, and bearing the money in person, Jihei was about to step out

---

[1] A person retired from active life, or a hanger-on.

of doors when who should appear but his father-in-law Gozaémon, fur hood in hand, asking, " Is Jihei in ? "

" Ah ! " exclaimed Jihei and O-San in bewilderment, " unlucky meet . . . welcome in."

The old man snatched the package from the boy's back, abruptly sat down and spoke with asperity :

" Sit down, woman. Son-in-law, you cut a fine figure clad in finery and swaggering about with a sword. One would take you for a rakish millionaire, not a paper dealer at all. You are off to Sonézaki, I suppose : very conscientious of you indeed. You evidently have no need of a wife. Divorce O-San ; I have come to take her back."

Jihei was speechless with confusion.

" Father," said O-San softly, " how brave of you to venture out to-day in spite of the cold weather. Do take a sip of tea ! " She proffered her father a cup of tea and continued, " Not long ago mother and Magoémon Sama called and at their earnest entreaties my husband repented of his conduct and, shedding hot tears, wrote a vow to the effect that he was giving up Koharu. That paper he handed to mother. Haven't you seen it yet ? "

" Is this what you mean by a vow ? " exclaimed Gozaémon producing a paper from his bosom. " A foolish prodigal writes vows everywhere and on every occasion. Remembering this, I regarded the paper with doubt, and my doubt I am sorry to say has been justified. How shamefully, Jihei, you have sworn by Bonten and Taishaku ! You would do better to write a letter of divorce than a vow ! "

So saying he tore the paper to pieces and scattered the remains on the floor. Stupefied, the pair regarded each other without speech. A short pause followed. Then Jihei bent his forehead to the ground.

" Father-in-law," said he, " your anger is quite reasonable. I can find no word of excuse for myself, but, of your mercy, permit me to continue as O-San's husband. So much am I indebted to O-San that, even if I should become a beggar or an outcast obliged to live on the leavings of food bestowed by others, yet should I be sure to treat O-San with respect and not to let her suffer whatever I might suffer. The reason will become known to you in course of time if I work diligently to restore my property. Until that day please overlook my past and permit me to continue as O-San's husband. Such is my entreaty."

Jihei burst into tears and pressed his face against the mat.

" Nonsense ! " roared Gozaémon. " How can O-San be an outcast's wife ? Come, write a letter of divorce and be quick about it. I will count the tools and clothes O-San brought at her marriage and affix the seal [1] to them."

He made as if to advance to the chest-of-drawers, but O-San hurriedly barred his way, crying, " Don't, father, my clothes are all right. You need not count them."

Gozaémon thrust her away, pulled open a drawer and to his great surprise found it empty. He tried another and another, but the result was the same. Next he examined the wicker basket, the long chest and the clothes box, but not a rag was to be found in them. The old man's eyes grew furious, while the young pair withered in shame and humiliation.

" I am doubtful about this *furoshiki*," said Gozaémon. He untied the wrapper and put the clothes to disorder. " Fool ! You intended to pawn these, didn't you ? Upon my word, Jihei, you are a beast and not a man thus to strip your wife and children to their skins and go courting a courtesan on the proceeds ! Pickpocket ! Robber ! My wife is aunt to you, but I am no kin of yours. There's no reason why I should suffer loss on your account. I will regain through Magoémon everything belonging to O-San. Come, write a letter of divorce and be quick about it."

---

[1] To seal clothes means to attach to them a piece of paper with a seal upon it, to prevent possible substitution of other clothes in their place.

MR. FUKUSUKÉ (OSAKA) AS *O-SAN*   MR. GANJIRŌ AS *JIHEI*
" Dragged away by Gozaémon, O-San departed reluctantly and in tears."

[*face p.* 250

Against these imputations Jihei found no word of defence. At last he said : " It isn't with a pen that I will write a letter of divorce. See ! " He laid his hand upon his sword-hilt. " Farewell, O-San."

O-San seized his sword and clung to him.

" Father," she pleaded between her sobs, " why don't you heed my husband's words ? Selfish you are and hard-hearted. Though Jihei Dono is no kin of yours, yet my children are your grandchildren. Have you no feeling for them ? I will not accept a letter of divorce."

" So be it ! " exclaimed the old man, seizing O-San by the hand. " I require no letter of divorce. Woman, come with me."

" I will not go," said O-San, snatching her hand away. " I don't give him up, nor does he give me up, and would you have your daughter wash her dirty linen in public by daylight ? "

" And why not ? " inquired Gozaémon, seizing O-San's hand again. " I fully intend to take you back. And, what is more, to publish the fact throughout the entire neighbourhood."

Then she shook him off, but, once more captured, she slipped, and her toes happening to touch the sleeping children they awoke and tearfully reproached their grandfather.

" Grandpapa, why do you take away our dear mummie ? Without mummie whom shall we have to sleep with ? "

" Ah, my children, not one day since you were born have I failed to sleep between you. Now I must go to grandpapa's. So, from to-night, sleep with your papa, my darlings. Husband dear, never forget to see that the little ones take their Kuwayama [1] pills every morning before breakfast. Ah, how miserable I am ! "

---

[1] Pills for children : a patent medicine sold at Osaka. Its method of preparation, a Korean secret, was introduced into Japan by Kuwayama, a retainer of Taikō. Translator's note.

Students of Elizabethan drama may here recall some hint of parallel between

Dragged away by Gozaémon, O-San departed reluctantly and in tears, leaving the sorrow-stricken children. Upon the face of Jihei came an expression of contrition and great despair as he followed father and daughter with his eyes.

III

The small hours were come at Sonézaki ; not a soul was astir ; the stillness was unbroken save by the faint, eerie murmur of the Shijimi River. The moon of mid October shone with such brilliancy as to dim the sign-lantern of the tea-house Yamato-ya.

Passed the fire-watchman, beating his clappers and crying in sleepy tones, " Have a care !   Have a care ! " and the very sound of the clappers seemed to have something sleepy in its monotony.   He had hardly passed when a tea-house maid and a palanquin arrived before the Yamato-ya.   The maid opened the door and vanished within to be faintly audible, saying, " I have come from the Kinokuni-ya with a palanquin to bring Koharu San home." After a brief colloquy she emerged and addressed the bearers :

" Koharu Sama will rest here the night.   You will be wanted no more. . . .   Ah, there's something else I'd for-gotten to say.   Madame, please take special care of Koharu Sama.   Now that the ransom for her has been received from Tahei Sama she is an important charge.   Please do not let

these words and the words of the loveliest of all tragic women in English drama, John Webster's Duchess.   See *The Duchess of Malfi* :—

> Duchess : I pray thee looke thou giv'st my little boy
> Some sirrop for his cold, and let the girl
> > [*Cariola is forced off.*]
> Say her prayers ere she sleep.   Now, what you please :
> What death ?
>
> > Act IV, Scene II, line 109, Sampson's edition.
> > Reviser's Note,

her drink too much." Having said this she made off, the bearers having preceded her.

The night was so far advanced that even the tea-kettle of the tea-house was now at rest and the dim beam of a solitary lamp set by the kettle, streaming through a chink of the doors, glittered upon the frost that littered the street.

" It's still some time till dawn," the proprietor's voice was heard saying, " I had therefore better let my servant see you to your door. Ho! Jihei Sama is going home. Wake Koharu Sama up. Come, call her ! "

" There is no need for that, thank you, Dembei," remarked Jihei, throwing open a side door and stepping out. " Don't let Koharu know. If she knew I should be detained until dawn. I am taking advantage of her present deep sleep to steal away. When the sun is well up wake her and let her go home. When I get home I shall go up to Kyoto to do some buying. Since the transactions will be important, it is not at all certain whether I shall be able to get home precisely by the settlement day. So, from the money I handed you just now, please subtract my dues to you ; pay eight *ryō* to the Kawachi-ya, due to them for last month's moon-viewing party ; give a silver coin to Saiyetsubō as my contribution to the fund for a family Buddhist altar which he has bought. Let me see, is there anything else ? Ah, yes . . give five pieces of silver as a tip to Isoichi the buffoon. That's all. Good night, Dembei. I'll call again on my return from Kyoto."

He took two or three steps and then returned.

" One moment, I've forgotten my sword. Well, Dembei, a merchant takes such a piece of forgetfulness easily enough ; a samurai would, I suppose, commit *seppuku*." [1]

" It was wrong of me to have forgotten about your sword,

---

[1] The samurai was wont to call his sword his soul. If therefore he forgot his sword he would be like to kill himself for very shame.

sir, since it was I took it in charge. Pray forgive me. Here it is, all complete with its *kogatana*." [1]

"Thus armed," said Jihei, adjusting the sword in his dress, "I am already beyond the reach of harm. Good night again."

And with this parting Jihei made off.

"A safe journey to you ; good night, sir."

The guest departed ; the latch descended with a click ; and there was universal silence as before.

Jihei, who had only made as if to go away, soon stealthily retraced his steps and, clinging to the door of the Yamato-ya, was breathlessly peeping in when, to his consternation, he descried a figure drawing near. Hurriedly he crossed to the opposite house and hid himself in shadow until the unsuspecting newcomer should have passed by. It was Magoémon, flour merchant, the mill of whose mind was still grinding chaff on account of his brother.[2] Sangorō followed, bearing Kantarō on his back.

At the sight of the sign-lantern he hastened to the door of the Yamato-ya.

"Yamato-ya San," said he knocking on the door, "Kamiya Jihei is within, isn't he ? I wish to see him a moment."

Jihei started at the voice, but kept still.

"Jihei Sama's not here," a sleepy male voice answered from within. "He left not long ago, saying that he was going up to Kyoto."

No further exchange ensued. Magoémon burst into tears.

"That's strange," he communed with himself. "If such is indeed the case I ought to have met him on my way hither. Gone to Kyoto has he ? I don't see why. I begin to fear. I wonder if he has gone with Koharu."

His head sank upon his breast. Once again he struck upon the door.

---

[1] The long slender knife worn in the sword-sheath.   [2] A play upon words.

" Who's that, at this time of night ?   We're all abed, I tell you ! "

" I'm sorry to disturb you but I must ask you another question. Has Koharu Dono of the Kinokuni-ya left yet ? Hasn't she gone with Jihei ? "

" No, Koharu Dono is asleep upstairs."

" Now I feel easy," said Magoémon. " There's no fear of his committing suicide with the woman. I wonder where he's hiding now, giving us such anguish. Surely he cannot realize how all his family and relatives are consumed with fear and pain. Afraid that his father-in-law's reproaches may drive him to rashness I have brought Kantarō with me as an inducement to make him abandon any silly project on which he may be bent. I have searched and searched for him so long and all in vain. I wonder why 'tis so ? "

This soliloquy was audible to Jihei in his hiding-place a few steps away.   He held his breath and wept in silence.

" Now, Sangorō, don't you know any other place where the fool goes every night ? "

" I do indeed," answered the idiot, who took the title for himself, " but I cannot tell you for shame."

" You know ?   Where ?   Come, tell me."

" Don't find fault with me when I have told you. The place I visit each night all in a hurry is a flash-house at Ichinokawa."

" You fool !   What's that got to do with the matter in hand ?   Well, let's search the by-street. Don't let Kantarō catch cold, poor child. How cold you must be getting, and all because of good-for-nothing papa. The cold is all you suffer now ; may it be the worst that happens to you on this adventure."

Behind Magoémon's scorn, compassion was to be felt and

thus he made his way toward the by-street [1] with the idiot.

When his brother had retreated to some distance Jihei ran out of his hiding-place to stand on tip-toe and cast a longing eye after the receding figure.

" How kind you are, my brother ! " he whispered to himself. " You cannot suffer this wretch, guilty of the Ten Sins [2] though he be, to go to death, but follow him to the last. What mercy is yours ! "

Again and again, clapping his hands, he made obeisance to the retreating figure.

" I entreat your further mercy. Pray look after my children."

Overcome by tears, he could speak no more ; but, after a short pause, added softly, " Let me give way to no regrets, now that I am resolved to die. Koharu awaits me."

Advancing to the side-door of the Yamato-ya he peeped through the chink, when a dim figure caught his eye. Surely it must be Koharu. He coughed softly as a signal that he was waiting without, but, to his terror, all the answer he got was the sudden click-clack ! click-clack ! of a pair of clappers. It was the watchman returning from his round who, plying his clappers, cried out, " Have a care ! Have a care ! "

The startled Jihei hid himself once more to let the man go by ; and then again stood before the door which, at this moment, began stealthily to open from within.

" Koharu ? "

" Is it you waiting there, Jihei Sama ? I want to join you quickly."

The more impatiently she essayed to slide the door open

---

[1] There is a triple play upon words here in the original connected with the use of the word back : " at the *back* of Magoémon's scorn . . . a *back*-ground of compassion . . . to the *back*-street ".

[2] The " Ten Sins " according to Buddhist scriptures are :—Killing, theft, adultery, idle talk, duplicity, abuse, adorned speech, greed, wrath and prejudice.

the harder she found the operation.   Her purpose was to open it silently, but the door, rolling on its wheels, gave an alarming creak.   She shrank back in despair.   Jihei aided her, but since his hand shook with fear little progress was made. Little by little the door began to slide away—a quarter of an inch, half an inch, an inch.   " Hell an inch ahead " [1] was in store for them, yet they did their best in " the absence of the ogre ".[1]   At last to their joy and relief Koharu succeeded in stealing out.

Hand in hand the desperate lovers walked like persons in a trance until they had put the place of her bondage behind them.   Then they came to a standstill, wondering which direction to take.   Should they proceed north or south, east or west ?   After considerable hesitation they decided to go opposite [2] the direction of the moon borne upon the current of the Shijimi River.   They continued walking east.

Even as the manuscript of the *nō* play is written in the Konoé [3] style and *yarōbōshi* [4] are ever of a light purple, so frequenters of houses of ill-fame are doomed to love suicide.

Such could not but be Jihei's fate.   Dying to-night with his love, to-morrow the news would be spread over the world ; illustrated pamphlets containing a detailed account of the tragedy—pamphlets printed on just such paper as he himself was accustomed to deal in—would publish far and wide a posthumous shame and ignominy.   True, he expected this ; once grasped by the icy hand of death, however, that hand he could not shake off.

" On this fifteenth night of October," said Jihei to Koharu

---

[1] These two phrases are popular sayings. " Hell an inch ahead " means " any peril may occur at any moment."   Here of course it implies that the pair must suffer the agonies of death in a few minutes.   " The absence of the ogre " here implies the absence of any observer.

[2] That is upstream.

[3] The Konoé style : a style of calligraphy originated by Konoé Nobumoto, a Court noble.

[4] Yarōbōshi : the headgear of actors playing female parts.

as they went forward, " the moon shines brightly enough, yet not brightly enough to illumine the darkness of our minds. This frost which now covers the ground and which will vanish with to-morrow's light, how long-lived is it compared to the brief span of our love ? And not less swiftly than the shining water of the Shimizu River flows away, will the sweet odour that is about our bodies dissolve upon the air. This Tenjin Bridge which now we cross takes its name from the God Tenjin who, when a man, Kwan Shōjō, was exiled to Kyūshū. So loth was he to part from a plum-tree in his garden that he composed an ode addressed to it ; whereon the tree, affected by his verses, took one night's wing through the air to the place of his exile. Shame is it that I, born the vassal of so mighty a God, am obliged to kill you and myself. This doom is come on us because I have not sense and judgment enough to fill a *shijimi* shell. Short our lives have been, short as an autumn day, short as Shijimi Bridge itself. Ah, grief ! Our vow to live together till grey had come into the hair, how vain it was : before there has been three years' joy between us, we must die by our own hands. This night, this very night, you who are but nineteen and I but twenty-eight ! A cruel end is ours ! . . . A weary way our walking has been ! Here stand we already on Hades' path."

" Ah ! " exclaimed Koharu tremulously, clinging close to Jihei, " is this already Hades' path ? "

Sadly the pair looked upon each other, yet saw each other but for a moment, their eyes being dimmed with tears. For very agony because of the grief, and what was to come upon his wife and children, Jihei's heart was heavy ; but not a sign betrayed it. By walking northward he might have caught a glimpse of his house, but he had been careful to take the southern road. Now, after crossing another bridge, they found themselves beside the landing-place of the Yodo River, which

MR. GANJIRŌ AS *JIHEI*   MR. JAKUÉMON AS *KOHARU*

MR. GANJIRŌ AS *JIHEI*, HIS FAVOURITE CHARACTER

is called Hachikenya. Fearful of the arrival of the ferry from Fushimi, they pushed on till they came to the spot where the Yamato River flows into the Yodo. Thinking over "the affinity of water and fish," Jihei found some consolation in the reflection that, to the very last moment, they could enjoy a greater affinity.

"I have been wrong!" Jihei exclaimed. "What have I to regret? Not in this world can we wed each other, but remember, not only in the next world shall we be husband and wife, but also in the world beyond, in the world beyond that, and so further and ever further. By virtue of the holy Fumombon in the *Hokékyō* Scripture, of which I have made one transcription [1] every summer, we shall doubtless be mounted on the jewelled dais in paradise. When we have thus become Buddhas and have attained the power of saving human souls, let us protect those who inhabit the house of ' I die daily,' [2] that never may they commit suicide for love's sake."

Shallow was his brain who sought to console himself by such foolishness. Now faint light began beyond the mountain peaks. In the creek of Noda a mist was rising; the bells of temples began to toll. At the sound, Jihei said, " Koharu, we can hesitate no longer. Come, let us on to death." Counting their beads, that were bedewed with tears, the couple reached the sluice-gate of a rivulet running by the bamboo grove of the Daichōji Temple at Amijima, the spot he had selected for their suicide.

" Dear," said Jihei, " wheresoever we may wander we can find no spot appointed as man's place of death, therefore let us make this our place of death." He took Koharu by the hand and kneeled down upon the ground.

---

[1] In olden times pious priests wrote during the three summer months a copy of the Fumombon, a book of the Hokékyō Scripture. This godly act was called *gegaki* or " summer-writing ". Laymen often followed the priests' example.

[2] Literally, the men and women of the demi-monde quarter.

" You speak true, Jihei Sama," she said, leaning upon him in tears, " but this thought came to me as we walked. Should it be reported ' Face against face, side by side, Jihei and Koharu were found dead ' what would O-San Sama think of me ?   Surely she would say in anger, ' Is not that the way of a faithless wanton to have broken her vow to leave my husband and to have no share in his death and yet to have enticed him to commit suicide beside her. A liar to the end ! ' I dread O-San's scorn, jealousy and resentment more than the re-proaches of thousands of others. This alone of all things would trouble my peace in the next world. Therefore kill me here and do you do the deed elsewhere."

" Not I ! O-San was taken from me and divorced by her father's act. She and I are now strangers. I owe her no duty as a divorced wife. Have I not this moment declared we shall be husband and wife in the several worlds to come ? Who then will censure us or who feel jealous of us, if side by side we die ? "

" But on whose account was she divorced ? Why would you not have us die upon different spots ? Do our bodies descend together to Hades ? Albeit we die upon different spots and what though our bodies be picked dry by kites and crows, yet let our souls bear each other company and take their flight, wing by wing, to hell or to paradise, or hell or paradise it be." She sank to the ground and wept bitterly.

" Ah, yes, my dear, yes. Our bodies are compact of earth, water, fire and wind and when we die are rendered back to nothing. Here will I prove to you that never in the Five Existences, nay, in the Seven Existences, shall our souls be separate."

Suddenly he unsheathed his sword and severed a lock of his jet-black hair. " See, Koharu, while this hair remained uncut I was O-San's husband, known to men as Kamiya

Jihei ; now that it is cut I stand up a bonze [1]—a priest who has put the world by and has nor wife nor child nor treasure. I am O-San's husband no longer, nor does any duty bind you to her."

" What joy is mine ! " said the girl.   And, taking up the sword, she shore away her inky locks ordered in the fair style of Shimada.

" A nun you are now and have forsaken the world," said Jihei.   " Neither is any more bound by duty to O-San. We may die together where we please, and it were well perhaps to die on different spots according as you have wished—one may be upon a mountain and the other under a river.   Yes, let us take it that this ground above the sluice-gate is a mountain.   Your place of death it may be, even as this stream may be mine.   Thus, though we die upon the same point of time, manner and spot shall be different, that thus we may declare our sympathy with O-San.   Give me your waist-band."

She handed him her girdle of light purple.   He fastened it to the crossbar of the sluice-gate and tying its ends made a loop. Watching what he did she was seized with sudden terror.

" Is that your way ?   Ah, horror !   Since apart we must die but little longer can I enjoy you, come hither "—they grasped each other's hands—" the point of the sword is swift and pains not, what pain must be yours if so you hang ! I grieve for you."

" Words !   Words !   Where lies the difference, since pain must be, between the silk or steel about the throat ?   Let not such idleness vex your last moments.   Do rather what is meet.   Cast your eyes in worship toward the light of Buddha,[2] sloping westward.   Keep constant your eyes upon

---

[1] The head of a Buddhist priest is shaven.   In former days a layman cut off his hair in order to enter the priesthood.

[2] The Pure Land or paradise, *Saihō-Mida-no-Jōdo*, that is " Mida's Pure Land in the West ", is held by Buddhists to exist over the western edge of the world and the moon is held to be the halo of Buddha.

it. Never forget the West. If aught remains unsaid, say it before you go."

" Nothing. But are you not troubled at thought of your two children ? "

" My children ! My children ! You make me weep again. I see them sleeping soundly, happy in ignorance that their father is about to die. Fair babes, I cannot forget you ! "

He bowed his head. The voices of the crows, risen in a cloud that moment from the tree-tops, cried so mournfully that it seemed they pitied the poor pair.

" Hark to the crows, Koharu. These are they who conduct us to Hades. Is it not spoken that whenever a vow of fidelity is written on the back of a Goō [1] paper three crows of Kumano die upon the mountain. Many copies of our vow have been written—one copy at the beginning of each month —many a crow must we have slain. The crows which used to cry ' *Kawai ! Kawai !* ' (my darlings ! my darlings !) to-night seem to cry ' *Mukui ! Mukui !* ' (Retribution ! Retribution !) To whom is this retribution for sin due ? Do I not know it—for me only, me only, are you to suffer the agonies of death. Forgive me now this thing."

" No. Myself I do it for my own self's sake."

She clung to him with sobs. The cold wind froze the tears that Jihei had shed among the locks upon her temples.

Behind them the booming of the bell in the Daichōji Temple proclaimed the break of day. Time was their foe. Jihei arose.

" Let us leave," said he, " no trace of tears upon our dead faces."

" I shall not."

Each forced a smile. Jihei raised the sword, but, frost-benumbed, his hand trembled and suddenly he grew dizzy. He could not do the deed.

---

[1] See former note.

" I cannot. Why haste ? "

" Be quick. Stay not."

Courage struck out to him from her and the prayer breathed upon the wind from the temple strengthened him to say " *Namu Amida Buddha* ".

Steel sank in throat. He pressed her down. Leaning backward she writhed in terrible agonies. Jihei perceived the stroke had failed. It smote his sight. He braced himself and thrust till flesh met sword-guard. One moment, and she ceased to breathe—her soul flitting away like the dream at dawn that is suddenly broken. He set the corpse upon its right side with the head to the north and the face turned west, as the rites of the Lord Buddha prescribe, and covered it with his *haori*. Then he brushed away his tears, picked up the girdle, set his head within its loop and, upon the wind-borne sound of that passage in the scripture which runs " *Uen muen naishi hōkai byōdō riyaku* " (those related or unrelated to us—all in the universe shall alike be saved), he said, " May we two come to rebirth together within the lotus.[1] Namu Amida Buddha," and hanged himself in the stream. A few moments' agonies were his and then his soul dissolved even as the morning dew.

Fishermen, going out to their work under the dawn, descrying the corpses, cried in consternation, " Hither ! There is death in this place. A double suicide for love ! "

The melancholy news was swift in spreading ; many an eye there was filled with tears at telling of " The Double Suicide at Amijima ".

[1] This literal rendering of the Buddhist expression *Ichiren takushō* signifies : " May we enjoy perpetual bliss together in paradise."

NO. 1

MASAKIYO, THE HERO OF THE EIGHT CAMPS, A PUPPET PLAY BY NAKAMURA GYOGAN

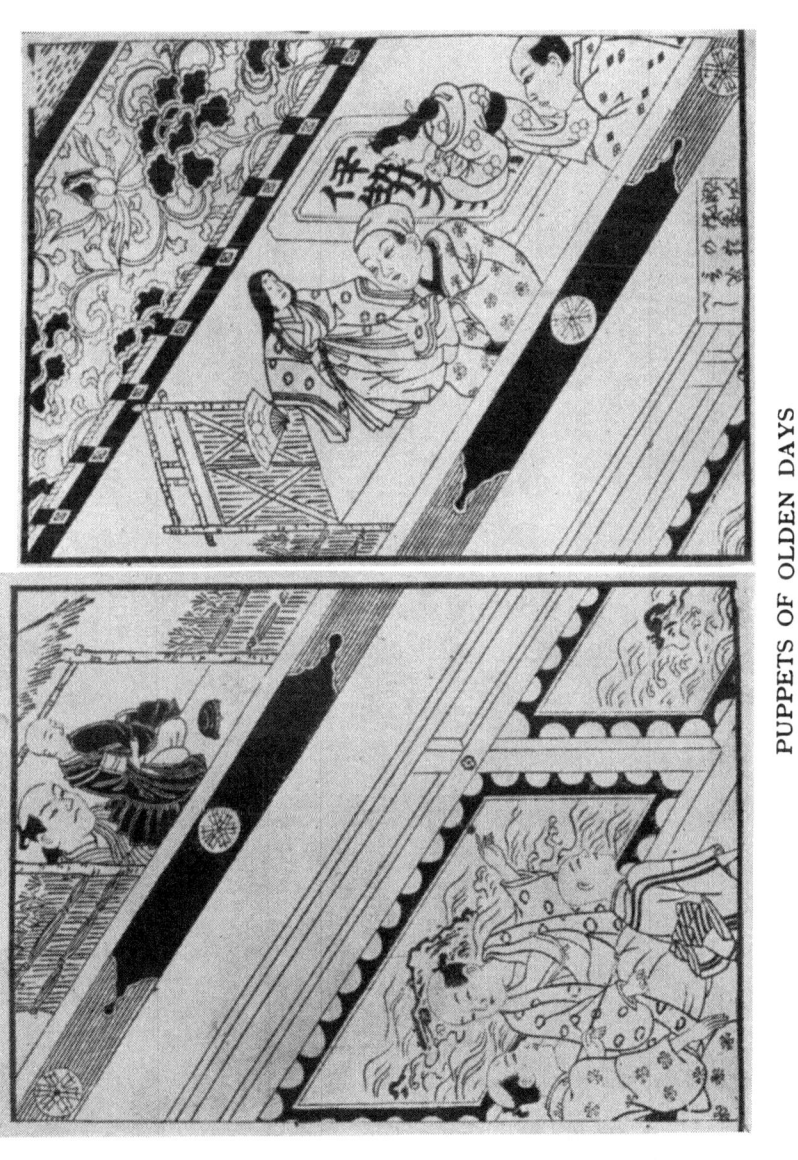

PUPPETS OF OLDEN DAYS

From an illustration in an old book, *The Seikyoku Ruisan.*

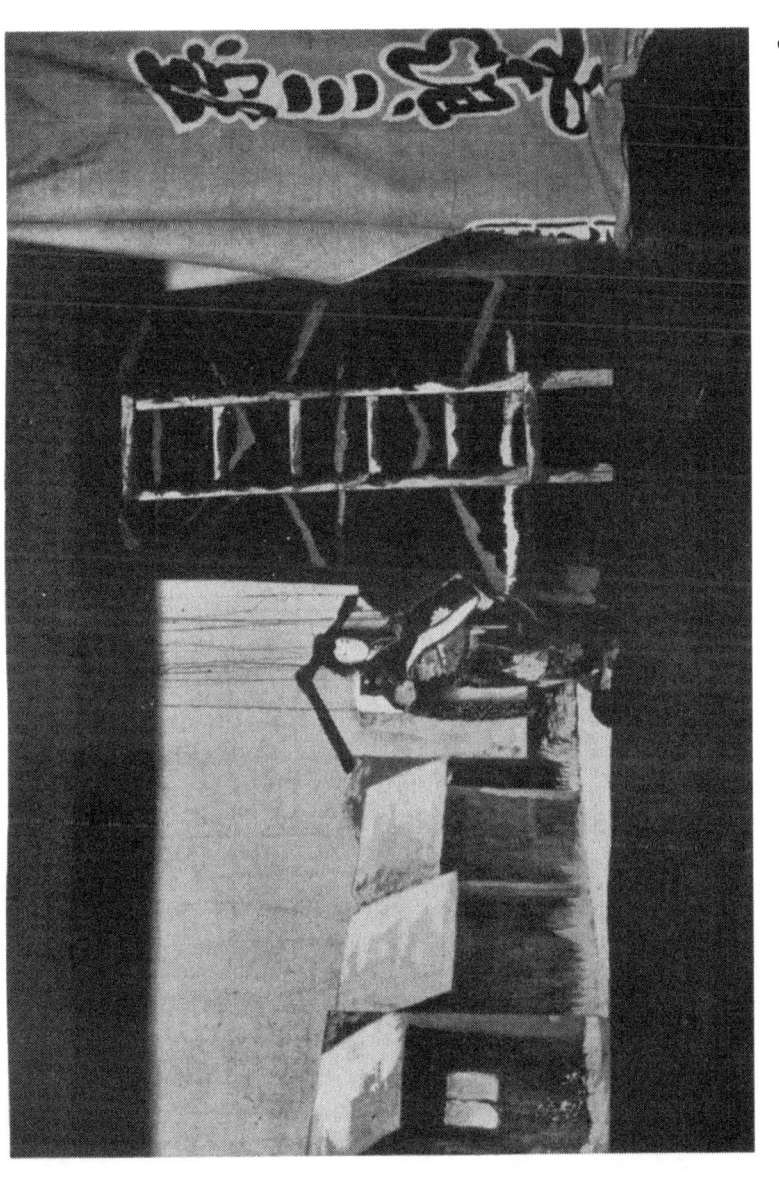

O-SHICHI, THE GREENGROCER'S DAUGHTER, PRODUCED BY MR. MAGOSABURŌ YŪKI'S COMPANY AT THE KEIO UNIVERSITY AUDITORIUM, ON FEBRUARY 2, 1924

A SCENE FROM *THE STORY OF HŌJŌ JIRAI*, PERFORMED AT THE TOYOTAKÉ-ZA

From an illustration in *The Annals of Puppet Performances*

TOYOTAKÉ WAKATAYŪ, THE CHANTER-IN-CHIEF OF THE TOYOTAKE-ZA (facing the bookstand)

THE ADVENTURES OF THE HAKATA DAMSEL

(*Hakata Kojorō Namimakura*)

THE ADVENTURES OF THE HAKATA DAMSEL

(Hakata Kojorō Namimakura)

I

If you must soon set sail, my love,
O do so in the dead of night!
Even one glimpse of silver sails
Would change to sorrow my delight.

SHIMONOSEKI in Nagato Province is the largest port on the beautiful Inland Sea. The city is situated where the outer sea enters by the western inlet. Morning and evening thousands of ships call there, laden with rich merchandise from China and Holland. Millions of *ryō* change hands in that city daily. Gold coins without number—we need not speak of silver—roll hither and thither. The harbour might be called a world of gold.

One autumn evening a large cargo ship lay at anchor in the offing far from the bustle of the city. Sunburnt sailors lay at their ease upon her decks. The remainder of her crew, a rough lot, capable, if their appearance did not belie them, of fighting ogres should the need arise, stood on the poop on watch against the outer sea, scanning it for incoming sails. There was about their bearing something at once alert and anxious and the eyes of certain of them were haggard. At length one who happened to be the chief of the group and was named Kezori, his second name Kuémon, a native of Nagasaki, addressed his companions in his peculiar dialect.

" What, my men ! Isn't Ichigorō and Sanzō's boat in

sight yet ? I don't like the look of it. This weighs so on my mind, I can't get a wink o' nights. If this affair of ours turns out successful we'll run to Hakata, ransom some rare lasses out of Yanagi Street and make off to Osaka with them." He paused. " Did I tell you, by the way, that at the request of one of our sailors I have granted a passage to a young travelling merchant who is on his way to Hakata. He's to occupy the front cabin. If our affair doesn't prosper, we shan't of course go to Hakata. I do wish I could get good news so that we could set sail at once. Meanwhile let us invite the merchant up on deck and kill time by a chat with him. Go down, one of you, and fetch him up."

" Ay, ay, gov'nor," came the prompt reply. One of the group descended while the others spread mats upon the poop, sifted Chinese tea into the pot and otherwise busied themselves—all this to serve their leader. It might be remarked what affection and loyalty these rough men had for their chief. Ere long the merchant made his appearance, a young and courteous man, who, kneeling respectfully before Kuémon and placing his hands politely on the mat, informed the captain how delighted he was to see him, how grateful he was for a passage and concluded by asking him to forgive his want of civility in not having appeared on deck even before the summons to make known his gratitude.

" You are too polite," returned Kuémon kindly. " That's right. Don't stand on ceremony. Make yourself at home. We who live in the same ship and take our rice out of the same tub needn't look upon each other as strangers, but may well consider ourselves related. For myself, I come from Nagasaki, my name's Kezori Kuémon and I am a trader in a small way of business. These are my comrades and every man says what he likes without thinking twice about it. You will find them friendly and ready enough, I daresay, for a chat."

He introduced his men one by one to the merchant.

"This is Yaheiji, native of my own town. These are Ogura Denné and Naniwa Niza, both Osaka men. The fellow I sent down to you is the barber, Heizaémon is his name and he comes from Tokushima. If you want a shave, I daresay he will oblige. And now may I ask in my turn where you hail from?"

"Well, I was born in your own city of Nagasaki, but while I was still a child we moved to the Imperial Capital, where I still live. My father's name is Komachiya Sōzaémon and my name is Sōshichi. Every year I pay a business visit to Hakata. It is a great pleasure to me to make your acquaintance, sirs. I hope you will forgive any shortcomings I possess as a mere landlubber of a passenger."

Greetings over, tongues wagged more freely; courteous postures relaxed; until at length all lay upon their bellies, resting their faces upon their hands. Nor was it long before hearts thawed, even as morning hoar-frost before the sun. Soon they were as friends of many years' standing.

"Friends," said Kuémon at last, "nothing so beguiles the monotony of a seafaring life as freely telling the tale of our experiences. Let me tell you of a fight I had with a Satsuma man when I was twenty-seven. Listen, now. It's not a made-up thing, but a real hard fact. Every year at the festival of the tutelary god of Nagasaki, that is from the seventh to the ninth of September, the local dance and certain Chinese children's dances, among a variety of other amusing performances, are given at the Suma Shrine. During this festival, while I was making my way toward the Shrine, I happened upon a green boy of a Satsuma samurai—stout young fellow all the same—who was rolling about pretty drunk. As we passed each other the tip of his scabbard struck my side. In a trice I seized his scabbard and twisted it with all my might. He turned a somersault and fell to

the ground with a thud.   The reason why I lay such emphasis
on that somersault is because it's a custom among the Satsuma
samurai to put to death that one of their number who has
been flung down by a man of another clan, directly he gets
home.   My antagonist, who probably thought he might as
well die there on the spot as at home, drew his long sword.
'Wretched foolery!' I cried and, shouldering him, I gave
him another fall.   He hit his head against a rugged stone
and I saw his skull was broken.   No, the word 'broken' is
taboo on board this ship.   Let me see—yes, that'll do—his
skull was bruised.   Blood and tears gushed out.   I saw him
carried by a coolie to his inn holding his head together with
both hands.   Then I was mighty proud of myself, but now
I remember the deed with pity.   I might well have refrained
from such brutality.   The people of the capital, I suppose,
being gentle, never give way to such violence as that, do they,
my young friend?"

The company had listened with no little interest to this
story, narrated as it had been in a loud voice and with a
wealth of vivid gesture.

"Come, my young friend from the capital," continued
Kuémon, "tell us some of your reminiscences.   I'm going to
ask each of you to tell his tale in turn.   One always hears
great tales of love affairs in the capital.   You have a romance
or two I'll be bound.   Won't you oblige?"

"Do, do," chimed the others.

The good-natured Sōshichi could not but yield to their
repeated demands.

"Well, er—my father Sōzaémon is so strict with me in
everything that I can't spend even a copper as I'd like to at
Kyoto and Osaka.   During my yearly trip to Hakata, however, I do succeed in visiting the gay quarter of Yanagi Street.
On my very first meeting with a beautiful girl of that street,
named Kojorō, we fell in love with each other and at last we

made a vow to the effect that I would spare no pains to ransom her this year and she vowed that she would become my wife."

"Enough," broke in Kuémon, not without a touch of derision in his voice, "I don't care to listen further. We too visit the gay quarter of Yanagi Street. When you ransom your Kojorō we'll accompany you as your attendants. We hope you'll favour us, my lord, with such presents as are proper to the occasion."

Kuémon rose upon his knees and cast a scornful glance at the young merchant. His comrades laughed among themselves.

"Bravo! A handsome gallant!"

"Ransomer of Kojorō!"

"Hurrah for a lady-killer!"

The exasperated Sōshichi restrained his rising temper with difficulty.

"Well, sirs," said he clearing his throat, "I caught a chill this morning and it's turned to a headache. Pray excuse me. We will continue our chat later."

He made his bow and returned to his cabin, his heart big with wrath and mortification.

"He seems to me to be a fool to pretend to have a cold in his head when his purse is in such a healthy condition that he can afford to ransom a courtesan."

Even as Kuémon spoke a swiftly moving boat appeared at a distance. Her rowers pulled with a will and it was not long before she came alongside. In great excitement Kuémon and his comrades cried, "Ahoy! Sanzō and Ichigorō! How did it turn out with you?"

"Never been so lucky in years. We received the goods you were after and paid the price, to the complete satisfaction of both sides. It won't be long now before we deliver you the goods, in reference to the tally."

This was welcome news.   Kuémon ordered down the sailors to receive the goods.

" Ay ! Ay ! Sir," they responded heartily and set about loading the goods.   The first articles were one hundred and five tiger skins, no less gay than these men's hearts.   Next appeared five boxes of best quality ginseng, weighing forty pounds.   The sailors were as lively as if they had already swallowed this quantity of medicine.   Then were taken in forty pods of musk and two hundred pieces of damask in seven chests.

" Did none of the watchers see you ? " inquired Kuémon anxiously.

" Not they.   Here are fifteen boxes of striped silk gauze, twelve rolls of satin, seven pails of lacquer, one hundred and thirty pounds of tortoise-shell as bright as a full moon.   That's the lot.   No, I am wrong.   Here are eighty coral beads, big as morning stars.   All these goods are entered in the invoice and here is a note of identification for next year.   They ask you to send them a ship next summer, sir."

The chief received the note and held it up to his forehead. He appeared pleased.

" Bravo ! Ichigorō and Sanzō ! You have done well. Take a rest.   Now, men, give them some *saké*."

" Our best congratulations, gov'nor," returned the new-comers.   " We hope you will see your way to rewarding us handsomely.   Now let us have plenty of *saké*."

They boarded the ship, which slowly moved further out into the offing, one pool of gold under the full moon.

As he who follows this story will by now have guessed, Kuémon and his band were smugglers—unlicensed importers of Chinese and Dutch goods, known in a general way as " pirates " and liable to severe punishment on detection.

Kuémon assembled the crew on deck and spoke in a whisper : " Listen ! When we took those goods aboard that young fellow below saw fit to thrust his head out of a port-hole and from the look he had I fancy he was not without his speculations, in fact I am inclined to think he was suspicious. I don't know if you others noticed it, but so it appeared to me. If he is allowed to go on sleeping quietly down there, sooner or later he'll peach on us and that'll be the end of us. We'd best not cut his throat and spill blood, though; it might bring bad luck just as we're putting out on this important expedition. You will therefore strangle him and throw his body in the sea. Remember he has a servant, so don't be off your guard."

" Certainly, gov'nor. Now then, look sharp about it ! "

" Ay ! Ay ! "

'Twas but a moment's work for those ruffians to make ready for the brutal deed. They wound their kerchiefs round their heads, tucked up their sleeves and skirts and stealthily descended the hatch. Not one of them but imagined their evil intentions to be quite unsuspected by their would-be victims. The Kyoto merchant and his servant seemed to be endowed, however, with a sixth sense—the sense for danger. The servant made a desperate leap for the deck, only immediately to be overpowered by two of the sailors who closed upon him. They lifted him to arm's length overhead and with a loud " Yo ! Ho ! " heaved him headlong overboard and the poor fellow descended to Davy Jones's locker.

" So much for him ! But where's Sōshichi ? Nose him out, boys, nose him out ! "

" Here ! " Out rushed Sōshichi, a pole in his hand. " Devil-dogs of pirates ! I have your secret ! Die if die I must, but I will not die alone ! "

So saying he laid about him with his weapon. One of the crew seized him from behind only to be flung down, but, falling, the sailor took him by the leg and Sōshichi tripped and fell sprawling on the deck. The pack fell upon him, seized him, lifted him up and hurled him headlong into the deep.

" Now that that's settled we can take a rest in peace."

They laughed heartily and at once busied themselves preparing the gear for the voyage.

Sōshichi, however, was not so easily disposed of as they imagined. He was not drowned yet. In fact, when he awoke from the stupor caused by the fall he found himself lying miraculously unhurt in the dinghy belonging to the ship. He felt his bones : nothing broken. And what joy to learn that he had escaped a danger more terrible than the jaws of a shark or boa-constrictor. Not a moment did he lose in unfastening the painter and in rowing himself some distance away.

" Ahoy ! You rascals ! " he cried as he plied the oar. " Be so good as to take notice that I, Sōshichi, thank you for your trouble. The day is coming when I'll get my own back—and don't you forget it ! " He rowed with all his strength and was soon lost to sight.

.   .   .

The scene shifts to the front apartment of the Okuda-ya, a famous brothel in Yanagi Street in the city of Hakata. The brilliant lights flooded the new green mats and gorgeous red curtains. Gay enough it was in there as the two young girl attendants on courtesans danced to the music of a *samisen* which Yokuichi, a blind minstrel, was playing. Suddenly the girls ceased dancing.

" Stop, Yokuichi San," they said angrily. " How can we dance to such a rhythm ? If you don't know the music of the *zenidaiko* dance you ought to have told us so before we started. Izaémon San of Nagasaki, mind you, knows all about it. We won't dance any more."

" How can you hope to improve if you're so idle ? Dance on until I stop playing. Now then, dance."

" No, we won't dance, whatever you may say. And as for you, instead of playing [1] the *samisen* you'd do better to play [1] blind-man's-buff ! "

" What ! Play blind-man's-buff ! Don't you try making a fool of me ! Blind as I am I can chastise you for all your eyes."

The enraged Yokuichi, holding his instrument aloft, pursued the frightened girls up and down the room. At this moment Shirozaémon, the proprietor of the house, appeared.

" What are you up to, Yokuichi ? It isn't worthy of you to torment children. Girls, if you persist in making all this noise I'll tell the supervisor to scold you. Come, Shigénojō, to-day being the thirteenth anniversary of the death of Kojorō's mother, she has taken a day off and is praying for the soul of the departed in her room. And you, her attendant, ought to be with her, burning incense to the spirit of the dead. In any event, why all this noise ? "

" Well, sir, while we two were practising the *zenidaiko* dance this Yokuichi here came and disturbed us by playing the samisen. And so——"

" Worse and worse," broke in the proprietor. " There are right hours and wrong hours for practice. Go in and wait on Kojorō. Be off, the pair of you ! Now, Yokuichi, Gen Sama of Dazaifu is in the front room upstairs. You had better go and pay your respects to your patron."

" Excellent ! I will go and take a piece of silver off him. If you please, sir ! "

Elated at the prospect of receiving a little money, the blind minstrel groped his way upstairs. The girls and Shirozaémon retired.

Out in the street, hard by the door, stood a shabbily dressed man, no other than Sōshichi, but pale and haggard

---

[1] A play on the words here.

now. Having escaped with his life off Shimonoseki it was not without great difficulty that he had found his way to Hakata, the city of his heart's desire. Now that he stood without the house he sought he was in a sorry plight, for his adventures had so reduced him that he now possessed nothing but his own body and was so ashamed of his condition that he dared not visit his acquaintances in the city. His passion for Kojorō had drawn him hither, but in the gay quarter where gold, and gold alone, reigned supreme, the penniless youth felt the meanness of his appearance and suffered a corresponding humiliation. He had meant to knock, but now he hesitated and only continued standing, his heart beating a tattoo within him, and from time to time peered through the gate or shrank back from it in fright lest perchance the servants might espy him.

"Be off, you beggar there!" cried a harsh voice. "We have given away all the kitchen scraps."

The passionate lover in Sōshichi felt cowed. "It's no better than a beggar I appear, is it?" he said to himself. "Alas, what shall I do? If I ask them to let me see my Kojorō they are sure to refuse me and, did I succeed in seeing her, it would only bring disgrace on her I must give up the idea; yes, I'll leave without seeing her."

He had but taken a few steps when a voice cried, "Wait a moment!" It was Kojorō's girl attendant Shigénojō. "To-day being a day observed as sacred by my *tayū* [1] san, I'll give you a copper as alms." [2]

She surveyed Sōshichi not without wonder as she proffered him the money. "A mighty fine beggar indeed! Why, he's dressed in silk . . . ah, I know you! Confess, you are Sōshichi San of Kyoto, now aren't you? *Tayū* San, come quick! Here's Sōshichi Sama come abegging!"

---

[1] There were four classes of courtesans. The highest were called *tayū*.

[2] It is customary on the anniversary of a death to distribute alms to the poor. This is held to bring peace to the departed soul.

The girl peered into his face. Her cry of astonishment still more humiliated Sōshichi. He shook his head with vigour and prepared to move off in haste. But the girl, taking him by the belt, detained him, crying, " I won't let you go ! Wait ! "

Meanwhile Shirozaémon and his hirelings had rushed out upon the scene. Kojorō came too, and running up to Sōshichi, snatched away his *kasa* [1] and gazed into his face.

" It really is Sōshichi San ! What fun ! You are very welcome, my dear. How on earth did you come to be in such a plight ? "

Already, even before he had told his story, she was in tears. She addressed herself to the proprietor.

" May I have a private talk with Sōshichi San ? "

" Certainly. You are quite at liberty to do so. Sōshichi Sama is a patron of ours from of old. If you should need anything, sir, please don't hesitate to mention it."

Kojorō took her sweetheart by the hand and hastened with him into the front room. No sooner was the door shut than she clung to him weeping. " Why didn't you let me know it was you earlier, my love ? What can have brought you to such a condition ? Has your father disinherited you ? There must be some special reason or other. Do tell me. Do you still think of me as a courtesan ? True, I continue in service, but long ago I considered myself your wife. Though both should be reduced to such penury as to have to beg, yet never will I break my plighted word. To-day is the thirteenth anniversary of my mother's death. Since I have chanced upon you on this day of all days I can hardly doubt that my parents in the spirit have brought about this joyful meeting. Can't you just say to me, Sōshichi San, ' How is it with you, my dear wife ? ' "

Kojorō spoke in tearful tones. It was evident that she

---

[1] A hat with a hanging brim.

was carried away by passionate love. In her voice there was an ecstasy of joy not without a hint of reproach. Her swimming eyes bore witness to the candour of her heart.

" My dear Kojorō," returned Sōshichi trembling, " it is good of you to say so. I am very glad to find you looking so well. It grieves me very much that, after a year's separation, instead of presenting myself finely dressed and with good news upon my tongue, I should have to bring you unpleasant news. Pray listen. When I was making my way here carrying, according to my custom, my annual large stock of goods, I had the misfortune to chance to take passage in a smugglers' vessel. Before my very eyes the villains saw fit to drown my servant in the sea. I all but shared his fate, yet managed to escape the jaws of death and it has not been without considerable suffering that I have managed to make my way hither. Such being the case, not only my goods and my fine clothes, but even my money were left in the ship. Finding myself without a penny I have been reduced to disposing even of some of the clothes off my back—a wretched business indeed ! Last year, you remember, I promised that I would ransom you this ; but my ill-fortune has been such that I have lost the money intended for this purpose. I am indeed sorry that I cannot keep my word and in my own grief can only too well imagine your anguish and disappointment. It was to look upon your face once more and to assure you of my heart-sickness that I have dared to come here despite the fact of being well aware of what a shabby-looking creature I am."

Kojorō displayed no sign of great sorrow at this melancholy recital, but rather appeared buoyant, inwardly delighted perhaps at an opportunity to prove her fidelity.

" Thank you for giving me your confidence," she returned calmly. " Money is not of account, but life is everything. It is a joy to me that you are still alive. Once my mind is

THE ADVENTURES OF THE HAKATA DAMSEL, PRODUCED AT THE
ICHIMURA-ZA
MR. KIKUJIRŌ AS *KOJORŌ*   MR. KIKUGORŌ AS *SŌSHICHI*

[*face p.* 278

made up it is no hard matter for me to support you. The question in fact doesn't worry me at all, though I sympathize with your sufferings. I fear you must feel the cold. You seem to have grown very thin."

She laid one sleeve of her flowing overdress upon his shoulder, then tightly embracing him burst into tears.

The voice of a servant without was heard crying briskly. " Hullo there ! Here are *daijin* [1] sama ! "

" Guests have arrived. Come this way."

She took him by the hand. The pair entered the inner room.

The guests proved to be none other than the smugglers. Kezori Kuémon was at their head. Yaheiji followed him with five subordinates. They filed into the room with happy shouts. Each was gorgeously attired in rich imported cloths : woollen, satin, damask and velvet. Though their hair was dressed after the Japanese fashion, their costumes were a fantastic medley of the Japanese and Chinese styles. They ascended the front room and seated themselves in a row, Kuémon appropriating to himself the place of honour. He had arrogated to himself the part of lord and paymaster combined and now addressed himself to the proprietor with an air of importance.

" You remember us, I presume ? Hitherto we have frequented the small houses in this city, but, as you may observe, we are now made men and intend accordingly to play the part of *daijin* from this day forth. On our way hither we have glanced in upon Eguchi of Ichimonji-ya, Katsuyama and Usugumo of Maru-ya, Misao of Abura-ya, Ogura of Izumi-ya and Ōiso of Kuruma-ya. If you will be so good as to be go-between we will ransom them for our comrades. Kindly

---

[1] A rich man who spends extravagantly in the gay quarter is called a *daijin*. A *daijin* signifies literally " a great spender ". Etymologically the word is probably originated from another word of the same pronunciation meaning " a minister of state ".

make arrangements to-night, we cannot wait till to-morrow."

" You're in a great hurry, sir."

So saying Shirozaémon made as if to go. Kuémon inter-cepted him.

" Don't go. If you go there will be no one in charge. You can send someone, can't you ? "

" Certainly, sir."

The proprietor hurriedly took brush and paper, wrote a series of notes and dispatched them by a messenger, then he turned to the maids and servants.

" Make haste and bring soup. Open the sliding doors that this room and the next may form a large banqueting hall. Don't let the children cry. Give my wife her medicine. Get a move on you ! "

" Is your wife ailing, Shirozaémon ? That's too bad. Hand me over that box there. Take care of your health. The only way to keep well is to take ginseng. I have some here in this box if you care for it."

Kuémon opened the box and produced a packet of large ginseng roots of the finest quality. From this packet he extracted about a pound's weight of roots and handed it to the proprietor.

" How many children have you, Shirozaémon ? "

" A girl and two boys, sir."

" A proper number. These corals are small but weigh two ounces a pair. Let your sons have them as ornaments. Here are three rolls of damask and five rolls of satin for your daughter. This scarlet silk crêpe here will do as lining. These coins will pay for silk wadding."

These things he threw out one after the other in such quantities and with such expedition that Shirozaémon, receiving them and lifting [1] them to his forehead, felt his arms grow positively tired.

---

[1] A polite way of expressing gratitude.

" Pardon my saying so, sir," exclaimed Shirozaémon, his eyes nearly popping out of his head, " but your opulence and liberality are so astounding that I can hardly find words in which to express my gratitude. May I venture to inquire when and how you acquired such enormous wealth ? "

To this leading question Kuémon returned but a random answer.

" Your surprise is natural enough," he replied off-hand. " The truth is, finding my trade at Yedo but a humdrum affair I visited the temple at Sayo-no-Nakayama and rang a successful peal on the famous Bell of Muken at the temple. As a consequence I suddenly became a millionaire, but you mustn't run away with the idea that a mere anybody can ring that bell without trouble. You have to practise some severe austerities or ever you get to ringing it at all. In the temple they keep a book called ' The Millionaire's Bible ' with a long list of these austerities in it. Let me recite the contents to you."

" A rare book, I'll be bound," said the proprietor, slapping his thigh. " Since I have no objection to emulating your good fortune, please recite the words."

" Excellent. Now listen."

Kuémon ceremoniously produced a paper of dubious appearance from his bosom and read aloud :

" The Millionaire's Bible.

" He that would learn the history of this Bell of Muken, let him know that there once lived in India a bird with a pot of money whose name was Gwakkai, well known, too, as being a close-fisted sort of fellow. The Lord Buddha, who had it in his mind to snatch this brand from the burning, cultivated the habit of calling round every morning dressed up as a begging friar to give him the ' how d'ye do ', but his luck was out, for every time he got the straight tip to skedaddle,

with the door slammed in his face. Then the Lord Buddha
got a great idea and the next time he was walking round that
way he turned up all tricked out as a whacking great image of
shiny gold. No sooner had His Stinginess run his eye over
that stunning image—and mind you it was just the colour
of gold—than he was all of a flutter to rip off the golden
leaves. This time he opened the door readily enough to the
Lord Buddha and the Lord, having it all his own way, soon
succeeded in converting him. In brief, the upshot of the
matter was that the old hunks, who had never given a thought
to anything but himself before, soon found himself putting
up the ready to have this Bell of Muken cast. And if you
want the proof of the story, here it is. You ring that bell
and the greedy soul of the fellow can't leave it, there's so
much money tied up in it, so that when you ring it it says
' *Oshiya! Oshiya!* ' or ' Oh, how I hate parting! ' Folks
who hear the toll of the bell get rich quick in this world,
but in the next are apt to find themselves sitting on the hobs
of the Muken hell. You can gather from this that this old
bell isn't to be rung for the mere fun of the thing. Here's a
list of all the nice little things you have to do before you can
get a successful ring. To begin with you mustn't parade
about in silk or in pongee. Even cotton is not allowed for
your quilt. Straw matting is more ' comme il faut ' As to
food, you must swallow tea-skilly twice a day and keep your
nose out of the side-dishes, for the idea is that this sort of
ration is the sort of thing to give one a helping hand in a life
of devotion and assists the purification of mind and body.
Then again, you have to work all day and every day throughout the year, and that with all your might. Don't leave even
an old boot to lie if on the road you find it and when you fall
on your nose, you've got to mind you don't get up without
something in your hands, even though it's only a handful of
dirt. See that you get up at the crack of dawn. Don't

lend money without receiving an I.O.U. It's so much to your credit if you don't buy what you desire. You'll lose by not working by moonlight. The fellow who works as if he meant it will never be hard up. Cut the firewood fine before you use it. Throw nothing away, not even the ashes. Use soot from the pan when you paint your eyebrows. Rice-straw is a sovereign remedy for a leg gone to sleep.[1] A dried up well's no bad place to keep ladders in. The saving man will use a rat's tail as a gimlet sheath. An umbrella should be dried at once after being used. The wise man never lends any of the following : dried bonito,[2] a pestle, an earthenware mortar, a whetstone, a quern, a druggist's mortar, for every time you lend any one of these things, it is sure to come back worn, however small the wear may be. We must be frugal and satisfied with our conditions, remembering that there are others not so well off as we are. If you observe these precepts faithfully many a mickle will make a muckle until at last you grow to be a millionaire. Of this there can be no shadow of doubt whatever. If, having assiduously practised every one of these austerities, you then ring the Bell of Muken, depend upon it you will then be a millionaire and your fortune will be that of a millionaire, not only in this world but in the next."

This humorous recitation over, Shirozaémon smiled and said, " That's a real fact and not a fable, but were the whole world to behave as this Bible instructs it, my business would be at an end ! "

Kojorō, who had given ear to all this from behind the paper doors in the next room, was lost in amazement and whispered to Sōshichi, " What a mint of money he must have ! Did

---

[1] There is a superstition among common folk that when a leg goes to sleep an application of rice-straw to the forehead will cure the numbness.

[2] The Japanese dry fillets of this fish. They may be seen in the shops and have the appearance of wooden blocks, the shape of the section of an enormous orange. They can be dropped on the earth without breaking. The Japanese shave off flakes from them against the steel of an especial kind of plane sold for the purpose.

you hear him say he was going to ransom half a dozen courtesans ? And he seems to have heaped on the master one valuable thing after another, for all the world as if silver and gold were dirt to him. Isn't it enough to make one envious ? Even when my people were living in poverty I never even dreamed of wanting to get money which I couldn't earn in a fair way, but to-day I long to be able to lay my hands on a large sum and how I envy those courtesans who are going to be ransomed. One shouldn't be jealous of a man in good fortune, none the less I should like to see what sort of man he is."

She peered through the chink between the paper doors. A surprise awaited her.

" Why, he's a friend of mine ! He's the man who kindly gave me his promise that he would help me if I were ever in need of help. I'll go in to him and ask him for a loan."

She was about to enter, but Sōshichi stopped her.

" No, my dear. You know nothing of this man beyond the house, and what is more, those strangers with him would overhear you. How can a courtesan demean herself by requesting a loan [1] of her patron ? Don't you feel the disgrace of it ? "

" That depends upon circumstances. As I told you a little while ago, my Chikugo [2] patron has all but promised Sadoya that he will ransom me next month. It is therefore with extreme longing that I have awaited your visit, only to be disappointed. Were I handed over to another I would not live. Pray, where is the disgrace in a loan if it be repaid ? Do please leave the matter to me."

So saying she twitched her sleeve from his grasp, great tears

---

[1] Strange as it may seem, courtesans of olden days enjoyed considerable respect and avoided mean behaviour, deeming it beneath their dignity to borrow money from their patrons. Their position had perhaps something in common with that of the Greek Hetaerae.

[2] She did not like the Chikugo man and she was determined to kill herself were she handed over to him.

glistened in her eyes, nor could Sōshichi refrain from tears. At length she wiped them away, slowly entered the next apartment and gracefully seated herself at the side of Kuémon. At the unexpected vision of so much beauty these rough customers made haste to trim themselves up. Then unanimously they turned upon her sheep's eyes, so that an unseen beholder would surely have been put in mind of " ogres viewing beautiful flowers ".

" What a pleasure it is to me to see you, Kuémon San," began Kojorō lightly. " I happen to have a great favour to ask of you. A very heavy misfortune has befallen me and I consequently find it necessary to get myself ransomed at once. As ill luck will have it my lover hasn't the money required at the present moment. Would you be so kind as to keep the promise you made me some time ago and lend me enough money to effect my ransom until the whole sum comes along ? Do be so good, Kuémon ! "

" What delicious frankness, Kojorō," returned Kuémon with joy. " There's no one but hates to ask another for a loan, yet you have dared to take the bull by the horns. I am glad of it. You won't have to ask me twice I'll let you have even a thousand *ryō*, why, ten thousand if you want it ! Now, Shirozaémon, I am going to ransom Kojorō. She shall go wherever she chooses. Yes, I'll pay her ransom money. And I engage her services until the other courtesans arrive. Come, be merry, friends ! Sing and drink ! "

Kuémon and his companions needed no second invitation, but Kojorō stayed them.

" One moment, sirs. My lover is behind these doors. I'll bring him in to thank you, Kuémon. Don't break your word, sir."

" Upon my honour as a man and a merchant, I never lie. Bring your lover in."

Overjoyed, Kojorō left the apartment.

" See, *tayū* san have come ! "

Scarcely had the announcement been made when Katsu-yama, Eguchi and Ōiso showed their lovely faces. The room grew gay.

" Good day, sirs," they cried merrily. " Usugumo San, Misao San and Ogura San will follow us presently."

" Welcome, girls ! " Kuémon's companions grew suddenly uproarious and gazed upon the courtesans with rapture.

" Now, Shirozaémon," remarked Kuémon, " take these girls into another room a while for we've some business to do here. And don't let the second lot of girls come in either."

" Certainly, sir. Come with me, girls."

The three submissively accompanied the proprietor.

For a while Sōshichi pondered whether to show his face or no, but at length, urged by Kojorō, he opened the doors and entered the apartment. Great was the consternation of both Sōshichi and the roughs when they met face to face.

" Kojorō's sweetheart ! Is it you ? I remember you."

" So we meet ! I have longed for this moment. What, all of you here ? These fellows are———"

Kuémon's retainers sought to prevent his further speaking.

" Not a word more ! " they cried. " Cut him down ! "

They had leapt to their feet. Cups, bottles and pans rolled hither and thither, spilling liquor and soup upon the mats.

" A quarrel about a woman ! It's going to be serious."

Panic-stricken maids and servants looked on in terror, their faces white as linen. Kuémon did not budge.

" Not so much fuss," he cried calmly. " I have a plan, comrades. Do you go in to the girls. I'll settle this matter alone."

" No, no ! We'll deal with him ! Better not leave you alone with him."

" Nonsense ! " returned Kuémon with a glare. " Do you

think I am the sort of man to take an easy licking ? If you remain there'll only be a riot. Get out and be quick about it."

" Very well. We leave it to you."

Kojorō, who had not the slightest idea of what had occurred between them, was astonished at the unexpected turn events had taken, but none the less continued courageously to sit by Sōshichi, glancing first at one face and then at the other.

" Well, young man," Kuémon calmly began, " breathe but one syllable of what passed the other day and you will be undone. Not one word. No need to enlarge upon my trade, you know it ; but if your life has any value for you whatever suffer those doings to pass in silence. If you show any signs of objecting you may take it that there will be serious trouble. Therefore suffer things to stand as they are. If I in my own person see fit to ransom Kojorō, your promise will be empty and poor Kojorō's kind intention pass for nothing. She has put herself to the humiliation of asking me for a loan of money for your sake, isn't that so ? It would be a shame to disappoint her. Bearing your interests in mind I sincerely advise you to join us in our business. If you see fit to do this I will not only ransom Kojorō for you, but place at your disposal five hundred ryō, no, even one thousand ryō, in order that you may take your ease with your girl without calling on your father for assistance. Perhaps you will wonder at the offer, considering that the more numerous our comrades are the more disadvantageous it is to us. Yet in our trade nothing counts like luck, and since you indeed appear to be a lucky fellow in having escaped the perils of not long ago, I feel sure that your joining us will contribute to the prosperity of our business. I therefore entreat you to join us. Indeed I most humbly insist that you do so, Sōshichi Dono."

Kuémon spoke as one who pleads. Nevertheless his hand was on his sword-hilt and he appeared ready to use the weapon should the young man refuse. Sōshichi found himself in a terrible dilemma. If he joined the smugglers' gang, he would be a violator of the national laws, and run the risk of losing his life. If he refused he would not only have to render his sweetheart to another, but that other would be his murderer. Death awaited him upon either course. Should he heed the law or obey the promptings of love ? He was at a loss.

" Well, Sōshichi San," remarked Kojorō in a soothing tone, " what Kuémon's business may be I do not know, but it is obvious that when one man rides in a palanquin and another carries it, both go the same road, though their manner of passing the time is different. I think Kuémon San means well by you since he is making this offer of money and appears to be doing everything else he can for you. Won't you say ' yes ' and join him and live with me as husband ? But if your joining him means your ruin, return him a definite refusal. Remember that if I cannot be your wife I will live no longer. Whether you make me your wife or cause my death depends upon your ' yes ' or ' no '. Since this is not a small question, do not be in a hurry to make your reply."

With that she thrust her hand into his bosom and was surprised to find him wet with perspiration.

At last Sōshichi made his resolve.

" I consent, Kuémon Dono," he said in a determined voice, " I will join you and obey your every order. I have heard that at Nagasaki it is the custom to drink *saké* mixed with blood when one makes a vow. To testify to my sincerity I will draw blood from my arm."

He made as if to bare his arm. Kuémon intercepted the gesture.

" No need of that. Your sincerity is sufficiently apparent. Come in now, comrades."

His subordinates instantly returned with their fair companions. Sōshichi exchanged a cup of fraternity with each of them.

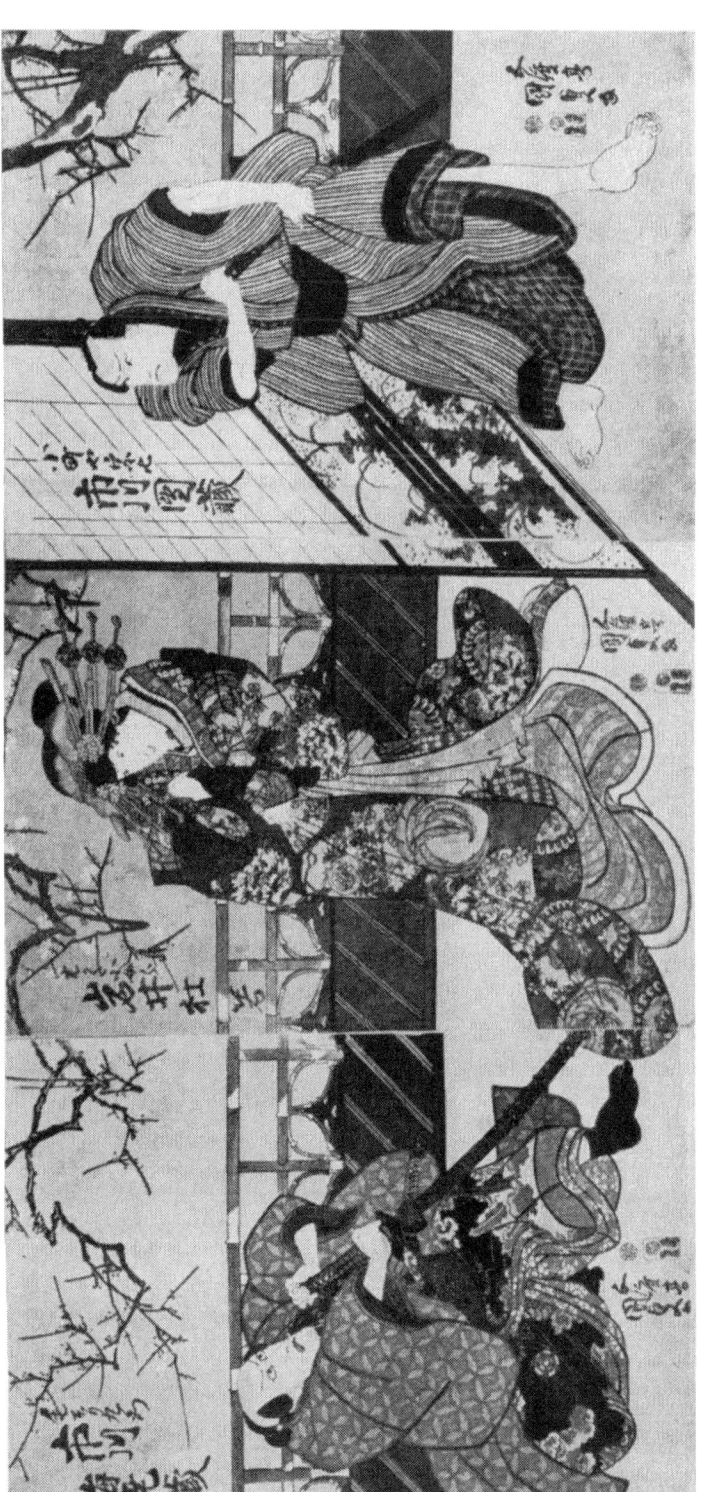

THE ADVENTURES OF THE HAKATA DAMSEL, PLAYED BY CELEBRATED ACTORS OF OLDEN DAYS

From a colour print by **Kunisada** (Gototei)

"Nevertheless his hand was on his sword-hilt and he appeared ready to use the weapon should the young man refuse."

[*face p.* 288

" You must feel in fine feather, Kojorō Dono," remarked Kuémon patronizingly. " Now, Shirozaémon, what does the total ransom money amount to ? "

" Here is the bill, sir."

Kuémon received the bill and ran his eye over it.

" So the ransom of Kojorō Dono and the other girls amounts to one thousand, four hundred and fifty *ryō*, does it ? Well, here's one thousand five hundred, Shirozaémon. The odd sum's a nuisance. I give you the balance of fifty *ryō*." The whole sum of one thousand five hundred *ryō* in silver and gold was accordingly then and there piled up.

" This vow of brotherhood suits me nicely," said Kuémon. " Now, comrades, every one of you treat this young man as more than a brother. Come, a song, a song.' Thereupon that rude company broke into chorus :

> Where the great green chestnuts spread,
> And the cot among the rocks is,
> Where the shade is cool o'erhead
> And grass pleasant underfoot,
> Lie we down, lie we down,
> Lie we down, boys, with our doxies,
> Head by head on chestnut root.

The song was suddenly interrupted by the cry of a night-watchman.

" Hi ! Shirozaémon Dono ! A murderer has taken refuge in this quarter and all the visitors are to be examined. Let no one forth. See, the constable is approaching."

Watchman and proprietor left incontinently.

Kuémon and his companions, albeit proud of their self-possession, turned a trifle pale.

" This looks bad. Is there not, I wonder, some other route to our ship ? Never mind the expense."

" The earth appears solid enough, alas ! Isn't there some mode of going through the air ? "

T

" Oh, that we had the harness of invisibility ! " [1]

Sōshichi, taking Kojorō by the hand, sat still, drawing his breath with difficulty, while he fixed an anxious look on the front door. At this moment there arose, uncertain whether in this house or the next, a tumult, the sound of rushing feet and stamping, followed by the loud cry, " We arrest you ! "

The sinister exclamation was not without its effect upon the company : all were stiff with terror.

" Have no fear, sirs," remarked Shirozaémon returning. " A wretch who murdered a postman, while playing the high-wayman at Tonomachi Street in this city, has been arrested next door and taken to the Bailiff's office : a matter which in no way concerns you, sirs."

The smugglers exchanged glances, not unaccompanied by sighs of relief.

" There's no point in stopping any longer, Sōshichi Dono," said Kuémon, " we'll away to the capital. Come now, comrades, let's be off. Girls, you will follow us to the wharf in palanquins. Farewell, Shirozaémon."

" Farewell, Shirozaémon Dono," echoed Kuémon's companions.

" Farewell, sirs. A thousand thanks for your patronage. Pray visit us again."

II

An auction was in progress at the house of Komachiya Sōshichi in Shinsei Street of the capital. Everything was being put up for sale, from wardrobes, chests, swords and hanging pictures by famous artists to cupboards with their

---

[1] Tradition asserts that in ancient times there existed straw coats and sedge hats which, like the magic caps in a western fairy tale, conferred upon the wearer the benefit of a temporary disappearance from sight. These were called *kakurè-mino* (hiding straw coats) and *kakurè-gasa* (hiding hats).

contents, pots and pans, etc., yes, even the mats and the household Buddhist shrine itself. Things were at such a pass that it seemed as if they would sell the very dirt and ashes if they could. The whole neighbourhood had gathered; bidding was brisk among the noisy crowd. The owner of the house, Hishiya Kaémon, rushed forward, crying indignantly to the aged man who was acting as auctioneer.

" What an outrage! This house of mine is rented to Komachiya Sōshichi, a travelling merchant. He and his wife have gone to Osaka on business; this old woman has been left behind as caretaker. They asked me to be responsible for the contents of the house during their absence. They are expected back to-day or to-morrow. Are you pleased to think you are doing your duty as caretaker, old woman? Now, old man, what and who are you? Are you so old that you don't know the customs of the capital? What madness is this that you should trespass inside another man's house and sell all its contents without so much as reporting the matter to the Street Meeting Office.[1] Do you imagine that I, an alderman of this street and the owner of this house, will suffer such an outrage to pass unchallenged? I intend to have both of you cross-examined. You will be so good as to come with me to the Meeting Office next door. Come now, let there be no delay about it." He endeavoured to hurry them but the woman only wept with bowed head. The old man respectfully replied.

" Honoured sir, as a householder and an alderman, you speak with a good show of reason. I wouldn't think of disobeying you, but pray condescend to listen to what I have to say. I am Sōshichi's father, by name Komachiya Sōzaémon. I am a native of Nagasaki, but I have been living for twenty years in the capital. By trade I am a merchant. My re-

---

[1] *Machi Kaisho* or " Street Meeting Office " was an office wherein the public affairs of a particular street were transacted. Every street had such an office.

sources are but small and consequently my business is not prosperous. So I live miserably enough in the suburbs. As you are probably aware, my son Sōshichi is in the habit of visiting Hakata as a travelling merchant. Recently his letters have become more and more rare, a thing that has filled me with anxiety, more especially when I have considered the rumours concerning his movements that have lately reached me. Rumour averred that he had earned an immense sum in Kyūshū, had ransomed a Hakata courtesan and was living in a splendid house on Shinsei Street. Outwardly his mode of life was humble, so the rumour ran, but in reality he lived a life of luxury. Astonished at the news, I paid a visit to this place for the first time last night and was amazed to find everything that had been asserted true. Above all the value of the household effects overwhelmed me. I questioned this woman about Sōshichi's affairs, but she could tell me nothing. I daresay you have much experience as a merchant. I have been in business all my life, old as I am, but as far as my experience goes I consider it impossible for a humble merchant to become a millionaire in so short a while. In old days Sōshichi showed such appreciation of his filial duty that he let me know whenever he had earned even so small a sum as ten or fifteen *ryō*, but now it would appear that he is doing his best to hide this great property from me. It's quite impossible for me to think he has earned the money fairly and in his progress from bad to worse, involving as it must you and his other neighbours, he cannot escape a shameful death. I have therefore seen fit to put his things up to auction for a mere song in order to make him realize that ill-gotten goods never prosper and to endeavour to induce him to proceed upon honourable courses. I do this out of sheer affection for my son, sir. Carried away by my desire to dispose of these things I entirely overlooked the fact that the correct procedure was to report the matter to you and the Meeting Office.

I most humbly beg your forgiveness for such laxity   I beg to return you this house with thanks, on Sōshichi's behalf."

The householder's indignation evaporated before the other's pleading. " Your explanation is sufficient, old man," he returned, nodding his appreciation of the facts of the case, " but since this house is rented under the signature of a surety I want a declaration from you, lest trouble should arise, and I should like this woman's seal affixed to it.   Pray come with me to the Meeting Office."

In less than no time Kaémon had ordered every remaining thing to be carried away. The house stood empty. The outer gate was closed and a placard was pasted up reading " House To Let ". The three repaired to the office.

The courtesan formerly known far and wide as " Kojorō of Hakata " was now a contented merchant's wife. Her husband, Sōshichi, was a nouveau-riche after frequent ups and downs on the stormy waters of a dangerous trade. The fortunate pair, accompanied by three servants, returned from their brief visit to Osaka. The sight of their house struck them for a moment completely speechless. The *noren* [1] was wanting and the notice " House To Let ", drawn in bold, black letters, stood upon the gate.

" What can have happened ? "

They forced the side-door, entered, and were still more astonished to find the house entirely empty : not a kettle to warm water in, not a mat to sit upon. A solitary bird cried disconsolately in the garden. They were too over-whelmed with surprise to cry like the bird, but simply gazed at each other open-mouthed. Something seemed suddenly to strike Sōshichi's mind. He felt as if the soles of his feet were pierced by pointed bamboo stumps and, crestfallen, seated himself upon the bamboo floor.

[1] That is, a sign-curtain.

" My dear," said Kojorō excitedly, " there's no good in sitting down and taking your ease. The householder is a very good friend of ours and his wife and I are on such intimate terms that when I last saw her the other day she asked me to present her with a pair of Osaka clogs as a souvenir. It's very unreasonable of them, considering the friendliness of our relations, to have emptied our house in our absence. I'll go at once and ask an explanation of them."

She made as if to go out. Sōshichi stopped her.

" No," said he with gloomy composure, " such negotiations are not for a woman. Remember that this house is a rented house in name only : it was in extremely bad condition when I took it over and accordingly I repaired it entirely at my own expense. And only lately I bought planks to have the floor repaired. As to the rent, I have paid two or three months' rent in advance. I have never been in arrears with it. What is more, we've been liberal in our relations with our neighbours. And now, in spite of all that, this wrong has been done us : our property has been taken from us and our old caretaker is missing. I cannot believe that this is the doing of the householder or of any other neighbour. It seems to be probable that our money and valuables, entrusted to the care of friends, have given rise to official suspicion. In any event we are in imminent danger and accordingly cannot linger here even for one night. Alas ! All is over with me ! My doom has come at length." He called his servants to him—a man and two maids—and thus addressed them :

" My dear servants, under present circumstances I can no longer retain your services. I am sorry to part from you, but I have no option but to discharge you. I give you this purse which contains some change : share it. Farewell."

With that he threw them a cretonne purse ; it was accepted with gratitude. " Many thanks, master. It would be rude to decline your offer. We grieve for you and your fortunes. Farewell, master and mistress."

They felt the purse and were agreeably surprised to discover that it contained eight or nine *ryō* in gold. Then, without exhibiting the least shadow of regret, the cold-hearted servants took themselves off.

The old caretaker, who had perceived the return of her master and mistress, stole out of the Meeting Office.

" Oh dear, oh dear ! Master and mistress," she said sorrowfully. " Your honourable father came last night and was much surprised and grieved to see the value of your property. He said to me, ' Greed must have driven Sōshichi to join a gang of pirates. Evidently he considers gain, however unfairly earned, a blessing. Ere long he will be crucified. He has disregarded my precept that money, fairly earned, be it only a penny one has turned by peddling turnips and radishes, is worth more than millions of *ryō* gotten by ill means. I'd very much like to know how he can afford such expensive surroundings. They're a danger to my son, that's what they are.' Then sadly enough he summoned a dealer in second-hand articles and with his assistance sold off your belongings dirt cheap, locked the house up, and took his way to the Meeting Office, where he made his humble apologies to the officers. All this trouble did he take on your behalf. I am very sorry both on your account and on your father's."

At these words Sōshichi burst into a torrent of tears. After a brief silence he said gravely, " My good woman, I am wondering what has become of the note of identification I kept in the case of the ink-stone ; should that note come to the eye of strangers it would occasion my ruin. Can it, do you think, have passed with the case into the hands of a dealer in second-hand articles ? "

" No, sir. The case was indeed sold, but the note is in your father's pocket-book. Don't be anxious on that point, but busy yourself in a fashion I consider more useful, namely, in losing not a minute in escaping from this quarter. Since the Meeting Office is likely to send for me at any moment, I had better get back If we continue to live, chance may bring us together again. Pray take good heed to yourselves, master and mistress. Farewell."

Reluctantly and sorrowfully she returned. Sōshichi sat with a vacant expression upon his face for a moment, then exclaimed :

" Now that our secret has reached my father's ears, it must already be known to the public. Nothing can be done. My dear, we had best fly and keep flying as long as may be. I have a friend in the town of Yokkaichi in Isé Province ; let us take our way in that direction. It is now close upon four o'clock. Come, get ready for starting, Kojorō."

At this moment a gruff voice cried, " Is Sōshichi in ? "

And the next moment the side-door admitted a grim giant who proved to be Kezori Kuémon.

" You've closed the doors early ! "

" What ! Is it Kuémon Dono ? " the perplexed Sōshichi stammered. " What brings you to the capital ? Well—er—come up—now, Kojorō, bring the tobacco tray. Bring tea."

" Silence, Sōshichi," said Kuémon, casting a suspicious look about him. " It was but four or five days ago that we met at Osaka when we promised to meet in the capital and now you seem to be removing, eh ? Why and whither are you going ? It makes me anxious."

" You need have no fears. I have just returned from Osaka and haven't had time yet even to wash my feet. The fact is, my father is such an old man that I can no longer live apart from him : accordingly we've agreed to live together and all my belongings have been taken to his residence. That's why everything here is in confusion. Where are you

putting up ? I'll soon let you know my new address. Well—
er—excuse us a moment."

The couple prepared to make off, but Kuémon interposed.

" One moment ! You look startled and ill at ease.
Strange ! Remember, the season of our trade is returning.
Since I mean to set out for Nagasaki to-morrow I have come
for the note of identification we entrusted to your care. Give
me the note before you go out."

" Certainly. But because the note is so precious I put
it in a box, sealed the box, and entrusted the same to my
father. I will presently send it to you."

At this Kuémon turned colour.

" What ! " he burst out angrily. " You have entrusted
the note to your father ? Remember that in the quest of our
fortunes we are in the habit of making voyages over three
thousand miles of waves and that note constitutes the only
surety in our traffic. Its value is only second to that of our
lives. And can you really mean that you have entrusted
it to your father ? Don't utter such nonsense ! I believe
it is your intention to secede from our circle and to monopolize
the trade. For such a purpose you plan to abandon us
without my knowledge. There's no doubt about that. You
have that note on your person, I'll be bound. I will take it
from you by force."

With these words he lost no time in fastening the latches
of the main door and of the side door, then he advanced into
the middle of the room. Kojorō was frightened.

" Kuémon Sama," she pleaded, " how can there be double-
dealing between us who are as close as fish and water ? I will
not fail to hand you that note in two or three days. Will you
please go now."

She tried to push him gently out of doors.

" A beggarly nuisance ! " cried Kuémon, and seizing her
by the arm he threw her to the floor.

Sōshichi lost his head.

" A fine way to treat a helpless woman, when you could treat me as you will ! "

He laid hands upon his sword.

" You can't frighten me, young man. I mean to have that note and have it I will, no matter how ! "

He had scarcely spoken when his sword left its sheath. Sōshichi jumped back, drew his, and in a flash steel tingled on steel. Thrust and cut were sure, but the old bamboo floor being rotten in some parts both had considerable difficulty in fighting, for their feet ever and again caught in the decayed bamboos. Squarely matched, neither could injure the other : did Kuémon cut at Sōshichi's right, Sōshichi leapt to the left ; when Sōshichi thrust at Kuémon's left, Kuémon dodged to the right. And at each thrust and parry the swords glittered like icicles.

Despite the danger, more terrible than that of treading upon ice that is thawing beneath the spring-tide sun, Kojorō placed herself between the fighters and tried to knock away Kuémon's weapon with a broom. Her feet caught in the bamboo flooring ; she stumbled ; fell down. Over her the swords continued to flash.

The sound of the fight became audible to the neighbours, but they were too terrified to intervene. Not so Sōzaémon. His affection for his son forbade passivity. He rushed to the doors.

" Sōshichi ! Stop fighting ! I will give you the note of identification."

But the fighters were too excited to pay heed. He pushed against the doors, beat against them with both hands, but they would not open. He peeped through the chinks and was horror-struck to behold the struggle at its height. With an exclamation of terror, and twisted up with anguish, he ran round to the rear of the house.

Within doors Kojorō, who had removed a paper door to serve both as a shield and weapon, endeavoured to batter down Kuémon's sword ; but, her strength proving insufficient, she fell down with the door upon her back. Kuémon seized his chance to thrust at her. But his feet caught in the frame of the door and he too fell. As he lay he tried to stab her through the door. Sōshichi lifted his weapon.

" Kill Kojorō and I kill you ! "

At this juncture a small hole was broken in the wall ; a hand was thrust through, waving a roll of paper. The paper arrested the attention of the combatants. To his surprise and joy Sōshichi perceived the paper to be the note of identification.

" Look at that, Kuémon ! " cried Sōshichi. " Now that it is restored to you you can have no further quarrel with me. Let us cease our useless struggle."

Both swords were forthwith sheathed. Touched by his father's affection, Sōshichi lifted the note and the hand that bore it to his forehead in token of gratitude. Then, taking the note from the hand, he offered it to Kuémon saying, " Here is your note, Kuémon."

Kuémon received it and carefully examined it.

" Yes, this is the note. I acknowledge its receipt. Forgive my rashness, Sōshichi, and never harbour ill-feelings toward me again. Remember our trade is one carried on at the risk of our lives and that it is our custom to renew our friendships the very moment we sheathe our swords. You look pale and seem worried. Have courage. Do not lose your self-possession though a mountain crumble to pieces beside you : for otherwise you cannot prosper in our calling. Come to Nagasaki when our trading season opens and meet us there. Farewell, Sōshichi and Kojorō."

So saying, Kuémon took himself off composedly enough.

Sōshichi helped Kojorō to her feet. Great tears coursed

down his face. " Did you understand what passed, my dear ? How great is my father's compassion ! Thanks to it we are saved from death. Well may you prostrate yourself before the breach in the wall ! "

" What compassion ! What kindness ! I am indeed grateful. It grieves me that this wall prevents me from seeing your father's face. What misery is mine ! I am out of breath and cannot speak. How I should love some hot water, nay, even cold water."

She panted ; but to her great regret not a tea-cup nor a ladle was to be found in the empty house.

" I am very thirsty ; what shall I do ? "

Her words reached Sōzaémon's ears. His hand reappeared through the wall and in the hand was a cup containing tepid water. At sight of this kindly hand the couple cried, " Thanks, father, how good of you ! " They grasped the hand affectionately " Not even a cup of *saké* bestowed by a nobleman, not even a sovereign medicine, not even the libation of a tutelary deity can compare with this cup of water ! " They received the cup reverently and drank from it by turns.

" Dear father-in-law," said Kojorō, grasping the hand once more, " I am delighted to take your hand, but I am sorry I cannot see your face. Please understand that, though I have not yet your approval, I am your daughter-in-law. Please forgive Sōshichi San's error and condescend to see him and permit me to have a first and last glance at your face."

So saying she pressed the hand to her face again and again and burst into tears. Albeit Sōzaémon's face remained invisible they could easily imagine his deep grief from the agitation of his hand. Presently the hand shook itself free of Kojorō's grasp. A purse was thrown in and the hand vanished in such a manner as to suggest that the pair should retire forthwith. Now that they found it impossible to address their father they again gave way to tears.

" It is true compassion on his part to make a present of money for travelling to an unfilial son," said Sōshichi, holding the purse in his hand, " and it would be all the more unfilial to refuse the favour."

Each held the purse in turn to their foreheads in token of gratitude.

" It is now so dark that no one can perceive us leaving. Let us set out at once, my dear."

They tucked up their clothing as a preparation for the journey and left the house not without tears. Sōshichi could not tear his eyes away from the house next door. He stood at its gate to murmur, " Old woman, can't you manage to let Kojorō have a glimpse of her father-in-law ? I too wish to thank him for the money he has given me to help us on our journey."

Low as he spoke, the whisper was not lost upon the old woman. She made as if to come out to him, but Sōzaémon called to her from within.

" What are you about, old woman ? I deserve no thanks. Why, I did no more than throw into the next house money raised by disposing of the articles in it. Sōzaémon taught his son how to do business. He does not acknowledge the existence of a son who gets his living by unlawful means. Wretched and pitiable Sōshichi's condition is ! Call to mind that Heaven, the sun and moon, the Gods and Buddha do not willingly punish a man, but that man it is who offers himself for punishment by them. Nature has provided food for all. When man comes into the world he finds that which will nurture him—his mother's breast—those who engage in a lawful occupation find that Heaven does not fail, but provides nurture appropriate to one's station in life. Often may a man seem to live in luxury and comfort upon ill-gotten gains, but this is only appearance, not reality. Sooner or later the nurture of Heaven will fail him ; he will find himself an orphan in the world ; drag out a profitless existence and die at length the death of a dog. Such indeed is only too often the case. The dog eats his food from the ground and envies not the cat sleeping quietly by a fireplace inasmuch as he is content with his own status. Alas, that I should find a fool below a dog in this respect. I fancy I can see his final doom. My very anger makes me pity him."

Despite his harsh words it was evident that he could not control his tears.

" Sōshichi, if once more you wish to be considered Sōzaémon's son, tread the path of righteousness however poor you be. In this way only can you escape the death of a wretch. Take care of your life, that you die not before Sōzaémon. Fail not to attend his funeral in mourning garments. Thus alone shall I be happy in my coffin and acknowledge you as my son. Till then, farewell. Be gone quickly."

With these words he wept so bitterly that the sound of his crying pierced the hearts of the listeners. It was with sorrow that the pair took their hesitating leave.

III

Four days after leaving the capital Sōshichi and Kojorō found themselves at Seki, a post-town in the province of Isé. There the foot-worn travellers halted before a stone image of Jizō, a guardian god of children. Fervently were they praying to the deity that he might soften Sōzaémon toward them when palanquin bearers accosted them.

" Cannot we serve you, sir ? "

" That may be. We are going to the province of Owari. How much will you charge to carry us to the next stage ? "

" It is five miles to Ishiyakushi, the next stage, so we ask you for *korori*." [1]

Sōshichi was startled.

" I don't know how much *korori* is."

" A hundred *mon*, sir."

" Too much. Come down to seventy."

" Very good, sir."

With the care-worn fugitives within their palanquins the bearers presently began a rapid march, keeping time in their steps to the cries : " *Sokosei !* "—" *Katasei !* "—" *Makkasei !* " Mile succeeded mile, until Oiwaki was reached, where it was customary to change palanquins and bearers. The carriers therefore stopped. Kojorō stepped out promptly, but Sōshichi would not get down, so great was his fear lest the bearers' sign " *korori* " should prove a bad omen. His mind might be said to be fettered [2] with apprehension ere his body was tied [2] to the detective's cord.

" Well, Kojorō," said Sōshichi, " you had better change palanquins and go ahead of me."

" I will."

" And wait for me at a place called Yokkaichi."

" I will, my husband."

Kojorō, all unaware of Sōshichi's fears, changed palanquins and let herself be carried ahead. A few minutes later a palanquin arrived from the next stage. The newcomers addressed Sōshichi's bearers.

" Isn't your passenger the companion of the young woman who's just gone on ? Let us exchange passengers."

" That'll suit us nicely. Now, sir, we're going to do an exchange. Please descend."

[1] *Korori*, a sign among the bearers, was also used in the following sense : " His head, being cut off, rolled down *korori*."

[2] A play on words.

The bearers lifted the blind of the palanquin for Sōshichi. The passenger of the other palanquin had already stepped out. He was lightly dressed in drawers and leggings, carried a packet in his hand and a *hayanawa* [1] in his belt. Sōshichi but glimpsed at him and shuddered. He turned his face away and covered his head with a *tenugui*.[2] Hurriedly he descended and with a brief " Thank you, bearers ", stepped into the other palanquin and quickly pulled down the blind.

" I'm in a hurry," he said in a tremulous voice. " I'll give you extra ; start quickly."

He had hardly uttered these words when a shrill voice cried, " We arrest Komachiya Sōshichi ! "

The next moment a strong hempen cord had been wound round his palanquin. The terror-stricken captive struggled in the palanquin but to no purpose ; and he could but cry like a caged [3] bird. Armed detectives, lying in ambush, emerged and surrounded him.

" Prisoner, you know what charge we arrest you on. The official information asserts that there are eight in your gang. We have come to arrest you. Do you permit yourself to be arrested, or shall we have to bind you by force ? "

To this the prisoner made no reply, but was heard to address a plaintive prayer to Amida Buddha.

" No," said the first detective, " let us take him as he is to the next stage and bind him when we get there. That's more convenient. Now, bearers, move off."

"Certainly, sir, but inasmuch as he can't escape death, why don't you bind him here ? "

So murmuring, the bearers approached the palanquin

---

[1] A cord for binding criminals.

[2] A towel.

[3] Japanese words for cage and palanquin have the same sound : *kago*. Here the author makes a clever use of his favourite device, a play upon words, in this case untranslatable into English.

and lifted it, when, to their amazement, blood dribbled down *gaba-gaba* from it, instantaneously forming a scarlet patch upon the ground. The occupant uttered a groan of pain. The affrighted coolies cried, " The prisoner has killed himself in the palanquin ! Come and look ! "

The palanquin was hastily set to earth. The bearers drew apart. The detectives unwound the cord from the palanquin and raised its blind. Sōshichi, with fixed eyes, was gasping after a mortal fashion. The long blade plunged in his right side was buried to the hilt. Its point protruded from his left. The detectives were speechless with terror and dismay.

Kojorō, bound, was brought back. Seeing her husband's plight she was struck with unspeakable grief. She trod the tide of blood. She thrust her face into the palanquin.

" I am here, Sōshichi San. Kojorō is here, Sōshichi. I was bound a few minutes ago. Till last night we slept together. We had a vow to die in the same hour. And now, despite our vows, you have died alone, leaving me behind to suffer by myself. That is selfish of you. But never mind that now. You must be in pain ; I see you are in great pain."

With these words she wept and, sinking down, placed her face in the dying man's lap. Intelligence returned to the eyes of Sōshichi.

" Ah, Kojorō," he gasped, " are you bound ? I am a wicked man who has broken the national laws and disobeyed my father. I have so narrowed the compass of the wide world that my own home could no longer be a home to me and have wandered to this place till at last I am caught in a heavenly net—quite naturally and justly. Were I brought to my home and there executed I should bring disgrace on all my relatives and prove doubly undutiful to my father. With this thought in my mind I have done the deed you see.

U

This is just retribution I now receive for having joined Kezori Kuémon's gang of smugglers and having lived above my station.   And since in the eye of the law a wife cannot escape connection with her husband's crime, you are bound, undergo dishonour and are made to suffer—all of which is caused by my own wicked nature.   But for Sōshichi you would not have suffered thus.   Poor girl!   How great must be your grief! You have to sacrifice your life on account of the man with whom you have lived for but a short space of time.   Pray forgive me, Kojorō."

Sōshichi breathed with difficulty.   Death second by second drew nearer.   The stern detectives, taking pity upon the sorrowful pair, spoke gently.   " When you reach prison you will not be suffered to see each other.   Man must help man.   Take your fill of speech now."

The more Kojorō listened to Sōshichi's kind words the more sorrowful she grew.

" Sōshichi San, my dear, you are not to blame.   For whose sake is it you have done what you have done ?   Out of eagerness to prevent Kojorō passing into another's hands you joined Kuémon and forsook even your father.   At the risk of your life you became my husband, so dearly have you loved me.   So overcome am I at your goodness to me that I cannot find even in Chinese or Hindoo, still less in Japanese, fit words to express my gratitude.   Were my hands but unbound I would prostrate myself before you ere I die."

Anguish took her.   She wept so bitterly that she seemed almost to lose consciousness.

" Now," gasped Sōshichi, " now comes the last moment we behold each other in this life.   In the next world, remember, we shall be husband and wife.   Namu Amida Buddha."

The voice that prayed was faint.   Then he drew the sword

from his side and almost in the same moment ceased to breathe. Piteous was Kojorō's cry. "Husband, stay [1] for me a moment! I would accompany you! Sooner or later I shall be slain. Officers, have mercy! Slay me here—slay me, I entreat you!"

She wailed and rushed hither and thither in the frenzy of madness. At this moment a police superintendent and his underlings arrived, convoying Kezori Kuémon, his followers and their respective courtesans. All were bound. All had been captured in one place or another. The leader of the party unrolled a scroll and read as follows :

"Prisoners, I read you an Imperial mandate. Listen to it with gratitude. Forasmuch as you have committed the crime of smuggling in connection with great ships in the offing in defiance of the national laws, you richly deserve capital punishment. But in honour of his coronation, His Majesty the Emperor is graciously pleased to pardon you and to release you from such a penalty."

The gratitude of the prisoners knew no bounds. They cried out for joy. The police superintendent addressed the courtesans.

"Forasmuch as your profession compelled you to become the companions of these men you are guilty of no crime. Henceforward you can go whither you choose. Now, men, set these women free."

The constables released the women. The courtesans caressed the abrasions the cords had caused.

---

[1] Lovers of English poetry will recall the lovely lines of Henry King's (1592–1669) Exequy on His Wife :—

> "Stay for me there : I will not fail
> To meet thee in that hollow vale.
> And think not much of my delay :
> I am already on the way,
> And follow thee with all the speed
> Desire can make, or sorrows breed."

Reviser's Note.

" The power of His Majesty the Emperor," they exclaimed, " is great indeed ! Our hands are freed from the cords. We feel like birds escaped from their cages."

But Kojorō, albeit set at freedom like her companions, continued to weep. At length she lifted her head.

" Sorrow it is that my husband Sōshichi has forsaken me and his soul winged its way to the other world or ever the compassion of this edict could be made known to him. This life is not now worth while the living for this ' Kojorō of Hakata ', who is just like a bird which has lost its mate by death.[1] Officers, have mercy ! Slay me ! "

The bitter tears fell.

" Your grief is natural," said the sympathetic superintendent. " Though your husband was one of a gang of ruffians, he joined them out of youthful folly and infatuation. It follows therefore that his offence was small. We regret that his impetuosity should have led to his suicide. We grieve on your behalf, but nothing is to be done. Your best course will be to serve your father-in-law in Sōshichi's place and busy yourself in prayers for the peace of the departed soul. Now, my men, treat the prisoners as the Imperial edict commands."

Of the smugglers who had escaped death some were branded or tattooed upon the face, others had their ears or

---

[1] I refer the reader to John Webster's *Dutchesse of Malfy*—that beautiful extended passage (Act 4, Scene 1, lines 60–90) wherein the Dutchesse, having been deceived by the counterfeit dead hand of Antonio presented her, expresses her abhorrence of life. For example :—

Bosola.   Come, you must live.
Dutchesse. That's the greatest torture soules feele in hell,
         In hell : that they must live and cannot die.

See also Sophocles' Electra (Campbell's translation) :—

         " Nay, death is not so hateful as when one
         Desiring death is balked of that desire."

                                        Reviser's Note.

noses cut off that they might not repeat their offences. Then they were set free.

The rumour of the adventures of the hapless Hakata damsel did not take long to spread far and wide. It remained a topic of conversation for generations afterwards.

A SCENE FROM *THE DESIGN OF CHRYSANTHEMUMS*, BY MOKU-AMI
From a colour print by Toyokuni

[*face p.* 310

THE SOGAS' JANUARY, A KABUKI PLAY, BY SEGAWA JOKŌ THE SECOND,
PERFORMED BY FAMOUS ACTORS OF OLD JAPAN

From a colour print by Toyokuni the First

A MARIONETTE PERFORMANCE

Notice that these, minor puppets are operated only by showmen of less importance who wear black hoods and robes to render themselves inconspicuous.

JŌRURI CHANTERS READY TO SING

THE TETHERED STEED

(Kwan-Hasshū Tsunagi-Uma)

THE TETHERED STEED

(*Kwan-Hasshū Tsunagi-Uma*)

I

In February of the second year of the Eien era (A.D. 988), during the reign of the Emperor Ichijō the sixty-sixth monarch, Minamoto-no-Yorimitsu the Shogun, attended by his brave retainers Watanabé-no-Tsuna and Sakata-no-Kintoki, proceeded to the palace in response to an Imperial summons occasioned by the daily apparition of a goblin horse within the Imperial precincts. Particulars of the creature were supplied by Fujiwara-no-Kanéié, the Regent. The Shogun and his retainers, after fitting preparations for its destruction, awaited the phenomenon.

Noon was come when, on a sudden, precisely at the Hour of the Horse, the sky became overcast, a storm accompanied by thunder and lightning got up, and there appeared in the gardens a black charger of powerful build, having a flowing mane rugged as the ridges of a mountain range, towering ears great as conches, eyes bright as polished mirrors of copper. Right loudly he snorted ; terribly he neighed ; hither and thither he raged. Black clouds of dust sprang from beneath his hoofs as he trampled the lawns and dashed between the trees. Into the air he leapt and made as if to wing his way into the palace. Tsuna and Kintoki, hurling themselves upon him from right and left, exerted their superhuman might to stay him. But, in a moment shaking them off, the beast raged to and fro the more furiously. Perceiving the apparition to be beyond the power even of his retainers, Yorimitsu, when he had thrice in a loud voice declared, " I am Minamoto-no-Yorimitsu the Shogun, the Lord of Settsu and a descendant of the august Emperor Seiwa ! "—set an arrow to his great bow, bent the bow to its utmost extent, and shot. Pierced through the muzzle, the phantom gave one loud groan and crashed to earth. Next instant the beast had vanished and, to the admiration and boundless joy of the Regent and his courtiers, the storm ceased.

When the Regent Kanéié had made an end of praising the exploit of Yorimitsu and his retainers, he summoned to his presence a famous doctor of divination, for he wished to ascertain the whereabouts of the goblin. The doctor consulted an occult volume and presently it became known that the hiding-place of the monster lay south-east of the palace. Yorimitsu, his retainers and the courtiers, assisted by lower officials, made their way to an ancient treasure-house standing upon the spot indicated and subjected it to a prolonged search. Extreme was their surprise to discover therein an ancient coffer in which the Shogun's arrow had buried itself up to half its length. Upon the lid of the coffer no inscription was to be found save the brief words " March of the third year of Tengyō era ". Terror seized the entire party, but after some reflection Yorimitsu slapped his thigh and exclaimed, " I have it ! That was the date on which the rebel Taira-no-Masakado was overthrown during the reign of the Emperor Shujaku. This was his crime—by pretending to be a Prince Imperial he succeeded in raising an army in the Eastern Provinces, to the end that he might usurp the throne, only at last to suffer death at the hands of the Royal army. One night, so the story goes, a sinister star fell into his stable and transformed itself into a swift steed. The rebel deemed it an omen tokening success to the enterprises of his villainous ambition. He set up the horse as a god of war, worshipped it, and adopted as the crest upon the curtains of his pavilion a tethered steed. This coffer, I feel sure, contains the curtain of his pavilion which Fujiwara-no-Hidésato, commander-in-chief of the Royal troops, brought back as trophy when he returned victorious. I have received a report that Yoshikado, the youngest son of the deceased traitor, now grown to manhood, has gathered a band of malcontents about him and is busy amassing treasure by pillaging villages, a sure sign of a proposed rebellion. We may suppose that the evil spirit of the vindictive Masakado has been transmitted to his son and has breathed a soul into the steed upon his pavilion curtain, with the result that we have seen the cursed goblin." On this the mysterious coffer, tightly locked though it was, was opened in the presence of the Emperor and the Regent. Its contents proved to be exactly such as Yorimitsu had indicated. The Emperor, struck with profound admiration at the doughty deed and at the sagacity of the Shogun, graciously bestowed upon him a beautiful wine-cup, together with a mandate entrusting to him the management [1] of all affairs of state, and directed him soon to appoint an heir to the office and possessions. The Emperor also commanded Lord Ebumi, the Prime Minister, to take custody of the pavilion curtain.

Yorimitsu, who had no son of his own, saw nothing for it but to make one of his younger brothers, Yorinobu and Yorihira, his heir. But so nearly equal in character and ability were they, that Yorimitsu found it impossible to choose between them, and therefore determined to solve the problem by an appeal to the divine will of the God Hachiman, patron deity of the Minamoto family. The ceremony was held in the grand hall of his palace upon the evening of a lucky day

[1] In those days the Shogun was the *de facto* ruler, while the Prime Minister was but a figurehead.

especially selected for the purpose.   The shrine was set upon a dais and before it were laid a variety of offerings.   On a desk in the centre of the hall stood a large quiver filled with arrows having white feathers and arrows having black, thirty-three arrows of each kind, which symbolized the office of the Shogun who was guardian of the sixty-six provinces that constituted the Empire of Japan.   A great brightness filled the room by reason of those waves of holy light with which the many candles glistened.   Lady Yorimitsu, attended by her maid-of-honour Kochō,[1] a girl of supreme beauty, summoned to her presence the Shogun's trusted retainer Hirai-no-Yasumasa and thus addressed him :   " You and other chief retainers of His Highness the Shogun are presently to gather before the altar ; the candles will then be put out and each of you will be required to pick in the darkness an arrow from the quiver, the doing of which shall prove an oracle.   If the white feathered arrows thus drawn outnumber the black, Yorinobu shall be heir ; if not, Yorihira shall succeed.   You or one of the ' Greatest Four '[2] should by rights be director of the ceremony.   But, forasmuch as men are subject to the suspicion of being under the influence of party spirit, my maid Kochō here is to preside over the rite. . . .   Be so good as to tell my brothers-in-law to come here separately and offer their prayers to the deity."   She then retired into the inner apartments.

No sooner had Yasumasa departed towards the rooms of the Shogun's brothers than Kochō's heart began to beat like the clapper of an alarm bell and a fire crept in her veins, for it seemed to her that now or never was the night on which to disclose to Yorinobu her ardent and long-established passion.   Ere long the handsome warrior appeared, attired

---

[1] " Little Butterfly."

[2] Kintoki, Tsuna, Suétaké and Sadamitsu, the bravest of the Shogun's retainers, were called his *Shitennō*, or " Big Four ".

in the utmost splendour, and the sight of him sitting in a dignified manner before the altar troubled her eyes. As she listened in a trance to the murmur of his prayer, there emanated from his clothes a delicious odour of incense and this odour seemed to waft her into the air. No sooner had the maid, attracted as by a charm, drawn near to him, than she leaned against him and, utterly losing her head, all but embraced him on the spur of the moment. Despite all his native self-possession, Yorinobu was nevertheless surprised.

" Excuse my rudeness, my lord. I slipped against you by accident."

She drew back and gazed shyly downward a moment, then, controlling her beating heart as best she might, she continued in a whisper, " Many a time have I intended to reveal my secret to your lordship, but whenever I met you face to face my heart failed me and I dared not confess it. Your lordship may well understand how I feel."

" I understand, girl," returned Yorinobu, nodding his head and showing no signs of surprise, " I have heard that you are intimate with the family of the Prime Minister, Lord Ebumi, and you often call at their residence. I believe what you call your secret to be a message from Lady Eika,[1] eldest daughter of the Premier. As regards this matter we have by frequent correspondence come to a mutual understanding, yet I am sorry my station in life hardly permits me to comply with her eager request that I meet her by stealth. Since I have already acquainted the Shogun and his wife, it cannot be long, should the question of heirship be decided in my favour, before I can openly take her to wife ; therefore carry my salutations to Lady Eika and tell her to abide the time in patience. And now, if we talk any longer, I fear we may be overheard. Let us again speak together at some other time." With that Yorinobu hurriedly made his

---

[1] " Singing."

way into the inner rooms. Stupefied with disappointment, the maid found herself bereft of speech and looked as one who dreams that she dreams.

"Alas!" she said, when she had recovered. "All these long years have I yearned for him with such passion that oftentimes I could hardly sleep. With my eyes set upon the prospect of happiness my duties have proved no burden at all to me. Indeed this has enabled me to work harder than my comrades and I have fervently prayed to the gods and to Buddha morning and evening that I might attain my desire. And this—this is the result! Hateful Lady Eika, to be so frank and confidential with me and yet to have kept such a secret as this from me! A vixen! 'All's fair in love and war.' I will not hesitate to use every means to thwart her purposes, though I die in the process. Never will I rest content till I have avenged myself upon her."

She was still a prey to the flames of jealousy when Yorihira entered the room. She instantly approached him and whispered, "Kindly excuse an inopportune request, my lord, but permit me to deliver an urgent message from . . . the truth is that Lady Eika, daughter of Lord Ebumi, has long nursed a secret passion for you, a longing so extreme as to cause her to pine away. Each time I see her the love-sick girl begs me to contrive some means whereby she may, while yet there is life in her, meet you in secret. Hapless creature that she is! If you feel any pity for her I will do my best to arrange——"

"One moment," Yorihira interrupted. "To be frank I fell in love with her at first sight, on the occasion of a New Year Party at Court, but coming to hear of her exchanges with my brother I was greatly disappointed and now believe my love's cause to be hopeless."

"No, no, my lord," returned Kochō encouragingly, "that they exchanged notes is true, but they found themselves mistaken in their attachment. Her love toward you, however, is sincere and springs from the very depths of her heart. Why should I deceive you ? By the gods, I am speaking the exact truth. Abandon your doubts and believe me."

" I trust that what you say is true and that I shall not prove a traitor to my brother, and I beg of you to serve as a ferry-boat between our loves."

The maid secretly sighed her relief and the satisfaction she felt in observing that the young warrior had fallen an easy prey to her wiles.

At that moment the water-clock struck the appointed hour and the Shogun's consort and Yorinobu, followed by Yasumasa and twenty-seven other chief retainers of the Shogun, all clad in ceremonial costume, appeared.

The company seated themselves. At her lady's command Kochō declared the ceremony commenced and, lifting a fan of silken gauze, immediately extinguished the candles. In silence and in darkness warrior after warrior proceeded to the quiver and drew each an arrow. When the rustling of clothes and of footsteps had continued a few minutes, Mita-no-Jirō Tomozuna, cousin of Watanabé-no-Tsuna, stepped forward to take his arrow. Hard by the quiver the sweet odour of incense emanating from Kochō's garments proved irresistible to one already under the influence of the saké that had been served in honour of the occasion. Over-whelmed by the spell of a potent and intangible voluptuous-ness that in the darkness made his senses swim, Tomozuna, hardly cognizant of what he did, drew her tightly to him. Kochō was startled, but, being quick-witted, instantly determined to seize this opportunity of demonstrating her single-hearted devotion to Yorinobu. She seized in her hands the string of Tomozuna's headgear and, drawing her dirk, cut it off ; then she pushed him away.

" Ah ! " she cried vehemently. " Here is a wretch who

catches at me before the very altar, under cover of the darkness. Lights! Lights! The profaner must be known, for I have cut off the string of his headgear in token of his guilt."

All present were amazed. In a moment Tomozuna had become sober. He turned pale. " Abominable hussy," he thought, " heartless wench! Shall I slay her? Or shall I make reparation by self-slaughter?"—he grasped the hilt of his sword—" but I would not die alone."

At this juncture the voice of Yorihira was heard crying, " Do not bring the lights yet; I have an idea. Warriors, cut the strings of your headgears, and when you have so done, forthwith give a signal cry. Then let the lights be brought."

The samurai lost not a moment in obeying the command. When the hall was once more brilliantly illumined, the headgear strings of all the warriors had disappeared Thus was Tomozuna saved from an infamous death by the ready wits of the cunning Yorihira. The large-hearted lady spoke not a word concerning the affair, but ordered the arrows picked by the warriors to be brought her. When her examination had been concluded she exclaimed, " A miracle! As you can see for yourselves, not a single white-feathered arrow can be found among these twenty-eight. See how just and impartial the divine will has been in choosing the elder brother, Lord Yorinobu. The result of this night's ceremony will be duly reported to the throne and then upon some day of luck Lord Yorinobu will be appointed to the heirship. Rejoice, all of you! Remain in this hall and make merry over the saké [1] offered to the deity."

With these words the lady and her brothers-in-law withdrew amidst tumultuous cheering in honour of the long life and prosperity of the Minamoto family.

Late one night when the sinking moon shed a sickly light

[1] *Saké* offered to a deity on such occasions is generally afterwards shared by the family as a form of congratulation.

Sakata-no-Kintoki, one of the Greatest Four of the Shogun, was patrolling the streets. He wore the disguise of a pedlar, for the capital was riddled with Yoshikado's followers, who nightly committed robbery and murder. As he paced close under the earthen wall of the mansion of the Prime Minister, Lord Ebumi, he suddenly felt his face touched by a strange something. He discovered it to be a daffodil dependent from a fine cord hung over the wall.

" What can this be ? " exclaimed the warrior in wonder. " A charm against plague or robbery, I suppose. But folks generally use garlic. This tasteful substitute is worthy of Lord Ebumi the poet."

With these words, scarcely thinking what he was doing, he gently jerked the cord. Whereupon a woman's voice was heard within making a faint response. His curiosity was aroused. He repeated the pull and found himself offered a tangible answer, for presently a pretty maid emerged from the wicket. She peered at Kintoki as he stood there in the shadow of the wall.

" Welcome, my lord," she whispered. " For love's sake, I see, you have this disguise. I pray you come in, my lord. My lady impatiently awaits you."

So saying, the maid approached him. Her consternation was considerable when she perceived his grim red face and saucer-like eyes. She gave one short cry of dismay, then rushed within and fastened the gate.

Scarcely had she done so when Kintoki's fellow night-watchman, Watanabé-no-Tsuna, arrived at the spot. Many soldiers, armed with iron rods as well as swords, and bearing bright lanterns upon poles, attended him in processional formation. Kintoki, unaccompanied as he was by henchmen, rallied his comrade upon the ostentation of his march. Tsuna made an unanswerable rejoinder. Kintoki was silenced and they went their respective ways.

X

They had been but a little while gone and the streets had fallen completely silent again when two figures stole to the wall of the Premier's mansion. They were Kochō and Yorihira. Yorihira was disguised as a woman wearing a *kazuki*.[1] " Kochō," whispered Yorihira, " I owe you my thanks for bringing about this meeting."

" Why thank me, my lord ?   To attain my purpose I must use every means at my command to bring their relations to an end.   That is the reason that I have arranged this for you. It is I, not your lordship, should say ' Thank you '.   I will use only the first half of your name, saying simply ' Yori Sama '.   Lady Eika and her maids will then believe that you are Lord Yorinobu.   You will have to haste lest you be discovered.   When you have both awakened she will have become assuredly yours, however much she may complain of your stratagem.   See this flower !—it is her ladyship's signal."

With these words Kochō pulled the cord, when the maid opened the door as before.   Guided by her the two went within.

The moon had set.   It was pitch-dark.   A group of figures clad in black approached the wall.   They were Yoshikado's generals, Yasusuké and his son Tokiakira, and their respective followers.   Both Yasusuké, a younger brother of Hirai-no-Yasumasa, and his son, had been retainers of the Shogun, but the vileness of their characters had prompted their liege lord to exile them.   Their present purpose was to surprise the mansion of Lord Ebumi that they might steal the pavilion curtain decorated with the crest of a tethered steed, which had been confided to the Premier's keeping.

Yasusuké conferred in whispers with his son, then, knock-

---

[1] The *kazuki* or *katsugi* was a large and flowing coat worn over the head and reaching down to the waist, so that it served as a veil.   In days of old, ladies of high birth wore it when walking out.

ing upon the gate the while, he shouted, " Ho ! Within there ! An urgent message from His Highness the Shogun ! "

But the warders of the gate, rubbing their sleepy eyes, only answered, " Our master's away to-night, being on duty at court," and would not open.

" Your master's absence is of no account to us," returned Yasusuké sternly. " Forasmuch as her ladyship Eika has become betrothed to Lord Yorinobu, who has just been appointed heir to the Shogunate, I am come as the bearer of a present from his lordship. The saying goes :

> ' Who to the doing of a deed,
> Good in itself, adds also speed,
> Does verily a good indeed.'

I, Watanabé-no-Tsuna, despite the darkness of midnight, have hastened on this errand. Open the gate and be quick about it ! "

At so peremptory a demand the thoughtless porters immediately flung wide the great gate.

Yorihira started up in bed. He had heard the shouted announcement of an urgent messenger bringing a betrothal present. He confessed all to Lady Eika and poured out prayers that she would forgive the infatuation of his deed. The girl was speechless with amazement, but, after some reflection, returned in tones of unshakable resolve, " It's no use crying over spilt milk, my lord. Once having given herself to a man, even though giving herself under misapprehension or suffering herself to be beguiled, a woman should stick to him all her life. I no longer have any desire to wed your brother. If we escape together before the presents of betrothal have been exchanged no infamy of betrayal will attach to us. I am quite willing to abandon my parents for the sake of the love we have shared this night. Don't forsake me, dear Yorihira Sama."

She clung to him with tenderness. Kochō was at their side before they were aware.

" A brave resolve ! " said she. " As for me, I will plead with your parents. Harbour no regrets, but flee at once. I will accompany you till day dawns."

Eika lost no time in making herself ready. The three stole out by the postern gate.

On a sudden all was uproar and confusion within. Shrieks arose and a noise of splintering shutters and the crash of paper doors broken through. Blood-bedabbled samurai and servants rushed out. Lady Hagi, wife of Lord Ebumi, emerged from the great gate bearing the pavilion curtain beneath her arm and crossed swords with Yasusuké. Bravely enough she fought him for a while, but his son rushed forward and knocked her sword from her hand. A moment later he had pinned her to the ground. Yasusuké snatched the curtain, bade his son dispatch her, and rushed within. Tokiakira was about to behead the poor lady, when Tsuna and Kintoki, driving like squalls across a bay, precipitated themselves upon the wretch and bore him to the ground. While Tsuna helped the lady to her feet and tended her, Kintoki prised up the chin of Tokiakira pinned beneath his foot. " That drone, Yasumasa's nephew, eh ? " he cried. " Your fits of thieving, which not even your uncle's excellent remedy could relieve you of, I will cure by massage. It will mean a little pain for you of course. Summon up your courage."

With these words the hero, with one hand, wrenched off his head. Then he pitched the body inside the gate. Scared out of their wits at this wonderful display of strength, the other wretches, with the exception of Yasusuké who leapt upon the roof [1] of the great gate, lost not a moment in taking to their heels.

" Infamous fellow ! " cried Yasusuké, upright upon the

---

[1] Some gates have tiled or thatched roofs over the doors.

roof. " I call upon you to keep in mind that it is a crime to resist one who will be Regent to Yoshikado, the aspirant to the throne. Observe the courtesy proper toward a man of high station. You rascal ! "

" If that is what is troubling you, Your Highness the Regent," Kintoki returned with a laugh, " and you desire high rank, we will translate you to higher spheres and no mistake about it ! "

The eyes of the heroes exchanged a sign. Kintoki and Tsuna laid their hands upon the pillars of the gate, braced themselves, and lifted the gate. Right and left the earthen wall rumbled to the ground. Yasusuké, upon the roof, was raised aloft till the gate-posts were all but on the shoulders of the pair. Shaking with fear, the braggart coward clung to the crest tile.

" Good sirs, good sirs," said he, while his tears pattered on the tiles, " it's far too high here and I am feeling dizzy. Please, please !—I will give the curtain back. Save my life, good sirs ! Oh, please save my life ! "

" A baseless Regent indeed ! " cried Tsuna and Kintoki. " A fine thatch to keep the rain out ! "

A while they carried the gate about ; then, having tormented the would-be Regent to their satisfaction, they tore off the pillars to right and left. Tiles, timber and earth descended in a mass ; dust like black smoke started up ; and Yasusuké, flung head over heels on to the pavement, was cruelly crushed out of shape

II

The magnificent mansion of the Shogun commanded a fine view of Mount Hiéi, " the Fuji of the Imperial Capital ". Its gardens boasted a miniature hill adorned with fantastic rocks, trees of lovely shape, and a large pond fed through a bamboo pipe with the clear water of the Kamo river.

Late one afternoon several young maids were busying themselves sweeping and dusting the rooms of this mansion. For, following the elopement of Lady Eika, the Ex-Emperor had graciously arranged to bestow upon Yorinobu the hand of a court lady named Iyo-no-Naishi, a lady no less beautiful than Eika. Their wedding ceremony was to take place this very night.

" What can Kochō be about ? " grumbled one of the maids. " It is very lazy of her not to have shown her face yet. Kochō San ! Kochō San ! " she cried fretfully.

Kochō appeared. Her eyes were flushed with much weeping, her cheeks pale, and the powder upon them streaked by tears. The maid who had called Kochō cast a suspicious glance at her and remarked sarcastically, " What makes you look so glum on this happy occasion ? We, as you can see, have finished our tasks, while your part of sweeping the gardens remains undone. You had better be quick about it, and when you've done it you can play hide-and-seek or anything else you like at your leisure."

Kochō was thrown into such deep disappointment and agony at finding herself confronted with a new and powerful antagonist when she had successfully rid herself of Lady Eika, that she was but little affected by her comrade's cynical observations. She remained in a reverie.

" Now, Kochō San," cried another, " look, there's a big blue spider on that *yatsudé*.[1] An awful beast ! Its poison will kill a man. To think of such a creature being in front of the bride's apartment ! It's your duty to take it away or it may find its way into her dishes."

These words seemed to bring the love-sick girl to her senses —at any rate some happy idea seemed to cross her mind.

---

[1] The Fatsia Japonica.

The voice of the chief maid was heard. " A messenger has just announced the arrival of the bridal party. Make haste to the first hall ! "

The maids hastened within.

Stealthily Kochō stepped down into the garden and, catching the spider on a bamboo broom, without showing a sign of fear, wrapped it in a silk handkerchief. A horrible imprecation issued from her flower-like lips.

" Blue spider, blue spider ! They say that though you are only a mere insect, you possess miraculous powers, inasmuch as you can foretell the good or evil that is to be and can do many other things. They say that when your poison touches the lip, even of a hero possessed of superhuman strength, that man instantly dies a painful death. Receive my soul into your inch-long body and with your poison slay Iyo-no-Naishi between sunset and to-morrow's dawn ! Spin from your body a myriad threads that will so tightly bind together my lover Yorinobu Sama and myself that these bonds will not be loosed for all eternity. With all my being I make this prayer to you, the so little and the so mighty." Her invocation ended, she turned about and beheld all the rooms and corridors brilliantly illumined by candles and heard the sounds of merry-making. She had but taken two or three steps as though to return when a sudden signal-like whistle was heard without. Instantly she was all attention, glanced about her, and then, stealing to the water-pipe, applied her mouth to its spout from which the water had now ceased to flow.

" Brother," she spoke into the pipe, " you called me, did you not ? I am your sister—Kochō."

She applied her ear to the spout as though expecting a response.

The man she thus addressed was none other than Yoshi-kado, ringleader of the would-be rebels. He was now standing some way off in the dry river-bed whence the pipe took its course. Kochō was his sister and had entered the service of the Shogun's consort in order that she might play the spy. She was to convey to Yoshikado news of any opportunity for the assassination of Yorimitsu and his brother Yorinobu.

Yoshikado replied through the pipe. " Is it you, sister ? Yes, it is your brother speaking. What fools this Yorimitsu and his followers are ; they appear to have no idea that I am in their neighbourhood. Those idiots, the Greatest Four, are far away now searching for me and the samurai left behind as defenders are all poltroons. They will, I am sure, get dead drunk to-night on the *sake* served at the wedding and so be off their guard. There could not possibly be a better opportunity for assassinating Yorimitsu and his brother, imprisoning the Emperor and usurping the throne, and thus realizing the most cherished aspirations of our dead father. Watch for a chance to aid us and guide me in at the proper moment."

These words struck Kochō to the heart. Long ere this such cruel aspirations had perished as far as she was concerned, since Yorinobu, on the slaying of whom her brother was set, had become the object of her affections. How could she reconcile herself to contriving his death ? She became lost in thought.

Under cover of the darkness the Shogun's consort, to whom Kochō's absence from the feast had appeared strange, stole up. Perfectly unaware of her presence, Kochō made answer, " Brother, all is not yet quiet here. I am very much afraid that it will be impossible to find a chance to-night and were we to fail in our attempt it would only prove our sure destruction. In my opinion it is perfectly possible to wait some other and more favourable occasion. We had best bide our time in patience. When a good chance comes our way I will not fail to let you know. You had better turn back to-night, brother."

" I can't, I tell you, coward sister," cried Yoshikado angrily. " Let to-night go, and how can we be sure that another opportunity will occur ? Take your courage in both hands, sister, and guide me in."

No sooner had the lady heard these words than she drew her dagger, rushed upon the girl and dealt her a powerful stroke with it upon the shoulder. Kochō gave a shrill cry of pain and leaned backward. The lady made another stroke, seized her by the hair and pinned her to the ground. Hirai-no-Yasumasa, who had heard the cry, rushed out lantern in hand and was astonished at what confronted him. At the other end of the pipe Yoshikado, applying his ear to the orifice, impatiently awaited the answer. The lady, no whit discomposed, heaped her reproaches on the girl.

" Hateful woman ! Not only have you aimed, or so it would appear, at the death of Iyo-no-Naishi, but it has been your intention to guide a bandit. Vile doings ! Confess all ! You can no longer escape death."

" Guide to a bandit ! " Kochō gasped. " The insult is too great. I had resolved never to confess my secret, however mortal the torments to which I might be subjected ; but the ill name of a bandit's accomplice would disgrace the fair reputation of my noble ancestors. That is a prospect I cannot face ; I will therefore disclose my secret. I am the daughter of Taira-no-Masakado, a descendant of the Emperor Kwammu, and sister to Yoshikado. I entered your service under a false name, that I might spy out the movements of the Shogun and his brother, and thus assist the realization of my brother's ambitions. But while I watched an oppor-tunity for their destruction I was unfortunate enough to become the prey of passion. Slave as I am of my love for Lord Yorinobu, I have now quite forsaken my original attitude and these several months I have solely devoted myself to winning him. It was I who beguiled Lord Yorihira into eloping with my rival, Lady Eika. No sooner had I succeeded in ridding myself of her than I was confronted with another powerful rival, whose appearance here to-night is the cause of my despair. I was determined to poison Iyo-no-Naishi. She, however, has gained her life while I have lost mine. Assuredly this is heaven's punishment for my having disobeyed my dead father and my brother. Now that I can no longer win him I will do my utmost as an evil spirit and as a reborn mortal to prevent Lord Yorinobu and Naishi from dwelling together in happiness. I will not rest content till they are parted." Her eyes had a glare; her hair bristled. She sprang frenziedly to her feet and made as if to rush within; but Yasumasa lost not a moment in springing upon her. Her head fell to the ground. Meanwhile the lady applied her mouth to the pipe.

"Brother," she said in a feigned voice, "I am sorry it has taken me so long to find out how the land lies. The whole batch of them, the Shogun and his retainers alike, are now fallen dead asleep with drinking. You might set a light to them and they wouldn't wake up. This is our opportunity. Steal in through the south wicket which I will leave open; but be quick, quick!"

Yoshikado leapt for joy at so urgent a summons. "I thank you for your trouble, sister. I go at once."

The lady ordered Yasumasa to open the wicket and both went within.

Ere long Yoshikado glided in and, groping his way through the darkness of the garden, approached the brilliantly-illumined inner chambers. Yasumasa, veiled in a *kazuki* that he might have the appearance of Kochō, drew to the villain's side and suddenly grappled him.

"Bolder than your appearance!" Yoshikado exclaimed. "None the less, the Greatest Four are far away. Yasumasa? Resist me and you die, fool!"

He shook himself free. Yasumasa closed again. A well-matched pair, they wrestled upon the ground ; and now one had the advantage and now the other. So struggling, Yasumasa seized a chance to leap backwards and, drawing his sword, cut at his antagonist, who received a slight wound in the side. His adversary flinched. Yasumasa knelt upon him and, obtaining a lock upon his arm, made as if to rise and march him off. At this moment, wonder of wonders— Kochō's head leapt into the air and fitted itself upon her trunk. The frightful apparition stood upright. It seized Yasumasa by the nape and separated him from his prisoner, who instantly disappeared into the darkness.

" A great chance missed ! " Yasumasa cried, freeing himself. " Cursed be the wretch who interfered with me ! "

He glared behind him, and lo, Kochō's head and trunk separated each from each ! The body fell to the ground and there was no more apparition.

Yorihira and Eika, whom Kochō had so cleverly manœuvred, made their way the morning after leaving her father's house, in a northward direction toward Mount Kurama that they might seek sanctuary in the Buddhist temple upon the mountain, for Yorihira was acquainted with its superior. Not even the chill of the falling snow and the wind's icy blast sufficed to cool the ardour of their passion, which increased as they trudged on through fields and scattered villages. On the plain of Ichiharano, whither at length their weary limbs had borne them, they encountered six or seven giants, whose appearance they could but distrust. Supporting wicker baskets upon their backs, these giants were driving forward an ox heavily laden with a money-chest, a mirror-stand, swords, spears and halberds and, as they passed by, indulged in jeers at the expense of the weary lovers— " A pretty bit of goods ! Our hearts are quite captured."

One of them reached out his hand and took Eika by the waist-band. With an exclamation of horror she thrust his hand away and drew closer to Yorihira. " A dull-witted wench ! " cried the ruffian. " Let her know that we are not the sort of folk who fall a prey to the charms of woman, however lovely she may be. It is your beautiful clothes that fascinate us. Now you know what we are after ! We intend, before we let you proceed, to strip you naked. Young man, you are a handsome fellow enough in all conscience, but your handsome sword has more attraction for us than your person. You will both be so good at this instant to remove your clothes and to hand over your sword. Refuse, and we shall be compelled to give you a taste of the steel, and that would be a pity, for soiled clothes do not command so good a price. Life is precious. Doubtless you will be readier to part with your clothes than your lives." He turned to his companions. " That is true, comrades, isn't it ? "

Yorihira shielded the trembling Eika, then he said, " If you are in such need of my sword, I will give it you. Take this——"

He had hardly spoken when in a flash he drew and cleft the head of the terrible bearded giant. The other ruffians drew and slashed at him. The young warrior, of great strength and a notable swordsman, cut and hewed right and left. The ruffians, altogether outmatched, were about to take to their heels, when a giant, seemingly their chief, emerged from a neighbouring bush and seized Eika by the arm, crying, " Young man, fight as you do, and this is what will happen ! " He levelled the point of his sword against Eika's breast. Yorihira halted. " One moment ! Be not rash ! " he cried. " That lady is my wife whom I have won at the sacrifice of my rank and fief. I offer no further resistance."

He threw down his sword and stood motionless. A cold

sweat had gathered upon his body; agony clouded his forehead.

"So?" returned the leader, nodding sagely. "At first sight I knew you for a man beyond the ordinary. I, myself, in point of fact, am not a mere bandit. You see before you no other than a rebel famous throughout Japan, Shōguntarō Yoshikado, son of Hei Shinnō Masakado. These many years have I been troubling my brain to discover such a hero as yourself and win him over to my cause. I cannot but admire your courage and skill in swordsmanship. I entreat you to join me. Refuse, and I will slay your wife. Her life hangs on your answer. Take counsel with yourself before you reply."

Yorihira, stupefied at this sudden turn of events, stood a moment speechless. "Luckless chance!" Yorihira returned, grinding his teeth with rage. "Are you indeed Yoshikado the rebel? I am Yorihira, third son of Minamoto-no-Mitsunaka. This lady is Lady Eika, eldest daughter of the Prime Minister, Lord Ebumi. Formerly she was the about-to-be-betrothed of my brother Yorinobu. But by the caprice of fate she became united to me and we are now flying together. It was my intention to destroy such as you and by so doing to earn the forgiveness of my brother and of the Shogun. Alas! that my hope should prove vain and that I should find myself in such a predicament as this! My doom is sealed. What shall I do? How luckless my chance!"

"Yorihira Sama," exclaimed Lady Eika, "be of good courage. How will your honour as a knight fare if for woman-sake you should espouse the cause of a traitor? If your love for me is true love, leave me to be slain, and get honour for yourself by slaying this fellow. That is my prayer."

She burst into sobs. Yoshikado laid his hand upon her mouth.

"Will you join me, Yorihira," he demanded, "or shall I slay this woman here? Return me a swift answer: yes or no. Answer now, this moment."

"I join you," replied Yorihira with resolution, "even though I be branded as a rebel and my whole life go down in ruin—for I cannot suffer my love to be put to the sword merely for the sake of my good reputation. I cannot lower myself to condoning such a selfish course of action. I am willing to desert my own people and throw in my lot with you. I am your friend, Yoshikado."

Overjoyed at this reply, the rebel chief released Lady Eika.

"Well spoken, Yorihira. I thank you for your prompt and hearty consent. With the nobility of your descent I am well acquainted; as to my own, I am a descendant of Prince Kazurawara, son of the Emperor Kwammu, from which circumstance you may perceive that it is only reasonable that I should aspire to the throne. You cannot therefore be said to commit any crime in assisting me toward the realization of my ambition. Let us pledge each other."

So saying, he strode up to the ox, slit its ear with his dagger and caught the blood in a cup, from which each drank in turn. The pledge given and taken, Eika wept bitterly.

Kidōmaru, Yoshikado's scout, suddenly returned.

"My Lord," he panted, "I beg to report that Minamoto-no-Yorinobu, who is now visiting the temple of Mount Kurama, will return by this road."

"Excellent news!" cried Yoshikado, dancing for joy. "An opportunity to avenge the death of my sister Kochō! We will slay him as a blood-offering to the god of war. But Yorihira, dare you help me slay your brother?"

"Why such a question after such a pledge? Let me, in proof of my sincerity, deal him the first stroke."

"You satisfy me. Kidōmaru, you will slaughter this

ox and hide in its belly. You will keep still enough for Yorinobu to mistake it for an ox that has died out at pasture. When he approaches it, you will take him by surprise."

Kidōmaru proceeded to obey, while Yoshikado, accompanied by Yorihira, took ambush behind a hill.

Presently Yorinobu appeared, mounted and accompanied by some thirty warriors marching in slow procession, and, as he advanced, now and again shaking the snowflakes from his sleeves, he recited a poem upon the subject of the beauty that snow always possesses. Suddenly he reined in his horse.

" Look, Watanabé-no-Tsuna, yonder is a strange sight. Surely I beheld the belly of that dead ox stir—or was it my fancy ? "

" Very strange, my lord So strange a thing were best not suffered to remain uninvestigated."

With these words he set arrow to bow, drew the arrow to its head and let fly. The arrow pierced the carcase, but as it whizzed downward Kidōmaru emerged and made as if to challenge Yorinobu to fight. Nevertheless Tsuna seized him, trampled on him and wrenched his head off. A whistle sounded among the hills and the next moment more than three hundred men in armour, commanded by Yoshikado, emerged from ambush. The war-cry was raised and all precipitated themselves upon Yorinobu and his followers. A hot fight ensued, which ended in a crushing defeat of the rebels, the majority of whom fell fighting and with whose blood the snow was soon dyed scarlet. As for Yorinobu, he rode away in search of the rebel chief, who had fled the press. Tsuna was about to follow his liege lord when Yorihira rushed from under a pine-tree, which the weight of snow had bended, and blocked his path.

" Tsuna, you and I are no strangers. To-day a certain reason has induced me to make Yoshikado's cause my own. Do not stir."

He cut at Tsuna. The astonished hero, remarking that this man had been his former lord, contented himself with assuming the defensive. At length, seizing a chance, Tsuna beat down Yorihira's defence, pinned him to the ground and tied his hands behind his back. Lady Eika ran up.

"Already bound ? " she exclaimed between her sobs. "O ! Tsuna Dono, Lord Yorihira's treachery is all to be laid to my charge and you would therefore do well to slay me in his stead. Is not a warrior's honour imperilled if he bind his former lord ? "

It was at this moment that Mita-no-Jirō-Tomozuna, Yorihira's foster-brother, who garbed as a traveller, had started in search of the eloping pair, made his appearance and, astonished at what he beheld, intervened.

" *Yai*, Tsuna," he roared, " are you mad ? What monstrous deed is this to bind your lord ? Lord Yorinobu did of course love Lady Eika, but she had not become his wife. Lord Yorihira cannot therefore be said to be guilty of adultery in flying with her. Loose his lordship at once."

Tomozuna pressed upon him.

" Overhasty fellow," replied Tsuna pushing him off, " it is Lord Yorihira, not I, who has gone mad. Lord Yorihira, having seen fit to ally himself with Yoshikado, was infamous enough to attack Lord Yorinobu as Lord Yorinobu was returning from Mount Kurama, and the result was the sharp fight just ended. Lord Yorihira is without doubt the rebel's second-in-command and it is therefore just that he should be bound and by me. Have I not given you sufficient reason for saying that he is mad ? "

The astonished Tomozuna clung to Yorihira.

" Is this true ? The pity, the shame of it ! What made you act so ? "

Yorinobu, who had failed to find his arch - enemy, returned.

" Tomozuna," he said sternly, " you too are a rebel when you condole with Yorihira, a proven traitor."

" Rebel ?—a cruel title ! " returned Tomozuna. " It grieves me to think that I, the foster-brother of this man here, and his guardian, should have known nothing of his flight and of his alliance with the rebels and of his capture. I am ashamed to avow how careless, how ill-advised I have shown myself to be. It is surely my bounden duty now to inquire of him how he found himself in a situation that could lead to such a crime as this. I therefore beg this boon of your lordship—that you will place Lord Yorihira in my charge until such a time as I have ascertained the motive of his terrible crime "

He prostrated himself. Yorihira, without a word, motioned him aside and, advancing upon Yorinobu and Tsuna, inclined his head forward as though suggesting execution. Yorinobu paid not the slightest attention.

" Tomozuna," said he, " my brother has proved guilty of so awful a crime that he ought not to be suffered to draw another breath in this world. Swayed, however, by your entreaty, I grant him a reprieve. Moreover, were it rumoured that I had slain my brother for ill-will borne him in that he had stolen away my bride, this would ill become me in the face of the world. Your mother, moreover, is Tsuna's aunt, and you are a grave and serious person. I therefore place Yorihira and Lady Eika in your charge. Guard them with care and await the instructions of the Shogun."

Having so pronounced, Yorinobu with Tsuna and his other followers withdrew. The eyes of Tomozuna, speechless with joy and gratitude, followed the retreating figure of the magnanimous general.

Y

III

Yorihira and Lady Eika, state prisoners in the hands of Tomozuna, spent several days in his house. Meanwhile a conference at the Imperial Court brought its deliberations to a close with the finding that the noble culprit could not escape the due punishment for treason. The Emperor therefore ordered Yorimitsu to carry into effect whichever of the alternate sentences of death or banishment he should deem more suitable. Bowed down with shame and grief at his relation's monstrous crime, the Shogun finally decided upon capital punishment.

The same conference decided that Lord Ebumi was to be considered responsible for his daughter's relations with a traitor and it was concluded that he should forfeit his rank and with his wife be exiled from the capital. The pair had been haled before the Supreme Court, sitting in the hall of the Shogun's mansion; the verdict was pronounced and the officers of the guard were on the point of relieving the ex-Premier of his official headgear, when Lady Ebumi intervened and, clinging to their sleeves, spoke between her tears : "One moment, sirs. I do not consider the sentence pronounced upon us unreasonable ; but I must speak out the truth—Lady Eika is not the daughter of the Premier. She is the daughter of my first husband and I brought her to my present husband's house when she was but five years old. Lord Ebumi is an utter stranger to her and I alone am responsible for her misconduct. I therefore entreat you to inflict upon me any condign punishment you think fit. Let this action of mine plead for him and relieve him of punishment."

"An end to idle words !" broke in Lord Ebumi. "Albeit

I am not related by blood to Lady Eika, yet for many years have we called each other 'Father' and 'Daughter' and I have come to love her as if she were indeed my daughter. Let us suppose she had not behaved as she has, and had become Lord Yorinobu's consort; would I then fail to acknowledge her as my daughter? We three—husband and wife, parents and child—have a right to share our joys and sorrows. Treat me, even for loving-kindness' sake, as a stranger and I shall resent it."

To these reproaches the lady made no reply but continued weeping bitterly. The officers were touched, but none the less were compelled to inform her, albeit as gently as they were able, that there was no disobeying the Imperial command. Then they stripped her lord of his headgear and robe. Armed soldiers conducted the erstwhile Lord Ebumi and his spouse to beyond the gate.

This touching scene had not long been concluded when an ancient warrior, whose hair was snow-white, who wore two swords with red sheaths and was altogether dressed after a very old fashion, halted before the porch.

"Sasamé is my name," he told the porter. "I have come to present in person a petition to Lord Yorimitsu."

Without further words he entered and passed up the steps into the hall. The porter and the samurai on duty were taken aback.

"Hey you, you rude old fellow," cried the samurai, "one moment!—whether your business is public or private, you can't enter without our permission. Before you beg an audience of our lord, you must acquaint us with the object of your visit."

"Nonsense!" replied the old man, emitting a loud roar of laughter. "Mine is an affair of vital public importance and I cannot acquaint such as you with it. It is imperative that I speak to Lord Yorimitsu in person. Permit me to enter."

He spoke hoarsely. His great voice reverberated through the halls. The samurai had had enough of him.

" A madman surely ! Drive him away."

Scarcely were the words spoken when armed men rushed up and surrounded the ancient. He ran an ironical eye over them.

" A terrible to do and no mistake ! " he remarked sarcastically. " All this fuss over an old man who is no better than a locust ! What, I should like to know, would you do if you were to encounter a young and robust enemy ? Do you suppose that an old creature like myself, nothing but a pair of perambulating shin-bones, would trouble you with a visit were I scared of staves and pikes ? Go on—hit me, stab me, if you think you can gain credit for it."

" Surely this is the rebel Yoshikado's spy come to assassinate our lord. Make an end of him."

They were about to attack him when a loud voice announced the approach of the Shogun. Yorimitsu, attended by pages, appeared.

" So your name is Sasamé, is it ? "—he mused. " A name with which I am not acquainted, a man whom I do not know . . . but from your fearless fashion of requiring to be able to see me in person, I conclude that you have a matter of true importance for my ear. Speak without hesitation."

The old man prostrated himself. His tone was reverent : " I thank your lordship for your great condescension in granting me an audience. Pardon my boldness if I deem it strange that you, who are so lenient as to overlook the rudeness of my behaviour, should not yet bestir yourself to save your own brother, Lord Yorihira, from death. Youth is prone to error. If you take the sword to your relatives whenever they err you will soon lose all of them. Lord Yorihira, her youngest child, was his mother's greatest darling. If therefore you suffer him to die you will not only cause the spirit of your mother great grief, but will thereby become an unfilial son. And how can an unfilial son expect to govern the Empire with success? I therefore most humbly entreat your lordship to save Lord Yorihira from capital punishment and to await his repentance. I hope you will remember the promise you once made me to the effect that you would grant any one petition I might make during my lifetime."

" Yorihira's defection," rejoined Yorimitsu, not without a look of surprise, " is a terrible crime. In such a case as this there is no room for the influence of any personal sentiment of mine. I would have you realize that even the parents of his mistress, Lady Eika, have but just now been exiled by Imperial order. How then can the culprit himself escape punishment? As for the promise, I remember it. But I gave it to Watanabé-no-Tsuna's aunt, who was nurse to Yorihira, in recognition of her distinguished service in raising the hero Tsuna for me. To her I gave it and to none else, and I have no such bond with an old man of your name. Be gone, therefore."

" Surely your lordship remembers the promise? Well then, I will reveal to you my identity : you see before you no other than Tsuna's aunt in disguise. I do not know whether such treatment arose from the fact that your lordship remembered the promise made, but when my son Tomozuna and I of late repeatedly sought an audience, that I might present my petition to your lordship, that audience was invariably refused. The keenness of my disappointment has induced me to resort to this ruse. So much have I changed since last you saw me that to-day you can hardly recognize me and I have taken advantage of this further to disguise myself in the habit

of a man in order to gain an audience. I beg you to forgive
my deception and my rudeness. Permit me to prove to you
that I am Tsuna's aunt."

So saying, the old woman stripped from her the upper
portion of her clothes, when, to Yorimitsu's extreme surprise,
he was granted an opportunity of verifying the assertion by
indubitable ocular evidence.

The Shogun's consort, who had, all this while, been
observing the scene through the chinks of the partition,
hastened in accompanied by a maid-of-honour and took the
old woman by the hand.

" I am delighted to see you, Tsuna's aunt. I fully
appreciate your kind efforts on my brother-in-law's behalf,
but you must remember that Yorihira is not without justice
considered a traitor in that he joined the forces of the rebels ;
and inasmuch as he is my husband's brother by blood it is
become all the more impossible to pardon him. I also have
pleaded for him, only to be severely rebuked by my lord,
who insisted that if Yorihira were pardoned justice would
go out of existence. I have therefore ceased my importunities
and I can only hope that, having followed my example,
you will return to your home."

With these words, aided by the maid, she rearranged the
old woman's garments and gently patted her on the back.
Tsuna's aunt, however, was not appeased, but, drawing close
to Yorimitsu's knees, spoke with vehemence.

" You are stony-hearted, my lord. Will you break your
word for the sake of a barren justice ? Very well, then,
I will plead no more. When I perceive that Lady Eika's
very foster-father has been banished by reason of Lord
Yorihira, I can only conclude that this old nurse of his, who
may in some sort be said to be his mother, and Tomozuna
his foster-brother, that these two, I say, both richly deserve
capital punishment. I make you this prayer. Slay me and

expose my head that the public may realize to the full the justice and impartiality of your administration."

"Noble words, woman," returned Yorimitsu, overcome with admiration. "Your courage and loyalty are truly worthy of one who is the aunt of Tsuna. For the sake of my promise and in recognition of this courage and loyalty of yours, I will place Yorihira, who was to have been executed to-morrow, under your charge for a week. If during that interval owing to your admonitions, he displays indubitable signs of repentance, I will petition the throne that he be pardoned. If he does not display such signs, I will send officers duly to carry out the sentence at cockcrow on the fourth of next month, by which time the week will have expired. You understand me?"

At these words the old woman burst into tears of gratitude, and, after assuring the Shogun and his consort of her intention to do her utmost in the matter, she departed in the best of spirits.

Day and night Tsuna's aunt earnestly expostulated with Yorihira, advising him to repent and obtain forgiveness of the Shogun, but to no purpose. The stubborn hero spoke no word and to all her admonition turned a deaf ear. With grief and anxiety she beheld the fatal week draw to a speedy close. The curtains of night fell upon the last day. Her patience was exhausted. She produced a bow, her valued possession, the very bow which Yorihira's dead father had carried against rebels, and used it to rain repeated blows upon him.

"This bow, Lord Yorihira," she said in tears, "is the soul of your dead father Lord Mitsunaka. You do well to consider it his whip of chastisement. Listen, if you have ears; see, if eyes you have. It is only natural that, since you are fool enough to have turned traitor in order to keep a petty pledge, you should be callous to the troubles of others. Alas, it is solely on account of you that your father-in-law Lord Ebumi and his wife have been exiled by Imperial order and that their daughter Lady Eika has become an unfilial child. And yet for all this you do not repent. I can only conclude that you bear a grudge against your brothers because you were not appointed heir to the Shogunate. Yours is a crooked spirit. Well, let me, in place of your revered father, beat the wickedness out of you.''

With that she once more raised the bow, but Yorihira seized her by the arm and, with a melancholy look, exclaimed : '' Dear nurse, the chastisement you mete out to me through the instrumentality of my father's bow grieves me so sorely that I am compelled to open my heart to you. It is not that I cannot distinguish right from wrong, but you must know that neither does the scorched seed bud nor the fallen flower return to its native branch. What though my life were spared ?—how could I face public censure and the scorn of my brothers and retainers, I, who stole away Lady Eika who was to be my brother's bride ? There is, too, another affair which is of even greater importance ; I would have you know that I, descended from the Emperor Seiwa, drank a draught of ox's blood with Yoshikado, a descendant of the Emperor Kwammu. Should I break this pledge and desert his cause, how can it be but that people will say : ' When his sweetheart was taken prisoner by the rebel chieftain, Yorihira would not fight a duel with him, but treacherously joined him to save her from death. Such a coward is a disgrace to the Minamoto family ' ? Again, were I shameless enough to live on despite such ill-fame, my brothers' reputation would thereby be compromised. It would, however, redown to their credit if I caused folk to say ' Yorihira kept his pledge even to death. He is worthy of his noble lineage.' Sometimes it happens that a warrior seems to wander from the path of righteousness, though in reality he does no such thing. Gold is the most precious of treasures, but to a man exhausted with thirst upon a lofty mountain thousands of gold coins are not worth a handful of water. In summer, too, coarse linen is exalted above brocade. Thus comes it that it is my intention to wipe out one disgrace by another and by one guilt to clear myself of another. It is my trust that you can enter into my feelings and sympathize with me, dear nurse."

" You have my heartiest sympathies, Lord Yorihira," the old woman returned, throwing the bow aside. " Why did you not unbosom yourself to me before ? How foolish, how thoughtless have I been, who, in my ignorance of my lord's intentions, have beaten and abused him ! May my tongue fester ! May my arm break ! I entreat your forgiveness, my dear lord."

She burst into tears, but after a while resumed, " I have no time to weep. Ere long the officers will be here. I fear that they will compel us to defend ourselves against them here in this very house and that none of us can hope to survive. Let us therefore enjoy a feast of farewell in the inner room. Tomozuna, bar the gate. Come in, all of you."

The company went within. And as the feast, accompanied by the old woman's pathetic singing and dancing, took its course, the night wore on. At length, mixed with the sound of a shower drumming upon the window, there was heard a series of faint raps upon the gate-door. Lady Eika, perceiving the noise, slipped out and advanced to the gate.

" Who knocks at so dead an hour of night ? " she demanded in a whisper.

" It is my daughter Eika, is it not ? " answered a voice without the gate. " I wish to speak with you. Pray open the door."

The voice of her mother was unmistakable. The girl's heart leapt.

"Is it you, mother? So long separated, much I wish that I might obtain were it but a glimpse only of your sweet face; but I grieve to say that the gate is tightly fastened. What can have brought you here at this hour of the night? Lord Yorihira's life must end at cockcrow. I also am doomed to the same fate. It is only a matter of a short while ere the troops that will dispatch him arrive. Imagine my surprise and grief at hearing that both my father and mother had been exiled and the noble house of Ebumi ruined —all on my account. My iniquity is too great for me to hope for pardon. The last moments draw near. Delay but a little longer and danger must indubitably overtake you. Haste away, dear mother."

She leaned against the wall and sobbed bitterly.

"Luckless Lord Ebumi," said the old woman, "I don't know how to apologize to him; not even my death could atone for your ill-doing. You can imagine how I feel. But now that Lord Yorihira's life draws to its close, little it matters at whose hand he dies. I came hither to-night as proxy for Lord Ebumi to ask for his head ere the execution occurs. Should my husband be able to present Yorihira's head to the throne, I feel sure he will be pardoned and restored to the enjoyment of his rank and office. I am aware that the request I am about to make is cruel, but I entreat you to guide me within that I may accomplish the assassination of Lord Yorihira. I know you love your husband as dearly as I do mine; but if you suffer me to kill your husband you will at least be able to fulfil your duty toward your foster-father. Come, girl, guide me in; or shall I make an unguided assault and so court certain failure? If I find myself unable to do either I will never return, but slay myself here. The hour grows late; render me an answer promptly: yes or no! Make haste, make haste!"

She emphasized the urgency of her demand by rattling

her dirk up and down in its scabbard so that the hilt clashed against the mouth of the sheath, but she received no answer from Eika, who found herself at an entire loss.

"Come, daughter, answer promptly! Shall I force my way in without assistance or am I to slay myself where I stand? Not a moment remains for further reflection. Make haste, make haste!"

Eika writhed with anguish. Should she suffer her mother to assassinate her husband she would be a wicked wife. Should she disobey her mother she would be doubly undutiful toward her parents. At last she came to such a resolve as she deemed would enable her to extricate herself from this predicament. "You have my willing consent, mother," she answered with forced laughter. "Fortunately my husband drank himself into a stupor at the farewell feast we have held this night. He is now dead asleep in the front room by the porch. During his long confinement he has allowed his hair to grow so long that it now hangs over his shoulders. When the moment comes I will extinguish the light in his room. When this signal has been given, steal into the room, and when you feel your hand upon his long hair, stab him. In this fashion you cannot fail to kill him."

She had hardly concluded when her mother replied, "I am glad, daughter. I shall thank you all my life. I will steal in immediately."

"Not so. Not yet. Should anything occur to Lord Yorihira before cockcrow, Tomozuna and his mother, who have him in their charge, would incur great blame. Do not be so impatient. Await my signal, I beg you. Fare you well, mother."

She hurried back to her room and, taking a razor from her toilet-case, cut her jet-black hair so short that it barely reached her shoulders. Then she proceeded to the front room and kneeled down in tears.

Outside Lady Ebumi, fixing her eyes upon the eastern sky, awaited the cockcrow with such patience as she could summon. She had not been waiting long ere there was heard the neighing and trampling of a troop of horse yet afar off. Soon great paper lanterns, bright as stars and borne upon poles, came in sight. These were followed by a company of about fifty mounted warriors. Startled, Lady Ebumi instantly removed her hat and mantle and, scaling the wall with great difficulty, groped her way up to the roof of the gateway, whereon she crouched scarcely daring to draw a breath. Ere long the posse arrived before the gate. Their commander, Kintoki, who was in full uniform, alighted, stepped up to the gate and knocked upon its door.

" Ho ! Within there ! " he cried loudly, but with courtesy. " I, Sakata-no-Kintoki, am come as a messenger of His Highness the Shogun. Since Lord Yorihira has not yet seen fit to send his apologies to His Highness, I am strictly enjoined to persuade him into self-dispatch and to bring his head back with me. It is however my earnest prayer and my hope that his lordship will at once retract the vow he made with the rebel chieftain and sue forgiveness of his honourable brother. It is with this express purpose that I have arrived ere cockcrow. Tomozuna and Tomozuna's aunt, spare no pains to prevail upon him, that he may return in my company to the palace of His Highness."

At these words the lady upon the gate-roof found herself very ill at ease. Obviously she could not proceed to her bloody act before cockcrow, yet further delay must inevitably frustrate her plans. In desperate straits, she thrust her face into the pine branches overhanging the gate-roof and twice gave a loud *kokkekō*. Upon this all the cocks in the neighbourhood clapped their wings and crowed amain. Unobserved in the tumult and excitement that ensued within and without the gate, she leapt down into the courtyard and, finding to her joy the light extinguished, she felt her way within. Hardly had she entered when the paper doors were dyed scarlet.

"Oho, there!" she called. "I, Ebumi Tamenari, have dealt the first blow to Minamoto-no-Yorihira, the greatest ally of the wretched rebel Yoshikado!"

"What brazenness! What an insult!" thundered Kintoki in consternation. "Hateful aunt and cousin—to have permitted a weakling of a court noble secretly to enter and thus to bring disgrace upon the Shogun's messenger! Wait, I will open the door with a key of my own fashioning."

He put forth all his strength against the door; under the strain the hinges cracked. Then he kicked the door; at which the bolt broke in two and the door swung open. Kintoki and his troops rushed in. Tomozuna's mother ran out and hurriedly opened the paper doors of the front room. Behold! between Eika and her astonished mother, who bore a blood-stained dirk in her hand, crouched blood-bespattered Tomozuna, holding together with his hand a terrible wound in the neck. Lady Ebumi was speechless with sorrow and amazement. Tomozuna crept to the verandah and, hard-spent, spoke as follows: "Lady Ebumi, Kintoki and my mother, your surprise is quite natural. If you wish to know the truth I will tell it you—I have suffered myself to be struck by Lady Ebumi. This heroic woman, bent upon slaying Lord Yorihira thus to obtain the Imperial pardon, begged Lady Eika's assistance. That unhappy creature, Lady Eika, finding herself in such a dilemma, resolved to die at the hand of her mother. She cut her hair short and was awaiting in the darkness the mortal stroke when I, perceiving what was happening, and struck with admiration and pity for the young lady, so contrived as to receive the mortal stab in her place. Lady Ebumi, present but my head to the throne and I am sure your husband will receive his pardon, for I am

Lord Yorihira's chief retainer and guardian. There is however another end for which———"

" How rash a deed, Tomozuna ! " broke in Yorihira, who had but this moment entered. " That you should act as substitute and die in my stead is not to be thought of. You have died in vain indeed ! "

" You are mistaken, my lord," gasped Tomozuna, " it was not my intention to perish as your substitute. That a warrior who has repeatedly, but all in vain, remonstrated with his lord should slay himself is but the custom. Again and again have I remonstrated with your lordship, but you have ever turned a deaf ear to my advice For this reason have I resorted to these desperate means. Should my death induce you to forsake the path of error, nothing, I think, could so contribute to the welfare and prosperity of the Minamoto family and to the public good. Then indeed I should not die in vain. My lord, my mother, my cousin and the rest of you, ere I breathe my last, I have a tale for you. You will recall how on a certain night in February last the ceremony of choosing the Shogun's heir took place. On that night, unable to resist Kochō's charms, I trifled with her under cover of the darkness, with the result that she not only cut the string of my headgear but loudly called attention to my misbehaviour. Shame and despair ordained that I should slay myself, but Lord Yorihira in his mercy commanded all the samurai present to cut the strings of their headgears. Thus was I suffered to escape detection and an ignominious death. Gratitude prompted me to await an opportunity to requite his lordship's benevolence. It was my hope that he would march against the rebels, thus affording me an opportunity to fight for him. Alas ! How profound was my sorrow and disappointment when I discovered that he had himself turned rebel ! Kintoki, save his lordship repent of his errors and apologize to his honourable brother, I shall not be able to die in peace. For it is this thought alone and no other that is a torture to me in my last moments. O my mother, O Kintoki, do your utmost to induce my lord to repent, such is my dying request."

"Lord Yorihira," sobbed the old woman, "yours is a heart of flint! While my son yet draws his breath let him hear those three syllables 'I repent' pass your lips: a requiem more potent for good with him than the prayers of a thousand priests."

Yorihira, stubborn though he was, could resist no longer. He burst into tears and, taking Tomozuna by the blood-stained hand, spoke with passion: "A thousand pardons, my dear Tomozuna. I regret with all my heart that my obstinacy should have caused the death of so brave and loyal a retainer. Here do I solemnly declare, by Shō-Hachiman, that I entirely and absolutely annul my pact with Yoshikado and humbly beg forgiveness of my brothers. Tomozuna, set your mind at ease. You have not died in vain. I am infinitely grateful to you, dear Tomozuna."

"I thank you, my lord. Now I regret nothing. I can die in peace and joy. Come, Kintoki, I pray you behead me."

"Ah, no!" cried the lion-hearted Kintoki. "I know not how to behead so brave, sympathetic and loyal a samurai as yourself. Do you behead him, aunt."

"Fie upon you! I have no need of your assistance." The dying warrior breathed a "Namu . . ." and, fixing a smiling eye upon his mother, decapitated himself with his own sword, to the extreme horror and grief of all present. The old woman took up the bleeding head and lavished every mark of affection upon it.

"My dear son, you are at last in my arms again—for the first time since you were weaned at the age of five."

She applied the head to her face and bosom and wept the bitterest tears.

IV

Kintoki's detailed report on the suicide of the loyal Tomozuna, on Lady Ebumi's heroic deed, and, above all, on Lord Yorihira's heartfelt repentance and apology so profoundly moved the Shogun Yorimitsu that he forthwith obtained Imperial permission to reprieve Yorihira from capital punishment and to restore Lord Ebumi to his rank and office. Yorimitsu repaired to the Government Office whither he summoned Yorihira and Ebumi. Great was their joy and gratitude when they learned that the Imperial pardon had been extended to them. The ensuing mutual congratulations were crowned when, in the very midst of the company's rejoicings, news arrived that the arch-rebel Yoshikado had been captured and was now in the courtyard of the Office. The happy Shogun, accompanied by his brother and Lord Ebumi, stepped out on the verandah to view the prisoner, who, with his hands bound, was kneeling, guarded by his captors, Suétaké and Sadamitsu, two of the Shogun's Greatest Four. Yorimitsu highly commended the exploit of his brave retainers and informed all present that from time immemorial every such traitor had eventually encountered the same fate as the prisoner they now beheld. He added in conclusion—" This deep-dyed criminal, having defied the Imperial authority, even as his father did before him, shall in due time be executed. Meanwhile cast him into prison."

Yorihira interrupted : " Now that I have severed my connection with Yoshikado and am myself so graciously pardoned, it were an easy matter for me to chastise the prisoner here. But, since I have a particular purpose in view, I beseech you to deliver him up to my keeping for a while."

His petition being immediately granted, Yorihira descended to the prisoner whom he addressed in kindly fashion : " Having regard for the pact I made with you and for the fact that you did spare Lady Eika's life, I give you quarter and set you free. From now on we are enemies. Your head is in your own keeping until my sword severs it on the battlefield. So be off, Yoshikado." With that he cut the cords that bound the prisoner.

" An honourable warrior in very deed ! " exclaimed Yoshikado with a smile. " I am captivated by your faith-keeping and kindliness. I am inclined to think it will not be long ere we meet upon the battle-field. Farewell, Yorihira."

He was about to depart when the Shogun bade him halt one moment.

" You are a deep-dyed villain to have set the royal authority at naught. But that you should pay special homage to your father's spirit is admirable. I will make you a parting present."

He produced the pavilion curtain, upon which was the crest of the tethered steed.

" This, your father's curtain, is quite useless to the Minamoto family. To you, however, it is a god of arms. I return it you ! "

With these words he cast the curtain to the ground. Reverently and gratefully Yoshikado took it up.

" I thank you for this precious gift. I shall not fail to requite your favour with my sword. Know that I shall shortly raise an army in Mount Katsuragi and capture Yorihira. But even though I may return his body to the Minamoto family, yet his head shall remain with me for ever as my ally."

He bade farewell to the Minamoto brothers and strode away.

Day and night the dreams of Iyo-no-Naishi, wife of Yorinobu, were haunted by the spectre of Kochō. Slowly she languished, until the several distractions devised by the wives of the Greatest Four had all in turn proved unavailing and the chief physician felt compelled to declare the case beyond his power. The wives of the Greatest Four, however, did not cease to rack their brains and at length hit upon a happy expedient. It was the custom to light a big bonfire on Mount Higashiyama on the night of the sixteenth of July. The bonfire was always shaped like the Chinese character for " Great ", in shape somewhat resembling a cross. The object of this peculiar bonfire was that it might afford a guiding light to souls astray in Hades and conduct them back to the right path. It was decided to kindle a similar bonfire in the artificial hill in the garden before the noble sufferer's apartments—thus at once to afford her consolation and to appease Kochō's spirit and so restore the Shogun's consort to health. An excavation in the shape of the particular character was made in the hillside and the cavity filled with much firewood. At nightfall the women, torches in hand, set a light to the wood. So bright was the blaze thus kindled that noonday seemed re-established. The fire illumining rocks, trees and flowers gave to the whole scene an indescribably beautiful appearance. The lady was much intrigued and a sudden rosiness returned to her cheeks. Meanwhile the wives prayed for the peace of Kochō's soul. Then, after several hours' gay converse with their mistress, they retired.

The Milky Way had grown pale, the hour of dawn drew nigh, the bonfire was all but dead, when from the low red embers a ball of bright flame shot upward and as rapidly fell to the ground. From the heart of the ball the ghostly figure of Kochō glided forth and, drifting effortlessly, even as a cloud upon the wind, advanced toward the lady's bed-chamber and violently struck upon the paper doors. The lady awoke.

" Strange ! " she murmured. " Who's there ? "

" I am a maid in the service of His Majesty, the ex-Emperor. Intelligence of your illness has reached his ears and His Majesty has graciously conferred upon you several supreme Chinese and Japanese remedies. I have brought them hither. Take them quickly, my lady."

Not without misgiving as to why such a messenger should have come at so strange an hour, Naishi opened the doors. Overcome with horror at encountering that very figure which had so often haunted her dreams, she uttered a loud shriek and leapt back. But the apparition advanced remorselessly upon her. " Fool of a Naishi," it exclaimed in terrible tones, " I am the spirit of Kochō, that Kochō who fell a prey to love for your husband and I am no less also the spirit of the Greatest of all the Spiders. Fathomless is my hate of you, of you my rival in love. I,—I am purposed to inflict upon you all the sufferings that are mine in Hades."

Hardly had the awful voice ended when from the creature's finger-tips issued innumerable webs, which instantly twined themselves about the lady. Vain were her struggles—they did but serve to knit the bonds the tighter. She suffered agonies. She stumbled about the room, all but in collapse. Vast gusts whistled through the garden trees ; the water in the artificial pond made its incommunicable sound ; will-o'-the-wisps gleamed and were gone in the darkness ; the roll and rattle of thunder added to the pandemonium.

On this the four wives immediately perceived that a calamity must have taken place. Halberds in hand, they rushed into Naishi's chamber and were astonished at the plight in which they found her. With great difficulty they saved her from the webs which threatened to strangle her and carried her to her bed. Once back on the verandah, they

were glancing in every direction, when Kochō's figure arose
bolt upright behind them.

"Foolish women," quoth the spectre, shaking with anger,
"know that I am the spirit of a ground-spider that has
dwelt many, many years in Mount Katsuragi. It was my
purpose to usurp the possession of the Great Empire of Japan
that I might make it one huge abode for my family. To
attain this purpose I espoused the cause of the rebel Yoshikado
and possessed his sister Kochō, but to my ill-fortune the girl
fell a prey to love and so I lost my temporary dwelling. None
the less I will display to you my powers."

The spectre had no sooner spoken than the women sprang
upon it, brandishing their weapons. When they lunged at its
skirts it leapt in the air; when they thrust at its right, it
appeared to their left. Did they cut at its back, it stood
before them. When they surrounded it, it changed its nature
and became a blaze of fire. Next it dispersed itself into red
and green jack-o'-lanterns which spread throughout the
gardens and vanished and flashed hither and thither by turn.
Anon these jack-o'-lanterns floated like a mist from branch
to blossoming branch. Now the spectre maiden appeared
standing before them and laughing, laughing hysterically. A
moment later it seemed to vanish, only to appear again
beckoning to them from the distant verandah. So magical
were its powers, moving in so many forms, that the heroic
women were at last reduced to gaping at it.

At this moment Yorinobu, accompanied by Hirai-no-
Yasumasa, rushed forward to the attack, brandishing a
sacred sword, the heirloom of the Minamoto family. He
hung it at Naishi's pillow, to ward off evil spirits. Then both
heroes leapt from the verandah and, taking up their stand
in the garden, glared at the sky. Instantly the storm ceased,
only to be followed by millions of cobwebs which poured
down from heaven as in an unnatural shower. Hither and

thither they spun themselves about the warriors who were soon at a loss to rid themselves of the silvery threads.   Then was it that there occurred a miracle of miracles—thunder rolled within the confines of the lady's chamber, the sacred sword sprang from its sheath and, vaulting into the night above the gardens, flickered to and fro in the darkness.   Again and again it stabbed at something above that was hidden, a bloody dew descended, the webs, dissolving, were no longer seen, and a shrill voice was heard crying upon the upper air, " Forgive me, I come no more ! "

The sword pursued the fleeting voice, but, when the voice became at length inaudible, the sword sprang back into its sheath.   No sooner had this miracle been achieved than the illness immediately fell from Naishi and she was as one who has awakened from an endless dream.   Thus was the haunted palace changed to a palace of joy and merriment.

V

Two expeditions, each composed of several hundreds of troops, and commanded by Hirai-no-Yasumasa and by Yorinobu and Yorihira respectively, were dispatched against the monster spider with orders to accomplish its destruction. Tracking the monster by the trail of its blood, they marched toward Mount Katsuragi in the province of Yamato.   Kintoki led the van.   The terrible monster was nothing to him who, clad in ordinary clothes, shouldered a huge bamboo broom as his sole weapon.   His appearance excited continuous laughter among the heavily-armoured soldiery.   Standing at the foot of the mountain, they descried, fluttering upon its summit, the pavilion curtain crested with the tethered steed. The sight inspired them with redoubled courage, for they hoped to achieve a double prize, the monster and the arch-rebel. They commenced the ascent amid blowing of conches, beating of drums and chorus of war-cries. They discovered to their amazement that the rocks and trees of the slope were thickly twined with silken webs. From the darkest heart of the forest there emerged an immense spider, whose eyes shone with the cold glare of a mirror and whose legs bristled with hairs like iron nails. Emitting with every breath a gust of fire, the angry monster rushed down upon the army. The terror-stricken vanguard were about to take to their heels, but even this the spider prevented, for it flung about them a showering web in which the soldiers found themselves entangled Then, seizing certain of them with its giant legs it proceeded to suck their blood. Kintoki, in his rage, tore and kicked his way through the threads and sprang upon the monster. Instantaneously it vanished, leaving in its stead an enormous *kobukuro*, or pouch containing its young. This the hero promptly broke in pieces, when, from within it, issued myriads of young spiders which sprang upon the troops and threw them into confusion, while all about, among the bushes and in the shadows of the rocks, elf-fires danced and gleamed so brilliantly that the whole mountain seemed afire. While this adventure was going forward and Kintoki was valiantly wielding his big broom against the webs and the young spiders, Tsuna and Sadamitsu and other soldiers attacked the enemy on the other side of the mountain. So well did they acquit themselves and so many of the enemy did they slay that the rebel chief, Yoshikado, was compelled to run for his life. In his flight he came to the front slope where, being intercepted by Kintoki, he was about to be captured. At this moment the dim figure of Kochō was discerned close to Yoshikado, who became suddenly possessed of a miraculous strength, and, felling the Greatest Four to the ground, towered to his full height and stared fiercely about him.

Then it was that Yorinobu shouted : " Beware of Yoshikado, O Greatest Four ! I'll be sworn he is dowered with the monster's powers." Forthwith he drew the sacred sword and, invoking divine protection, hurled it at Yoshikado. Instantly Kochō's figure vanished. The monster reappeared in its place. The superhuman strength of Yoshikado left him. In a moment Tsuna and Sadamitsu precipitated themselves upon him and held him down. Kintoki and Suétaké mounted the spider's back. Not a leg could the monster stir. At the sight the whole army raised a shout of triumph and a lusty cheer for the Minamoto family echoed about the mountain.

PRINTED IN GREAT BRITAIN BY
THE EDINBURGH PRESS, 9 AND 11 YOUNG STREET, EDINBURGH

For Product Safety Concerns and Information please contact our EU
representative GPSR@taylorandfrancis.com
Taylor & Francis Verlag GmbH, Kaufingerstraße 24, 80331 München, Germany

www.ingramcontent.com/pod-product-compliance
Lightning Source LLC
Chambersburg PA
CBHW052348020726
47503CB00001B/157

* 9 7 8 0 4 1 5 8 4 9 4 5 6 *